THE HISTORY OF STAUNTON HIGH SCHOOL SPORTS

(1908 – 2012)

By:

Steven F. Moore

Tradition never graduates.

Steven F. Moore

∞ INFINITY
PUBLISHING

All rights reserved. No part of this book shall be reproduced or transmitted in any form or by any means, electronic, mechanical, magnetic, photographic including photocopying, recording or by any information storage and retrieval system, without prior written permission of the publisher. No patent liability is assumed with respect to the use of the information contained herein. Although every precaution has been taken in the preparation of this book, the publisher and author assume no responsibility for errors or omissions. Neither is any liability assumed for damages resulting from the use of the information contained herein.

Copyright © 2012 by Steven F. Moore

ISBN 978-0-7414-7717-0

Printed in the United States of America

Published August 2012

INFINITY PUBLISHING
1094 New DeHaven Street, Suite 100
West Conshohocken, PA 19428-2713
Toll-free (877) BUY BOOK
Local Phone (610) 941-9999
Fax (610) 941-9959
Info@buybooksontheweb.com
www.buybooksontheweb.com

Dedication

This book is dedicated to my parents, George and Cheryl Moore. My father left this world much too soon, but not before he impressed upon me the importance of character and service above material possessions. My mother is my hero. The work ethic and selflessness she displayed in raising three young boys are attributes I can only hope to emulate with my own children.

Acknowledgements

With so many resources needed to complete a project of this magnitude, I want to thank anyone who provided me with research materials. Many people provided me with scrapbooks, yearbooks, and personal stories, and without your input this book would not have been possible. Patricia Long, my former teacher and eventual colleague, in particular deserves praise. Her collection of yearbooks was invaluable in my efforts. I am also indebted to Andy Easton. The information he provided was priceless, and I hope it is not lost on this audience how much history he has documented on South Central Conference and Macoupin County high school sports. I also want to thank anyone affiliated with the Staunton Public Library for assisting me with microfilm, copies, and other tasks. My many hours sitting in the Genealogy Room were more bearable because of you. Additionally, I need to thank Linda Hawkins, Cheryl Moore, and Elisabeth Moore for agreeing to review this book for me. If errors are found in the text, it is undoubtedly my fault, as not every suggested change was adopted. Finally, I want to thank my wife and children for their support. This project resulted from hundreds of hours of research and writing and, without acknowledgement and patience for the time constraints, I could not have finished it in a suitable manner.

Table of Contents

Chapter 1	Classes of 1908 – 1919	1
Chapter 2	Classes of 1920 – 1929	9
Chapter 3	Classes of 1930 – 1939	23
Chapter 4	Classes of 1940 – 1949	37
Chapter 5	Classes of 1950 – 1959	49
Chapter 6	Classes of 1960 – 1969	63
Chapter 7	Classes of 1970 – 1979	77
Chapter 8	Classes of 1980 – 1989	95
Chapter 9	Classes of 1990 – 1999	119
Chapter 10	Classes of 2000 – 2009	155
Chapter 11	Classes of 2010 – 2012	195
Attachment 1	Team Accomplishments	215
Attachment 2	Individual Accomplishments	239

Introduction

This project began out of curiosity about the history of Staunton High School athletics. Being a huge fan of prep sports, I have attended multiple events at various area venues. In doing so, I began to observe how well some communities honor their sporting success and, in comparison, how little Staunton has documented and celebrated its own achievements. I therefore was motivated to uncover the accomplishments of past teams at SHS. While I initially planned on focusing only on team aspects, as I uncovered more information, I began documenting personal accolades, which to my surprise ended up being a major component of this book.

At first my research was just for fun, a personal hobby used to compare success across sports programs and to verify recollections of "the good old days" (I soon found out that just like fishing stories, memories of team and personal accomplishments tend to grow over time.). Eventually, I realized that a lot of people in the community would like to see what I had found, so I decided to write this book in order to share the information. After just a few weeks of writing, I was sure I had bitten off more than I could chew. Not only am I not a writer by trade, but hours upon hours of research seemed to only lead to more questions about the past. But, eventually the manuscript took form, and the book began to write itself based on what I had discovered.

It was difficult to decide how to organize the material, but eventually I chose to do it by graduation year, with each sport being covered alphabetically instead of by season or gender. Also, it was hard to determine what information should be included for each section. I strove to incorporate items such as the season record, conference results, coach's name, senior participants, team highlights, and individual awards. In addition to All-Conference, All-County, All-Area, and All-State accolades, I also included major team awards, such as Most Valuable Player (MVP). Due to concerns over space, quality, and consistency, I excluded most in-season honors and minor team awards. However, I did include available player statistics and individual records when appropriate.

I apologize for leaving anybody out of the document. I did not intentionally omit information, as my goal was to include as much of Staunton High School's athletic history as possible. However, covering over one hundred years of multiple sporting events is quite a task, and in the end I simply could not find everything that I wanted to include. In my defense, I did make several pleas for information in the community by word of mouth, online, and through the local media, yet very few people came forward with relevant material. Maybe after being overlooked in this book, more people will come forward with documented information for potential future editions. Finally, it is worth noting that my reporting is only as accurate as the information found in my sources. Since I relied heavily on yearbooks and newspaper articles, I am at the mercy of the people who initially provided that information.

CHAPTER 1

Classes of 1908 – 1919

Overview

Though students had been receiving an informal education in Staunton since the 1880's, Staunton High School did not officially offer classes until the 1894-95 school year. Thirteen years later, SHS participated in the Macoupin County Meet, the first time the school sent student-athletes off to competition. In the early part of the century, the event was comprised of two portions: oratory and track. While the oratorical portion, which took place in the morning, was the main feature, due to the nature of this book the focus will be on the sporting side of the meet.

By the 1911-12 academic year, Staunton fielded its first team sport, as football became the activity of choice in the community. While track has never been considered a major sport at SHS (and in fact was disbanded at one point for more than a decade), football immediately gained a loyal following in the community and to this day is still considered the main athletic attraction in town.

Class of 1908

Track (Boys)

Staunton High School's first formal athletic contest occurred in 1908. The event was the Macoupin County Meet. Since the event represented the only time athletes competed during the year, the team did not officially have a coach. However, superintendent Bill Eccles escorted all of the participants, and therefore he has been designated as the coach for Illinois High School Association (IHSA) purposes.

Although 1908 marked the first time that Staunton participated at County, it was in fact the fifth annual production of the meet, and thus Macoupin County schools had been competing against one another since 1904. Staunton had just one winner that year, as Leslie George took home 1st place in the standing broad jump. He thus became the first decorated athlete in the history of Staunton High School. It is worth noting that the top three finishers in each event at County moved on to the Inter-County Meet in which the best of Macoupin County faced off against their Montgomery County counterparts. Unfortunately, no athlete from SHS was able to take home gold at that meet, as Macoupin County lost to Montgomery County at the event, which was hosted by Staunton.

Class of 1909

Track (Boys)

SHS fared much better at the 1909 Macoupin County Meet, as the school had more experience with how the competition was conducted, and thus was able to more effectively prepare in the weeks leading up to the event. The athletes also had excellent support from the community, as did most county schools. In fact, in the early 1900s the Macoupin County Meet was the highlight of the school year since community bragging rights were on the line. The preparation and support proved useful, as Staunton took home 1st place in four events, including the 100 meters, 200 meters, discus, and shot put under the direction of Bill Eccles.

Class of 1910

Track (Boys)

Staunton High School placed 2nd overall at the 1910 Macoupin County Meet. SHS was led by championship performances from Leslie George (50 meters) and Bob Woods (triple jump). Superintendent Bill Eccles escorted the team that season.

Class of 1911

Track (Boys)

SHS won its initial Macoupin County Banner in 1911, finishing 1st overall due to strong performances in the oratorical session. The squad was not overly impressive on the track, as Art Goff was the lone gold medal winner, though he did set a county record in the standing broad jump. Sponsor Bill Eccles and the community must have been proud of the participants, as the banner was displayed in the store windows of various local businesses on a rotational basis.

Class of 1912

Football

Though a Staunton city team had begun playing games in 1908, there was no formal high school football team in place until 1911. Much credit must be given to superintendent Bill Eccles who was instrumental in forming the program and, in fact, became its first coach. The first football players in SHS history were Will Allen, Walt Fischer, Frank Godfrey, Harry Hopper, Will Hyndman, Tie Kinnikin, John Luker, Leland Mitchell, Ernst Reschetz, Roland Russell, Reith Sawyer, and Will Volentine. Given that mascots were not adopted at area schools for more than twenty years, local squads tended to be nicknamed by their school colors. In Staunton's case, those colors were myrtle and maroon, and the team was thus known informally as the Green Wave or Maroons for years to come. In fact, the local junior high still keeps maroon as a school color, though its teams are known as the Terriers.

Unfortunately, the first game in school history was a loss to Bunker Hill Military Academy (BHMA) by a score of 17-3. The Staunton squad rebounded in the following game, easily defeating Bunker Hill High School (57-0). A scoreless tie with Troy and a loss to Edwardsville followed before SHS ended its season with another loss to BHMA (17-0). Therefore, the inaugural football season ended with a record of 1-3-1, an inauspicious start to what became the focal sports program for the school and community over the next century and beyond.

Track (Boys)

The track team was unable to defend its overall crown at the Macoupin County Meet in 1912, and Bill Eccles' unit walked away without a winner in the athletic portion of the event.

Class of 1913

Football

The second year of Staunton High School football saw a change of fortunes for coach Bill Eccles' 1912 team. A more experienced squad fared much better than their predecessors, as the team finished with a record of 3-2 on the season. Staunton opened the year with yet another loss to Bunker Hill Military Academy, this time by a close score of 8-6. SHS registered its first win with a 3-0 shutout victory over Edwardsville, avenging a loss from the previous season. Staunton followed up that win with two straight victories over BHMA, the latter game by a score of 33-0.

Due to travel hardships, as well as the fact that very few community high schools fielded teams in those days, one can understand why SHS played its neighbors to the west on more than one occasion during the season. However, the Green Wave travelled for the last game of the year to Greenfield, a football powerhouse in the early 1900s and beyond. One can only imagine the hardships involved with playing football in those days. In addition to the high rate of injury before modern equipment, the travel involved in competing against a team from Greenfield certainly took its toll. In order to play their opponent, the Staunton players had to leave very early in the morning to catch a train to Carlinville before being transported west in order to play in a late afternoon affair. All excuses aside, SHS dropped the game to Greenfield (20-0) in shutout fashion but still ended the year with the school's first winning season in any team sport.

Track (Boys)

The Macoupin County Meet of 1913 proved to be very good to Staunton High School, as the team won the Literary Cup, Literary Banner, and Relay Cup, in addition to several 1st place finishes in the track portion of the meet. In those days the only relay that took place at a track meet was the 800 meter relay. Staunton's team of John Auer, Harry Hopper, Tie Kinnikin, and Nessel blew away the competition, bringing the Relay Cup home to Staunton for the first time in school history. Other county champions included Frank Godfrey (shot put), Handshy (400 meters), Kinnikin (800 meters), and John Luker (1600 meters). The squad was directed by Bill Eccles.

Class of 1914

Football

Bill Eccles' 1913 football team finished the season with a mark of 5-2, setting a school record for wins at the time. Captain Frank Godfrey, along with fellow seniors John Auer and Harry Hopper, led a team of sixteen players into the season's inaugural contest with Edwardsville. The matchup was witnessed by more than one hundred spectators at Wall's Pasture in Staunton. SHS defeated Edwardsville by a tally of 6-0, and they also defeated Bunker Hill Military Academy by the same score in Week 2. Unfortunately, a Week 3 loss to Greenfield made history, as Staunton came out on the wrong side of an 81-0 shellacking, the worst loss in school history. However, wins over Blackburn College (26-0) and Carlinville High School (43-6) followed. The Carlinville game marked the first-ever meeting between the two biggest cities in Macoupin County and sparked a rivalry that continues to this day. The season ended with a 19-6 loss to Edwardsville in Week 6, followed by another victory over Blackburn College in Week 7, this time by a score of 32-6. On a side note, with no titles to play for, the winner of the annual game between Staunton and Carlinville became the unofficial champion of Macoupin County, and SHS took home the prize in 1913. It is interesting to note, however, that each school seemed to lay claim to the title regardless of how they fared against the other Macoupin County schools during the year.

Track (Boys)

The 1914 Macoupin County Meet was disappointing for coach Bill Eccles, as his team was unable to defend its overall crown. Only one athlete, Murrell Funderburke, brought home gold for SHS. Blowing away the competition, he set a county record in the 1600 meters.

Class of 1915

Football

The 1914 football team was coached by Bill Eccles and led by seniors John Ackers, Al Davis, and Bill Hyndman. The squad matched the previous season's win total, finishing 5-2-1 on the year. The season began with a Week 1 victory over Virden (26-7), followed by a shutout of Palmyra (34-0). After losing 20-6 to Alton Western Military Academy, SHS defeated Edwardsville (14-6) the very next weekend. Unfortunately, there would be no repeat as Macoupin County champions, as the boys in myrtle and maroon were soundly defeated by Carlinville (36-0). A 3-3 tie with Edwardsville was followed up by shutout victories over Palmyra (39-0) and Litchfield (32-0), capping off a very successful season for the program.

Track (Boys)

Though SHS and sponsor Bill Eccles took home the Literary Cup and Literary Banner, no athlete was able to capture a championship at the 1915 Macoupin County Meet.

Class of 1916

Football

The 1915 football team continued the accent of the program under coach Bill Eccles. The squad finished 6-1 on the season, breaking the old record for wins in a year. The only loss was to Palmyra (41-18) in Week 2 of the season. A Week 1 shutout victory over Litchfield (38-0) was followed by the Palmyra loss, which prompted a five-game winning streak to close out the campaign. Victories over Carlinville (51-6), Edwardsville (27-7), and Pawnee (19-17) preceded a second victory over Edwardsville in Week 6, this time by a score of 40-6. SHS closed out the year with a victory over Mt. Olive on Thanksgiving, sparking what later became a holiday tradition for the two schools.

Track (Boys)

Superintendent Bill Eccles had to be delighted with his orators in 1916, as Staunton once again took home the Literary Cup and Literary Banner from the Macoupin County Meet. In addition, SHS featured one of the premiere athletes at the contest. Murrell Funderburke set county records in both the 400 meters and 800 meters, easily bringing home championships in both events.

Class of 1917

Football

Little is known about the football team of 1916, as the squad was disbanded after just three games played, most likely due to lack of numbers in the program. After losing to Litchfield (60-0) and Benld (16-6), SHS defeated Edwardsville by a score of 13-7 before cancelling its remaining schedule. The 1-2 team was coached by Bill Eccles.

Track (Boys)

Staunton was shut out at the 1917 Macoupin County Meet, as no individual was able to capture gold at the event for the school and sponsor Bill Eccles.

Class of 1918

Football

Bill Eccles' 1917 football program consisted mostly of freshmen, and the inexperience of the team was displayed in early shutout losses to Benld (32-0) and Hillsboro (26-0). The team also lost to Litchfield before the program was disbanded for the second straight year. Though the most apparent causes were player youth and a lack of numbers on the squad, there likely was another factor at play as well. High school principal Noble Newsum, who later became the school's first-ever basketball coach, was called to serve his country in World War I. The district was unable to fill Newsum's position quickly, and thus Eccles, the superintendent of the district, took on more administrative responsibility at the expense of the football program. Although the 0-3 season goes down as Staunton's first winless campaign, the record is excusable given the context of the situation and lack of games played.

Track (Boys)

Little is known about Bill Eccles' 1918 track program, other than the fact that the squad was very young. Several freshmen gained valuable experience at the Macoupin County Meet, which they eventually curtailed into successful careers by the time they graduated from the school.

Class of 1919

Football

The 1918 football season was cancelled at Staunton High School, as it was at most area institutions. The culprit was the flu epidemic that swept the nation, shutting down most schools for several weeks, and some even longer.

Track (Boys)

The 1919 track team finished 3rd at the Macoupin County Meet under the direction of Bill Eccles. Byron Bozarth, a junior, captured gold in the 1600 meters.

CHAPTER 2

Classes of 1920 – 1929

Overview

Information dating back to the early 1900s is very hard to come by, especially since yearbooks were not common publications at Staunton High School until the latter part of the century. In fact, the first-ever SHS yearbook was published for the 1920-21 school year. It was a quality piece that included a surprising amount of detail about the students. Unfortunately, it was not produced again until 1924 and stopped being published soon thereafter. One can only presume why there were no annuals for over twenty years. The Great Depression certainly played a role, as there would have been a lack of funds available for students to purchase the yearbook, as well as few advertising dollars available to help cover overhead expenses. A push to conserve paper during wartime was likely a factor as well. Regardless, Staunton was not alone in its plight, as most community high schools in the area did not publish yearbooks during the era. The original SHS yearbook was titled the *Myrtle and Maroon*, named after Staunton's school colors at the time. At some point the yearbook became known as the *Echo*, as it still is today.

In addition to the construction of what is now the current high school building (the Class of 1925 was the first to graduate in the new facility), the 1920s saw two new sports added to the athletic offerings in the district. Boy's basketball began in 1920-21, and the baseball program was likely launched two years later. While basketball has, in general, never gained traction in the community, baseball is well-rooted in Staunton's past. However, the focus on the sport has generally been at the city level, and in fact the high school only competed in baseball sporadically in the first few years. Thus, despite the fact that no other program at the high school has won as many conference championships, baseball has rarely garnered much attention at SHS. Coupled with the fact that season results were often unattainable by the yearbook deadline, one can understand why baseball records have been difficult to uncover. Although not a sporting change, it is worth mentioning that football enjoyed a decade of supremacy unlike any other, as the program went 72-14-5 in the 1920s. Included in the mix was the 1923 team that set state and national records for offensive dominance on its way to a perfect 10-0 season.

The decade also saw the formation of the South Central Conference (SCC) for the 1926-27 school year, of which Staunton was a charter member. In fact, SHS remained in the league until 2009-10, when the school switched to the Prairie State Conference for three seasons before rejoining the SCC. Other original members of the SCC included Carlinville, Gillespie, Hillsboro, Litchfield, Mt. Olive, Nokomis, Pana, Shelbyville, and Taylorville.

Class of 1920

Football

The 1919 Staunton football team finished 5-1-1 on the season. The Maroons started the year out on the right foot, getting by Edwardsville 13-0 in Week 1. However, Carlinville defeated Staunton 8-0 in Week 2, thus denying SHS of the unofficial Macoupin County championship. The team members took their anger out on Litchfield in Week 3, racking up a record 73 points in a shutout victory over LHS. Wins over Edwardsville and Divernon followed before Staunton once again defeated Litchfield, this time by a score of 38-0. A 7-7 tie in Week 7 against Virden ended the successful campaign.

The 1919 football team was coached by Bill Eccles. His team featured Byron Bozarth, Art Grabruck, Jess Hastings, Clarence Heinz, Earl Heinz, Max Jones, Howard Linton, Art Lippold, Charley McGaughey, Ervin McLauchlan, Bill Nixon, Clayton Peel, Tom Sansone, and Mel Stiegemeier. Bozarth later returned to SHS and led the football and track programs to great success.

Track (Boys)

The 1920 track team finished 2nd at the Macoupin County Meet, which was won by Palmyra before a crowd reported to be in the thousands. No individuals won county titles for SHS and sponsor Bill Eccles, though Byron Bozarth, Jess Hastings, and Max Jones all qualified for the State Meet, which was held in Jacksonville. Bozarth, a senior, later returned to his alma mater to guide both the football and track teams.

Class of 1921

Basketball (Boys)

The first basketball team in school history was formed for the 1920-21 season. The squad, directed by principal Noble Newsum, finished with a record of 7-9. However, the first season could be considered fairly successful given the circumstances. SHS did not have an indoor court to practice on in those days, as the current high school and its gymnasium were not constructed until a few years later. Therefore, the players and coaching staff braved the elements, conducting practices outdoors during the winter, though local businesses with enough space donated use of their buildings from time to time. Despite the losing record, it is worth mentioning that Staunton won its first basketball game in school history, defeating Litchfield by a score of 22-18. SHS finished 4th in the Macoupin County Tournament in 1921, with freshman George Oehler being named All-County. Seniors on the squad included Jess Hastings, Al Martinelli, Ervin McLauchlan, and Ken Smith.

Football

The 1920 Staunton football team had a very successful season behind the play of seniors Al Martinelli, Charlie McGaughey, Ervin McLauchlan, Charlie Ross, and Ken Smith. The squad, coached by Bill Eccles, finished the year with a record of 7-1-1, outscoring their opponents 310-45 and capturing the unofficial Macoupin County championship. The group in myrtle and maroon started the year with three straight shutouts, defeating Litchfield (48-0), Benld (82-0), and Divernon (35-0). Staunton's only defeat came in a tough game at Hillsboro where it fell by a score of 20-7. SHS came back in Week 5 to defeat Carlinville (20-6) before settling for a scoreless tie with Virden in Week 6 of the season. Staunton finished the year with three straight victories, including another win over Litchfield (60-3), as well as triumphs over Palmyra (21-2) and Mt. Olive (37-14).

Track (Boys)

The track team returned a nice blend of talent and experience for the 1921 season, including seniors Jess Hastings and Ervin McLauchlan. Glen Hasting, Max Jones, George Oehler, Roland Sawyer, Armond Sherman, and Cliff Stiegemeier rounded out the team. At the Macoupin County Meet, McLauchlan (javelin) and Jones (1600 meters) set records in their respective events, while Sherman also brought home a county title in the standing broad jump. Staunton also made some noise at State that year, as McLauchlan placed 2nd in the javelin and Jones placed 3rd in the 1600 meters. The Staunton athletes were coached by Bill Eccles.

Class of 1922

Basketball (Boys)

With no yearbook published and newspaper articles spotty at best, it is hard to find a complete record for the 1921-22 basketball team. However, it is known that the squad defeated Livingston twice in the regular season, as well as beating Virden and Benld once each. Losses came to Gillespie and Morrisonville. At the Macoupin County Tournament, Staunton defeated Virden and Gillespie before falling to eventual champion Mt. Olive, thus ending the season with an incomplete record of 6-3 under coach Noble Newsum.

Football

Coach Bill Eccles' 1921 football team finished 7-3 on the year. It was Eccles' last season with the team, though he certainly was not forgotten for the impact that he had on Staunton football. As superintendent of the district, he not only formed the program but, by experiencing success, he set the foundation for the record-breaking seasons that followed. Interestingly enough, Eccles had run for public office years earlier but was defeated in the election. Had he won the position, it is difficult to say what might have become of Staunton High School football.

Back to 1921, the Maroons started the year off right with a shutout against Benld (19-0). After losing a heartbreaker to Mt. Olive (10-7), Staunton reeled off three more shutouts over Gillespie (13-0), Granite City (64-0), and Litchfield (21-0). Losses to Greenfield (38-15) and Virden (21-19) ensued, though the Virden loss came with much controversy. Apparently, in the final minute of the game and SHS leading by a small margin, Virden ran a play that the refs blew dead. The Staunton players stopped on the whistle but Virden did not, instead running in a touchdown to take the lead. Unfortunately, the Staunton bunch could not win the argument over the blown call, and the touchdown stood, resulting in a victory for Virden. Regardless, SHS finished the season strong, winning games over Palmyra (26-6), Carlinville (10-7), and exacting revenge on Mt. Olive (51-19). Football members that season included Gwylim Bozarth, Cliff Conway, Ed Fritz, Glen Hasting, Ed Hofstetter, Harry Jeanes, Max Jones, Delbert Lloyd, Adam Marquis, Harris May, Harry Miller, George Oehler, Harlow Panhorst, Gerald Roberts, Art Ruffini, Roland Sawyer, and Cliff Stiegemeier.

Track (Boys)

The 1922 track squad placed 2nd at the Macoupin County Meet. Max Jones (800 meters) and Roland Sawyer (50 meters) won their respective races at the event, thus giving coach Bill Eccles two champions that year.

Class of 1923

Baseball

Though it is possible that baseball began at Staunton High School prior to the 1923 season, no records indicating this have been found. However, what is known is that the 1923 team was coached by Paul Miller. In addition to his duties as school principal and classroom instructor, Coach Miller also directed each sport available at SHS during the 1922-23 school year. Many of his teams were considered among the best in the area, and his first baseball team was no different, finishing a sparkling 9-0 on the season.

Basketball (Boys)

Only partial results were obtained for coach Paul Miller's 1922-23 basketball team, though it is known that Staunton defeated Shurtleff College, Litchfield, and Carlinville. A loss to Mt. Olive also occurred, leaving the team with an incomplete record of 3-1.

Football

For the first time in school history the football program had someone other than Bill Eccles at the helm. Paul Miller guided the 1922 team, a squad that finished with a mark of 9-1 overall and set a standard for the following season's record-setting team. The year began with a Week 1 victory over Benld by a score of 28-3. Shutouts over East St. Louis (20-0) and Litchfield (31-0) ensued, followed by a victory over rival Gillespie by a score of 28-3. A 65-0 shellacking of Auburn preceded a Week 6 route of Virden (40-6). Staunton hit the century mark for the first time in school history in Week 7, as SHS pounded Granite City by a score of 101-0. It was not the last time Staunton broke the 100-point barrier, and in fact the mark was shattered the very next season on two separate occasions. Unfortunately, the fun ended the very next week, as the Green Wave suffered its only loss of the season by a score of 33-13 to Carlinville. A solid victory over Alton Western Military Academy (13-0) followed, and Staunton also took care of business in the annual Thanksgiving game against Mt. Olive. SHS had many outstanding players in 1922, but two in particular garnered media attention. Dave Wilson was named 1st Team All-Central Illinois by the *Illinois State Register*, while Fred Arnicar was named to the 2nd Team.

Track (Boys)

Paul Miller's 1923 track program featured just five participants, all juniors. However, each was an exceptional athlete who helped SHS to a very successful season. Glen Hastings, John McBrien, George Oehler, Roland Sawyer, and Cliff Stiegemeier led the team to victory at the McKendree College Invitational, an event that featured more than twenty local teams, and at that time was considered the premier track meet in Southern Illinois. At the Macoupin County Meet,

Hastings (400 meters), Oehler (discus) and Sawyer (standing broad jump) all won their respective events, leading the team to a 2nd place finish.

Class of 1924

Baseball

The SHS baseball team finished the 1924 season with a spotless 8-0 record, defeating Gillespie, Litchfield, Virden, and Mt. Olive twice each. Seniors Glen Allen, Glen Hastings, George Oehler, Roland Sawyer, and Cliff Stiegemeier led first-year coach Gilbert Lane's undefeated team.

Basketball (Boys)

Due to the success of the football program, Gilbert Lane's 1923-24 basketball squad got a late start to the season. Nevertheless, the team showed no rust early, winning their first four games of the year. The Maroons played .500 ball the rest of the way, finishing with a record of 11-7. Staunton played for the championship at the Macoupin County Tournament that year, only to be upended by Chesterfield by a score of 20-19. Edwardsville eventually eliminated SHS in the District Tournament. Seniors at SHS included Glen Allen, Glen Hastings, John McBrien, George Oehler, Roland Sawyer, Cliff Stiegemeier, and Harry Yauornick. Stiegemeier returned years later to direct the basketball program at Staunton after spending several years coaching at Mt. Olive.

Football

The 1923 football team was quite simply the most dominant in school history and certainly could be considered one of the best in Illinois history. The boys in myrtle and maroon steamrolled nearly every team they played, finishing 10-0 on the season. In fact, most games were not even close, as coach Paul Miller's squad outscored its opponents by a score of 494-23 on the season, allowing just one team to cross the goal line. Furthermore, in a 233-0 drubbing of Gillespie, SHS set state (still stands) and national (since surpassed) records for most points (233) and touchdowns (30) in a game. In fact, the game was so humiliating for Gillespie that the school refused to compete against Staunton in any activity indefinitely, including football, basketball, and debate. South Central Conference officials eventually required the two schools to renew their rivalry beginning in 1928-29.

The season started with a very difficult game against Alton Western Military Academy, and SHS won a defensive struggle by scoring on a blocked punt for a 7-0 victory, the first of eight shutouts on the year. Carlinville came calling in Week 2, and a crowd of more than two thousand fans saw Staunton hold on for a 26-20 victory. The schedule remained difficult in Week 3 as Staunton ventured to St. Louis to take on Cleveland High School, somehow coming away with a 10-3 victory over the host school. The season ended with seven straight shutouts, starting with a Week 4 victory over Benld (18-0). After slaughtering Litchfield (113-0), SHS defeated Virden (9-0) and Girard (20-0) before the aforementioned matchup with Gillespie. A Week 9 victory over Mt. Olive (38-0) capped off a perfect regular season. Although the score of the Mt. Olive game looks respectable on paper, in reality it would have been much worse if the whole game had been played. About halfway through the contest, Mt. Olive's coach and players reacted to a perceived bad call by walking off the field, resulting in a forfeit. Ironically, SHS had requested that the annual Thanksgiving game be postponed anyway, due to the heavy rain and wet conditions of the playing field. However, the Mt. Olive coaching staff insisted on playing but, as stated, did not finish the game.

Being champions of the Central District, SHS arranged a postseason game with Carbondale High School, champions of the Southern District. The Staunton defense once again rose to the challenge, posting yet another shutout in a 20-0 victory. After the game, several media outlets bestowed upon Staunton the title of state champion. In an unlikely turn of events, Carlinville was being considered by some to be the best team in Illinois at the time, despite the early loss to SHS. Obviously, the community of Staunton was not happy with the claim and vocalized as much. The back and forth in the media strained relations between the schools, and in fact Carlinville eliminated Staunton from its schedule for two years thereafter.

Regardless of any media posturing, Staunton had achieved a season for the ages, and for their excellent play Cliff Stiegemeier, Mel Stiegemeier, and Art Ruffini were named 1st Team All-Central Illinois by the *Illinois State Register*, while Gerald Roberts made 2nd Team. George Oehler and Dave Wilson were also commended for their fine play, taking home Honorable Mention status. Senior members of the historic 1923 team were Erwin Grabruck, Glen Hastings, Oehler, Roland Sawyer, Roberts, and Cliff Stiegemeier. Hastings, Oehler, Sawyer, and Cliff Stiegemeier were four-year letter winners, and Oehler continued his career at Washington University in St. Louis. Cliff Stiegemeier eventually returned to his alma mater and led the football program to success as its head coach.

Track (Boys)

The 1924 track program featured the same five participants as the previous season, but this time Glen Hastings, John McBrien, George Oehler, Roland Sawyer, and Cliff Stiegemeier were determined seniors looking to surpass the success of the prior year. SHS again captured the title at the McKendree College Invitational, the premier track meet in Southern Illinois at the time. Though it is unclear how the community received the previous year's title, this time the championship was considered such a feat that the following Monday was declared a holiday from school. The student body stormed Main Street, pulling an old buggy with the track team in tow. With principal Paul Miller serving as the team's coach, it is likely the students had the administration's blessing to carry on in such a manner.

SHS took home 2nd place overall at the Macoupin County Meet, though the squad did finish 1st in the athletic portion of the event. Early county meets featured an oratorical competition in addition to the athletic one, and thus Carlinville's mastery of the former contest gave them the overall team title. Sawyer had an outstanding year, breaking the meet record in the standing broad jump, while Hastings took home titles in the running broad jump and 800 meter run.

Class of 1925

Baseball

Gilbert Lane's 1925 baseball team featured seniors Fred Arnicar and Gwylm Bozarth. Apparently the team was only able to schedule two contests on the season (Edwardsville and

Alton Western Military Academy), and in fact after the season the program apparently went dormant for nearly two decades for unknown reasons.

Basketball (Boys)

The 1924-25 basketball team, directed by Gilbert Lane, was led by seniors Gwylm Bozarth, Delbert Lloyd, Vic Patterson, and Art Ruffini. Despite not having a gym available at the school for practice until late in the season, the squad still finished 7-8 on the year. Mt. Olive served as the team's nemesis during the season, as the boys in purple in gold defeated SHS on four separate occasions, including knocking SHS out of both the Macoupin County and District tournaments.

Football

Staunton High School welcomed a new coach for the 1924 football season. Byron Bozarth, a Staunton graduate, took over the reins of a program coming off of one of the best seasons in Illinois history. Due to the success of the previous year, SHS had a hard time finding games and had to do some travelling in order to play a full schedule. Despite the graduation of some very talented players, SHS still had a strong senior class led by Fred Arnicar, Gwylm Bozarth, Delbert Lloyd, Dan McGaughey, Vic Patterson, and Art Ruffini.

The season began against Kirkwood High School in Missouri, a team which Staunton shut out by a score of 38-0. Week 2 saw rival and neighbor Benld come to town, and the two schools played an excellent game, settling for a 6-6 tie. In Week 3, the Green Wave defeated Alton Western Military Academy (16-7). With no opponent willing to play the team in Week 4, tiny Modesto agreed to take on SHS. As a favor, Staunton started its second unit against the feisty Modesto squad, but it backfired, and the boys in myrtle and maroon fell behind by two touchdowns early in the game. The first unit was then called upon, and they easily handled their competitors in a 45-14 victory. After a scoreless tie with Hillsboro in Week 5, SHS took on St. Louis University High, shutting out the much bigger squad (10-0). The only loss of the season came in Week 7 at Lincoln, with SHS falling by a score of 28-5. The campaign ended with consecutive shutouts over Mt. Olive (13-0) and Benld (7-0), leaving Staunton with an overall record of 6-1-2. After graduating, Arnicar and Ruffini both enrolled to play football at Centre College in Danville, Kentucky. Ruffini eventually returned to Staunton and become head coach of the football and track programs.

Track (Boys)

The 1925 track team was one of the most successful in school history, as the unit finished in 8th place overall at State. Additionally, the Staunton squad tied Webster Groves High School for the championship at the exclusive Washington University Track Meet, an event that included some of the biggest schools in the St. Louis area. Finally, SHS finished 2nd at the McKendree College Invitational.

The squad, coached by Byron Bozarth, included seniors Fred Arnicar, Bob Maynard, and Art Ruffini. Arnicar won the Macoupin County Meet in the shot put and discus before placing 2nd at State in the shot put. Dave Wilson won a county title in the 400 meters, and he eventually finished in 3rd place in that event at State. Finally, Jim Peele took 4th at State in the hurdles. Ruffini returned to SHS years later and directed the track program, in addition to his tenure coaching football in the district.

Class of 1926

Basketball (Boys)
The 1925-26 Staunton basketball team was coached by Byron Bozarth. The team featured Dave Wilson, a 2nd Team All-Tournament selection at the Macoupin County Tournament. The team finished with an unofficial record of 5-4, as it is likely the squad played more games than were reported.

Football
The 1925 football team, directed by Byron Bozarth, was a formidable squad. The team finished 7-1, with the only loss coming to Alton Western Military Academy (AWMA) by a score of 6-0. Staunton began the season with two close wins. A Week 1 affair with Kirkwood resulted in a 12-6 victory, followed by a 13-0 win over Greenfield. The Week 3 loss to AWMA preceded five straight victories, with four coming via shutout. Staunton defeated Pana 28-0 before beating St. Louis University High (26-0). Another win over Kirkwood, this time by a score of 34-6, followed, and wins over Hillsboro (33-0) and Benld (27-0) closed out the season. One of the standouts on the team was Roy Awe, a senior who went on to play football at Illinois College.

Track (Boys)
Coming off the previous season's 8th place finish at State, coach Byron Bozarth's track team looked forward to repeating its success from the prior year. Unfortunately, little is known about the season, though it is clear that the squad was unable to duplicate the success of the one that came before it.

Class of 1927

Basketball (Boys)
The 1926-27 basketball season seems to mark the first time that the school and community rallied around the program, providing ample resources, opportunities, and support needed for success. Perhaps not coincidentally, it was also the first year of the South Central Conference, with Litchfield eventually emerging as the champion of the league. Staunton, led by first-year coach Carroll McBride, did not disappoint its stakeholders, finishing 15-10 overall, thus setting a school record for victories in a season up to that point.

The highlight of each basketball season in that era was the Macoupin County Tournament. Although the current version of the tournament still holds some allure, with fewer schools competing, and with so many other entertainment options for people in modern society, crowds are sparse on most nights. Such was not the case in the 1920s, as the tournament was the showcase event of the winter season, drawing huge crowds to the host gymnasium with sixteen teams competing for bragging rights. Among the schools battling it out for the title were Benld, Brighton, Bunker Hill, Carlinville, Chesterfield, Gillespie, Girard, Hettick, Medora, Modesto, Mt. Olive, Palmyra, Scottville, Shipman, Staunton, and Virden.

Staunton began the tournament with a relatively easy victory over Virden before winning a close matchup with Benld. In the semifinals, SHS drew Chesterfield, which despite its small enrollment, was a force to be reckoned with on the basketball court in the 1920s. Unfortunately, SHS dropped the game by a score of 21-19. Staunton went on to capture 3rd place by easily defeating Brighton, and Chesterfield lost in the championship game to Mt. Olive, which captured its third straight county title. One of the standouts on Staunton's team was Walter Grabruck, a senior who went on to play basketball at Centre College.

Football

The 1926 football season saw two firsts: the first year for head coach Carroll McBride, and the first year for the South Central Conference, of which Staunton was a charter member. However, despite being a ten-team league, the setup was a bit haphazard, as many conference foes did not actually settle games on the field. In fact, Staunton, which closed at 5-4 overall, only played five SCC games, finishing 2-3 in those affairs. The season began with a shutout victory over Litchfield. Solid wins over Edwardsville (8-0), East Alton-Wood River (48-0), and Greenfield (9-6) gave the team high hopes, and a shutout of SCC foe Carlinville (27-0) added to the excitement. However, it was all downhill from there, as a 20-0 loss to Benld preceded setbacks to Hillsboro (7-0), Pana, and Mt. Olive (6-0). Thus, after having started the season 5-0, Staunton went on to lose four straight games, setting what was then a record for most losses in a season. Mt. Olive went on to win the inaugural SCC football title in 1926.

SHS featured two standout players in the form of seniors Walter Grabruck and John Horky. Both players moved on to Centre College to continue their careers. In addition to participating in football at the school, Grabruck also played basketball. Meanwhile, Horky became a campus icon and eventually had a building named after him at Centre College, as well as an award that is still given annually in his honor.

Track (Boys)

Under first-year coach Carroll McBride, the 1927 track season saw Staunton continue its upward trend in the sport, as several individuals qualified for State. At the Macoupin County Meet, Wellman France won the high jump. He also won District in that event and eventually placed 6th at State. In addition, France teamed up with Howard Meyer, Bob Ramseier, and Irwin Spotti on the District champion 800 meter relay team. The relay team also advanced to State, as did George McLauchlan (pole vault), Don Overbeay (discus), and Spotti (hurdles).

Class of 1928

Basketball (Boys)

The 1927-28 basketball team was coached by Carroll McBride, and the squad was quite simply the best in SHS history up to that point. The program accomplished many firsts, including the first 20-win season, the first Macoupin County championship, and the first postseason title, as SHS won the District Tournament. Unfortunately, the boys in myrtle and maroon were unable to win the South Central Conference despite finishing 21-6 overall and 8-2 in league play.

Staunton was led into action that season by four outstanding players: Bernie Aschbacher, Wellman France, John Oehler, and Don Overbeay. Aschbacher, France, and Oehler were each named 1st Team All-County, while Overbeay was named to the 2nd Team. At County, Staunton defeated Girard, Virden, Chesterfield, and Gillespie on its way to the title. At District, SHS took out Morrisonville, Mt. Olive, Irving, and SCC champion Hillsboro in winning the school's first District title. France and Oehler were named to the All-District Team at the conclusion of the event. At Sectionals, Staunton played very well in the first game, defeating Lebanon to advance to the next round. Unfortunately, the next opponent was Witt, a squad that had narrowly defeated SHS twice earlier that season. This matchup was no different, as Witt once again took care of SHS on its way to an eventual appearance at State. After the season, Aschbacher (Honorable Mention), France (1st Team), Oehler (2nd Team), and Overbeay (1st Team) each made the All-Conference squad.

On a side note, SHS exacted revenge on two ex-coaches during regular season action. Paul Miller, coach of the legendary football team of 1923, had moved on to Alton High School where he was put in charge of the basketball program. After losing to Alton early in the year by one point, SHS easily defeat the much larger school later in the season. Also, Byron Bozarth, a Staunton graduate who eventually coached basketball, football, and track in his hometown, was now working at Granite City High School. While SHS defeated Bozarth's squad that season, he in fact enjoyed many successful years at GCHS, ultimately winning a state championship in 1940.

Football

Staunton captured its first South Central Conference football championship in 1927. Gillespie shared a piece of the crown, as both teams were undefeated in SCC play. However, GHS upheld its ban of competing against teams from Staunton, due to the 233-0 thrashing that occurred in 1923. Despite repeated attempts by SHS to determine the championship on the field, the game never happened. However, writers and critics believed that the game would have been no contest, as Staunton, along with Virden and Hillsboro, was believed to be one of the best teams in the state, with Gillespie barely in the conversation. Others chose to look at comparative scores between common opponents. For instance, SHS defeated Mt. Olive 39-0 in the last game of the season, just one week after Gillespie narrowly beat Mt. Olive by a score of 6-0.

Staunton finished 8-0-1 overall in 1927, including 4-0 in the SCC, with all four conference victories coming via shutout. The record marked the program's second undefeated campaign in its history. Week 1 opened with a non-conference game against Edwardsville, a team that SHS easily defeated by a score of 47-0. Week 2 provided the only blemish on Staunton's record in a 7-7 tie with Virden. The fact that Staunton was able to garner a tie was a surprise to many, as Virden returned basically its whole starting lineup from the previous season, a group that was not scored upon all year. A 56-0 tune-up in Week 3 over Livingston preceded SCC play, which Staunton opened with a 13-0 victory over Litchfield. Wins over Greenfield (32-0), Carlinville (27-0), Girard (53-6), Hillsboro (14-0), and Mt. Olive (39-0) followed, and when the season was over SHS had outscored its opponents 232-13.

Carroll McBride directed SHS football in 1927, and team members included Bernie Aschbacher, August Costa, Wellman France, Otto Horky, John Jersin, Tom Kinnikin, Bill Moss, George McLauchlan, Howard Meyer, Roy Miller, John Oehler, Don Overbeay, Bob Ramseier, Will Saottini, Irwin Spotti, and Bill Straud. Aschbacher, Miller, Oehler, and Overbeay all attained All-Conference 1st Team status, while France and Ramseier were also honored by being named 2nd Team All-SCC. Aschbacher and Overbeay continued their football careers at Illinois College.

Track (Boys)

Not only did SHS win the athletic portion of the Macoupin County Meet for the second time in school history, but in 1928 the team also took home the overall title, bringing the Grand Prize trophy, Field Meet trophy, and Relay Cup back to Staunton. Moreover, Carroll McBride's crew also made history by winning the initial South Central Conference Track Meet. Finally, the dream season continued, as the track team won the District championship for the first time in the program's history.

County champions in 1928 included Wellman France in the high jump, long jump, and hurdles. France actually set a county record in the high jump, which interestingly enough was a better mark than the record set at State that same year. Howard Meyer won County in both the 100 meters and 200 meters, while the 800 meter relay team of Meyer, Bob Ramseier, Irwin Spotti, and Harry Walters tied the meet record in winning that event. With the SCC Meet being in its inaugural season, each Staunton winner actually set a conference record. Winners included France (long jump, hurdles), Meyer (50 meters, 100 meters, 200 meters), Spotti (400 meters), and the 800 meter relay team of Meyer, Ramseier, Spotti, and Walters. Finally, although the team as a whole placed 1st, Meyer was the only SHS athlete to win at the District Meet, doing so in both the 100 meters and 200 meters and setting a meet record in the latter event. He moved on to State in both events, eventually winning 3rd place in the 100 meters. France also advanced to State, and he too took home a 3rd place medal, with his honor coming in the high jump.

Class of 1929

Basketball (Boys)

Having graduated four starters from the previous year's record-setting team, the 1928-29 basketball squad struggled to find consistency during the season. Staunton finished with an overall record of 7-14, including 5-9 in the South Central Conference. However, the Macoupin County Tournament showed promise, as SHS defeated Virden and Modesto to advance to the title game for the second year in succession. Staunton's opponent for the crown was Chesterfield High School. Unfortunately, Staunton lost in the championship 9-5, and in fact the game set a record for the lowest scoring championship in Macoupin County Tournament history. John Oehler was named 1st Team All-County, while Bill Moss and Harry Walters were both named 2nd Team. The club was coached by A.R. Pruitt in his only year with the program.

Football

Staunton repeated as South Central Conference champions in 1928, this time led by A.R. Pruitt in his only season at the helm of the football program. The 8-2 Staunton team finished 4-0 in the SCC. Week 1 saw SHS once again defeat Edwardsville handedly, this time by a score of 40-6. Shutouts over East Alton-Wood River (18-0), Litchfield (15-0), and Greenfield (13-0) preceded a key matchup with Carlinville in Week 5, which Staunton was able to win in close fashion by a score of 18-13. SHS suffered its first loss of the season in Week 6 to Virden (6-0) before defeating Hillsboro (18-0) and Benld (7-0). Granite City, led by former SHS alum and coach Byron Bozarth, nipped the Green Wave in Week 9 by a score of 18-0. However, the biggest game of the season came on Thanksgiving, as SHS played its annual grudge match with Mt. Olive. This game had more on the line than usual, as a Staunton victory would wrap up a share of the SCC. Mt. Olive played an excellent game, but SHS responded to the pressure by coming through with a 6-0 victory to close out the season and a conference championship. Unfortunately, for the second straight season Staunton had to share its crown, as Taylorville also swept through its portion of the conference slate. Letterman on the 1928 SCC champions included Libro Airola, August Costa, Corbett Dietiker, Otto Horky, Tom Kinnikin, Jim McGaughey, Howard Meyer, Bill Moss, Bob Moss, John Oehler, Bob Ramseier, Elmer Schnaare, Elmer Spotti, Irwin Spotti, and Harry Walters. The Spotti brothers moved on to continue their careers at Missouri University of Science & Technology in Rolla. Meanwhile, Oehler played football at Purdue University before competing professionally for the Pittsburgh and Brooklyn organizations.

Track (Boys)

The 1929 track team matched the success from the previous year, but this time under a different coach, as A.R. Pruitt took over the program for one season. By the end of the year, SHS found itself once again South Central Conference and Macoupin County champions, and eventually finished in 7th place at State, the best result in program history.

At County, the team brought home the Championship Cup, Athletic Cup, and Relay Cup, mostly due to success in the field events, though several competitors also fared well in the oratorical portion of the meet. The day belonged to Staunton's Howard Meyer. Meyer won five events at County, becoming perhaps the first and only athlete to accomplish such a feat. Given that athletes are now only allowed to compete in four events in any given track meet, it is probable that the accomplishment will never be matched. Meyer won the long jump, 50 meters, 100 meters, 200 meters, and was also on the winning 800 meter relay team. He was joined on that team by Bob Ramseier, Irwin Spotti, and Harry Walters. Ramseier also took gold in the 400 meters for SHS. At the SCC contest, Meyer again was impressive in winning the 100 meters, 200 meters, and 800 meter relay, joining Ramseier, Spotti, and Walters on the unit. Ramseier also captured the 400 meters, and he was joined in the winner's circle by John Masser (pole vault). Ramseier (400 meters) and the 800 meter relay team eventually took 5th place at State. Meanwhile, Meyer just missed out on becoming Staunton's first state champion, as he had to settle for 2nd place in the 100 meters and 4th place in the 200 meters.

CHAPTER 3

Classes of 1930 – 1939

Overview

Though SHS continued to field successful teams into the 1930s, perhaps the most important happening of the decade came off the playing field, as Staunton's first and only mascot was chosen during the 1935-36 school year. Before that time, local teams had always been referred to by their school colors. However, mascots were taking hold across the state, and the administration left it up to the student body to vote on proposals. Norm Norvell, a junior at the time, successfully lobbied for "Bull Dogs", which later was changed to "Bulldogs". However, the school retained its colors of myrtle and maroon for several years.

Despite average team success during the decade, as well as the context of the Great Depression, participation in high school sports continued to thrive into the 1930s in Staunton. In fact, a survey conducted during the 1930-31 academic year showed that only 7% of boys in the district did not play sports, and that most athletes participated in at least two activities. It is worth noting that a few individuals competed in tennis during the decade. While not much is known about the popularity or staying power of the sport, it is known that at least four individuals qualified for the State in the 1930s. Interestingly enough, the first "S" Club was formed at the school during the decade. The organization, which was later discontinued, reached its heyday in the 1960s.

While basketball was not very popular in Staunton at the time, perhaps the biggest event in the area was the annual rendition of the Macoupin County Tournament. During the 1930s the tourney included sixteen schools. Each year, teams from Benld, Brighton, Bunker Hill, Carlinville, Chesterfield, Gillespie, Girard, Hettick, Medora, Modesto, Mt. Olive, Palmyra, Scottville, Shipman, Staunton, and Virden competed for county bragging rights. Finally, the South Central Conference has experienced tremendous change throughout its history, and the first such shakeup occurred in 1932-33. That season saw the SCC fall to nine teams with the departure of Shelbyville. Litchfield followed suit two years later, leaving the organization with eight teams. However, the SCC went back to nine teams in 1935-36, as Benld was welcomed to the fold.

Class of 1930

Basketball (Boys)

Staunton welcomed a new coach for the 1929-30 basketball season, as Judson Jones took over the program. SHS graduated many key competitors from the prior two seasons, and unfortunately youth and inexperience took their toll as the team suffered to a record of 4-18, including 2-10 in the South Central Conference. The team's win total came in a six-game span, as the squad opened the year with twelve straight losses and finished with four straight defeats. A stretch of strong play came at the Macoupin County Tournament, as the team thrilled fans with many close games before bowing out in 4th place. The event started with a close win over Mt. Olive (18-17). SHS then narrowly defeated Benld in overtime by a score of 17-16. Unfortunately, Modesto ended the team's title hopes with a 9-7 victory, after which SHS was soundly defeated by Carlinville. Out of the four wins in the campaign, three came against Mt. Olive.

Football

After the flu epidemic forced the 1918 season to be cancelled, SHS reeled off ten straight winning campaigns, many of which were spectacular seasons. However, Staunton stumbled to a 1-6-1 record under coach Judson Jones in 1929, including 0-5 in the South Central Conference in his first season on the job. The lone victory came in Week 1 when SHS defeated Granite City by a score of 18-6. After a scoreless tie with Edwardsville, the Maroons went on to lose the rest of their games to Gillespie (7-6), Pana (51-6), Benld (17-7), Hillsboro (57-0), Carlinville (19-0), and Mt. Olive (7-0). Hillsboro captured the first of two straight SCC titles that season.

Though the team did not fare well on the field, SHS once again saw a large group of players participate in football. In 1929, the roster included Herman Bachelor, Winston Bachelor, Ernest Borsch, Art Bozue, Ed Burgoyne, Jim Burgoyne, Ted Charley, John Conway, George Courtney, Jim DeQuire, Elmer Graham, Al Haase, Clettis Hebenstreit, Bob Herschel, Mel Hiffman, Otto Horky, Lewis Jacobs, Rob Jones, Joe Kapilla, Junior Kaseman, Layton Lamb, Rich Lorenzini, Edgar Lorsen, Bill Marland, John Masser, Ted Melton, Leroy Miller, Bill Mosser, Joe O'Neal, Elmer Schnaare, Fred Schulte, Adler Spotti, Elmer Spotti, Myrl Stiegemeier, George Swain, Harry Walters, Walt Yaeger, and Fred Yauornik.

Tennis (Boys)

It appears that Staunton High School added a tennis team, or at least allowed individuals to compete, for the spring season of 1930. Al Haase and Fred Schultz were particularly effective, as they advanced to State in doubles and made a run for the title before finishing in 3rd place.

Track (Boys)

Staunton was unable to three-peat as South Central Conference champions in 1930, as the team fell to 3rd place in the standings under coach Judson Jones. John Masser was the lone bright spot for SHS, setting a conference record in the pole vault and later advancing to State in that same event.

Class of 1931

Basketball (Boys)

Coming off a poor season from the year before, the 1930-31 basketball team looked to improve under the leadership of Judson Jones. Coach Jones welcomed back six letter winners, including seniors Rich Lorenzini and John Masser, as well as underclassmen Corbett Dietiker, Stan Filipwcz, Ted Melton, and Adler Spotti. Although the team did not attain a winning season, the squad did improve, finishing 7-8-1 overall and 3-6-1 in the South Central Conference.

Ties in basketball are very rare, and in fact the one in 1931 was the only tie in the program's history. SHS played Gillespie in Staunton, and the boys in myrtle and maroon led 22-21 with just seconds left in the contest. At that point, a Gillespie player stole the ball and hit a half-court shot to seemingly win the game. However, the score table disagreed on whether or not the shot had beaten the clock. The referees eventually decided that overtime should be played to determine the winner. But, by that time the crowd would not settle down, and the same officials decided to end the game on the spot and call it a tie.

The Macoupin County Tournament was fairly uneventful for SHS, as Staunton defeated Virden before losing to Carlinville by a score of 11-10. However, one interesting note about the event is that 1931 marked the first year that tournament administrators decided to play all of the games at night. Instead of a two-day affair that saw games begin on Friday morning and end Saturday night, the tournament switched to a Wednesday-Saturday format due to low attendance. Though Staunton did not fare well, Masser took home All-County honors at the event, which was won by Chesterfield for the third straight season.

Football

The 1930 Staunton football team fared better than the previous year, finishing 4-4-1 overall and 3-2-1 in the South Central Conference. Judson Jones coached the team in his second season with the program. Though Week 1 saw the team lose to Palmyra by a score of 13-0, it is believed that the game was the first in Macoupin County history to be played under lights. SHS dropped a tough game to Edwardsville (12-6) in Week 2 but started off the SCC slate on the right foot with a shutout of Taylorville (18-0) in Week 3. In Week 4, Staunton and Gillespie played to a scoreless tie before Carlinville nipped Staunton (13-12) the very next week. Two shutout victories followed, as Staunton downed Litchfield (34-0) before pulling a big upset in defeating Jacksonville Routt (7-0). A loss to eventual SCC champion Hillsboro preceded the annual Thanksgiving game against Mt. Olive, with SHS winning by a score of 21-0.

Tennis (Boys)

The 1931 tennis team ventured to Collinsville and defeated the host squad to capture the District championship.

Track (Boys)

Judson Jones' 1931 track team finished 5th at the South Central Conference Meet, with only one individual, John Masser (pole vault), capturing gold. The team fared much better at the Macoupin County Meet, with Masser again winning the pole vault. However, this time he was joined in the winner's circle by Elmer Graham (hurdles), Ted Melton (long jump, 400 meters), and Bill Pervinsek (shot put). Walt Meyer, a senior, continued his track career at Illinois College.

Class of 1932

Basketball (Boys)

As the Great Depression set in, newspaper space became limited, and thus results for sports other than football are hard to uncover, and in reality some have probably been lost to history. In particular, basketball coverage suffered, perhaps because the community viewed basketball as a minor sport, or due to the fact that the program had not been overly successful throughout its history. Either way, it is very difficult to determine the record of several teams of the 1930s, and the 1931-32 season is no different. In the four results that were found, Staunton was 0-4 under coach Judson Jones.

Football

Judson Jones' 1931 football team got off to a very hot start, winning the first four games of the season. After a three-game losing streak, SHS closed with two victories and thus finished the season with a record of 6-3, including 4-2 in the South Central Conference. After the season, team members Elmer Graham and Layton Lamb were both named 1st Team All-Conference. Senior Ted Melton continued his football career at Millikin University.

Week 1 saw Staunton clobber Mt. Olive by a score of 45-0. The shutout victories continued the next two weeks, as both Palmyra (25-0) and Shelbyville (27-0) suffered losses at the hands of the Green Wave. Staunton was able to squeak by Gillespie (7-6) in a Week 4 matchup between the two rivals. Close losses to Nokomis (6-0), Carlinville (14-6), and Benld (7-6) ensued before Staunton pulled off an epic upset of Hillsboro in Week 8 by a score of 13-12. The Hiltoppers were undefeated coming into the game, and by many accounts they would surely beat a reeling Staunton squad. However, SHS held on for a close victory and went on to defeat Mt. Olive (12-0) for the second time on the season in the annual Thanksgiving game. The close losses to Carlinville and Nokomis came back to haunt SHS, as those two schools eventually tied for the SCC crown.

Track (Boys)

Judson Jones' 1932 track team had an average season, finishing 6th at the South Central Conference Meet and 4th at the Macoupin County Meet. However, the team did receive outstanding individual performances from two members, as Bill Pervinsek set SCC records in both the discus and shot put, while Ted Melton won a conference title in the long jump. At County, Pervinsek set a record in the discus while also winning the shot put, and Melton repeated as champion in the long jump. It is worth mentioning that in 1932 event officials determined to switch from awarding individual medals to instead giving out ribbons to each winner. Surely this was a cost issue, partly due to the economic situation that the country faced at the time.

Class of 1933

Basketball (Boys)

Though the program played a full schedule, only partial results were found for the 1932-33 basketball team. The squad finished 2-8 in those games under the direction of Judson Jones.

Football

On paper, the 1932 football season was one of the worst in school history at the time, as the squad finished winless on the year with a record of 0-5-4, including 0-4-3 in the South Central Conference. However, a closer look at the results reveals that every game on the schedule was competitive, and in fact the team only allowed 78 points the whole year. Unfortunately, SHS only scored once during the season in an age of defensive excellence. The team was coached by Judson Jones in his last year with the program. A bright spot for the club was the play of senior Layton Lamb, an All-Conference selection.

The season started with a 6-0 loss to Mt. Olive, followed by scoreless ties with Litchfield and Collinsville. Losses to Gillespie (15-0) and Benld (13-0) followed before the team battled

Carlinville to a 7-7 tie. Two straight losses to Pana (13-0) and Hillsboro (24-0) put Staunton in a precarious situation, as the boys in myrtle and maroon had to knock off SCC front-runner Mt. Olive to win their only game of the year. Though SHS did not win the game, it did play Mt. Olive to a scoreless tie, thus forcing the boys in purple and gold to share the league crown with Gillespie. On a side note, and unfortunately as a sign of the times, Litchfield dropped its football program after the season due to budgetary constraints.

Track (Boys)

Judson Jones' 1933 track team took 2nd place in the athletic portion of the Macoupin County Meet. However, the students scored well in the literary portion the previous day, and thus the school actually won the Championship Cup. In the sporting portion, Ted Charley took gold in the pole vault, as did the 800 meter relay team. At the South Central Conference Meet, Will Leonard took 1st place in the 400 meters.

Class of 1934

Basketball (Boys)

Coming off several disappointing seasons, the 1933-34 basketball team found itself under new leadership, as Cliff Stiegemeier returned to his alma mater to take over coaching duties at Staunton High School. His tenure saw a return to prominence of both the basketball and football programs.

The boys in myrtle and maroon finished the year with a record of 13-14, including 5-9 in the South Central Conference. Though not overly impressive on paper, the season marked the first time in six years that Staunton had won more than seven games. More importantly, SHS had excellent showings at both the Macoupin County and District basketball tournaments. At County, Staunton defeated Bunker Hill, Virden, and Medora before losing to Gillespie 25-22 in the championship game. At District, SHS defeated Waggoner, Livingston, and Gillespie before dropping a tight game to Litchfield. Interestingly enough, in that year the IHSA decided that both the District champion and runner-up were eligible to advance to Sectional play. Though Staunton lost to Clinton in the first game of the Sectional Tournament, the experience gained from postseason play paid dividends over the next few years. Starters on the team included Bauman, Joe Branka, Norm Meyer, Norm Stolze, and Westerman, with the latter two being named to the All-County team.

Football

Cliff Stiegemeier's first season running the football program was fairly successful, as the team finished 4-5 overall and 2-3 in the South Central Conference in 1933. Though the record did not live up to expectations of the program historically, it was a step in the right direction, as SHS was coming off the first winless campaign in school history. After the season, Frank Yakos was named to the All-Conference team.

SHS opened the season with a 47-0 shutout of Mt. Olive, a program that Stiegemeier had directed just one year prior. Week 2 saw the Green Wave lose to Collinsville in the final minutes of the game. The matchup was scoreless as SHS attempted to punt from deep in its own end with just over a minute remaining. However, a Collinsville defender broke through the line and blocked the punt, falling on it for the game's only score. Adding to the disappointment was the fact that Staunton's star quarterback, Norm Stolze, broke his foot and did not see significant action until the last game of the season. The team never recovered from the loss and had to reshuffle its lineup for the following week's SCC opener against Taylorville, a game that Staunton dropped by a score of 12-8. A Week 4 shutout of Gillespie (7-0) preceded a loss to Benld (14-6). SHS bounced back with a win over Girard (14-7) in Week 6. Though it was a non-conference matchup, the game with Girard was very important to the community because it marked the first-ever Homecoming game, with many graduates coming back for the weekend's festivities, which included a play, dinner, and musical entertainment. Back to the gridiron, Staunton lost consecutive SCC tilts with Hillsboro (13-0) and Carlinville (6-0) before rebounding with a Week 9 victory over Mt. Olive (25-7) on Thanksgiving. Hillsboro went on to win the SCC title, the first of three straight crowns for the school.

Tennis (Boys)

Staunton once again had a doubles team advance to State, as Art Ahrens and Roland Lippold placed 2nd at the District Tournament. Unfortunately, due to an untimely illness, the duo was unable to compete at State.

Track (Boys)

The 1934 track team, under the direction of Cliff Stiegemeier, enjoyed a reasonably successful season. Though the team placed just 6th at the South Central Conference Meet, Will Leonard brought home a title in the 400 meters, while the 800 meter relay team of Vic Bono, Pete Bono, Leonard, and Westerman also captured 1st place. At the Macoupin County Meet, Leonard and the relay team duplicated their championships from the SCC Meet. Also, Vic Bono won the 50 meters and 100 meters, and Norm Stolze took home the pole vault title. Finally, at District, Leonard took 2nd place in the 400 meters, qualifying for State in that event.

Class of 1935

Basketball (Boys)

Staunton had an outstanding team in 1934-35, tying the school record for wins, though the mark fell the very next year. The unit finished 21-5 and 8-2 in the South Central Conference, capturing the SCC title along with the Macoupin County championship. Cliff Stiegemeier, in just his second year directing the program, had high aspirations entering the season, as the team returned four lettermen in Joe Branka, Charlie Ferguson, Norm Meyer, and Rich Stolze. Joining them in the starting lineup was Frank Yakos, and the squad was rounded out by Vic Bono, Ed Furtwangler, Ernest Grimm, Norm Norvell, and Ray Stiegemeier.

The Macoupin County Tournament was an exciting time for the community. Staunton began action in the competition by defeating Girard by a score of 51-20. After disposing of Mt. Olive (23-16), SHS easily handled Hettick (34-19) to advance to the championship game. Waiting for Staunton in the title tilt was arch-rival Gillespie. The two teams played a methodical game, but SHS found a way to eke out a 10-6 victory, winning the county championship for just the second time in school history. Furthermore, for their outstanding conduct during the tournament, the fans of Staunton won the Sportsmanship Award. Unfortunately, despite having beaten Litchfield both times during the regular season, Staunton's campaign ended in an upset loss in the semifinals of the District Tournament.

Football

The 1934 football team continued the program's turnaround behind seniors John Crowder, Ed Furtwangler, Ernest Grimm, Kelly Simmons, Jim Tietze, George Wenner, and Frank Yakos. Coach Cliff Stiegemeier's team finished the season 6-2-2 overall and 3-1-1 in the South Central Conference. The season began with a Week 1 shutout of Mt. Olive (20-0). After a tough loss to Edwardsville (14-0), SHS crushed Girard (38-0) in Week 3. Week 4 welcomed the team's first SCC opponent, and Staunton held on for a close victory by winning 7-6 over Taylorville. A Week 5 loss to Nokomis (20-0) ended the team's hopes for a league title, though the boys in myrtle and maroon finished the season without losing again, as two straight scoreless ties (Benld and Carlinville) preceded wins over Springfield Feitshans (13-0), Mt. Olive (20-12), and Gillespie (13-0). Hillsboro won the conference title for the second straight year. For his outstanding play during the SCC slate, junior Vic Bono was named to the All-Conference 1st Team. Finally, it is worth mentioning that the matchup with Benld was especially intriguing, as their coach, Glen Hastings, was a former standout athlete at SHS. In fact, Hastings and Stiegemeier graduated in the same class and together had teamed up for the program's historic 1923 football season.

Track (Boys)

The 1935 track squad under coach Cliff Stiegemeier was extremely successful. The team finished 2nd in the South Central Conference, 1st in the athletic portion of the Macoupin County Meet, and sent two individuals to State. Vic Bono (pole vault) and Frank Yakos (800 meters) each captured gold at the SCC event, while Bono (pole vault, 200 meters), Ernest Grimm (1600 meters), Norm Meyer (100 meters), and Jim Tietze (400 meters) turned in winning performances at County. At the District Meet, Bono won the championship in the pole vault, advancing to State in that event. While Grimm did not win the 1600 meter run, he did place 2nd, thus advancing to State. Additionally, Grimm set a school record in the event.

Class of 1936

Basketball (Boys)

The 1935-36 basketball season was the best in school history up to that point, as the team finished 24-6 overall and 9-3 in the South Central Conference. SHS got off to a slow start, losing to Edwardsville and Benld early in the season. However, the team quickly hit its stride, including winning the championship of the first-ever Staunton New Year's Day Tournament. At the event, SHS defeated Gillespie before exacting revenge on Benld to win the title (Mt. Olive was the only other school participating). Staunton also avenged its loss to Edwardsville, handing the Tigers their first defeat midway through the season by a score of 26-24. Staunton's winning streak reached ten games during the Macoupin County Tournament before losing to Benld in the title game. The boys in myrtle and maroon reached the championship by defeating Gillespie, Mt. Olive, and Hettick before the Benld setback. However, SHS continued its strong play, winning six of seven games leading into Regionals. The Regional was a tense affair, as Staunton narrowly defeated Benld (14-13) and Mt. Olive (21-20) before disposing of Litchfield in the title game to win the school's first Regional championship. Unfortunately, SHS fell to Carlinville in the first game at the Sectional Tournament.

The 1935-36 basketball team was composed of Joe Branka, John Eller, Charlie Ferguson, Leroy Hart, Norm Meyer, Norm Norvell, John Spagnolla, Ray Stiegemeier, Rich Stolze, and Fred Williams. Though not a starter, Norvell was an important figure because he was responsible for the creation of the school's first and only mascot. His choice of "Bulldogs" was popular with the student body, and the mascot still represents Staunton High School to this day.

Football

The 1935 football team finished 7-2 overall and 4-2 in the South Central Conference. The season began with a Week 1 win over Mt. Olive (34-7) and a Week 2 shutout victory over Edwardsville (20-0). Following a 19-7 loss to eventual SCC champion Hillsboro, SHS defeated Virden (26-0), Pana (13-7), and Benld (19-6) in the annual Homecoming game. A 20-13 loss in Week 7 against Carlinville ended any aspirations of a conference title, though the team finished strong with shutouts over Gillespie (13-0) and Mt. Olive (8-0) to end the year. After the season, coach Cliff Stiegemeier said goodbye to seniors Vic Bono, Joe Branka, Larry Goehe, Rudy Moggio, Fred Smith, Rich Stolze, Steve Vlahon, and Earl Vogelsang.

Track (Boys)

Cliff Stiegemeier's 1936 track squad again had solid showings at both the South Central Conference and Macoupin County track meets. The team finished 4th in the SCC, with Vic Bono (pole vault) and the 800 meter relay team of Bono, Farris, Norm Meyer, and Rich Stolze capturing gold. SHS fared even better at County, finishing in 2nd place. Interestingly enough, 1936 marked the first time that Staunton played host to the Macoupin County Meet. Bono made his mark on the event, setting a meet record in the long jump and capturing 1st place in the pole vault and 50 meters. Meyer won a title as well, taking first in the 200 meters. At District, Bono finished in the top two in the pole vault and thus advanced to State for the second consecutive year in that event.

Class of 1937

Basketball (Boys)

Coming off the two best seasons in school history, Cliff Stiegemeier's 1936-37 basketball team seemed primed to continue its excellent run, especially with returning lettermen Charlie Ferguson, Leroy Hart, Norm Norvell, John Spagnola, Ray Stiegemeier, and Fred Williams leading the charge. Surprisingly, after a 2-1 start, SHS struggled through the season. The squad dropped nine straight games before defeating Carlinville in the Macoupin County Tournament. Though the final tally is incomplete, the team finished just 4-14 overall in known results, including just 3-9 in the South Central Conference. The season marked Stiegemeier's last at the school.

Football

For the first time in school history, the 1936 football team was known as the Bulldogs. However, SHS still sported myrtle and maroon as school colors and therefore was still referred to as the Maroons or Green Wave by many. Also of note, the roster included a future professional football player in the form of Emil Banjavcic. After graduating from SHS, Banjavcic moved on to the University of Arizona and was later drafted by the Detroit Lions.

Cliff Stiegemeier's squad had an outstanding season but fell short of its goal of a South Central Conference championship. The Dogs finished the year with a record of 8-2 overall, including a 5-2 mark in the SCC. The season began with five straight victories, with the Bulldogs downing Gillespie (13-0), East Alton-Wood River (19-6), Taylorville (12-7), Virden (18-12), and Benld (13-12). A heartbreaking upset loss to Carlinville (13-12) in Week 6 ended Staunton's hopes for the SCC crown. However, SHS returned to action in impressive fashion, winning three straight over Jacksonville Illinois School for the Deaf (27-7), Nokomis (14-6), and Stonington (21-0) in the one and only matchup between the two schools. Those victories set up a showdown with Mt. Olive in the annual Thanksgiving game. Mt. Olive came into the game undefeated, but SHS had beaten its neighbor six straight times. Unfortunately for the Dogs, the boys in purple and gold played well in defeating SHS by a score of 26-0. In addition to the 1936 SCC championship, Mt. Olive went on to capture the next two conference titles as well.

Track (Boys)

The 1937 track season was the last under the direction of Staunton alum Cliff Stiegemeier. Not much is known about the team, though it is worth mentioning that the program itself experienced a decline both in numbers and success. In fact, just a few years later the sport was disbanded for more than a decade.

Class of 1938

Basketball (Boys)

The 1937-38 season was one of the most peculiar in the history of the Staunton High School basketball program. Coming off a disappointing year, the Bulldogs found themselves with a new coach in Hubert Pierce but, unfortunately, the same early season results. In fact, the team dropped its first five games and thirteen of fifteen to begin the year. Things got especially bad at the Macoupin County Tournament, as SHS was knocked out in the first round, thus continuing its disappointing winter campaign. However, after County something clicked, and the team went on a nine-game winning streak, including three victories that resulted in a championship at the Regional Tournament.

SHS began the postseason with a huge upset over a 22-4 Litchfield team. After disposing of Benld, Staunton upset SCC champion Hillsboro to win the school's second Regional crown. The Bulldogs continued their surge with a 32-28 win over Mulberry Grove in the first round of Sectionals. Unfortunately, the season came to an end in the next round. The Dogs had nothing to be ashamed of, especially considering the poor start to the season. The year eventually ended with a record of 11-14 overall and 4-8 in the SCC behind seniors Walt Bechem, Dom Fortuna, Ray Pesavento, and John Spagnola.

Football

The 1937 football team found itself with a new leader, as assistant coach and SHS grad Art Ruffini took over the program. The team responded very well to Ruffini's system, especially defensively, as the Bulldogs registered five straight shutouts to begin the year. Week 1 saw Staunton take on East Alton-Wood River, and the Dogs came away with a 20-0 victory. South Central Conference play began in Week 2, as the Bulldogs took on Gillespie and captured a 12-0 win. Victories over Pana (6-0), Benld (7-0), and Hillsboro (7-0) followed, though a surprising 12-12 tie with Carlinville blemished the season record for the first time. Staunton squeaked out a non-conference victory over Jacksonville ISD (9-6), setting up another showdown with Mt. Olive to determine the SCC championship. However, for the first time in many years, Staunton and Mt. Olive did not play on Thanksgiving, instead opting for another holiday, Armistice Day, to mark the showdown. In front of more than two thousand spectators, an undefeated Mt. Olive squad downed Staunton (15-0) for the second straight year to win the conference title. Staunton thus finished 6-1-1 overall and 4-1-1 in the SCC under its first-year coach. After the season ended, Felchner, Ken Herbeck, and Ray Pesavento were named to the All-SCC 1st Team, while Bert Bono, Dom Fortuna, and John Spagnola were awarded 2nd Team honors.

Track (Boys)

Not much is known about the 1938 version of the track team, other than the fact that senior Dom Fortuna concluded his career with an outstanding campaign. Fortuna won the South Central Conference in the 200 meters and 400 meters. He also won the District championship in the 400 meters, thus advancing to State in that event. The team's coach was Art Ruffini.

Class of 1939

Basketball (Boys)

Although basketball was still considered a secondary activity by many in the Staunton community, the 1938-39 season was more anticipated than ever before. There were two reasons for excitement surrounding the sport. First, SHS returned several letter winners from the previous season's Regional championship team, including Livio Basso, Al Costa, Fred Hofer, Lou Mosele, and Dom Pesavento. Second, the sport had undergone major changes intended to increase scoring, such as the introduction of a better ball, as well as the alteration of rules that slowed the game down, such as having a jump ball after every made basket.

Coach Hubert Pierce's squad started the season much like they finished the prior one, on a hot streak. In fact, SHS won four of its first five games. Unfortunately, the start of South Central Conference play slowed the team down, and the boys in myrtle and maroon faltered to a 5-9 mark in the league to go along with a 10-14 record overall. Surprisingly, Staunton was eliminated in the first game of all three tournaments it entered, including the Pana Holiday Tournament, the Macoupin County Tournament, and the Regional Tournament. The season also marked the end of Pierce's tenure with the program.

Football

The 1938 football season was a good one for the Bulldogs, except when they played Mt. Olive. The Wildcats continued a dominant run in which they did not lose a game for the third straight year, including two wins over Staunton that season. The campaign began with a forfeit win over Nokomis. The first game decided on the field was against Mt. Olive in Week 2, a contest that SHS lost by a score of 31-6. Staunton managed a scoreless tie with Gillespie in Week 3 but could not find an opponent for the following week. In those days, SHS was known for its physical, determined play on the field, and thus very few teams of similar enrollment scheduled Staunton during the season. The Bulldogs displayed no rust from their time off, as SHS defeated Carlinville (20-13) in Week 5. Week 6 welcomed Granite City to the schedule. The Warriors were coached by Staunton alum and former leader of the SHS football program, Byron Bozarth. In fact, Bozarth mentored Staunton's Art Ruffini during the latter's senior year in high school. Teacher defeated pupil in this matchup, as Granite City shut out Staunton 12-0. SHS went on to win South Central Conference games over Taylorville (26-6) and Benld (6-0) before dropping the season finale on Armistice Day to Mt. Olive (26-6). With the win, Mt. Olive captured its third straight SCC title, though the 1938 title was shared with Hillsboro.

Ruffini's squad ended the season with a record of 4-3-1 overall and 4-1-1 in the SCC. Unfortunately, he had to say goodbye to a deep crop of seniors, including Jim Alexander, Bob Allen, Walt Bechem, Elmer Borsch, Al Costa, Bob DeGuire, Simon Hannig, Bill Hasse, Frank Hecko, Ken Herbeck, Fred Hofer, Harry Jacobs, Joe Jurek, Maurice McDermott, Frank Pernicka, John Saineghi, Udell Steinmeyer, and Walt Weiss.

Track (Boys)

The 1939 track team, coached by Art Ruffini, finished a disappointing 7th at the South Central Conference Meet, with no individuals capturing titles at the event.

CHAPTER 4

Classes of 1940 – 1949

Overview

Although it is not clear exactly when the change occurred, the 1940s brought new school colors to SHS, as myrtle and maroon were replaced by red and white. The switch in colors likely took place sometime in 1946. Though the reason for the change has been disputed, it is possible that it came as a result of a request (or requirement) from the United States Armed Forces. Apparently, there was a shortage of the compounds used to produce myrtle-colored dye, and thus school districts throughout the land were asked to switch colors to preserve the resources. Other theories include a desire to have a modern look, or a stab at altering the luck of the once-proud football program that experienced two winless seasons in the years leading up to the transformation. Either way, Staunton High School's days with myrtle and maroon as its colors were over, and the Bulldogs have sported red and white ever since the late 1940s.

Baseball was reintroduced as a sport at the school during the decade, and in fact the 1944 baseball team became the first program at Staunton High School to qualify for State. Unfortunately, the decade also saw track disappear from the fray. The first sport in which SHS students competed for the school, track was not reintroduced until 1953. As for the South Central Conference, it had gone almost a decade without change. But, the SCC made a drastic transformation before the 1944-45 school year. That year, the league was reduced from nine teams to five as Hillsboro, Nokomis, Pana, and Taylorville left the conference. Thus, the SCC was left with only Benld, Carlinville, Gillespie, Mt. Olive, and Staunton, a lineup that remained in place for twelve years.

Class of 1940

Basketball (Boys)

Returning lettermen Livio Basso, Art Brumme, Valentine Cool, and Merlin Menk welcomed a new coach to the 1939-40 basketball team, as Carl Mendenhall began his tenure running the program at SHS. Mendenhall's squad finished 10-12 in his first season, including 5-7 in the South Central Conference. The season had its ups and downs, but two impressive victories included wins over large school powers Collinsville and Edwardsville. After starting the season 2-0, Staunton dropped its first game of the year to Granite City, directed by former SHS coach and player Byron Bozarth. Granite City went on to win the state championship that season.

Football

Art Ruffini's 1939 football team once again showed great competitiveness, especially on the defensive side of the ball. Unfortunately, despite only one game being decided by more than a touchdown, the squad faltered to a 2-3-4 record overall, including 1-3-2 in the South Central Conference. Interestingly enough, the four ties were all scoreless affairs. SHS did battle with both Gillespie and Mt. Olive twice during the season, and each matchup ended without a point being registered.

The season started with one of those ties against Mt. Olive in Week 1. Week 2 saw Ruffini's team defeat Granite City (7-0), a program coached by his former mentor, SHS alum and ex-coach Byron Bozarth. A 7-6 upset victory over Hillsboro ensued, and visions of a conference title came into view. Unfortunately, those aspirations were quickly dashed with a Week 4 shutout loss to Pana (21-0), and in fact SHS did not enter into the winner's column again all season. After playing Gillespie to a scoreless tie, the Bulldogs dropped games to Benld and Carlinville (13-6). A rematch with Gillespie was scheduled in order to raise money for band uniforms, but this game too ended in a scoreless tie, as did the annual Armistice Day game with Mt. Olive. Benld, Carlinville, and Pana shared the South Central Conference title in 1939.

Track (Boys)

Though not much information has been found regarding the 1940 track team, it is known that the unit did not fare well at the Macoupin County Meet, as no individual was able to capture gold for coach Art Ruffini's crew. Unfortunately, it appears that the 1940 squad was the last to compete for the school for over a decade. The program did not resume competition until 1953.

Class of 1941

Basketball (Boys)

The 1940-41 basketball campaign got off to a discouraging start, as Carl Mendenhall's squad won just two of its first fourteen contests. However, game number fifteen went a long way in turning around the season, as the Bulldogs upset eventual Regional champion Edwardsville. The win over Edwardsville seemed to act as a springboard for the team, as the unit headed into the Macoupin County Tournament confident despite a poor seed. The play represented the team's demeanor, as SHS defeated Girard (30-26), Bunker Hill (40-26), and Chesterfield (38-34) to reach the championship game. Unfortunately, the Dogs faltered in the title match, eventually losing to Gillespie by a score of 45-29. The squad continued to play better down the stretch, finishing with a record of 10-17 overall, including 2-10 in the SCC.

Football

Coach Art Ruffini's football team faced a very difficult schedule in 1940, as nearly every rival South Central Conference school had several returning letter winners to guide their respective teams. However, the campaign got off to an excellent start with a victory over rival Mt. Olive in Week 1 by a score of 6-0. After losing to Granite City (12-0) in Week 2, SHS began SCC play with two consecutive ties against Taylorville (6-6) and Nokomis (0-0). A 31-19 loss to Gillespie in Week 5 ended the team's championship hopes, though the Bulldogs pulled a major upset over previously unbeaten Carlinville in Week 6 by a score of 13-6. A 26-7 loss to eventual SCC champion Benld preceded a non-conference win over Auburn (12-7). The Bulldogs played a poor game in the season finale, losing 31-13 to Mt. Olive in the second meeting of the season between the two teams. Thus, the squad finished 3-4-2 overall, with a 1-3-2 record in the SCC.

Class of 1942

Baseball

The 1942 baseball team is believed to be the first squad representing the high school in nearly twenty years. Though 3-M baseball thrived both before and after this time period, for unknown reasons the school was unable or unwilling to field a team. That changed in 1942, as Carl Mendenhall directed a squad that went on to win the District championship. SHS played just four regular season contests, earning splits with both Gillespie and Livingston. In postseason tournament action, SHS nosed out Gillespie before defeating Mulberry Grove in twelve innings to capture the title. Though the team fell in the first round of the Sectional Tournament to Taylorville, the program was building momentum for what became one of the best in the area over the next thirty years.

Basketball (Boys)

Despite returning just one letterman in the form of John Dal Pozzo, the basketball program continued where it left off from the end of the previous season, winning four of its first six games. Unfortunately, the team played subpar basketball the rest of the way, eventually finishing with a record of 11-15 overall and 5-7 in the South Central Conference. The end of the season also marked the end of Carl Mendenhall's time directing the program after three years at the helm.

Football

Art Ruffini's 1941 football team struggled to overcome heavy losses to graduation, and the squad faltered to a 1-6-1 overall record, including 1-4-1 in the South Central Conference. As usual, the season began with the first of two matchups with Mt. Olive, with Staunton coming out on the short end of a 19-0 contest. Another shutout loss followed, this time to Edwardsville (14-0). Week 3 began the SCC slate with a game against Hillsboro, one that the Bulldogs lost in close fashion (7-6). The team continued plugging away and was able to garner a 6-6 tie with Pana in Week 4, followed by the lone victory of the season in a 6-0 shutout of Gillespie in Week 5. Unfortunately, the Bulldogs closed out the season with three consecutive shutout losses to Benld (6-0), Carlinville (25-0), and Mt. Olive (19-0). Benld was predicted to win the SCC in 1941 for the third consecutive time, but many members of the team were injured in a bus crash early in the season, thus paving the way for Carlinville to take home the crown.

Class of 1943

Baseball

In his first year coaching the baseball team, B.H. Gibbons directed the program to its second District Tournament championship in as many years. After advancing to the title game due to a forfeit win over Alton Western Military Academy, the Dogs defeated Livingston 5-3 to advance to the Sectional Tournament. Unfortunately, Staunton dropped its first game at Sectionals, effectively ending the 1943 season.

Basketball (Boys)

The 1942-43 basketball program welcomed a new coach in B.H. Gibbons, and his leadership paid immediate dividends as the team finished with a winning record for the first time in seven years. After dropping four of the their first five games while the players learned Gibbons' system, the Dogs rebounded with six straight wins and eventually finished with a 15-11 record, including 5-7 in the South Central Conference. More importantly, SHS appeared in the championship game of both tournaments entered during the year. At the Macoupin County Tournament, the squad defeated Brighton (48-9), Medora (37-18), and Mt. Olive (32-26) before losing in the title game to Gillespie (28-21). The Bulldogs also advanced to the championship game of the Regional only to lose to Greenville by a score of 39-27. After the season, senior Walt Beinke was accepted into the United States Military Academy at West Point. "Colonel" Beinke returned to Staunton years later and dedicated many seasons to the golf program as a volunteer coach.

Football

Though nearly every game on the schedule was competitive, the 1942 football team became just the third in school history to fail to win a game, as the squad finished 0-7-1 overall and 0-5 in the South Central Conference. The season began in decent fashion, as the Bulldogs were able to battle Mt. Olive to a scoreless tie in Week 1. The only blowout on the year came in Week 2, as Staunton was outclassed by Edwardsville (32-0). The SCC schedule began with a Week 3 loss to Taylorville (7-0), and another shutout loss followed, this time to Nokomis (12-0). The Bulldogs also fell to Gillespie (13-6), Carlinville (12-2), Benld (13-6), and Mt. Olive (6-2) to wrap up the winless campaign. The loss to Carlinville helped the Cavaliers secure their second straight SCC championship. The end of the season also brought an end to the coaching tenure of Staunton alum Art Ruffini after six years directing the program.

Class of 1944

Baseball

The 1944 baseball season was historic for Staunton High School. The team, under the direction of B.H. Gibbons and behind the outstanding pitching of senior Fred Brenzel, became the first in school history to advance to State in a team sport. In addition to Brenzel, club members included Carl Dalton, Gene Dietiker, Bill Edwards, Bill Ficker, Walt Fritz, Junior Hebenstreit, Fred Monschein, Bud Neuhaus, Jack Shaw, Bob Spagnola, Jim Sullivan, John Vesper, and Marvin Winkel. Brenzel later returned to SHS and led the baseball team back to State in 1957, in addition to his fine accomplishments as football coach at the school.

The postseason began easily enough for the Bulldogs, as the team shut out Alton Western Military Academy (15-0) to win the District title. After defeating Lovington in the semifinals at Sectionals, SHS beat Springfield Lanphier 3-2 in thirteen innings to advance to State. Brenzel pitched the whole game for SHS, fanning 21 batters in the contest. In fact, in winning the game, Staunton defeated future Major League Baseball Hall of Fame pitcher Robin Roberts. Unfortunately, the Bulldogs were defeated 14-13 by St. Bede High School out of Peru in the first game at the State Tournament.

After the season, Coach Gibbons took Brenzel, Edwards, Neuhaus, and Spagnola to St. Louis for a formal workout with the Browns. All four individuals fared well at the audition, and Brenzel (pitcher) and Spagnola (catcher) were asked to come back and form a battery for upcoming team workouts. Brenzel eventually earned his degree from Southern Illinois University. While there, he competed in both baseball and football for the Salukis.

Basketball (Boys)

In his second season as head coach of the basketball program, B.H. Gibbons' 1943-44 Bulldogs finished with a record of 21-6 overall and 10-2 in the South Central Conference. The win total marked the fourth 20-win season in the program's history, and the excellent league finish represented the best result in the SCC for the Bulldogs in nine years. Both conference losses were to a Taylorville team that finished as undefeated state champions.

Despite the outstanding season, Staunton was unable to capture any hardware, with rival Gillespie once again playing the role of nemesis. The Bulldogs were led by seniors Fred Brenzel, Art Caldieraro, Cal Dalton, and Bob Pervinsek. At the Macoupin County Tournament, SHS defeated Brighton (32-7), Carlinville (36-34), and Virden (42-18) before dropping the title game matchup with Gillespie by a score of 39-25. Gillespie ended Staunton's season at Regionals, defeating the Dogs 31-28. Ironically, SHS had beaten Gillespie in both regular season matchups that year.

Football

Coming off just the third winless season in school history, Staunton welcomed a new football coach for the 1943 season. B.H. Gibbons, who was already coaching baseball and basketball for the district, added football to his list of duties. As with many coaching changes, the program's philosophy changed immediately, as Gibbons established the "T" formation on offense. Though it took the team a couple of weeks to get used to the new system, scoring output increased from the previous season. The team also improved in the win column, finishing 3-5 overall, including 3-3 in the South Central Conference.

The season began with consecutive non-conference losses to Mt. Olive (13-6) and Edwardsville (27-13). However, fortunes changed in Week 3, as Staunton pulled off a surprising blowout win over Hillsboro, defeating the Hiltoppers 32-0. Another win followed, this time over Pana by a score of 25-13. Unfortunately, the Bulldogs were unable to sustain the momentum, losing to Gillespie (13-6), Carlinville (32-6), and Benld before ending the season with a 13-6 victory over Mt. Olive. The season finale was a reversal of fortunes from the first game of the year when the Wildcats had defeated the Bulldogs by that very same score. The Bulldogs did not face Taylorville during the season, but it is worth noting that the Tornadoes took home the SCC crown that year. The Bulldogs featured just four seniors in the Class of 1944, as Fred Brenzel, Art Caldieraro, Bill Stiegemeier, and Vernon Striegel were looked upon to lead the young team. In addition to continuing his baseball career in college, Brenzel also ended up on the football team at Southern Illinois University. He eventually returned to SHS and served as long-time baseball and football coach at the school. Brenzel is still the football program's all-time wins leader.

Class of 1945

Baseball

Though overall results are incomplete, it is known that B.H. Gibbons once again directed the baseball program in 1945. The team began the season with a game against Belleville that was called due to darkness. The squad went on to sweep a doubleheader with Benld, and a win over Nokomis followed. Unfortunately, the Dogs were unable to win the District title for the fourth consecutive season, thus failing to make a repeat appearance at State.

Basketball (Boys)

The 1944-45 basketball squad finished the season with an impressive 27-5 record, including 7-1 in the revamped South Central Conference, winning the league title for the first time in over a decade. The win total was a school record for the program, though the mark was tied during the 1992-93 season. Seniors on the team included Bill Edwards, Art Jarman, Fred Monschein, Bud Neuhaus, Jack Shaw, and Bob Spagnola. Edwards continued his career at the University of Illinois where he played basketball for the Fighting Illini for two years. He then transferred to St. Louis University and was a member of the school's 1948 NIT championship team.

The season began with six straight victories, and the Bulldogs also enjoyed separate winning streaks of twelve and seven games. Interestingly enough, at the behest of area coaches, the Macoupin County Tournament that season was held in December. The coaches felt that having the tournament before the holiday break would add a better flow to the season's schedule. However, the experiment did not catch on, and the tournament was moved back to mid-January the following year. At County, SHS defeated Carlinville and Virden before succumbing once again to Gillespie for the tourney championship. The Macoupin County championship marked Gillespie's fifth in six years, with four of the titles coming at the expense of SHS. The lone SCC blemish came in the very next game, as Benld surprised the Bulldogs. The Dogs later exacted revenge on both teams, defeating Benld later in the season to capture the SCC championship, and once again in the Regional. Gillespie was a victim of the Bulldogs twice during the regular season, as well as in the championship game of Regionals, a game that SHS won 27-25 in overtime. After County, SHS suffered just one more defeat during the regular season in a close loss to Pinckneyville, a traditional powerhouse that finished the season with a 29-6 record. As mentioned, Staunton was able to capture the Regional crown with wins over Hillsboro, Benld, and Gillespie. The Sectional Tournament was held at Collinsville, and unfortunately the Bulldogs were matched with the Kahoks on their own court. Despite having defeated Collinsville two times earlier in the season, the Kahoks came away with a 49-48 victory, effectively ending Staunton's dream season. Collinsville eventually advanced to the State Tournament.

Football

The 1944 Staunton football team, under the direction of B.H. Gibbons, finished the season only 5-3, yet still captured a tie for the South Central Conference championship with a 3-1 record in the SCC. Due to wartime conservation efforts, SHS was forced to face some local opponents two times that season, and thus Mt. Olive and Benld competed against Staunton in both a conference and non-conference affair. The first game of the season saw the Dogs face Mt. Olive in Week 1, losing 14-6. Luckily for SHS, the first matchup of the season with the Wildcats was the non-conference affair. Staunton later defeated Mt. Olive on Armistice Day by a score of 12-6 to capture a tie for the SCC crown. Week 2 saw Staunton take on a tough Edwardsville squad, falling by a score of 12-7. SHS defeated Nokomis (26-7) in Week 3 before suffering its only loss of the SCC slate to Gillespie (14-13) the very next week. Despite being 1-3, Staunton continued to compete and, in fact, swept the final four games of the season, including wins over Carlinville (39-21), Benld (7-0 and 7-6), and the aforementioned Mt. Olive team. Benld, Gillespie, and Staunton each ended the year with one conference loss, and thus the teams settled for a share of the SCC title in 1944.

Seniors on the 1944 team included Joe Bahn, Nick Bahn, Ray Drevenak, Bill Edwards, Bob Fleming, Art Jarman, Bud Neuhaus, Hal O'Neil, Jim Payad, George Robertson, and Bob Spagnola. Considered one of the best players in SHS history, Spagnola was honored at the end of the season with All-State status after scoring 111 of the team's 117 points on the year.

Class of 1946

Baseball

For the first time in the history of the school, Staunton played host to a Sectional Tournament in 1946. Unfortunately, SHS did not advance to its own event, as the Bulldogs lost to Benld (6-1) in District Tournament action.

Basketball (Boy)

The 1945-46 basketball program had another successful season under head coach B.H. Gibbons. The squad finished the season 17-11 overall, including 4-4 in the South Central Conference. Furthermore, the Bulldogs won the Macoupin County Tournament for the first time in eleven years behind seniors Eldred Brauer, Bill Ficker, Walt Fritz, Junior Hebenstreit, Joyce Kessman, Chas Randle, John Vesper, and Mel Wolf. The Bulldogs began the tourney with a 30-19 victory over Palmyra, followed by a 53-19 drubbing of Brighton. In the semifinals, the Dogs met up with a Mt. Olive team that started the season 17-0, including two previous wins over the Bulldogs. However, SHS pulled a major upset, defeating the Wildcats 26-24. The Dogs went on to win the title by downing Benld (28-23) in the championship game.

One interesting game to note was a matchup with Collinsville midway through the season. The Kahoks had defeated the Bulldogs in Collinsville early in the year, but when it came time for the return trip to SHS, Collinsville refused to play in Staunton because of concerns over the size of the gym. The Old Gym, as it is now known, was certainly a cozy space for a big school to get used to, so the Bulldogs agreed to meet Collinsville in Worden. SHS played one of its best games of the year in upsetting a Kahoks team that finished with a record of 30-10 and advanced to State.

Football

Coming off a conference championship from one year prior, hopes were high in the community that the football team would continue its dominance in 1945. Unfortunately, SHS turned in arguably the worst season in school history to that point, finishing 0-7-1 overall and 0-4 in the South Central Conference. Not only was the campaign the fourth winless one in the program's history, but unfortunately the Bulldogs achieved a remarkable feat by failing to score a single point during the course of the year.

A scoreless tie in Week 1 against Mt. Olive started the season off in decent fashion, but unfortunately that was the only game that was close all year. Successive defeats to Edwardsville (31-0), Alton Western Military Academy (25-0), and Pana (39-0) ended the non-conference slate. The Bulldogs then dropped all four SCC games, including losses to Gillespie (39-0), Benld (32-0), Carlinville (21-0), and Mt. Olive (19-0). Benld went on to win the second of three straight SCC crowns. The 1945 season was the last for B.H. Gibbons as head coach of the football program, though he returned the next season as an assistant. Gibbons had to say goodbye to seniors Bernie DeGuire, Bill Ficker, Walt Fritz, Junior Hebenstreit, Ralph Jenkins, Joyce Kessman, Dick Russell, Al Stein, Bob Sullivan, Bill Swetlik, and John Vesper.

Class of 1947

Baseball

Though no results have been found for the 1947 baseball team, it is known that B.H. Gibbons directed the squad. It was his last season with the team after five years at the helm.

Basketball (Boys)

The 1946-47 basketball season was the fifth and final for coach B.H. Gibbons. With the Bulldogs finishing 11-15 overall, it was also his only losing campaign, an impressive run considering that he took over a program fresh off of six consecutive losing seasons. SHS did wrap up the season with a winning record in the South Central Conference, finishing 5-3 in league play. After starting the season with a record of 5-12, SHS won six of its next eight games before falling in the Regional Tournament to Litchfield.

The campaign itself was fairly uneventful, though it is worth mentioning that Coach Gibbons always tried to schedule the toughest competition possible. In addition to several schools out of the Southwestern Conference, SHS was also able to get games with small school powers Pinckneyville and Pittsfield. However, once again the Old Gym hindered Staunton's ability to obtain home-and-home matchups with non-conference opponents, as many of those schools refused to play on such a small floor with very limited seating.

Football

The 1946 football team welcomed a new head coach in Bob Maloney. However, a familiar face was around to provide some consistency, as B.H. Gibbons stayed on the staff as an assistant. Though Maloney only led the program for one season, it was an extremely productive one. Coming off a year that saw the Bulldogs go winless without even scoring a point, the 1946 version ended with a record of 6-1-1, including 2-1-1 in the South Central Conference. Before the annual opener with Mt. Olive, Maloney brought in a group of war veterans to scrimmage the Bulldogs in the preseason. The practice game served the team well, and it showed in their Week 1 victory over the Wildcats (19-7). SHS brushed off Edwardsville (26-7) in Week 2, and followed that victory up with non-conference wins over Alton Western Military Academy (27-21) and Pana (13-0). The SCC slate began in Week 5 against Gillespie, and the Dogs once again were victorious, this time by a score of 19-7. The lone loss occurred in Week 6 against Benld, which went on to capture the SCC title. The Indians defeated Staunton by a score of 25-0 to seal their spot as the class of the league. The Bulldogs took care of Carlinville (12-0) on Homecoming and finished the year with a 7-7 tie against Mt. Olive.

Class of 1948

Baseball

The 1948 baseball team welcomed new leadership, as coach Joe Jurkanin took over the program. Jurkanin stayed in the lead position for five years, eventually experiencing considerable success with the Bulldogs.

Basketball (Boys)

In his first year directing the basketball program, coach Joe Jurkanin welcomed back just three lettermen from the previous season in the form of Don Furtkamp, Harry Wriede, and Ed Yakos. Predictably, the 1947-48 campaign was a long one, as the team faltered to a 4-19 record, including a winless 0-8 in the South Central Conference. The lone wins were over Worden (twice), Bunker Hill, and Hettick.

Football

The 1948 football season marked the first time in many years that Staunton and Mt. Olive did not face off in the annual opener. It also marked the first year of coach Joe Jurkanin's tenure leading the program. Unfortunately, his initial season at the helm was a rocky one, as the Bulldogs finished with a record of 1-5-2 overall, including 0-3-1 in the South Central Conference. East Alton-Wood River represented Staunton's new Week 1 opponent, and the Dogs went toe-to-toe with the Oilers before dropping a 7-0 decision for Staunton's first loss in five meetings between the teams. The lone win came in a Week 2 squeaker over Edwardsville, as Staunton nosed out the Tigers by a score of 7-6. Though the Bulldogs did not win another game, they did compete very well throughout the year. For instance, in Week 3 the Dogs earned a 6-6 tie with a traditionally tough Alton Marquette team in the first-ever matchup between the two schools. A Week 4 loss to Pana (13-0) followed, but SHS responded by opening the conference slate by tying an undefeated squad from Gillespie (7-7). Unfortunately, the season ended with three straight defeats, as Benld (24-13), Carlinville (8-7), and eventual SCC champion Mt. Olive (17-0) all got the best of the Bulldogs.

Class of 1949

Baseball

Coach Joe Jurkanin began his second season with the baseball program in 1949, though no team results were found.

Basketball (Boys)

After a rough rookie season with the basketball program, Joe Jurkanin welcomed back some experience for the 1948-49 campaign, including returning lettermen Bob Coatney, Paul Eller, John Kotzman, and Dale Schmutzler. The experience helped early on as Staunton won seven of eight games after dropping the season opener to Worden. The hot start ended with an overtime loss to eventual champion Anna-Jonesboro in the first round of the Dupo Holiday Tournament. Unfortunately, the team cooled off down the stretch and eventually finished with a record of 11-15, including 5-3 in the South Central Conference.

Football

Joe Jurkanin's 1948 football team finished the season with just one victory for the second successive year, as the Bulldogs ended with an overall record of 1-7-1 and 0-4 in the South Central Conference. SHS returned just three lettermen from the previous season, as John Kotzman, Ken Wall, and Ed Yakos did their best to lead an inexperienced team into battle. The season began with a 25-14 loss in Week 1 to East Alton-Wood River. However, a Week 2 matchup with Edwardsville saw the Bulldogs continue to play the Tigers tough, somehow coming away with a 19-19 tie. Unfortunately, five straight losses ensued, including shutouts to Alton Marquette (14-0) and Pana (21-0). Week 5 saw undefeated and eventual SCC champion Gillespie soundly defeat the Dogs by a score of 51-14. Losses to Benld (19-7) and Carlinville (20-7) followed. SHS attained its lone victory in a Week 8 shutout of Nokomis (18-0) before the season ended with a tight loss to Mt. Olive (7-0).

CHAPTER 5

Classes of 1950 – 1959

Overview

In 1950, the current agriculture, wood, and metal shops, as well as the old cafeteria, were approved by voters, and construction was completed in time for the following school year. More importantly for athletic purposes, in 1956 the New Gym was dedicated. Not only did the development provide a much-needed update for players and fans, but it also increased indoor space for district activities. However, those were not the only changes at the school during the era, as track was reintroduced early in the 1950s and golf was added as a sport later that decade. One program that was stable during the era was baseball. Not only did the Bulldogs begin a streak of dominance that lasted for twenty years, but the 1957 team returned to the State Tournament for the program's second of three appearances.

The South Central Conference remained a five-team league through the first half of the decade, featuring Benld, Carlinville, Gillespie, Mt. Olive, and Staunton. However, Nokomis returned to the SCC for the 1956-57 school year. That same season, the affiliation also admitted the newly formed Southwestern High School. Located in Piasa and named after its location in Macoupin County, Southwestern was founded as a consolidation of the Brighton, Medora, and Shipman school districts. Thus, the SCC carried seven teams for the next few years.

Class of 1950

Baseball

Though the official season results are unknown, seniors Joe Mishanec, Don Ridenhower, Bill Sullivan, and Rich Saottini led the Bulldogs into battle during the 1950 season. The team was coached by Joe Jurkanin.

Basketball (Boys)

The 1949-50 Bulldogs were a young team that featured just one senior, Joe Mishanec. However, a strong group of sophomores gained valuable playing time during the season, paving the way for two straight successful campaigns. Coach Joe Jurkanin's team eventually finished the season with a record of 12-14, including 3-5 in the South Central Conference. Though the year was for the most part uneventful, a scheduling tweak is worth mentioning. With just five teams in the conference at the time, the SCC schools agreed to have a round robin event early in the year that also counted as conference games, thus allowing scheduling freedom for those respective regular season dates. Thus, instead of regular season matchups against Benld, Carlinville, Gillespie, and Mt. Olive, SHS filled its four openings with Coffeen, Madison, Northwestern, and Raymond. Each new game represented the first-ever matchup on the hardcourt between Staunton and the respective schools.

THE HISTORY OF STAUNTON HIGH SCHOOL SPORTS

Football

After winning its first two games of the year, the 1949 football team struggled down the stretch, finishing the season with a record of 2-6-1 overall and 0-3-1 in the South Central Conference. Early victories over Nokomis (27-6) and Virden (20-7) were encouraging, and though the Dogs were also competitive down the stretch, those were the only wins they registered on the season. A Week 3 shutout loss to Alton Marquette (14-0) started the slide, and the very next week SHS lost another close game, this time to East Alton-Wood River (19-13). After a Week 5 tie at rival Carlinville (12-12), Staunton closed out the season with losses to Gillespie (13-0), Benld (28-7), Edwardsville (35-25), and Mt. Olive (26-7). The Wildcats went on to win the SCC title. Senior Bulldogs on the 1949 squad included Bill Agoras, Jim Horne, Joe Mishanec, Bill Sullivan, and Merrill Travis. The team was coached by Joe Jurkanin.

Class of 1951

Baseball

Joe Jurkanin's varsity baseball squad in 1951 was led by seniors Willis Coatney, Vince Heigert, Ron Sternes, Ed Witherbee, and Art Yarnik. Though the team's record is incomplete, it is known that the squad won both the South Central Conference and District championships. In fact, 1951 began a stretch of seventeen out of twenty years in which SHS won either a conference or postseason title.

Basketball (Boys)

Coach Joe Jurkanin's junior-laden basketball team had an outstanding season in 1950-51. The team finished 19-10 overall, including a 5-3 mark in the South Central Conference. Unfortunately, rival Gillespie played the role of nemesis to perfection that year, knocking off the Bulldogs in the championship game of both the Macoupin County and Regional tournaments. Gillespie also won the SCC in 1951, with the Bulldogs finishing in 2nd place.

Football

The Staunton football team had a nice turnaround season in 1950, posting the first of two consecutive 6-2-1 seasons. The season actually began with six consecutive victories, including a Week 1 win over St. James High School out of Springfield (20-6). Staunton went on to record non-conference victories over East Alton-Wood River (20-7), Virden (34-0), and Alton Marquette (19-7). The Bulldogs stayed hot into the SCC slate, securing a Week 5 win over Carlinville by a score of 20-6. A 34-6 victory over Gillespie followed, though Staunton only managed a tie with Benld (21-21) in Week 7. The first defeat of the season was a non-conference loss to Edwardsville, though the key setback occurred in Week 9 against Mt. Olive. The Wildcats shocked Staunton on the last night of the season by a score of 12-7. The loss left Staunton with a record of 2-1-1 in the SCC, which was won by Benld.

The Bulldogs, coached by Joe Jurkanin, were led by two All-State players in Jake Vezzoli (1st Team) and John Johnson (2nd Team). Both Vezzoli and Johnson were named 1st Team All-Conference, joining teammates Dick Goehe, Dale O'Neal, Fred Stein, and Charlie Yakos. In addition to Johnson, Yakos, and Vezzoli, senior football players included Will Coatney, Bill

Colbert, Don Hebenstreit, Jim Huhsman, Henry Morgan, Don Schmutzler, Ron Sternes, and Ed Witherbee. Yakos eventually ended up at the University of Florida where he competed in football for two seasons.

Class of 1952

Baseball

Coach Joe Jurkanin's 1952 baseball team repeated as South Central Conference and District champions in his last year with the program. With the senior class set to graduate, SHS witnessed one of the best groups in school history leave the program. Senior baseball players in 1952 included Jim Anschutz, Dean Brauer, Jack Gockel, Dick Goehe, Delmer Jarman, Don Kotzman, Bob Owens, Dom Picco, Len Renner, Fred Stein, Walt Vesper, and Jim Zuchek. Gockel continued his baseball career for a short time at the University of Illinois.

Basketball (Boys)

The 1951-52 basketball season is considered one of the best in school history, as the squad finished with an outstanding 23-4 record, including 7-1 in the South Central Conference. The 7-1 mark in the SCC was good for a league title for the first time in seventeen years, and the group also captured the championship at the Macoupin County Tournament that same season. The year started out with eleven straight wins, but unfortunately Gillespie ended the winning streak and eventually the season for SHS. While the Dogs and Miners split regular season SCC contests, Staunton captured the Macoupin County championship over the Miners, while Gillespie won the Regional to end Staunton's superb season.

The Bulldogs were an offensive juggernaut, averaging 74 points per game, including surpassing the 90-point mark on four different occasions. Len Renner led the explosive bunch, tallying over 500 points on the season. Though his career statistics are incomplete, it is likely that Renner was the first member of the school's 1000 Point Club. Dean Brauer and Dick Goehe also averaged double figures for SHS. Brauer continued his career at Eastern Illinois University where he was nominated for All-American status as a senior. The varsity squad consisted entirely of seniors in 1952, and the group included Jim Anschutz, Brauer, Bob Cargnoni, Jack Gockel, Goehe, Don Horne, Delmar Jarman, Don Kotzman, Dale O'Neal, Renner, Fred Stein, and Walt Vesper. Many of the boys played significant minutes as underclassmen, and in fact Gockel and Jarman were four-year letter winners for coach Joe Jurkanin, who was wrapping up his fifth and final season directing the program.

Football

Joe Jurkanin's final year at the helm of the football program made for a successful season, as the squad matched the previous year's 6-2-1 record and captured a share of the South Central Conference championship with a 3-0-1 record in league play. The Dogs were led by an outstanding group of seniors in 1951, many of whom had been starters for two or three years. The seniors included Rich Albrecht, Jim Anschutz, Bob Cargnoni, Jack Gockel, Dick Goehe, Delmer Jarman, Don Kotzman, Dale O'Neal, Bob Owens, Dom Picco, Steve Pirok, Len Renner, Fred Stein, Walt Vesper, and Jim Zuchek. Picco and Goehe both moved on to play football in college. Picco ended up at Purdue, whereas Goehe attended the University of Mississippi. In fact, Goehe was a member of Ole Miss football teams that made Cotton Bowl and Sugar Bowl appearances in his time at the school.

SHS played a very difficult schedule in 1951, beginning the season with a 27-0 shutout win over Springfield Cathedral in the first meeting between the two schools. SHS also faced a new opponent in a Week 2 loss to St. Louis DeAndreis (13-7), as well as in a Week 3 victory over Decatur Lakeview (20-14). Staunton moved on to defeat Alton Marquette (20-7) and Carlinville (26-6) to continue the winning track. A 13-13 tie with SCC co-champion Gillespie in Week 6 was the only blemish on either team's SCC slate. The Dogs finished the year with a victory over Benld in Week 7 (12-7), a loss to mighty Edwardsville in Week 8 (33-21), and a victory over Mt. Olive (20-7) to close out the season.

Class of 1953

Baseball

The 1953 baseball team featured seniors Jim Bond, Dick Haase, Dean Hutchins, Jim Meyer, and Dave Wineburner. The squad was coached by former SHS standout Bill Edwards. Though Edwards was known more for his basketball exploits while in high school, he was a member of the 1944 baseball team that made an appearance at the State Tournament.

Basketball (Boys)

Fresh off an outstanding season, the basketball program welcomed a new coach for the 1952-53 campaign. Staunton alum Bill Edwards, a collegiate basketball player at the University of Illinois and St. Louis University, returned to Staunton to coach his alma mater. Unfortunately, SHS graduated its whole varsity team from the previous season, and the Dogs struggled to an overall record of 8-17, including 2-6 in the South Central Conference. After the season, the Bulldogs said goodbye to seniors Jim Furtkamp and Jim Vesper.

Football

The Bulldog football team was in rebuilding mode in 1952, as the program lost the bulk of its production from the previous season's conference championship team. The Bulldogs also welcomed a new coach to the ranks, as SHS alum Bill Edwards took over the program. However, Edwards had to miss the first few games as he finished out his military service to his country, and thus assistant Jonas Lashmet filled in for a good portion of the season. As could be expected given the graduation losses and coaching situation, the Dogs struggled to a record of 1-8, including 1-4 in the South Central Conference. Seniors on the 1952 squad included Jim Bond, Jim Courtney, Jim Furtkamp, Dick Haase, Dean Hutchins, Jim Makula, Al Pernichele, and Jim Vesper.

The year began with a shutout loss to Springfield Cathedral (18-0), followed by three more non-conference setbacks to Litchfield (43-12), Decatur Lakeview (21-7), and Alton Marquette (46-7). The losing streak continued into SCC play following a Week 5 loss to Carlinville (47-7) and a Week 6 drubbing by Gillespie (40-0). However, the Dogs entered the win column the very next week, defeating neighbor Benld (21-19) in a tight matchup for the team's lone victory of the season. After a 40-8 loss to Edwardsville in Week 8, SHS closed out the season and conference play with a shutout loss to Mt. Olive (47-0). Carlinville, Gillespie, and Mt. Olive shared the SCC crown in 1952.

Track (Boys)

For the first time in over a decade, Staunton High School fielded a track team for the 1953 season. Jonas Lashmet guided the program, but much credit must also be given to Bill Edwards. The school's athletic director, Edwards was instrumental in re-implementing the sport after many years without a team. Unfortunately, the program did not fare well at the South Central Conference Meet, finishing in last place.

Class of 1954

Baseball

After winning two straight South Central Conference titles, the Dogs fell in the league standings in 1953. However, Bill Edwards' baseball team climbed back to the top of the SCC in 1954, starting a streak of ten straight SCC crowns and thirteen titles in fourteen seasons. The season did not get off to a good start, as Staunton dropped contests to Litchfield and Edwardsville to begin the year. However, SHS reeled off twelve straight wins before succumbing to East Alton-Wood River in the District title game. Senior pitcher Bill Renner (6-2), junior Harry Zude (4-0), and freshman Wayne Masinelli (2-1) led the team to their final record of 12-3, including an undefeated 6-0 in the conference. Renner also led the team in hitting with a .381 batting average. Senior ballplayers included Larry Caldieraro, Bill Lorson, Pat Muenstermann, Renner, Len Roddick, and Ron Yarnik.

Basketball (Boys)

The 1953-54 Bulldogs were coached by Bill Edwards and led by seniors Bill Renner, Rich Fiori, and Dick Scheller. It was an up-and-down year for the team, as SHS hovered around the .500 mark for most of the season. In the end, the Dogs finished 12-14 overall, including 4-4 in the South Central Conference. SHS took 3rd at the Macoupin County Tournament, defeating Mt. Olive in its final game. The Dogs and Wildcats split games during the season, with Mt. Olive winning both regular season contests, and the Dogs taking the Macoupin County and Regional matchups. Gillespie won the county title that season for the second of four straight years.

Football

The 1953 football season began once again with a coaching change, at least on paper, as Jonas Lashmet took over the program for one season. Lashmet essentially served as the team's head coach the previous season while Bill Edwards finished up his military service. While the Dogs showed improvement in 1953, the team unfortunately lost several close games in sliding to 2-7 overall and 1-3 in the South Central Conference.

The year started off with a tough loss to Springfield Cathedral (12-7) in Week 1, and the Dogs fell to 0-2 with a 25-0 shutout at the hands of Litchfield in Week 2. SHS righted the ship with a 12-0 victory over Edwardsville in Week 3 but fell the very next week to SCC rival Gillespie (19-6). The loss began a three-game losing streak that included close setbacks to Carlinville (7-6) and Bement (13-6). SHS responded by defeating Benld (13-6) for its lone SCC victory of the season. The year ended with consecutive losses to East St. Louis Assumption (19-13) and SCC champion Mt. Olive (27-0). Despite the record, seniors Larry Caldieraro, Rich Fiori, Bill Lorson, Harry Mengelkamp, Pat Muenstermann, Bill Renner, Len Roddick, and Dick Scheller did their best to spark the squad. After graduation, Caldieraro played one year of football at Southern Illinois University.

Track (Boys)

Jonas Lashmet guided the 1954 track team in his last season with the squad. Harry Mengelkamp was the lone senior on the team and he helped guide the Dogs to a 4th place finish in the South Central Conference. SHS placed 7th at the Macoupin County Meet.

Class of 1955

Baseball

The 1955 baseball program welcomed a new coach to the fold, though he was not unfamiliar to the community. Fred Brenzel, a standout pitcher who led his team to the State Tournament in 1944, returned to his alma mater to direct the baseball and football teams. Brenzel's first season running the baseball program was a successful one, as the team finished 11-6 overall and 5-1 in the South Central Conference. The SCC record was good for 1st place in the league, giving Staunton its second conference championship in as many years. Four of the team's six losses were to large schools Edwardsville (three times) and Collinsville, though Gillespie and Litchfield also had Staunton's number. The 1955 Dogs featured a strong starting lineup, including Gene Bentrup, Bob Crabtree, Rich Dal Pozzo, Wayne Helm, Al Loeh, Leroy Luketich, Ken Monschein, and Marvin Stein. Wayne Masinelli, Ted Wenner, and Harry Zude provided the pitching for the SCC champions.

Basketball (Boys)

The Staunton basketball team got off to an inauspicious start to the 1954-55 season, dropping eleven of its first thirteen games, with most of the losses coming by a large margin. However, Bill Edwards' squad responded with better play down the stretch, winning five of the next eleven games, with the six losses coming by a combined total of fifteen points. The 7-17 Bulldogs finished 3-5 in the SCC and were led by seniors Jerry Bradley, Ken Monschein, Wayne Odorizzi, Marvin Stein, and Harry Zude.

Football

In 1954, the SHS football program welcomed Fred Brenzel as its new coach. Brenzel represented the team's fourth leader in as many years. However, the high turnover rate ended when Brenzel was hired, as he stayed on for sixteen seasons and eventually established the Staunton football program as one of the best in the state. The 1954 season started off very well with close victories over Springfield Cathedral (20-19) and Litchfield (12-7). After suffering lopsided losses to Edwardsville (28-12) and Jacksonville ISD (40-0), the Dogs opened SCC play with a 14-0 shutout win over rival Carlinville. After being blanked 12-0 by Gillespie, the Dogs roared back with a shutout of Benld (14-0). Unfortunately, Staunton ended the season with two straight losses, falling 53-13 to East St. Louis Assumption before losing to a tough Mt. Olive squad by a score of 13-6. The season thus ended with a 4-5 record, including 2-2 in the SCC, which was won by Gillespie and Mt. Olive. Seniors on the squad included Gerald Scherff, Len Scherff, Ken Monschein, Marvin Stein, Ted Wenner, Bob Fletcher, and Jerry Bradley.

Track (Boys)

As athletic director, Bill Edwards reintroduced track as a sport at Staunton High School in 1953. Beginning in 1955, he found himself running the program as its new coach. Fortunately, he inherited a solid squad, including major lettermen Jerry Bradley, Ron Buffington, Dave Denny, Ray Duda, Ralph Jacobs, Fred Lamb, Gerald Scherff, Len Scherff, Frank Stanko, and Gerald Yarnik. Minor lettermen included Dick Coyne, Chuck Frey, Rodney Jacobs, and Tony Zeppetella.

Class of 1956

Baseball

Despite an overall record of just 7-7, Fred Brenzel's Staunton Bulldogs captured their third straight South Central Conference championship by finishing 6-2 in the league. The SCC champions were led by seniors Gene Bentrup, Jim Brusack, and Mike Heigert.

Basketball (Boys)

In its last season using the Old Gym for home games, Bill Edwards directed the 1955-56 basketball team and seniors Arlen Anschutz, Ron Buffington, Ray Duda, and Bert Hendricks. However, it was also the last season for Edwards leading the basketball program, as the former SHS standout and collegiate performer wrapped up his fourth season at the helm. Unfortunately, it was not a good season for SHS basketball, as the team suffered to a record of 4-20 overall and 1-9 in the South Central Conference. Wins over Bunker Hill, Girard, and Benld came early in the year, and the team embarked on a twelve-game losing streak before beating Cahokia on the eve of the Regional Tournament.

Football

Despite encouraging results in coach Fred Brenzel's first year on the job, the Staunton football program took a step back in 1955, recording just the fifth winless season in the sport's history. The 0-8-1 Bulldogs finished 0-3-1 in the South Central Conference. Ron Buffington, Bob Davis, Ray Duda, Gilbert Hebenstreit, Leo Nardin, Roger Perrin, Frank Stanko, and Rich Voyas were seniors on the team. Stanko continued his career at Iowa State University.

The season began with a 19-0 setback against Springfield Cathedral, followed by a close loss to Litchfield (13-6) in Week 2. SHS suffered two lopsided losses to Edwardsville (40-19) and Jacksonville ISD (40-19) before beginning SCC play in Week 5 against Carlinville. Unfortunately, SCC action was not kind to SHS, as the Bulldogs were handedly defeated by Carlinville (40-0) and followed that loss with a 34-7 setback to Gillespie. Week 7 saw Staunton and Benld play to a scoreless tie, the only contest of the season not to end in defeat for the Bulldogs. A Week 8 non-conference affair with East St. Louis Assumption ended in a 55-19 loss. Finally, the annual Veterans Day game against Mt. Olive had major implications for both teams. While Staunton was trying to avoid a winless season, rival Mt. Olive was shooting for its fourth straight SCC championship. Though the Bulldogs hung tough in the contest, they eventually succumbed to the Wildcats by a score of 39-26.

Track (Boys)

Bill Edwards wrapped up his coaching career at SHS in 1956, leading senior track members Ron Buffington, Dave Denney, Don Denney, Bert Holloway, Leon Kelso, Roger Perrin, Frank Stanko, and Gerald Yarnik for the last time. At the South Central Conference Meet, Wayne Helm (800 meters) and Dick Coyne (pole vault) won their respective events for SHS, marking the first time in eighteen years that a Staunton competitor captured an SCC title.

Class of 1957

Baseball

Coach Fred Brenzel's 1957 baseball team was one for the ages, as the Dogs advanced to the State Tournament for the second of three appearances in school history (1944, 1957, 1994). The Bulldogs destroyed Mt. Olive (11-0) and Bethalto Civic Memorial (13-2) to win the District title before shutting down East Alton-Wood River (4-0) and Edwardsville (4-1) to become Regional champions. Poor weather made the field nearly unplayable at the Sectional Tournament, so diesel fuel was sprayed on the diamond and ignited, effectively drying out the field enough to play the games. SHS took advantage of the situation, recording close wins over Belleville (4-3) and Salem (4-2) to capture the Sectional title and advance the team to the State Tournament. Unfortunately, Staunton lost its first game at State, finishing 16-3 on the year.

Wayne Helm (8-1) and Wayne Masinelli (7-1) concluded their brilliant careers with excellent senior seasons, as they were nearly unhittable on the mound for the Dogs. In fact, the SHS pitching staff led the Bulldogs to their fourth straight league title by allowing just five runs during the 8-0 conference slate. Bob Crabtree joined Helm and Masinelli as seniors on the team, with Bill Birdsell, Rich Dal Pozzo, Art Hasse, Larry Kuba, Bill Lambert, John Lesich, Leroy Luketich, Joe Mancewicz, Russ Masinelli, Jim Yauornik, and Wayne Zude rounding out the squad. After the season, Dal Pozzo captured the Hitting Award, while Helm won the Pitching Award. Helm continued his baseball career for one season with the Giant's minor league organization.

Basketball (Boys)

On November 25, 1956, the Staunton Community Unit School District #6 held a building dedication for the elementary school, including a brand new gymnasium with a seating capacity of 1800. The Bulldogs thus opened the 1956-57 season in the New Gym, one of the best facilities in the area at the time. Staunton wasted no time breaking in the new facility, as the school hosted the Macoupin County Tournament for the first time, an event won by Carlinville. SHS also hosted the Regional Tournament at the end of the season.

Unfortunately, the team's play on the court did not live up to the standards of their new building. The Bulldogs finished the season 5-18 overall and 3-9 in the South Central Conference under Wayne Beach in his one and only year leading the program. After a 3-3 start, SHS lost nine straight before it secured another win. Unfortunately, a five-game losing streak followed, including a loss to Carlinville in the Regional Tournament, the team's fourth setback that season to the Cavaliers. Seniors and three-sport standouts Wayne Helm and Wayne Masinelli led the SHS attack.

Football

Fred Brenzel's third year as coach of the Bulldogs saw dramatic improvement in the program in 1956. The Bulldogs played .500 football, finishing the year 5-5 overall, including a 3-3 mark in the South Central Conference. The turnaround was led by seniors Noel Bond, Tom Coyne, Bernard Gaudi, Ted Hancock, Wayne Helm, Ralph Jacobs, John Lesich, Wayne Masinelli, Russ Schuette, and Marlin Valent. All-Conference members included Gaudi and Masinelli, as well as juniors Chuck Frey, Leroy Luketich, Jim Oettel, and Wayne Zude. Jacobs and Masinelli shared Offensive MVP honors, while Luketich was named Defensive MVP.

The Dogs had an unusual occurrence throughout the season, as they alternated wins and losses for the duration of the ten-week campaign. Week 1 saw the team drop a heartbreaking 13-7 decision to Springfield Cathedral, only to come back and defeat Litchfield in Week 2 by the very same score. After a 32-14 loss to Edwardsville in Week 3, the Dogs easily handled Highland (41-7) in the first-ever meeting between the schools. Staunton split SCC contests against Carlinville (lost 20-12), Gillespie (won 34-6), Benld (lost 26-7), Nokomis (won 26-7), Mt. Olive (lost 14-13), and Southwestern (won 28-7) to wrap up the season. The close loss to Carlinville was a key game in the SCC, as the Cavaliers eventually laid claim to the league title. Also of note, the game with Southwestern was the first meeting between SHS and the new consolidation of Brighton, Medora, and Shipman high schools.

Golf (Boys)

Although there is some indication that individual golfers competed for SHS prior to 1956, the school's first official team was coached by Bill Schuetze and comprised of senior Ken Costa and freshmen Dan Michki, Norm Wenner, and Wayne Hutchins. Costa finished in the top three at the District Tournament and he continued his play on the links at Western Illinois University on a golf scholarship.

Track (Boys)

The 1957 track team was coached by Wayne Beach. Coach Beach had a small but quality group that year led by seniors Noel Bond, Tom Coyne, and Ralph Jacobs.

Class of 1958

Baseball

Coming off an appearance at State, the Staunton baseball program continued to experience success. The 1958 Bulldogs finished 13-2 overall and 5-0 in the South Central Conference, winning the league crown for the fifth time in as many years. Losses to Litchfield in the first game of the season (5-3) and in the District Tournament (5-4) sandwiched thirteen consecutive victories. Senior catcher Leroy Luketich, who later played in the Pittsburgh Pirate's minor league system, took home the Hitting Award after leading the team with a .438 batting average. Seniors Art Hasse (.429) and Rich Dal Pozzo (.380) also contributed in a big way at the plate for SHS. Pitching Award winner Dal Pozzo led the staff with a 7-2 record. Freshman Rick France had a remarkable year on the mound for SHS, finishing undefeated at 5-0. Sophomore Don Brewer rounded out the pitching staff. Bill Birdsell, Dennis Bortko, Jim Oettel, Bob Roman, and Wayne Zude joined Luketich, Hasse, and Dal Pozzo as seniors on the squad. After graduating, Hasse enrolled at the University of Illinois where he played baseball for two years.

Basketball (Boys)

The Staunton basketball team welcomed back a strong group of seniors for the 1957-58 season, including Bill Burdsell, Art Hasse, Rodney Jacobs, Leroy Luketich, Rich Marquis, Ken Odorizzi, and Wayne Zude. However, the Dogs had to learn a new system, as first-year leader Enno Lietz tried to build a successful program. Lietz and his squad rose to the challenge, posting a record of 20-9 overall, including 10-2 in the South Central Conference. The league mark was good for a conference title, and the Dogs also captured the Macoupin County championship.

The Bulldogs opened the year 0-3 but righted the ship heading into the O'Fallon Tournament. At O'Fallon, SHS defeated Mascoutah and East St. Louis Lincoln before succumbing to Highland in the title game. Staunton went on to win nine straight games and fifteen of sixteen, including four straight at County. After defeating Livingston to begin Regionals, Staunton dropped a tight game to Bethalto Civic Memorial 56-53, ending one of the best seasons in the history of the program. The Dogs were led in scoring by junior Don Kasubke (13.4 points) and Odorizzi (11.2), while Hasse, Luketich, and Zude also contributed to a balanced offensive attack. After the season, Zude was honored with the Free Throw Award.

Football

The 1957 football season was successful by many accounts, as the team finished 6-3-1, posting its first winning season under coach Fred Brenzel. SHS was also very close to winning the South Central Conference that year, finishing second behind co-champions Carlinville and Mt. Olive with a 4-1-1 mark. Before the SCC portion of the schedule started, Staunton continued to play tough early season opponents. After losing to Springfield Cathedral 27-14 in Week 1, SHS roared back in Week 2, defeating Litchfield 41-12. SHS lost to Edwardsville 25-0 in Week 3 before rounding out the non-conference schedule by defeating Highland (42-20). Week 5 saw rival Carlinville come to town and narrowly defeat the Bulldogs by a score of 18-12. Staunton rebounded by going undefeated in the SCC through the remainder of the campaign, beating Gillespie (38-6), Benld (28-20), Mt. Olive (26-13), and Southwestern (20-7). However, a 6-6 tie with Nokomis in Week 8 prevented SHS from clinching a share of the league title, as the Bulldogs were unable to overcome a flu virus that crippled the team. Seniors on the squad included Emil Albrecht, Rich Coyne, Chuck Frey, Art Hasse, Gene Kalika, Leroy Luketich, John Moros, Jim Oettel, Ron Schuette, Gary Weidler, and Wayne Zude. Luketich captured the Offensive MVP award, while Oettel took home Defensive MVP honors. After graduation, Oettel continued his football career at Eastern Illinois University.

Golf (Boys)

The 1957 golf team consisted of six sophomore members under the direction of coach Bill Schuetze. Charlie Fritz, Wayne Hutchins, Dick Kapp, Dan Michki, Ron Rodeghiero, and Norm Wenner comprised the squad.

Track (Boys)

Despite the baseball team's success, Enno Lietz welcomed a large group of track athletes in 1958, his first year with the program. The team was anchored by seniors Art Hasse, Ron Schuette, and Al Welch. At the South Central Conference Meet, Dick Coyne took home gold for SHS in the pole vault.

Class of 1959

Baseball

The 1959 baseball season was a very successful, yet very odd year. The Bulldogs, coached by Fred Brenzel, finished the season with a record of 16-6. Included in the overall record was a 9-1 finish in the South Central Conference, which gave the program its sixth straight conference championship. In the postseason, SHS defeated Livingston by a score of 10-0 in capturing the District title. After disposing of Virden 13-9 in the first round of Regionals, the Dogs fell to Alton by a score of 9-0, seemingly ending the year for the team. However, as the seniors practiced for graduation and the underclassmen wrapped up their finals, the IHSA informed the school that Alton had used ineligible players during the game, and thus had to forfeit the contest. Adding to the craziness, the Dogs had to break out their equipment and uniforms and be ready to play Greenville in the Sectional that very day. Unfortunately, SHS dropped a pitcher's duel to the Comets, losing 1-0 to bring the season officially to an end.

Senior Russ Masinelli capped off his career in fine fashion by taking home the team's Pitching Award (7-1) and Hitting Award (.425). Rick France, a sophomore, finished 5-2 on the mound, while junior Don Brewer completed the pitching staff with a 4-3 record on the season. Sophomore Ken Hochmuth (.368) and junior Larry Kuba (.338) helped power the Staunton hitting attack. Keith Dooley joined Masinelli as the only seniors on the team.

Basketball (Boys)

Coming off a season that saw them win Macoupin County and South Central Conference titles, the 1958-59 Bulldogs, coached by Enno Lietz, were hit hard by graduation yet still managed to finish with a 13-13 record. Though the team finished just 6-5 in the SCC, the Bulldogs were able to take home a 2nd place finish in the Macoupin County Tournament, losing to Carlinville in the title game. However, at County, an important feat was accomplished when senior Don Kasubke poured in 45 points in an opening round win over Bunker Hill. The point total is believed to be a single game scoring record at SHS, one that has rarely been threatened since he graduated in 1959. With 575 points as a senior, Kasubke more than likely became just the second member of the 1000 Point Club at Staunton High School. He continued his basketball career at Southern Illinois University for two seasons. Though Kasubke, winner of the team's Free Throw Award, was the only player to average double figures, Jim Yauornik, Joe Mancewicz, and Larry Kuba were additional offensive threats for SHS. Joining Kasubke and Yauornik in the Class of 1959 were Rich Ficker and Bill Probst.

Football

Coach Fred Brenzel's 1958 football team finished the season with a 5-3-1 mark. However, the Dogs went 5-0-1 in the South Central Conference, capturing the first of four straight SCC titles. After opening the season with three consecutive non-conference losses to Litchfield (20-14), Edwardsville (26-6), and Jerseyville (20-6), the Dogs did not suffer another loss that year, rolling through the SCC with victories over Carlinville (18-7), Gillespie (12-7), Nokomis (40-25), Mt. Olive (26-7), and Southwestern (53-6). The only blemish on the conference slate was a scoreless tie with Benld in Week 6 of the season.

The youthful Bulldogs were led by several outstanding underclassmen, including 1st Team All-Conference selections Barry Deist, Larry Kuba, Fred Marquis, and Leroy Schulte. Kuba was the team's Offensive MVP, while Marquis and Schulte shared Defensive MVP honors. Meanwhile, Joe Mancewicz was named to the All-SCC 2nd Team, and Honorable Mention awards were given to Dick Kapp and Don Brewer. All honorees were underclassmen, as Charlie Jackson and Bob Scherff were the only seniors on the squad.

Golf (Boys)

Coach Bill Schuetze's 1958 golf squad was led by junior Dan Michki, the squad's low scorer for the season.

Track (Boys)

Enno Lietz directed the 1959 track team, which was led by thrower Norm Wenner. Wenner took 1st place in the discus at both the South Central Conference and Macoupin County Track Meets. Senior track members were Don Kasubke and Jim Yauornik.

CHAPTER 6

Classes of 1960 – 1969

Overview

The decade of the 1960s saw the baseball program continue its dominance, as well as football's return to prominence. Combined, the two sports won fourteen of twenty possible conference titles in the decade. Unfortunately, the basketball program fell on hard times and, in fact, failed to secure even one winning season in the 1960s. While no new sports were added during the era, golf did disappear as an option for SHS students.

The 1960s witnessed numerous changes to the South Central Conference. The first two years of the decade saw the SCC remain a seven-team league with Benld, Carlinville, Gillespie, Mt. Olive, Nokomis, Southwestern, and Staunton in the fold. The conference was back down to five teams beginning with the 1961-62 academic year when the Benld school district was annexed by Gillespie and Southwestern left to join the Illinois Valley Conference (IVC). The IVC later merged with another league to form the Western Illinois Valley Conference (WIVC). Two years later, the Springfield Feitshans Flyers were admitted into the South Central Conference, making the conference a six-team league. Unfortunately, Springfield Feitshans was swallowed up by Springfield Southeast High School at the start of the 1967-68 school year. In order to keep the league at six teams, the SCC extended an invitation to Virden, which was accepted.

Class of 1960

Baseball

Coach Fred Brenzel's 1960 baseball squad finished 11-7 on the season. Though unimpressive in regular season non-conference action (1-5 record), the Dogs were simply dominant in the South Central Conference, finishing 9-1 and capturing the league crown for the seventh straight year. In fact, SHS outscored SCC foes 146-36, including double-digit scoring in all nine league wins. The offensive juggernaut was especially impressive in wins over Mt. Olive (11-0 and 10-0), Gillespie (17-0 and 19-0), and Carlinville (32-8 and 16-1). Hitting Award winner Larry Kuba batted .588 on the year, which is believed to be a single-season school record. Junior Rick France hit .453 and also finished 6-2 on the mound in taking home the Pitching Award. Senior Bulldogs included Don Brewer, Ray Caldieraro, Kuba, Joe Mancewicz, Rich Monschein, and Dan Roland.

Basketball (Boys)

The 1959-60 basketball team was led by seniors Larry Kuba, Dan Roland, and Norm Wenner. Enno Lietz directed the squad in a season that saw the Bulldogs finish 12-16 overall and 7-5 in the South Central Conference. Unfortunately, the campaign resulted in a record below .500, the first of fourteen straight losing seasons for the program. SHS tried to salvage the campaign, making the Regional final before succumbing to Litchfield by a score of 85-63. At the postseason awards banquet, junior Rick France was presented with the Free Throw Award.

Football

The 1959 Bulldogs, coached by Fred Brenzel, finished the season 8-2 and a perfect 6-0 in the South Central Conference, thus repeating as league champions. The only two losses on the year came to large school powers in a 19-0 setback to Collinsville and a 32-0 defeat by Belleville (BHS did not split into two schools, East and West, until the 1966-67 school year). SHS victories on the season came against Litchfield (25-0), Southwestern (21-0), Jerseyville (14-7), Carlinville (18-7), Gillespie (43-13), Nokomis (53-12), Benld (13-6), and Mt. Olive (32-0).

Larry Kuba captured All-SCC and All-State honors in gaining 1414 rushing yards on the season, a school record that stood for more than forty years. Leroy Schulte, Barry Deist, and Joe Mancewicz joined Kuba as All-Conference 1st Team members, while Don Brewer (2nd Team), Dick Kapp (Honorable Mention), and Fred Brauer (Honorable Mention) were also rewarded for their play on the field. Seniors included Brewer, Ray Caldieraro, Bob Frey, Kuba, Mancewicz, Jack Perrone, Mike Skertich, Mike Smith, and Norm Wenner. Kuba and Mancewicz were named Offensive MVP, while Brauer was the team's Defensive MVP. Kuba and Mancewicz both continued their playing careers at the University of Missouri on football scholarships. Kuba played all four years at Mizzou before returning to SHS as a long-time teacher and coach.

Golf (Boys)

The 1960 golf team was coached by Bill Schuetze in his last year at the school. The team featured seniors Charlie Fritz, Wayne Hutchins, Dick Kapp, Dan Michki, Ron Rodeghiero, and Norm Wenner.

Track (Boys)

Enno Lietz directed the 1960 track team, which was led by seniors Ron Bond, Don Brewer, Stan Conroy, Myron Hoffstetter, Jack Perrone, Dan Roland, Mike Skertich, and Norm Wenner. Though they have since been surpassed, Brewer (100 meters), Hoffstetter (1600 meters), and Wenner (discus) set school records in their respective events. Wenner also took 1st place at the South Central Conference Meet and advanced to State in the discus.

Class of 1961

Baseball

Though the 1961 baseball team played just eleven games, the Bulldogs made the most of their opportunities, finishing 8-3 overall and 4-0 in the South Central Conference. The undefeated SCC slate secured the program its eighth consecutive league title. Fred Brenzel directed the squad, which included seniors Bill Day, Larry Drumtra, Rick France, Ken Hochmuth, Todd Lantermo, and Dean Oehler. Hochmuth won the Hitting Award (.381), while France (6-2) took home the Pitching Award for the SCC champions. With a career record of 22-6, France is perhaps Staunton's all-time wins leader on the mound.

Classes of 1960 - 1969

Basketball (Boys)

Coach Enno Lietz welcomed seniors Bill Day, Rick France, Leroy Schulte, and Don Sievers to the court for the 1960-61 basketball season. The squad finished 9-12 overall, with France taking home the Free Throw Award for the second straight season.

Football

The 1960 football squad swept through South Central Conference play, finishing a perfect 6-0 in league and winning the program's third straight title. In fact, the Dogs outscored SCC foes by a score of 214-32. The season actually began with two straight losses, as SHS dropped non-conference affairs to Collinsville (39-0) and Litchfield (20-7). A Week 3 win over SCC opponent Southwestern (42-12) preceded two more non-conference games, a loss to Belleville (26-12) and a victory over Jerseyville (18-14). Staunton finished out the campaign with five straight league wins, including defeats of Carlinville (19-7), Gillespie (53-0), Benld (27-0), Nokomis (47-13), and Mt. Olive (26-0).

Coach Fred Brenzel's 7-3 squad was led by All-Conference selections Len Bednar, Fred Brauer, Rick France, Dean Oehler, Leroy Schulte, and Mike Yakos, all seniors, and Barry Deist and Bill Knop, both juniors. Schulte capped off a brilliant career by becoming the first athlete in school history to capture All-American honors, thus cementing himself as one of Staunton's all-time football greats. As a result of being named to this elite squad, he was invited to play in the All-American game in Texas, and he eventually wound up at the University of Mississippi and played one season for the Rebels. Deist finished the year with 1259 yards rushing, and he and France were both named Offensive MVP, while Brauer, Schulte, and Yakos shared Defensive MVP honors. Seniors included Bednar, Brauer, Jay Costa, Bill Day, Larry Drumta, France, Todd Lantermo, Oehler, Schulte, and Yakos.

Track (Boys)

The 1961 track squad included seniors Fred Brauer, Bill Pernicka, and Mike Yakos, The team, coached by Enno Lietz, featured junior Barry Deist, a State-qualifier in the 200 meters.

Class of 1962

Baseball

Coach Fred Brenzel's baseball team won the South Central Conference title for the ninth straight time in 1962 behind the play of seniors Barry Deist, Bill Knop, Dave Robbins, and Dean Schulmeister. The squad finished 13-6 overall, including a perfect 8-0 in SCC play. After the season, Deist took home the team's Hitting Award, while Knop was named the Pitching Award winner. After playing football for one season at the University of Illinois, Deist resumed his baseball career at Truman State University in Kirksville, Missouri. After his playing days ended, Deist returned to SHS as a member of the teaching staff and later became one of the winningest baseball and football coaches in school history.

Basketball (Boys)

The 1961-62 Bulldogs, coached by Enno Lietz, ended the season with a record of 8-12. The season was somewhat of a disappointment for SHS, as the team had a nice blend of senior leadership to go along with talent at the lower levels. Unfortunately, senior leader Barry Deist was injured and unable to play the whole season. To add insult to injury, the Dogs lost many close games, including three contests to Gillespie by a total of four points. Ron Keene (14.9 points) and Norm Schmidt (13.1) led the Dogs in scoring, while John Luketich, Deist, and Eugene Diel also contributed to a balanced attack. Dave Robbins joined Deist, Diel, and Schmidt as seniors on the squad. Junior Ed Barnhart captured the Free Throw Award for the first of two straight seasons.

Football

The Staunton football program, under the direction of Fred Brenzel, continued its success in the 1961 season. The Dogs finished the year 7-2 overall, including 4-0 in the South Central Conference, thus winning the league title for the fourth straight year. Staunton began the campaign with consecutive shutouts after soundly defeating Virden (41-0) and Litchfield (19-0). Coach Brenzel's teams were known for taking on all competitors, regardless of size. One of the biggest schools in the state came calling in Week 3, as the Bulldogs faced Belleville High School. The Dogs kept the game close but eventually fell by a score of 20-12. After narrow wins over Jerseyville (18-14) and Carlinville (13-7), SHS posted three straight shutouts in clobbering Gillespie (33-0), Nokomis (53-0), and Mt. Olive (40-0). Unfortunately, the Bulldogs lost a shootout to Centralia in Week 9, falling 47-41 to the Orphans.

Senior Barry Deist led the Staunton juggernaut during the season, scoring 105 points and being named All-State for his efforts. Predictably, Deist was also named to the All-SCC 1st Team. What made the honor so impressive, however, is that he had been named All-Conference in each of his four high school seasons. A rarity in any sport, but especially football, it is possible that Deist is the only player in the program's history to achieve the feat. After graduation, Deist continued his career at the University of Illinois. However, he suffered a knee injury in practice at the hands of the legendary Dick Butkus and therefore finished his playing days at Truman State University. Deist, who also played baseball at Truman State, returned to SHS as a teacher and coach, directing both the baseball and football squads for long tenures. As for other members of the squad, Bill Knop and John Luketich were also effective offensively for SHS, and they shared Offensive MVP honors with Deist. Butch Duda, Bob Gaudi, John Monroe, and Knop led a defense that posted five shutouts on the season, with Gaudi and Monroe sharing Defensive MVP honors. Joining Deist, Gaudi, and Knop as seniors on the squad were Ross Bradley, Ron Langley, and Dave Robbins.

Track (Boys)

Seniors Jeff Balliett, Dave Cool, Barry Deist, Eugene Diel, Gary Heinemeyer, Bill Knop, and Dave Straub led a deep and talented track squad in 1962. The team, which took 2nd place at both the South Central Conference and Macoupin County track meets, was directed by Enno Lietz. The 800 meter relay team of Deist, Knop, and juniors Melvin Duda and John Monroe took home SCC gold. Monroe also captured a conference championship in the hurdles.

Class of 1963

Baseball

The 1963 Bulldogs enjoyed continued success under coach Fred Brenzel, winning the South Central Conference for the tenth time in as many years, a remarkable feat that will perhaps never be repeated at the school. The Dogs finished 15-6 on the season, including 7-1 in the SCC. Additionally, SHS captured the District and Regional titles before bowing out in the Sectional Tournament.

In the District Tournament, the Dogs narrowly got by Livingston (3-0) before defeating Gillespie (6-4) for the championship. The win created a matchup with Litchfield for the Regional title, one which SHS captured with a 3-0 shutout victory. The Sectional Tournament was hosted by Staunton, but unfortunately the Dogs bowed out early after losing to Springfield Sacred Heart-Griffin by a score of 8-1 in the first game. Granite City also won its first game and eventually defeated SHG in the title game. Seniors in the Class of 1963 included Ed Barnhart, Mike Bortko, Bob Eggebrecht, and John Luketich. Barnhart was the team's Hitting Award winner, while freshman Al Schuette won the Pitching Award. Remarkably, Schuette won the award in each of his four seasons playing high school baseball and is rightfully considered one of the best pitchers in SHS history.

Basketball (Boys)

Enno Lietz wrapped up his sixth and final season at the helm of the basketball program in 1962-63. The Dogs, led by seniors Ed Barnhart, Bob Eggebrecht, Bob Frank, Ron Keene, John Luketich, and John Monroe, competed well throughout the year before bowing out with a record of 11-16. Barnhart captured the Free Throw Award for the second consecutive season.

Football

Fred Brenzel's Bulldogs enjoyed another successful campaign in the fall of 1962, finishing 7-3 on the year. Unfortunately, a loss to Carlinville midway through the season cost the Dogs their fifth straight South Central Conference championship, and the team had to settle for 2nd place with a 3-1 mark in the SCC. The Bulldogs were led by senior MVP's John Luketich (Offense) and John Monroe (Defense), who joined fellow seniors Harry Aberdroth, Ed Barnhart, Mike Bortko, Melvin Duda, Bob Eggebrecht, Ron Keene, Jim Mueller, Dan Stinnett, and Ron Weidler on the team. Barnhart moved on to Culver-Stockton College in Canton, Missouri to continue his playing career. Meanwhile, Luketich played one season at Southern Illinois University.

The year began with a 13-6 victory over Virden and was followed up with a 34-0 shutout win against Litchfield. A three-game losing streak ensued, though the opponents were among the toughest in the state. Week 3 saw SHS drop a non-conference contest to Belleville (28-7). In Week 4, Jerseyville shaded the Dogs by a score of 20-19. The most heartbreaking loss of the year, however, was a 13-7 setback to Carlinville in Week 5. The Cavaliers went on to win the SCC that year, ending a streak of four straight titles by SHS and a 25-0-2 record since the program's last SCC loss in 1957 (also to Carlinville). However, the Bulldogs finished the season very strong, recording five straight wins. SHS defeated league foes Gillespie (26-6), Nokomis (52-6), and Mt. Olive (34-0), and also recorded two tough non-conference wins along the way.

A Week 7 shutout of Decatur St. Teresa was impressive, as was a 14-12 victory over Big Eight champion Centralia to close out the year.

Track (Boys)

The track team of 1963 was coached by Enno Lietz in his final year directing the program. The squad featured seniors Melvin Duda, Bob Frank, Ken Gerhardt, Ron Keene, John Monroe, Jim Mueller, and Ron Weidler. Monroe was the high point scorer for the squad, while Frank tied the school record in the high jump.

Class of 1964

Baseball

In 1964, for the first time in eleven years, Staunton did not win the South Central Conference in baseball. A remarkable run, the Bulldogs finished 67-6 in league play during the time period. Coach Fred Brenzel's team finished the 1964 season with a record of 11-7 overall, including 5-3 in the SCC. The season ended in the championship game of the District Tournament, as the Dogs defeated Gillespie and Livingston before succumbing to Granite City in the final. SHS was led by four-year letter winner Gerald Lotter, who joined fellow seniors Tom Guennewig, Dan Holmes, Jerry Kinnikin, and John Oettel on the team. Kinnikin took home the Hitting Award with a .354 batting average, while sophomore Al Schuette captured the Pitching Award for the second straight season.

Basketball (Boys)

The 1963-64 basketball team welcomed a rookie head coach to the fold, as Bill McCullough took over the program. His initial squad was led by seniors Dan Holmes, Jerry Kinnikin, Rollie Loewen, and John Oettel. Unfortunately, the season was not kind to the Dogs, as the team faltered to a record of 5-17 overall. One bright spot for SHS was the play of junior Roger Kuba, the team's Free Throw Award winner.

Football

The 1963 football team was the first unit to win at least nine games in a season since the record-setting 1923 squad. Fred Brenzel's club finished the year with a 9-1 record, including a spotless 5-0 mark in the South Central Conference. The undefeated performance in league play earned the Bulldogs their fifth conference title in six years. The nine wins tied for the second-most in school history, and in fact Brenzel's program achieved the feat on three other occasions.

The season began with hard fought non-conference victories over Virden (14-7) and Litchfield (20-7). The team's lone loss on the season occurred in Week 3 against Quincy Christian Brothers College High School (which later became Quincy Notre Dame), as the Dogs were shut out by a score of 10-0. After disposing of Jerseyville (27-0) in Week 4, SHS opened league play with two thrilling victories over rivals Carlinville (14-13) and Gillespie (14-7). A non-conference affair with Decatur St. Teresa resulted in a 32-0 shutout victory for Staunton in Week 7 of the season. SHS then returned to SCC play, taking care of Nokomis (34-6), Mt. Olive (47-0), and Springfield Feitshans (47-7) to lay claim to the conference crown.

The Dogs were relatively young in 1963, featuring just four seniors in the form of Tom Guennewig, Jerry Kinnikin, John Oettel, and John Silvester. Kinnikin was named Offensive MVP for his outstanding play as quarterback. He eventually landed at Illinois State University and played the same position for the Redbirds. Other rushing and scoring leaders on the season were Jim Malek, Roger Kuba, Silvester, and Dennis Kuba. Oettel took home Defensive MVP honors before moving on to play football at Bradley University. Other notable defensive standouts included Brian Machota, Roger Kuba, Guennewig, and Silvester.

Track (Boys)

Coach Bill McCullough welcomed big numbers for the 1964 track season. The group was led by seniors John Fischer, Rollie Loewen, Don Masinelli, Dennis Mayfield, and Bill McBrien.

Class of 1965

Baseball

The 1965 baseball team, under the tutelage of Fred Brenzel, had a remarkable run through the season. After losing their first game of the year to Breese Mater Dei, the Dogs reeled off eighteen consecutive victories. The team finished the year with an overall record of 18-2, including a 10-0 mark in the South Central Conference. Not only did Staunton capture the SCC title, but the Dogs were also District champions that year before falling to Southwestern in the Regional by a score of 2-0. Remarkably, Staunton played in seven games that were decided by just one run, winning each contest on their way to what was then a school record for victories. Senior baseball team members in 1965 included Jim Goldasich, Roger Kuba, Jim Malak, Bill Mitchelar, Gary Oehler, Don Ott, and Tony Silvester. Oehler was the team's Hitting Award winner, while junior Al Schuette won the Pitching Award.

Basketball (Boys)

In 1964-65, Bill McCullough's second season leading the basketball program, the team finished with a record of 7-15 overall and 3-7 in the South Central Conference. The lone senior member of the unit was Roger Kuba. Junior Rod Barnhart captured the team's Free Throw Award.

Football

The 1964 season was one for the ages, as the Bulldogs finished the year undefeated with a record of 9-0-1, including a 4-0-1 mark in the South Central Conference. The only blemish on the record was a 6-6 tie with SCC co-champion Gillespie in Week 6 of the season. The season served as just the third undefeated campaign in the program's history up to that point.

Fred Brenzel's squad started out the schedule with lopsided wins over Virden (40-6) and Litchfield (59-0). Up next was Christian Brothers College High School (CBC) out of St. Louis. In the first meeting between the two schools, SHS scored another shutout, this time by a score of 26-0. A defeat of Jerseyville (26-7) followed in Week 4, and thus the Bulldogs were 4-0 heading into the SCC opener against Carlinville. In what was expected to be a competitive game, Coach Brenzel's Bulldogs destroyed the Cavaliers by a score of 41-7. The 6-6 tie with Gillespie came one week later, dashing the team's hopes of a clean slate. Staunton finished the season with an upset victory over Alton Marquette (19-14), followed by easy wins over Nokomis (44-6), Mt. Olive (41-0), and Springfield Feitshans (31-0). On the season, Staunton outscored its opponents 333-46 and outgained them 3702-1335 in yards from scrimmage.

Based on the success of the team, several players took home personal accolades, including five Bulldogs who were named All-State. Seniors Dennis Kuba, Roger Kuba, Jim Malek, and Tony Silvester, as well as junior Jim Arico, were each named to the All-State team. Each of the five players also made 1st Team All-Conference, and they were joined by juniors Rod Barnhart, Ron Dustman, Larry Kleeman, and Lou Scroggins. Seniors Jim Goldasich and Gary Oehler, along with juniors Brian Machota and Al Schuette, were named All-SCC Honorable Mention. At the team's postseason banquet, Roger Kuba was named Offensive MVP, while Dennis Kuba, Machota, and Silvester shared Defensive MVP honors. Additional seniors on the 1964 squad included Dave Brown, Bill Mitchelar, George Oehler, and Dennis Smith. Roger Kuba continued his football career at Southern Illinois University.

Track (Boys)

Though most were underclassmen, coach Bill McCullough once again had a high turnout for track in 1965, including seniors Tom Holloway, Bob Martinelli, and Dick Tiburzi.

Class of 1966

Baseball

Fred Brenzel's Staunton baseball team captured its second straight South Central Conference championship in 1966, finishing 12-2 overall and a perfect 6-0 in league play. Seniors Jim Arico, Ed Baldoni, Rod Barnhart, Bill Braasch, Brian Machota, and Al Schuette paced the squad. Schuette won the Pitching Award for the fourth consecutive season, while juniors Brad Neuhaus and Tom Monschein shared the Hitting Award. One of the best pitchers in SHS history, Schuette moved on to the University of Iowa to participate in both baseball and football. In fact, he once threw a no-hitter for the Hawkeyes.

Basketball (Boys)

Bill McCullough's third and final season leading the Staunton basketball program saw the team go 9-13 overall with a 4-6 mark in South Central Conference play. Seniors Jim Arico, Rod Barnhart, Larry Kleeman, Mike McDole, Gary Ramach, Ken Rinderknecht, and Al Schuette sparked the squad. Rinderknecht took home the Free Throw Award for the 1965-66 season. He continued his basketball career at Washington University where he also competed in track.

Football

Fred Brenzel's 1965 football team continued its success on the field, winning its third straight South Central Conference title by going 5-0 in the league. The SCC championship was the seventh in the previous eight seasons for Staunton, and in 1965 the Bulldogs outscored league foes to a tune of 149-12. The Dogs ended the season with an overall record of 8-1.

Staunton once again began the year with a tough non-conference slate, and the Bulldogs nearly came out of the early part of their schedule unscathed. Week 1 saw the Dogs easily take care of Hillsboro (39-0), and they followed that game up with another shutout, this time against

Litchfield (14-0). The one and only loss of the season was a 20-18 setback to Quincy CBC. The Dogs defeated Jerseyville by a score of 21-7 in Week 4, and the conference campaign began with a Week 5 shutout of Carlinville (27-0). The next two games were extremely close. SHS recorded a safety against Gillespie in a 2-0 Week 6 affair that saw two GHS touchdowns called back due to penalties. The other tight matchup came in a 19-12 victory over Springfield Feitshans. The Bulldogs wrapped up the season with consecutive shutouts of Nokomis (42-0) and Mt. Olive (59-0).

SHS placed eight members on the All-Conference team, including seniors Jim Arico, Rod Barnhart, Ron Dustman, Glen Herbeck, Larry Kleeman, Brian Machota, and Al Schuette, as well as junior Dave Link. Ed Baldoni, Rink Calcari, Chris Kapilla, Jim Margaritis, Lou Scroggins, and Fred Straub provided additional senior leadership for the squad. Machota (Defense) and Schuette (Offense) were named Team MVP's at the annual sports banquet. After graduation, Arico continued his career at Truman State University. Meanwhile, Barnhart and Schuette continued their football careers at the University of Iowa, with Schuette also playing baseball for the Hawkeyes.

Track (Boys)

Bill McCullough, in his final season as SHS track coach, welcomed seniors Eric Bohlen, Glen Herbeck, David Holmes, Chris Kapilla, Larry Kleeman, Ken Rinderknecht, Lou Scroggins, Norm Senaldi, and Joe Valenta for the 1966 season. The Bulldogs finished 4th at the South Central Conference Meet. After the season, Rinderknecht continued his track and basketball career at Washington University.

Class of 1967

Baseball

Coach Fred Brenzel's 1967 baseball team only played twelve games, but the Bulldogs made the most of them, finishing 9-3 overall and 6-1 in the South Central Conference to three-peat as league champions. In fact, the SCC title marked the program's thirteenth such championship in the previous fourteen years, a span that saw the Dogs go 94-10 in SCC affairs. Statistical leaders Al Culp, Tom Monschein, and Brad Neuhaus sparked the squad. Seniors included Bob Barnhart, Culp, Monschein, Neuhaus, Mark Skertich, and Mark Wenner. Skertich later returned to the Staunton school district and served as the elementary principal for more than three decades. Monschein continued his baseball career at Illinois State University where he was a member of the school's 1969 national championship team.

Basketball (Boys)

Dave Davison took over the basketball program for the 1966-67 school year, and he welcomed seniors Al Culp, Jack McDole, Tom Monschein, and Tom Oettel as leaders of his team. The Bulldogs experienced an up-and-down season, ending the campaign with a record of 11-13, including 5-5 in the South Central Conference. The Bulldogs struggled in the early portion of their schedule but ended the regular season with five consecutive wins before falling to Carlinville (72-61) in the Regional Tournament. Monschein and Oettel were both named to the 1st Team All-Conference squad that year, and Culp was named Honorable Mention. Team

MVP Oettel averaged a double-double for the season with 15.6 points and 11.5 rebounds. Monschein (15.4 points, Free Throw Award) and Culp (11.6 points, 8.4 rebounds) also averaged double figures for the Dogs.

Football

Having graduated nearly every starter from the previous season, Staunton was supposed to be in rebuilding mode for the 1966 football season. However, in those days the Bulldogs didn't rebuild, they reloaded. The youthful squad experienced an excellent campaign, finishing the season with a record of 8-1-1 overall and 4-1 in the South Central Conference. SHS recorded wins over Springfield Feitshans (37-6), Gillespie (19-7), Hillsboro (28-6), Jerseyville (20-13), Litchfield (21-7), Mt. Olive (20-0), Nokomis (45-6), and Quincy CBC (21-6). The tie was a 13-13 battle against Belleville East. Unfortunately, the lone loss was an SCC affair with Carlinville, which the Cavaliers won by a score of 7-6. CHS thus took the conference championship back to Carlinville after Staunton had won it three straight years. However, coach Fred Brenzel's Bulldogs had nothing to be ashamed of, as they surpassed all reasonable preseason expectations.

The Dogs were led by seniors and All-Conference 1st Teamers Bob Barnhart, Tony Bechem, Al Culp, Gary Frioli, and Dave Link, while Ed Hilmes was named All-SCC Honorable Mention. Juniors Lyndall Kleeman (1st Team) and Phil Callovini (Honorable Mention) were also honored for their play during the SCC portion of the schedule. Joining the aforementioned players, additional seniors in the Class of 1967 included Dave Hall, Bob Karl, Mike Minkanic, Mark Skertich, and Mark Wenner. Barnhart continued his football career at Culver-Stockton College, while Link moved on to the University of Iowa. Meanwhile, Skertich returned to Staunton schools as elementary principal, a position he held for more than thirty years.

Track (Boys)

Though they have since been broken, there were two school records set by track athletes in 1967. Hank Fey, John Hochmuth, Dave Larcker, and John Pingolt were successful in the 800 meter relay, while Ron Barber set the initial school record in the 3200 meters in the first year that the event was added to the sport. Seniors on the team included John Ashley, John Davis, Harry Eller, Ed Fey, Dave Hall, Pingolt, and Steve Ziglar. The team, coached by Jim Haynes, finished 3rd at the South Central Conference Meet.

Class of 1968

Baseball

Coach Fred Brenzel's 1968 baseball squad failed to capture the South Central Conference championship, though the team did win the District Tournament. The Dogs dispatched of Mt. Olive 2-1 before downing Livingston 8-2 to take the title. Seniors Louie Crook, Lyndall Kleeman, Bryan Kinnikin, and Joe Mitchell spearheaded the effort. Kinnikin won the team Hitting Award, while sophomore Dennis Smiley won the Pitching Award.

Basketball (Boys)

Dave Davison had to rebuild his team for the 1967-68 season, as the squad was hit hard by graduation. As expected, the Dogs struggled for most of the year, eventually finishing with a record of 6-17. SHS had a balanced attack, as seniors Bob Braasch (16.0 points, 9.7 rebounds), Lyndall Kleeman (12.6 points, 8.6 rebounds), and Bryan Kinnikin (11.3 points, Free Throw Award) all averaged double figures for the team. Additional seniors included Hank Fey, Dave Larcker, and Joe Mitchell.

Football

The Staunton football team had an outstanding season in 1967, culminating in yet another South Central Conference championship for the program under coach Fred Brenzel. SHS finished the year 9-1 overall and a perfect 5-0 in the SCC, with the only lone loss coming in the last game of the season to Belleville East. The Dogs began the schedule with non-conference victories over Hillsboro (26-6), Litchfield (28-19), Quincy CBC (35-0), and Jerseyville (14-7). Staunton began the conference slate with a Week 5 matchup against rival Carlinville, and SHS came away with a 21-13 victory. The game represented the only time the Dogs surrendered points in SCC games, as they went on to shut out Gillespie (13-0), Virden (7-0), Nokomis (27-0), and Mt. Olive (55-0). Week 10 brought a stiff test with Belleville East. Unfortunately, Staunton was on the wrong end of a 40-0 shutout.

The squad was led by seniors Phil Callovini, Gary Herbeck, Bryan Kinnikin, Lyndall Kleeman, Jim Morris, Mike Pintar, George Przymuzala, and Jim Tiburzi. Kleeman, in particular, had an outstanding season, and he was rewarded for his efforts with Defensive MVP honors, as well as being named to the All-State team. Quarterback Kinnikin took home the Offensive MVP award at the annual sports banquet. All-Conference 1st Team status went to Callovini, Kinnikin, Kleeman, Pintar, Przymuzala, and junior Larry Grabruck. Herbeck and junior Tom Kolkovich took home All-Conference Honorable Mention honors.

Track (Boys)

Seniors John Caldieraro, Drennan Cloyd, Ed Felchner, Hank Fey, Kirk Kramer, Dave Larcker, Mike Streeb, and Jim Tiburzi led the 1968 track squad to a 2nd place finish at both the South Central Conference and Macoupin County track meets. Though the marks have since been broken, six individuals set school records that season. Larker (400 meters) and Streeb (800 meters) posted event records, as did juniors Bob Smith (hurdles) and Tom Stephens (3200 meters), as well as sophomores John Hochmuth (200 meters) and Jim Wilson (shot put). Larker took home Team MVP honors for a unit coached by Jim Haynes.

Class of 1969

Baseball

Fred Brenzel's 1969 baseball team was led by seniors Rick Allen, Don Best, Wes Campbell, and Tom Goldasich. Unfortunately, SHS failed to capture a conference or postseason title for the just the third time in nineteen years.

Basketball (Boys)

Dave Davison's 1968-69 basketball team finished the season 9-15 overall, including 7-3 in the South Central Conference. The SCC mark was the program's best league finish in several years, and it was even more impressive considering the Dogs started just one senior, Terry Best.

A 2nd Team All-Conference selection, Best averaged 11.0 points per game for the Dogs. The team's leading scorer and rebounder was Brad Bahn, a junior who also captured the Free Throw Award. Bahn, the Team MVP, was also a 1st Team All-SCC selection. Additional seniors on the squad included Larry Grabruck and Terry Meyer.

Football

Although the 1968 football team finished with a winning record of 6-4, including 3-2 in the South Central Conference, the season did mark the first time in ten years that the Dogs failed to win seven games or finish as one of the top two teams in the South Central Conference. The season started off in fine fashion, as the Bulldogs won three straight, including victories over Hillsboro (28-7), Litchfield (14-0), and Quincy CBC (19-7). However, three consecutive losses pushed the Bulldogs back to the .500 mark. Jerseyville started the slide with a 14-7 victory over the Dogs, while Carlinville (13-6) and Gillespie (15-7) also registered narrow wins over the boys in red and white. The Bulldogs righted the ship with a 13-7 victory over Virden in Week 7, and they followed up with wins over Nokomis (25-0) and Mt. Olive (59-6). The final game of the season saw SHS fall to Belleville East by a score of 31-0. Carlinville captured the SCC title in 1968.

Coach Fred Brenzel said goodbye to seniors Rick Allen, Don Best, Dean DeVries, Tom Goldasich, Larry Grabruck, Tom Kolkovich, Loran Kovaly, Mark Neuhaus, and Ron Williams. DeVries, Grabruck, and Kolkovich were each named All-Conference, as were juniors Al Conroy, Gene Frioli, Dave Russell, and Jim Wilson. Goldasich (Offense) and Grabruck (Defense) were named Team MVP of their respective units.

Track (Boys)

Jim Haynes coached the 1969 track team to 2nd place finishes at both the South Central Conference and Macoupin County track meets behind seniors Terry Best, Larry Grabruck, Terry Meyer, and Ron Saunders. At the SCC Meet, junior John Hochmuth was a champion in three events (200 meters, 400 meters, 1600 meter relay), while sophomore Gene Roehl captured two titles (800 meters, 1600 meter relay). Best won the SCC high jump title, Grabruck took home discus honors, and sophomore Nick Wineburner captured gold in the long jump. Joining Hochmuth and Roehl on the relay team was a combination of juniors Al Conroy, Dave Russell, and Kevin Sullivan. Hochmuth, Roehl, and Wineburner each won their respective events at County, while Grabruck took home shot put honors.

CHAPTER 7

Classes of 1970 – 1979

Overview

The 1970s saw the introduction of three sports programs for females at Staunton High School. Though the Girls Athletic Association (GAA) had been in existence for many years, the first official sport offered to females at the school was track in 1972-73. Volleyball was instituted two years later, and basketball got its start in 1978-79. While success in girl's basketball has been minimal, track and volleyball both achieved instant success upon inception.

On the male side, cross country and golf were both added in 1975. Though the initial cross country teams were competitive, the sport has historically been hindered by a lack of numbers in the program. Golf enjoyed a considerable amount of success upon its reintroduction and arguably became the school's premier sports program during the 1990s. Unfortunately, the 1970s continued to be tough on the basketball program, as the Bulldogs enjoyed just one winning season in the decade. Meanwhile, baseball and football teams remained very strong at the school, though the programs did not enjoy the same level of success achieved in previous years. One item of note is the beginning of the IHSA Playoffs for football in 1974. The initial standard for qualification was very rigid, since only sixteen teams spanning five classes were admitted. As such, a school basically had to win its conference or finish 8-1 and hope for an at-large bid. SHS made its first playoff appearance in 1977. While the Bulldogs have never played for a state title, one could argue that Staunton had one of the elite football programs in all of Illinois during the 1920s and 1960s. Though it impossible to know how events would have played out, it is conceivable that SHS would have competed for multiple state championships during those years.

The 1970s were relatively uneventful in terms of changes to the South Central Conference. In 1970-71, Southwestern was readmitted to the league after its departure from the Western Illinois Valley Conference. The Piasa Birds joined Carlinville, Gillespie, Mt. Olive, Nokomis, Staunton, and Virden to form an SCC that included seven teams. The lineup remained unchanged for ten years.

Class of 1970

Baseball

The 1970 baseball team was the last squad directed by Fred Brenzel. As was the case with most of Brenzel's teams, the Bulldogs were a championship unit, as the club finished 16-4 and captured South Central Conference and Regional titles. The SCC title represented Brenzel's thirteenth in sixteen years directing the program. The Bulldogs were led by seniors Monte Cely, Al Conroy, Jerry Crabtree, Jack Gai, Dennis Kellebrew, and Dennis Smiley.

Basketball (Boys)

The 1969-70 Bulldogs were coached by Dave Davison in his fourth and final year at the helm. The squad finished 8-16 overall, including 6-4 in the South Central Conference. Team

MVP Brad Bahn led the squad, and he was joined by fellow seniors Al Conroy, Jerry Crabtree, Roger Elmore, John Hochmuth, and Kevin Sullivan.

Football

The 1969 football team, in Fred Brenzel's final year leading the program, won yet another South Central Conference championship, finishing a perfect 5-0 in the league and 9-1 overall. In fact, the SCC champions are considered one of the finest teams in school history. Week 1 witnessed the Bulldogs defeat Hillsboro (48-6) before shutting out Litchfield in Week 2 by a score of 44-0. The Dogs won a squeaker over Quincy CBC in Week 3 (8-7) and also narrowly defeated Jerseyville in Week 4 (16-8). However, SHS had no trouble with the conference slate, as the Dogs easily defeated Carlinville (20-6), Gillespie (39-0), Virden (77-8), Nokomis (36-14), and Mt. Olive (50-0). The Lancers of Belleville East ruined Staunton's hope for a perfect season by soundly defeating the Bulldogs (28-8) in a matchup of undefeated teams.

SHS was led by seniors Tom Brown, Al Conroy, Jim Fey, Gene Frioli, John Hochmuth, Steve Jarman, Dennis Kellebrew, Dave Russell, Steve Sitko, Jon Tevini, and Jim Wilson. Defensive MVP Conroy anchored a feisty unit, while Offensive MVP Hochmuth gained over 1000 yards rushing on the season. Moreover, with 1603 total yards from scrimmage, it is believed that Hochmuth set a single-season school mark in that category, a record that stood for more than three decades. In fact, it is possible that he holds the school's career yardage mark from scrimmage. Regardless, given the statistics he accumulated for some of the best teams in the program's history, Hochmuth must be considered one of the best running backs to ever play for the Bulldogs. After the season, Brown, Conroy, Frioli, Hochmuth, Jarman, Kellebrew, Russell, and Wilson each were named All-Conference, joining juniors Mike Kozemczak and Craig Schuette on the 1st Team. Conroy finished the season with 883 yards from scrimmage.

Brenzel holds the longest tenure of any football coach in school history. His sixteen year career included a record of 107-43-5 and nine conference titles. Although there was not a postseason tournament during his era, one could speculate that many of Brenzel's teams would have advanced deep into the playoffs, perhaps contending for a state title along the way. Unfortunately, the Illinois High School Association did not have a playoff system in place until a few years after Brenzel's departure from the Staunton football program.

Track (Boys)

The 1970 track team was coached by Jim Haynes. Senior and Team MVP John Hochmuth repeated as Macoupin County champion in the 200 meters and 400 meters. He was joined on the squad by fellow seniors Dennis Bloemker, Tom Brown, Al Conroy, Doug Haenni, Barry Hainaut, Terry Kuethe, Jim Rucker, Dave Russell, Kevin Sullivan, Bob Tuey, and Jim Wilson. Hochmuth continued his track career at Eastern Illinois University.

Class of 1971

Baseball

The 1971 baseball season saw former SHS standout Barry Deist take over the program. In fact, Deist directed the Bulldogs for twenty-two years, the longest tenure in SHS baseball history. Deist's first senior class included Frank Barrett, George Bednar, John Caldieraro, Rich Caldieraro, Dennis Felchner, Gerald Moss, and Craig Schuette.

Basketball (Boys)

The Staunton basketball team welcomed a new coach for the 1970-71 campaign, as Don Miller stepped in to guide the program. Unfortunately, Miller's first season at the helm was rocky from the start, as the Dogs stumbled to a 5-17 record, including 3-9 in South Central Conference play. Senior Craig Schuette was a bright spot during the season, capturing Honorable Mention status at the Macoupin County Tournament, which was won by Southwestern for the first time. Joining Schuette as seniors on the team were Rich Caldieraro and Dennis Felchner.

Football

The 1970 football season ushered in a new era, as for the first time in seventeen years Fred Brenzel was not roaming the sidelines for SHS. His replacement was former assistant coach Bob Chiti. Like Brenzel, Chiti coached at Auburn before coming to Staunton. Interestingly enough, Chiti's first season at each school resulted in undefeated seasons, as the 1970 Bulldogs finished 8-0-1 on the year. The undefeated campaign was the fourth in school history, and the Dogs were also able to capture another South Central Conference championship by finishing 5-0-1 in league play.

Chiti's first game as head coach saw Staunton defeat Hillsboro by a score of 36-26. After disposing of Litchfield in Week 2 (26-0), the Dogs began conference play against Southwestern and defeated the Piasa Birds by a score of 40-22. SHS continued the winning streak with a Week 4 non-conference victory over Jerseyville (20-6) but recorded the only blemish on the season in a 6-6 tie with Carlinville in Week 5. Staunton went on to defeat SCC opponents Gillespie (26-8), Virden (55-6), Nokomis (46-6), and Mt. Olive (58-14) to capture the conference title.

Success on the field brought individual notoriety, and SHS players garnered several accolades after the season came to a close. All-Conference 1st Team members included seniors Rich Caldieraro, Dennis Felchner, Mike Kozemczak, and Craig Schuette, juniors Rick Tsupros and Don Warren, and sophomore Mike Dal Pozzo. All-SCC Honorable Mention members included seniors John Caldieraro and Gerald Moss. Caldieraro and Moss were joined by juniors Bob Guennewig, Ron Warren, and Mike Watkins on the squad. Furthermore, Schuette (1st Team) and Kozemczak (Honorable Mention) were named All-State in 1970. John Colley rounded out a small but quality senior class. After graduation, Felchner and Schuette continued their football careers at Southern Illinois University.

Track (Boys)

Jim Haynes returned as coach in 1971 for his fifth and final year directing the track program. Fortunately, he welcomed back a few champions that season, including South Central Conference winners Gene Roehl (800 meters), Jim Sitko (1600 meters), and Nick Wineburner (100 meters), as well as the 800 meter and 1600 meter relay teams. Wineburner, a senior, set a school record in the long jump during the season. Additional seniors on the track team included Rich Caldieraro, Dennis Felchner, and Roehl.

Class of 1972

Baseball

The 1972 baseball team, coached by Barry Deist, included seniors Rick Tsupros and Bob Vesper.

Basketball (Boys)

The 1971-72 basketball team, under the direction of Don Miller, finished 2-20 overall and 0-12 in the South Central Conference. Unfortunately, the overall record represents the worst season in the program's documented history. The club's victories came against Livingston early in the year and Northwestern in the first round of the Macoupin County Tournament. Bob Vesper was the lone senior on the squad. After the season, Vesper was named Team MVP and won the Free Throw Award, and he also captured All-Conference Honorable Mention honors. Sophomore Daryl Schuette joined Vesper as an Honorable Mention selection.

Football

Bob Chiti's second year guiding the Staunton football program produced a .500 record, as the squad finished 5-5 in 1971. However, each victory came in South Central Conference play, giving SHS yet another league crown with a 5-1 mark in the conference, though the Dogs shared the championship with Carlinville and Nokomis. The Bulldogs opened the season with non-conference defeats at the hands of Hillsboro (18-8) and Litchfield (21-8). However, SHS started off the league slate on a positive note by defeating Southwestern (14-12) in Week 3 of the season. Another non-conference loss, this time to Pittsfield (43-12), dropped the Dogs to 1-3 on the year. However, narrow victories over Carlinville (12-8) and Gillespie (14-12), followed by a blowout win over Virden (54-13), righted the ship. Unfortunately, SHS lost a close game to Nokomis (22-20), keeping the Bulldogs from an outright conference title. A victory over Mt. Olive (37-14) in Week 8 ended the SCC part of the schedule, while a 33-8 setback to Edwardsville closed out the year.

Despite winning the SCC, Staunton only placed two players on the All-Conference 1st Team, as seniors Rick Tsupros and Don Warren were honored by league coaches. Tsupros took home the Offensive MVP award, while Warren was named Defensive MVP. Seniors Bob Vesper and Mike Watkins, as well as juniors Paul Hiette, Mike Dal Pozzo, and Brian Rotsch were named All-Conference Honorable Mention. Rounding out the senior class were Bill Felchner, Bob Guennewig, Jim Hawkins, Steve Link, Tino Lopez, Joe Pirok, Rich Schubert, Jim Sitko, John Skertich, and Bill Vogt. After the season, Tsupros was named All-State, and he continued his career at Eastern Illinois University. Watkins also continued playing football after high school, competing for Illinois College as a member of the Blueboys.

Track (Boys)

Ward Derlitzki took over the track program in 1972, his only year with the squad. Seniors on the track team that year included Jim Hawkins, Steve Link, Dan Oettel, John Skertich, Mike Watkins, and Larry Ziglar. The 800 meter relay team of Mike Dal Pozzo, Dennis Crouch, Skertich, and Watkins won the Macoupin County Meet, while Dal Pozzo also took home conference and county championships in the 100 meters.

Classes of 1970 - 1979

Class of 1973

Baseball

The 1973 baseball team was dominant in league action, finishing 9-1 and capturing the South Central Conference championship under the tutelage of Barry Deist. One game of note was a contest with rival Mt. Olive late in the season. The game lasted twenty-one innings (two shy of the national record) and ended in a 0-0 tie due to darkness. During the game, Mt. Olive set a state record by striking out 31 Staunton hitters. SHS pitchers responded by setting down 25 Wildcats, and in the process the two teams combined for a state record (eighth nationally) for combined strikeouts in a game. Seniors on the squad included Al Callovini, Paul Hiette, Joe Kravanya, and Fred Stein. Callovini and junior Bill Marcuzzo shared the Hitting Award, while junior Vic Spagnola won the Pitching Award.

Basketball (Boys)

Despite welcoming eight seniors for the 1972-73 basketball season, Don Miller's squad struggled in his third season as head coach. The Bulldogs finished 3-21 overall, including 1-11 in the South Central Conference. Wins on the year came in games against Odin, Mt. Olive, and Northwestern. Al Callovini, Mike Dal Pozzo, Mark Dietiker, Dave Hering, Paul Hiette, Brian Rotsch, Fred Stein, and Del Stiegemeier all finished up their playing careers that season. The end of the year also brought to an end Coach Miller's tenure with the program.

Football

Bob Chiti's 1972 football team enjoyed yet another successful South Central Conference campaign, as the Dogs finished with a 5-1 record in the league. Unfortunately, a 14-6 loss in Week 6 of the season to Gillespie cost SHS its fourth straight title, as the Miners finished undefeated in the SCC. The Bulldogs wrapped up the season 6-4 overall.

The season started with a shutout loss to Hillsboro (20-0) but followed with shutout victories over Litchfield (25-0) and Southwestern (26-0). Another shutout occurred in Week 4 against Pittsfield, though the Dogs came out on the wrong end of the contest (25-0). A 22-8 victory over Carlinville in Week 5 preceded the Gillespie loss. SHS went on to win three straight games, including victories over Virden (22-7), Nokomis (20-15), and Mt. Olive (20-9). The Dogs finished the season with a Week 10 loss to Edwardsville (34-8).

Staunton placed several players on the All-Conference squad, led by 1st Team members and seniors Gene Felchner, Paul Hiette, Fred Stein, and Terry Tevini. Seniors C.J. Kellebrew and Joe Kravanya were named All-SCC Honorable Mention, as were juniors Randy Best, Norm Heigert, Curt Kellebrew, and Daryl Schuette. Offensive MVP honors went to Hiette, while C.J. Kellebrew took home the Defensive MVP award. Additional seniors included Al Callovini, Mike Dal Pozzo, Roger Friend, and Dave Slazinik. Felchner continued his playing career at Illinois College.

Track (Boys)

The 1973 track program welcomed a new coach, with Gale Bryan taking over the reins. Senior Del Stiegemeier was the South Central Conference high jump champion that season, and he was joined on the track team by fellow seniors Dave Bird, Mike Dal Pozzo, Gene Felchner, Dave Hering, Paul Hiette, Bruce Robinson, and Brian Rotsch.

Track (Girls)

Although the Girls Athletic Association (GAA) had been in existence for a considerable number of years, the 1973 track season marked the first time that Staunton High School officially offered sports for girls in the district. Patty Rupert directed the first squad in school history, though no seniors participated in the inaugural campaign.

Class of 1974

Baseball

The 1974 baseball team tried to defend its South Central Conference title, but unfortunately the Dogs fell to 8-6 overall and 5-4 in SCC action. Barry Deist guided the team, which was led by seniors Norm Heigert, Bill Marcuzzo, Daryl Schuette, and Vic Spagnola. Marcuzzo (0.87 ERA) and Spagnola (1.23 ERA) were brilliant on the mound for SHS, while sophomore Eric Pingolt led the team in hitting with a .360 batting average. Marcuzzo and Spagnola were both named to the All-SCC 1st Team, while Pingolt and Schuette attained Honorable Mention status. Marcuzzo continued his baseball career for four seasons at Western Illinois University, earning All-American accolades as a senior.

Basketball (Boys)

An amazing turnaround occurred during the 1973-74 basketball season, as the Bulldogs, led by first-year head coach Randy Legendre, reversed a severe losing trend. Coach Legendre's team finished 14-11 overall and 9-3 in the South Central Conference, making the team co-champions of the league with Carlinville and Nokomis. The improbable championship season came on the heels of fifteen straight non-winning campaigns, including six straight years of single-digit win totals. However, Legendre's teams became known for making the impossible possible, as he eventually guided the basketball program to the school's only team title in his second stint as head basketball coach.

The 1974 team got out of the gate with a quick start, spurred by seven straight victories. Unfortunately, five consecutive losses ensued, though eventually the team finished the season on a four-game winning streak before being eliminated from postseason play by Nokomis. Seniors Bill Marcuzzo, Dave Oettel, Jeff Schmidt, Daryl Schuette, and Dave Suhrenbrock led the turnaround. Schuette garnered All-SCC 1st Team honors, and he was joined on the All-Conference squad by juniors Mark Stein (2nd Team) and Don Sullivan (Honorable Mention).

Football

The 1973 football season got off to a promising start for coach Bob Chiti, as the Dogs won their first four games of the year. Unfortunately, key injuries unravelled the season, though the team still finished 7-3-1 overall and 3-2-1 in the South Central Conference. Interestingly enough, Staunton played eleven regular season games for the first and only time in school history that season.

The year began with a Week 1 victory over Bethalto Civic Memorial by a score of 28-18. A close win over Hillsboro (28-22) in Week 2 preceded victories over Litchfield (20-6) and Southwestern (6-0). SHS lost a hard-fought Week 5 game to Pittsfield (12-8) before battling

Carlinville to an 8-8 tie in Week 6. Gillespie knocked off Staunton by a score of 24-14 in Week 7, giving the Miners their second straight SCC title. However, the Dogs rebounded with victories over Virden (20-6) and Nokomis (48-6). A loss to Mt. Olive (20-16) wrapped up the league slate, though SHS finished the season with a 14-6 win over Chatham Glenwood.

Seniors on the 1973 squad included Randy Best, Norm Heigert, Bill Marcuzzo, Tim McBride, Mike Pirok, Jeff Schmidt, Daryl Schuette, and Dave Suhrenbrock. Heigert was the lone Staunton player to make the All-Conference 1st Team, though Best and Schuette joined juniors Bob Lietz and Don Sullivan in garnering Honorable Mention status. Schmidt was named the team's Offensive MVP, while Best took home Defensive MVP honors. After the season, Schuette continued his playing career at Western Illinois University for four years.

Track (Boys)

Gale Bryan's 1974 track team took home 4th place at both the South Central Conference and Macoupin County track meets. Seniors Randy Braasch, Bill Marcuzzo, and Daryl Schuette anchored the team. Schuette (high jump), junior Don Sullivan (triple jump), and sophomore John Clark (shot put) all captured SCC titles for the Bulldogs.

Track (Girls)

The second year of track at Staunton High School saw seniors Denise Gockel, Terry Hawkins, Mary Link, and Renee Sherfy lead the program to a very successful 1974 season. In fact, the unit won all five of its regular season track meets. The Lady Bulldogs, under the leadership of Patty Rupert, finished in 2nd place at the Macoupin County Meet. Paula Hering starred for SHS, qualifying for State in the long jump.

Class of 1975

Baseball

The 1975 baseball team finished the season 4-7 overall, which is possibly the first losing season in school history, though documented records for the sport are not very thorough. Coach Barry Deist's team did finish with a winning record in the South Central Conference (4-3) behind seniors Dwight Garrells, Bob Gay, Mark Stein, Don Sullivan, and Greg Yarnik. Sullivan won the Pitching Award, while junior Eric Pingolt led the team with a .352 batting average. Yarnik continued his playing career at MacMurray College.

Basketball (Boys)

The 1974-75 Bulldogs were coached by Randy Legendre. Unfortunately, the Dogs were unable to match the previous season's success, as they finished 12-14 overall and 5-7 in the South Central Conference. Furthermore, the program had to replace a big group of seniors the following season, including Glenn DeVries, Jeff Hebenstreit, Bob Lietz, Mark Stein, Don Sullivan, Joe Tosolin, and Greg Yarnik.

Football

The 1974 football team finished 4-5 overall and 3-3 in the South Central Conference under coach Bob Chiti in his fifth and final year directing the program. The first six games of the season resulted in shutouts, though SHS ended up on the short end in the majority of them. After losing 8-0 to Hillsboro in Week 1, the Bulldogs bounced back to defeat Litchfield (20-0) and Southwestern (36-0). A Week 4 setback to Pittsfield (20-0) preceded losses to Carlinville (28-0) and Gillespie (26-0). Staunton righted the ship in a Week 7 victory over Virden (22-10), though the Bulldogs fell the very next week in a close game against Nokomis by a score of 12-6. SHS did end the season on a high note, knocking off rival Mt. Olive (38-32) in Week 9. Carlinville took home the South Central Conference championship that season, the first of two straight titles.

Senior Jeff Hebenstreit was the lone member of the Bulldogs to garner 1st Team All-Conference status, and fellow senior Rich Bednar was awarded 2nd Team accolades. Seniors Ken Kleeman and Bob Lietz, as well as junior John Clark, received All-Conference Honorable Mention. Senior Bulldogs included Mark Albrecht, Bednar, Tony Cerentano, Jack Felchner, Dwight Garrells, Hebenstreit, Lietz, Brian Margaritis, Kevin Murphy, Mike Renner, and Don Sullivan.

Track (Boys)

The 1975 track team was guided by Gale Bryan and finished 3rd at both the South Central Conference and Macoupin County track meets. It was a fantastic year for individual accomplishments, as several school records were broken. Keith Gockel (300 meter hurdles), Greg Humphries (high jump), Bob Lietz (pole vault), Don Sullivan (triple jump), and the 400 meter relay team of Jim Beisner, Jeff Hebenstreit, Sullivan, and Brian Wall all set school marks. Humphries was named Team MVP and also won the SCC title in the high jump. Sullivan won a conference title in the long jump and also advanced to State in that event. The 800 meter relay team of Hebenstreit, Humphries, Sullivan, and Wall were also SCC champions. The following season's team had big shoes to fill, as Hebenstreit, Humphries, Lietz, Sullivan, and Wall all graduated in 1975.

Track (Girls)

The 1975 track team welcomed Donna Ruehrup to the coaching fold and, in doing so, touched off a series of spectacular seasons for the young program. The success included two straight Macoupin County crowns, as well as South Central Conference titles in six of her first seven seasons. In fact, Staunton has not won a Macoupin County or SCC championship since that time. Given the success of her track and volleyball programs, Ruehrup is rightfully considered one of the best coaches in school history.

The 1975 season was very impressive, as SHS won each regular season track meet that it entered. Sheila Pingolt was particularly notable, winning District in the discus and advancing to State in that event. The team also featured seniors Paula Hering, Mary Sue Stiegemeier, and Terri Streeb.

Volleyball

The 1974 volleyball team was the first of its kind in school history, and the squad made its mark immediately by winning the District Tournament. The Lady Bulldogs were coached by Sandal Herbeck in her one and only term as leader of the volleyball program. Paula Hering, Dorothy Johnson, and Mary Sue Stiegemeier were the program's first-ever seniors.

Classes of 1970 - 1979

Class of 1976

Baseball

Barry Deist's 1976 baseball team featured seniors Dennis Baum, Al DeVries, Lark Horton, Steve Hribernik, Terry Libbra, Eric Pingolt, and Phil Vesper. The team finished 11-9 overall, including 9-3 in the South Central Conference. The Dogs struggled early, dropping their first five games of the year. However, a six-game winning streak ensued, and a five-game winning streak later in the season accounted for Staunton's victory total on the year. Pingolt took home the Hitting Award with a .489 batting average, while Vesper and sophomore Bart Yakos shared the Pitching Award. 1st Team All-SCC members included Pingolt and juniors Ron Heflin and Dan McDole. Vesper and Yakos received All-Conference Honorable Mention, as did junior Kevin Barrett.

Basketball (Boys)

Randy Legendre's third and final year in his first stint leading the basketball program saw the 1975-76 team finish just 4-18 overall, with all four wins (against eight losses) coming against South Central Conference opponents. The Bulldogs were able to defeat Carlinville, Gillespie, Mt. Olive, and Virden behind the play of Team MVP and Free Throw Award winner John Clark. Clark received 2nd Team All-SCC honors after the season, while junior John Podwojski was named Honorable Mention All-Conference. Seniors in the Class of 1976 included Clark, Keith Gockel, Lark Horton, and Eric Pingolt.

Cross Country (Boys)

1975 was the first season that Staunton High School offered cross country. Eight members comprised the squad, led by Keith Gockel, the lone senior on the team. Gockel was joined by Rich Barber, Jay Edmiston, Ted Hancock, John Hering, John Maroso, Tom Spears, and Paul Zimmer. Spears eventually emerged as one of the top runners in school history.

Football

After serving several years as an assistant coach, the 1975 season represented Barry Deist's first year directing the football program. Deist, a former standout at SHS, graduated in 1962 and took his talents to the University of Illinois on a football scholarship. He eventually returned to his high school alma mater and led the football program for fifteen seasons, fielding many competitive teams along the way. In fact, given the current scenario in which a team generally only has to win five games to qualify for the postseason, Deist's teams would have done so in nine of those years. One such season was the 1975 campaign, as the team finished 5-4 overall and 3-3 in the South Central Conference.

The year started out on a high note, as the Bulldogs defeated Hillsboro 10-6 in Week 1. Week 2 saw Staunton register another close victory, this time by a score of 20-18 over Litchfield. A Week 3 shutout of Southwestern (31-0) followed, giving the Dogs three straight wins. Unfortunately, three consecutive losses ensued, with the Bulldogs dropping games to Pittsfield (28-6), eventual SCC champion Carlinville (43-14), and Gillespie (20-0). A 7-6 squeaker over Virden put the Dogs back above .500, but they dropped back to even in Week 8 with a 12-6 loss against Nokomis. SHS finished the season strong with a 45-8 victory over rival Mt. Olive.

All-Conference football players included seniors John Clark (1st Team), Al DeVries (1st Team), and Phil Vesper (2nd Team), as well as juniors Lou Cipriano (2nd Team), Mike Cockrell (Honorable Mention), Ron Heflin (Honorable Mention), and Tony Muenstermann (2nd Team). Clark, DeVries, Eric Pingolt, Randy Rhodes, and Vesper comprised the senior members of the team.

Golf (Boys)

After fifteen years without a team, Staunton High School fielded a golf squad for the 1975 season. Larry Kuba directed the program, and he ended up coaching golf for twenty-six years before retiring from the district in 2001. In fact, his tenure as head of the golf program is the longest of any coach, regardless of sport, in school history. He also racked up nearly three hundred career victories, which is the second most in school history across all sports. Kuba's initial team was led by seniors Steve Hribernik and Terry Libbra.

Track (Boys)

Coach Gale Bryan's 1976 track team lacked depth at the upper levels, with only Al DeVries, Keith Gockel, and Randy Rhodes representing the senior class. Gockel was voted Team MVP, while sophomore distance runner Tom Spears earned the most points for the club.

Track (Girls)

Donna Ruehrup's 1976 track team repeated as South Central Conference and Macoupin County champions. The team placed 3rd at the District Meet, with nine athletes advancing to State. The qualifiers included the 400 meter and 800 meter relay teams of Lynne Eddington, Karen Hering, Kathy Maxville, and Kim Maxville, as well as the 1600 meter relay team of Chris Cordani, Liz Link, Sarah Link, and Ellise Schuette. Sheila Pingolt (hurdles) also advanced to State, as did the 800 meter medley team of Hering, Kathy and Kim Maxville, and Schuette. Seniors on the squad included Cheryl Ahrens, Hering, Liz Link, Charlene Maxville, and Sue Travis.

Volleyball

Donna Ruehrup's first season directing the volleyball program was fairly uneventful, as the team finished 5-9 behind seniors Cheryl Ahrens, Cindy Beyer, and Patty Leyden. However, the volleyball team did not experience losing for long, as Ruehrup quickly turned the program into an area power and one of the most successful sports at Staunton High School.

Class of 1977

Baseball

The 1977 baseball team was directed by Barry Deist and finished with a record of 9-9 overall, including 6-5 in the South Central Conference. After beginning the season just 1-5, the Bulldogs reeled off eight wins in their next ten games before finishing the year with consecutive losses to Gillespie and Virden. Senior Kevin Barrett won the team's Hitting Award (.362) and junior Bart Yakos won the Pitching Award. Barrett, Yakos, and senior Mark Bono each took home All-Conference Honorable Mention honors. Meanwhile, junior Bob Snell was named 1st

Team All-SCC. Barrett and Bono were joined by seniors Gilbert Best, Ron Heflin, Dennis Krocker, and Dan McDole in the Class of 1977.

Basketball (Boys)

The 1976-77 basketball season got off to a solid start under coach Jerry Landrem. The unit won four of its first six games and was 5-4 after nine contests. Unfortunately, the wheels soon fell off, and the Bulldogs won just one game over their next fourteen contests, finishing the season 6-17 overall and 3-9 in South Central Conference play. The club was senior-laden, with Gilbert Best, Mark Bono, Tim Dustmann, Bob Garino, Dan McDole, and John Podwojski all set to graduate at the end of the school year. Bono won the Free Throw Award and was also named Team MVP. The season served as Landrem's only one as head coach after a few years as an assistant.

Cross Country (Boys)

The 1976 cross country team was led by seniors Jay Edmiston, Ted Hancock, John Hering, and Paul Zimmer. The squad also included junior Tom Spears and sophomore Bob Cargnoni. Spears, in particular, had an outstanding season, setting course records at the Staunton and Carlinville invitational meets. Gale Bryan served as the team's coach.

Football

In his second year at the helm, Barry Deist's 1976 football team duplicated its record from the previous season by finishing 5-4 overall and 3-3 in the South Central Conference. The season began with a tough loss to Hillsboro (14-10), but the Dogs recovered quickly with three consecutive wins over Litchfield (20-8), Southwestern (32-6), and Pittsfield (20-7). Unfortunately, Staunton's record fell to .500 after back-to-back losses to Carlinville (21-0) and Gillespie (35-21). The season ended with a victory over Virden (19-6), a loss to Nokomis (27-18), and a blowout win over Mt. Olive (40-0). Gillespie captured the SCC title that season and rode the momentum all the way to a 2nd place finish at State.

After the season ended, seniors Lou Cipriano, Ron Heflin, and Steve Wood all received 1st Team All-SCC accolades. 2nd Team members included senior Mark Bono and junior Randy Foster, while seniors Gilbert Best and Mike Cockrell took home 3rd Team honors. Sophomore Jay Meckles was named All-Conference Honorable Mention. Joining the aforementioned seniors as graduates in 1977 included Kevin Black, Bob Clark, Jerry Foster, Bob Garino, Dan McDole, John Podwojski, and Dan Sherfy. At the end-of-year banquet, Cipriano and Wood shared the Defensive MVP award, while Cipriano took home Offensive MVP honors.

Golf (Boys)

Coach Larry Kuba's golf team had an eventful season in 1976, finishing 10-2-1 in match play and winning the District Tournament, thus advancing to Sectional play. The trip to the Sectional Tournament was the first of five straight for the program. The youthful team included juniors Dave Hebenstreit, Tim Libbra, and Tim Williamson, as well as freshmen Kevin Banovic, Troy Graves, Mark Marcuzzo, and Bill Katich.

Track (Boys)

The 1977 track team had a successful season by finishing in 2nd place at both the Macoupin County and District track meets. In doing so, several individuals qualified for State. The

Bulldogs had three District champions in senior Jay Edmiston (1600 meters), John Hering (triple jump), and junior Tom Spears (3200 meters). Joining them at State were seniors Steve Wood (hurdles) and Paul Zimmer (200 meters). Hering also qualified in the long jump, as did the 3200 meter relay team consisting of Edmiston, juniors Mike Heinemeyer and Ed Ripperda, and sophomore Bob Cargnoni. Joining Edmiston, Hering, Wood, and Zimmer as seniors on the team were Mike Cockrell, Ted Hancock, Paul Koniak, and John Maroso. Hering led the team in points, while Zimmer was named Team MVP.

Track (Girls)

The 1977 track team won its third straight South Central Conference title under coach Donna Ruehrup, though the unit was unable to three-peat at the Macoupin County Meet. However, several members of the team made it to State, including sophomore Deone Courtney in the hurdles. Also, the 400 meter relay team of junior Lynne Eddington, sophomores Kim Maxville and Peggy Senaldi, and freshman Bonnie Bruhn qualified in that event. Seniors on the squad included Pamela Billings, Christine Cordani, Vickie Fiori, Cathy Maxville, and Ellise Schuette.

Volleyball

In just her second season directing the program, Donna Ruehrup led her 1976 volleyball team to a South Central Conference championship. The Lady Bulldogs finished 10-3 overall and 9-1 in the SCC, with each regular season game coming against conference opponents. Staunton fell to Raymond Lincolnwood in the District Tournament, ending the careers of seniors Sheila Pingolt, Ellise Schuette, and Valerie Yarnik.

Class of 1978

Baseball

The 1978 baseball team, under the leadership of Barry Deist, finished 6-7 overall and 4-5 in the South Central Conference. Senior Bart Yakos was named 1st Team All-Conference and also took home the team's Pitching Award, while junior Marty Cely won the Hitting Award. Bob Snell and Jack Vesper joined Yakos as seniors on the team.

Basketball (Boys)

The 1977-78 basketball team welcomed its third coach in as many years, as Larry Lux took over the program. The Bulldogs struggled during the season, finishing 5-15 overall and 2-10 in the South Central Conference behind seniors Dan Hartman, Mike Heinemeyer, Tim Williamson, and Free Throw Award winner Bart Yakos. After starting off with a record of 5-7, the Dogs dropped eight straight games to end the campaign. One bright spot during the year was the play of the club's underclassmen, including sophomore Brad Yakos, a 1st Team All-SCC selection. Lux stayed at the helm just one year, though he enjoyed a tremendous career at the junior high level, including winning an Illinois Elementary School Association (IESA) state title in 1983.

Cross Country (Boys)

Coach Gale Bryan's 1977 cross country team included seniors Rich Barber, Barry Mathenia, Tom Spears, and Mark Wood. A 4th place finish at the District Meet allowed the Bulldogs to advance to Sectionals for the only time in program history. Though the team's season ended there, Spears advanced to State as an individual. By finishing 30th overall, he secured his spot as one of the top runners in school history.

Football

The 1977 football team made school history as the program qualified for the Illinois High School Association's postseason tournament for the first time. The IHSA Playoffs were started during the 1974-75 school year, but it was very difficult to qualify initially, as a team had to win a conference title or receive an at-large bid by finishing 8-1 to gain entrance. Current standards are much more lenient, and in fact a team generally only needs five wins to advance to the postseason.

Staunton began the 1977 season with seven straight wins, including four shutouts in that span. The campaign started with a Week 1 victory over Hillsboro by a score of 20-6. A Week 2 shutout of Litchfield (25-0) preceded a close win over Southwestern (14-12). The Bulldogs handled Pittsfield (24-6) in Week 4 before recording consecutive shutouts of Carlinville (6-0), Gillespie (28-0), and Virden (20-0). The win over Carlinville was particularly exciting. With less than a minute remaining, the Cavaliers seemingly broke open a scoreless tie with a long touchdown run to win the game. However, a clipping penalty was called on the play, sending the contest into overtime. In the extra frame, senior Bart Yakos barreled his way across the goal line to give SHS the win, setting up a showdown for the South Central Conference championship with Nokomis. Unfortunately, the Redskins came away with a 26-8 victory over SHS. After soundly defeating Mt. Olive in Week 9, the Bulldogs anxiously awaited their postseason fate. Staunton did receive an invitation to participate in the IHSA Playoffs and found its way to the western part of the state to take on a tough squad from Hamilton. In a brutally physical matchup, SHS came out on the short end of a 12-6 battle, ending the season for the Bulldogs. The team thus finished with an overall record of 8-2, including 5-1 in the SCC.

Staunton placed several members on the All-Conference team, with seniors Brian Black, Mike Heinemeyer, Jack Vesper, Yakos, and junior Jim Holak taking home 1st Team honors. Seniors Randy Foster and Terry Garino captured 2nd Team accolades, while junior Jay Meckles was named Honorable Mention. Garino, Meckles, and Yakos shared Offensive MVP honors, while Vesper captured the Defensive MVP award. Seniors on the squad included Tony Banovz, Black, Paul Callovini, Tom Dal Pozzo, Foster, Garino, Dan Hartman, Heinemeyer, Tim Less, Mike McBride, Ed Ripperda, Bob Snell, Vesper, and Yakos.

Golf (Boys)

Coach Larry Kuba's 1977 golf team featured just two seniors, as Dave Hebenstreit and Tim Williamson led a young but talented unit. In addition to a 15-2 record in match play, the Dogs fared well at the Carlinville Invitational, with sophomore Mark Marcuzzo taking home medalist honors. The Bulldogs later advanced to Sectionals for the second consecutive season after finishing in 3rd place at the District Tournament.

Track (Boys)

The spring of 1978 was a good season for track, as both the boys and girls captured the South Central Conference crown. The boys were led by coach Gary Baxter in his first season with the program, and he welcomed seniors Rich Barber, Phil Blotevogel, Dan Hartman, Mike Heinemeyer, Ed Ripperda, Bob Schwandner, Tom Spears, and Mark Wood to the team. Spears qualified for State in both the 1600 meters and 3200 meters, taking home Team MVP honors in the process. He eventually signed on to run at Southern Illinois University-Edwardsville. The 3200 meter relay team of Hartman, Heinemeyer, Ripperda, and junior Bob Cargnoni also made it to State.

Track (Girls)

Donna Ruehrup's 1978 track team captured its fourth consecutive South Central Conference championship, with seniors Mary Best, Dawn Davies, Lynne Eddington, Diane Heigert, Sarah Link, and Jeanne Saunders providing leadership for the Lady Bulldogs.

Volleyball

Coach Donna Ruehrup's 1977 volleyball team had a very nice season, finishing 14-7 and winning the District title. The success was a precursor of things to come, as the program started one of the best postseason runs in school history. Graduating seniors included Diane Heigert and Sarah Link.

Class of 1979

Baseball

The 1979 baseball team recorded the program's second straight 6-7 season and also duplicated the 4-5 South Central Conference mark from the previous year. SHS played competitive baseball during the campaign, with five of the seven losses coming by just one run. Coach Barry Deist's squad included seniors Artie Billings, Jim Brown, Marty Cely, Bob Fletcher, and Jay Meckles. While Meckles took home All-Conference honors, the team also witnessed several underclassmen turn in outstanding seasons, including All-SCC members Brad Yakos and Tim Yarnik, both juniors. The Hitting Award was won by freshman Rich Fletcher, who finished with a .423 batting average. Meckles moved on to Western Illinois University and competed all four years for the school.

Basketball (Boys)

Mike Stivers took over the basketball program for the 1978-79 season, representing the squad's fourth coach in as many years. However, the coaching carousel ended there, as Stivers remained at the helm for thirteen years and won 213 games, both of which are program records. The season was a rebuilding one, resulting in a 7-22 record, including 6-6 in the South Central Conference. However, the foundation for future success was set, though the team had to say goodbye to seniors Jim Brown, Marty Cely, Bob Fletcher, Rob Marra, Jay Meckles, and Mark Sherfy.

Classes of 1970 - 1979

Basketball (Girls)

Though intramural and Girls Athletic Association (GAA) basketball had been around the school for many years, for the first time in SHS history basketball was offered as a sanctioned sport for females beginning with the 1978-79 season. Joe Dugan directed the first squad, which finished with a record of 1-10. With no seniors on the roster, the Lady Bulldogs were led by letter winners Bonnie and Brenda Bruhn, both juniors, and sophomores Evelyn Bean, Laura Booth, Stacy Stierwalt, Janis Treadway, and Diane Williams.

Cross Country (Boys)

The 1978 cross country team, under the direction of Gary Baxter, featured just one senior in the form of Bob Cargnoni. In Coach Baxter's final season at the school, Cargnoni turned in an excellent season, advancing to the Sectional Meet. Unfortunately, 1978 marked the last season that SHS offered cross country as a team sport for nearly three decades.

Football

Coming off the school's first-ever playoff appearance, the 1978 Bulldogs looked for sustained success under coach Barry Deist. The Bulldogs answered with another excellent season, as SHS initially finished 7-2 overall and 5-1 in the South Central Conference. However, it was later discovered that Hillsboro, a team responsible for one of Staunton's losses, had used an ineligible player and thus had to forfeit their victory over Staunton. With the ruling, SHS actually enjoyed its second straight 8-1 regular season. However, the Bulldogs were left out of the playoffs that year.

The season began with the aforementioned matchup against Hillsboro, with the Bulldogs suffering a 7-0 loss on the field, though the result was later overturned. A safety was the only scoring in a Week 2 victory over Litchfield, with the Bulldogs coming out on top by a score of 2-0. A 37-8 stomping of Southwestern in Week 3 preceded a hard fought 18-14 victory over Pittsfield. Technically, the only loss of the season came in Week 5 against Carlinville, but it was critical, as the Cavaliers upended the Bulldogs 13-7 to win the SCC. Carlinville ended up making a deep postseason run that year, finishing 2nd in the state. Staunton's season ended with four straight wins in relatively easy fashion against Gillespie (39-6), Virden (29-8), Nokomis (38-0), and Mt. Olive (48-13). However, as stated, SHS was not invited back to the IHSA Playoffs in 1979, and in fact the program did not return to postseason play until 1996.

The Bulldogs placed several members on the All-Conference team, including 1st Team members Bob Fletcher, Jim Holak, Jay Meckles, Mark Sherfy, and Al Tebbe, all seniors. Junior Rich Link was also named 1st Team All-SCC. Senior Bob Carter took home 2nd Team honors, while fellow seniors Mark Hebenstreit and Jim Strohkirch were named Honorable Mention, joining junior Tim Yarnik with that distinction. Additional seniors on the team included John DeGuire, Rick Fey, Dennis Peters, Glenn Sies, Kevin Snell, and Mike Vojas. After the season, Meckles was named Offensive MVP, while Hebenstreit and Holak shared Defensive MVP honors.

Golf (Boys)

Larry Kuba's 1978 golf team had an outstanding season, finishing 11-1-1 and advancing to Sectional competition after tying Auburn for 1st place at the District Tournament. The Bulldogs rolled through their regular season schedule, other than a tie with Carlinville and a loss to Auburn by just one stroke. The Dogs also won the Carlinville Invitational, with junior Mark

Marcuzzo taking home medalist honors for the second straight season. In addition to his honor at Carlinville, Marcuzzo also posted the lowest score at both the District and Sectional tournaments, and he eventually made a run at a state title, finishing 2nd overall. Jim Brown was the lone senior for the Bulldogs that season.

Track (Boys)

SHS was not able to repeat as South Central Conference champions in 1979, coach Gary Baxter's final season directing the program. He departed with seniors Bob Cargnoni, Bob Carter, John DeGuire, Rick Fey, Ken Haustein, Mark Hebenstreit, Jim Holak, Mike King, Brian Kuethe, Jay Meckles, Jim Morgan, Jim Sawicki, Mark Sherfy, and Kevin Snell. At the end of the year, Cargnoni was named Team MVP.

Track (Girls)

Donna Ruehrup's 1979 track team won the South Central Conference championship for the fifth straight year behind seniors Deone Courtney, Kim Maxville, and Peggy Senaldi. SHS also qualified two relays for State, including the 800 meter team of Brenda Bruhn, Maxville, Peggy Senaldi, and Diane Williams, as well as the 1600 meter team of Bruhn, Courtney, Patty Senaldi, and Peggy Senaldi.

Volleyball

The 1978 volleyball season was one for the record books, as the team set a school mark for victories and postseason advancement, though both were surpassed two years later. Coach Donna Ruehrup's squad ended up 25-2 overall, taking home South Central Conference and Macoupin County titles before embarking on postseason play. From there the team won the District and Sectional tournaments before falling in the Sweet 16 at the Super-Sectional.

Seniors on the 1979 team included Tammy Banovz, Kelley Chiti, Deone Courtney, Lisa Lovejoy, Peggy Senaldi, Linda Suhrenbrock, and Lori Williamson. Chiti, Courtney, and Williamson all took home 1st Team All-Conference honors, and Courtney and Williamson were also named All-County. Lovejoy, Senaldi, and Suhrenbrock were each named to the All-Conference 2nd Team, while junior twins Bonnie and Brenda Bruhn were named Honorable Mention.

CHAPTER 8

Classes of 1980 – 1989

Overview

The 1980s witnessed the emergence of basketball (boys) and volleyball (girls) as the marquee sports programs at Staunton High School. The basketball program overcame two decades of struggles to capture six South Central Conference titles during the era, not to mention multiple Macoupin County and Regional crowns. In fact, at one point the program experienced four straight 20-win seasons. The volleyball program was even more impressive, capturing numerous conference, county, and postseason titles, capped off with a trip to the State Tournament in 1980. The decade also witnessed the first individual state championship in school history, as Becky Coyne captured gold in the 100 meter hurdles in both 1985 and 1988. Unfortunately, cross country ceased to exist as a sport at SHS and, since that time, has never had enough members to field a full team. On the other hand, a few females began to participate in golf during the decade, though SHS did not officially field a team until 2005.

The South Central Conference underwent two changes during the 1980s. First, Litchfield and North Greene entered the SCC in 1980-81. Mt. Olive, a charter member of the SCC, left the league that same year, and thus the SCC became an eight-team conference. In 1985-86, Triad, a school district made up of Marine, St. Jacob, and Troy, came aboard. However, that same season Nokomis, North Greene, and Virden opted out of the league, leaving the SCC with just six teams.

Class of 1980

Baseball

Given the success experienced during the year across multiple sports, the Class of 1980 must be considered one of the best groups to come through Staunton High School in quite some time. The baseball team, coached by Barry Deist, had an outstanding season, finishing 16-4 overall and 10-2 in the South Central Conference. The Bulldogs were led by seniors Fred Brenzel, Bob Chiti, Rick Haase, Mark Marcuzzo, Kevin Sievers, Brad Yakos, and Tim Yarnik. Yakos led the team with a .529 batting average, while Brenzel hit .442 on the year. Brenzel, Yakos, and Yarnik were all strong on the mound for SHS and, along with Sievers, received 1st Team All-Conference honors. Marcuzzo was named All-SCC Honorable Mention, as was sophomore Rich Fletcher. Yakos (Eastern Illinois University) and Yarnik (Millikin University) continued their baseball careers upon graduating from SHS, and Yakos also played one season of football in college.

Basketball (Boys)

Mike Stivers' second year coaching the Staunton basketball team witnessed the program's best season in more than twenty years. The 1979-80 Bulldogs not only won the Lincoln Land Christmas Tournament but also captured South Central Conference and Macoupin County crowns. Staunton finished the season 19-7 and 10-2 in the SCC.

Seniors on the club included Troy Graves, Rich Link, Mark Marcuzzo, Brad Yakos, and Tim Yarnik. All five seniors were recognized as All-Conference performers, with Yakos and Yarnik receiving 1st Team honors, Marcuzzo obtaining 2nd Team accolades, and Graves and Link securing Honorable Mention status. Marcuzzo, Yakos, and Yarnik were also named All-County that season. Both three-year starters, it is likely that Yakos and Yarnik each went over the 1000-point mark for their careers, perhaps becoming just the third and fourth players in school history to secure the exclusive total. As a team, Staunton had the biggest scoring differential in the area, defeating opponents on average by 29 points per game.

Basketball (Girls)

In just the second year featuring a team at the school, the 1979-80 basketball squad improved to 6-11 on the season behind seniors Bonnie and Brenda Bruhn. The unit was coached by Joe Dugan in his last season with the club. One interesting happening during the campaign was the introduction of the female portion of the Macoupin County Tournament. The inaugural event was won by Carlinville, and in fact the Lady Cavaliers won two straight crowns and three of the first four county titles. As for the Lady Bulldogs, junior Janis Treadway was named Team MVP for the first of two straight seasons.

Football

Barry Deist's football program continued its solid play during the 1979 season. The unit finished the year 7-2 overall and 4-2 in the South Central Conference, outscoring opponents 217-52 on the year. The season began with four consecutive victories, with SHS knocking off Hillsboro (23-20) and Litchfield (35-14), while also shutting out Southwestern (40-0) and Pittsfield (6-0). Unfortunately, ten points kept SHS from an undefeated season. In Week 5, Carlinville outlasted SHS for a 7-0 win, and arch-rival Gillespie defeated the Bulldogs 3-0 in overtime to hand Staunton two consecutive defeats. The Dogs rebounded with a three-game winning streak with victories over Virden (38-8), Nokomis (39-0), and Mt. Olive (26-0). Carlinville edged out Gillespie for the SCC title that season.

Several seniors received awards following the season, including All-Conference 1st Team selections Tom Allen, Rich Link, Brad Yakos, and Tim Yarnik. Todd Anderson took home 2nd Team honors, while Bob Chiti, Craig Neuhaus, and Joe Stranimeier were named All-SCC Honorable Mention. Yakos led the squad with 803 yards rushing, while Yarnik caught 30 balls for 456 yards. Seniors on the team included Allen, Anderson, Jim Booker, Brenzel, Chiti, Jeff Clark, Jim Foster, Mike Kuethe, Todd Libbra, Link, Neuhaus, Mike Peters, Kevin Sievers, Stranimeier, Yakos, and Yarnik. In addition to playing baseball for two seasons in college, Yakos also competed in football for one year at Eastern Illinois University.

Golf (Boys)

The 1979 golf team was the first in program history to advance to State. After winning the District championship and placing 3rd at Sectionals, coach Larry Kuba's squad finished 7th at the State Tournament. Senior Mark Marcuzzo led the team to a 12-2 record in match play, and he was also the District medalist before placing 10th at State. Marcuzzo continued his golf career at Southern Illinois University-Edwardsville, attaining All-American status his senior year. Other members of the high school team included seniors Kevin Banovic, Troy Graves, and Rick Haase, as well as juniors John Bond and Mark Vesper. Adding to what was already an illustrious season, Haase recorded the first hole-in-one in SHS history that year. In a match against

Hillsboro at the Staunton Country Club, Haase sank his tee shot on the sixth hole from 186 yards out.

Track (Boys)

The track program welcomed a new coach for the 1980 season, as Randy Legendre took over the squad for one year. He welcomed a deep and talented group of seniors to the team, including Tom Allen, Doug Boster, Jim Foster, Mike Kuethe, Kevin Sievers, and Brad Yakos.

Track (Girls)

Unfortunately, Donna Ruehrup's track team did not win the South Central Conference Meet for the sixth straight time in 1980, as the team instead finished in 3rd place overall that season. The unit also placed 2nd at the Macoupin County Meet. Although the Lady Bulldogs failed to bring home a championship, there were several notable personal accomplishments. First, freshman Dori Hartman advanced to State in the 800 meters. Also, two school records were broken during the season. First, junior Mary Henke set a high jump record. Additionally, the 1600 meter relay team consisting of sophomores Tina Schlemer and Cindy Yarnik and freshmen Sharon Cargnoni and Hartman broke a school mark. The lone seniors on the team were Bonnie and Brenda Bruhn. Junior Evelyn Bean was voted Team MVP at the conclusion of the season.

Volleyball

The Staunton volleyball team experienced another 20-win season in 1979 behind seniors Bonnie Bruhn, Brenda Bruhn, and Debbie Gockel. Coach Donna Ruehrup's squad won the championship at the Triad Invitational but was unable to win South Central Conference or Macoupin County titles, instead finishing 2nd in conference and county action. However, SHS did win the District Tournament for the third straight year, advancing to Sectional play where they lost to Vandalia to close out the season with a record of 20-5. During the year, the Bruhn sisters were named to the All-County team. After the campaign ended, Defensive MVP Bonnie Bruhn and junior Diane Williams were both named 1st Team All-Conference. Offensive MVP Brenda Bruhn and junior Mary Henke were named to the All-SCC 2nd Team, while juniors Evelyn Bean and Janis Treadway took home Honorable Mention status.

Class of 1981

Baseball

With only two seniors on the roster, the 1981 baseball team struggled to a 4-13 record. John Bond (All-SCC Honorable Mention) and Mark Vesper (All-SCC 1st Team) did their best to lead the Bulldogs, who were coached by Barry Deist. Junior Rich Fletcher was also named 1st Team All-Conference, and he shared the Hitting Award with Vesper. Junior Dean Schulmeister captured the Pitching Award.

Basketball (Boys)

The 1980-81 basketball team finished 11-12 overall and 8-6 in the South Central Conference. Don Engelke and Mark Vesper were the only seniors on a team that featured juniors Tom Coyne and Bruce Kasubke. Coyne, the team's Offensive MVP, averaged 18 points per game during the season. For his efforts, he was named 1st Team All-SCC, Honorable Mention All-County, and 3rd Team All-Area by WSMI Radio. Meanwhile, Kasubke won the Free Throw Award (76%) and was named Defensive MVP. The Bulldogs were coached by Mike Stivers.

Basketball (Girls)

The 1980-81 basketball campaign was a season of firsts for the Lady Bulldogs. Not only did SHS finish with a winning record (13-8) for the first time in school history, but it also represented Larry Kuba's first season leading the team. Kuba stayed on for more than two decades and left as the program's all-time wins leader with 192 career victories. The Lady Bulldogs were led by senior and Team MVP Janis Treadway, who was also named 1st Team All-Conference and 1st Team All-County. Seniors Diane Williams and Evelyn Bean were awarded All-SCC Honorable Mention status, while Williams also took home the Free Throw Award. Joining Bean, Treadway, and Williams in the senior class were Laura Booth, Diana Bruhn, Mary Henke, and Stacy Stierwalt.

Football

Barry Deist's 1980 football team was a very young squad featuring just four seniors, as Gregg Ashley, Jim Bianco, Ken Billings, and Ron Siebert provided leadership for the young team. With most of its firepower from the previous season having graduated, inexperience took its toll on the Bulldogs, and the team finished just 2-7 overall, the program's worst finish in twenty-five years. Both wins came in South Central Conference play, as the Dogs finished 2-5 in an SCC slate that was eventually won by Litchfield. The title represented the only SCC football championship in LHS history.

The season started with a 14-0 loss to Hillsboro, followed by a 25-16 setback against Columbia in Week 2. SHS posted its first win of the season in Week 3 when the Bulldogs defeated the Spartans of North Greene in their first-ever SCC contest. After a tough loss to Virden (13-6), Staunton pulled out a 7-6 victory over Nokomis in Week 5. Unfortunately, that victory was the last of the campaign for the Bulldogs, and the team dropped consecutive games to Gillespie (26-0), Litchfield (34-0), Southwestern (6-2), and Carlinville (28-8) to close out the season. Juniors Lonnie Colley (Defensive MVP) and Rich Fletcher (Offensive MVP) were both named 1st Team All-Conference, while Siebert was named Honorable Mention. After the season, Colley was also awarded All-State Honorable Mention status.

Golf (Boys)

The 1980 golf team, coached by Larry Kuba, saw the Bulldogs reach Sectionals for the fifth consecutive season after winning another District championship. The team finished 7-5 on the year and was led by seniors John Bond and Mark Vesper. Bond was the District medalist that season.

Golf (Girls)

Though there was no official team, junior Patti Ruffini competed as an individual during the 1980 season. She was coached by Larry Kuba.

Track (Boys)

The 1981 track team was coached by Dave Martin in his first season with the program. Though Martin did not have any seniors on the squad, he did have some talent in letter winners Russ Best, Charlie Black, Bart Brauer, Lonnie Colley, Bruce Kasubke, Kelly Pieper, and Tom Scherff. Kasubke took home Team MVP honors, and he also set a school record in the triple jump.

Track (Girls)

The 1981 track team won the South Central Conference Meet for the sixth time in seven years behind seniors Evelyn Bean, Laura Booth, Diana Bruhn, Mary Henke, Stacy Stierwalt, and Janis Treadway. Bean and Henke shared Team MVP honors, while sophomore Dori Hartman (800 meters) and freshmen Nikki Coyne (800 meters) and Kim Mueller (long jump) qualified for State. In fact, Coyne was the District champion in the 800 meters. The Lady Bulldogs were coached by Donna Ruehrup.

Volleyball

Coach Donna Ruehrup's 1980 volleyball team enjoyed a magical season that saw the squad make it all the way to the State Tournament for the first and only time in the program's history. The 28-3 Lady Bulldogs also won the Macoupin County Tournament as well as the South Central Conference title with a spotless 14-0 record. The team was led by seniors Evelyn Bean, Diana Bruhn, Mary Henke, Stacy Stierwalt, Janis Treadway, and Diane Williams.

The Lady Bulldogs won their first nineteen games of the season, including Macoupin County victories over Southwestern, Virden, and Carlinville. The first loss of the season came against powerhouse Breese Mater Dei in the championship game of the Triad Invitational Tournament, and the team dropped its second consecutive contest in a game against Bunker Hill. Other than a five-set exhibition match against 34-2 Sacred Heart-Griffin, the Lady Bulldogs did not lose again until State. The team's postseason run included a District championship with wins over Livingston and Bunker Hill, a Sectional title with wins over Riverton and Raymond Lincolnwood, and a Super-Sectional victory over Virginia. At State, SHS ran into an excellent Quincy Notre Dame team in the Elite Eight and came out on the losing end of that contest. QND ended up breezing through the weekend on its way to a state title.

After the season, Treadway was named Offensive MVP, while Henke took home Defensive MVP honors. At County, Bean, Stierwalt, Treadway, and Williams were all named to the All-Tournament team. All-SCC 1st Team honorees included Bruhn, Stierwalt, and Williams, while Treadway was named to the 2nd Team. Furthermore, the club's victory total still stands as an overall school record at SHS across all sports. After the season, Bean continued her playing days at Greenville College. In addition to volleyball, she also participated in softball and ended up coaching both sports at the collegiate level, first at Lewis & Clark Community College and later at McKendree University.

Class of 1982

Baseball

Barry Deist's 1982 baseball team finished just 9-7 overall and 7-5 in the South Central Conference. However, due to parity in the league, the Dogs captured a share of the SCC title for the second time in three years. The Bulldogs were led by seniors Tom Coyne, Rich Fletcher, Dean Schulmeister, Barry Wriede, and Phil Yarnik. Fletcher continued his baseball career at Southern Illinois University-Edwardsville, competing all four years for the Cougars.

Basketball (Boys)

Mike Stivers' 1981-82 basketball team won a Regional championship for the first time since 1945. However, the season started out in lackluster fashion, as the Dogs struggled to gain traction early in the year. But, SHS caught fire at the Macoupin County Tournament, defeating Carlinville (70-51), Girard (51-45), and Bunker Hill (45-43) to take the championship for the second time in three years. Interestingly enough, SHS dropped a game to Carlinville right before the tournament and lost to Bunker Hill by a score of 72-55 earlier in the season. After County, Staunton kept its hot streak alive, eventually recording thirteen wins in fourteen outings to close out the season. In addition to the Regional title, the hot streak allowed SHS to capture the South Central Conference championship as well. At Regionals, the Bulldogs defeated Litchfield (49-38), Alton Marquette (58-49), and Bunker Hill (40-36). The Dogs fell at the Vandalia Sectional to Hillsboro (57-48) to close out the season.

Staunton finished the year with an overall record of 19-8, including 10-4 in the SCC. Unfortunately, SHS had to say goodbye to seniors Charlie Black, Lonnie Colley, Tom Coyne, Rich Fletcher, Bruce Kasubke, and Kelly Pieper. Team MVP Coyne averaged 17 points and 8 rebounds per game, capping off a nice career for the Bulldogs. Fletcher took home Defensive MVP honors, while Pieper won the Free Throw Award (74%). While Coyne was the lone player to make the All-Conference 1st Team, Fletcher (2nd Team), Black (Honorable Mention), and Kasubke (Honorable Mention) were also honored by league coaches. At the Macoupin County Tournament, Coyne was named tourney MVP, and he was joined on the All-County team by Pieper, an Honorable Mention selection. Finally, both Coyne (1st Team) and Kasubke (2nd Team) were included on the WSMI Radio All-Area squad. Coyne went on to play basketball for three seasons at Missouri Baptist University in Creve Couer.

Basketball (Girls)

The 1981-82 basketball team was coached by Larry Kuba and featured only one senior, Donna Windisch. The Lady Bulldogs finished the campaign with a record of 6-12. Windisch was voted Team MVP by her peers, while sophomore Sharon Bodi led the team in scoring. Fellow sophomore Mary Hering won the Free Throw Award with a 57% clip from the line.

Football

Coming off an uncommonly rough season, the 1981 football team returned to form by finishing 6-3 overall and 4-3 in the South Central Conference. The Bulldogs, coached by Barry Deist, were led by seniors Charlie Black, Bart Brauer, Wayne Bruhn, Lonnie Colley, Chris Costley, Rich Fletcher, Ken Highlander, Bruce Kasubke, Kelly Pieper, Dean Schulmeister, Barry Wriede, and Phil Yarnik.

The Bulldogs began the year with a close victory over Hillsboro (8-7). After defeating Greenville (33-18) in Week 2, the Dogs took down North Greene by a score of 34-15. SHS ran its record to 5-0 with victories over Virden (61-20) and Nokomis (13-6). Unfortunately, the Bulldogs dropped three of their next four games. In Week 6, Gillespie, on its way to the SCC title, downed the Dogs by a score of 27-15. Staunton bounced back with a 47-0 shutout of Litchfield in Week 7, but a loss to Southwestern (20-8) in Week 8 preceded a tough defeat to Carlinville (33-28) to end the year.

After the season, SHS placed several players on the All-SCC squad, including 1st Team members Black, Brauer, Colley, and Fletcher. Also making All-Conference were Costley (2nd Team), Wriede (2nd Team), and Yarnik (3rd Team). Fletcher rushed for more than 1000 yards on the year, becoming one of the few Bulldogs in school history to eclipse the exclusive mark in a season. For his efforts, he was named to the All-State 1st Team.

Golf (Boys)

The 1981 golf team finished the year with a 2-7-1 record, representing the lowest win total in the program's recorded history. In fairness, the mark can be attributed to the lack of matches played during the season, as Staunton competed against just ten opponents, the lowest total in program history. The Dogs were led by seniors Tom Coyne and Darren Graves and coached by Larry Kuba.

Golf (Girls)

Patti Ruffini once again represented the only female on the 1981 golf team, which was coached by Larry Kuba. By finishing 3rd at District, Ruffini became the first female golfer in school history to compete at the Sectional Tournament.

Track (Boys)

The 1982 track team, coached by Dave Martin, included seniors Bart Brauer, Lonnie Colley, Bruce Kasubke, Tony Masinelli, and Kelly Pieper. Additional letter winners included Jeff Angle, Lance Bates, Mike Cipriano, Rich Deal, Don DeVries, Jim Gasper, John Luketich, Sam Miller, Tom Scherff, Mark Stierwalt, and Rick Wall.

Track (Girls)

Donna Ruehrup's track team featured just one senior in 1982, Donna Peters. However, the Lady Bulldogs had a solid season behind letter winners Gerri Anderson, Sharon Bodi, Nikki Coyne, Lisa Kasubke, Kim Mueller, Dawn Rudy, Jamie Seketa, Dimitria Sies, Sheri Windau, and Lynn Yakos. Team MVP Yakos wrapped up an outstanding season by qualifying for State in the high jump.

Volleyball

The 1981 Staunton volleyball team was coming off a season that included the only State Tournament appearance in program history, as well as a school record for wins across all sports. Coach Donna Ruehrup's team had a great encore in store, finishing the year 26-2 overall. In fact, the season winning percentage (.929) still stands as the best in SHS volleyball history. Additionally, the Lady Bulldogs once again captured South Central Conference, Macoupin County, and District championships before losing just their second game of the season at Sectionals. Seniors on the club included Lori Henehan, Donna Peters, Donna Windisch, and

Cindy Yarnik. Peters was named Defensive MVP, while Windisch took home Offensive MVP honors.

Class of 1983

Baseball

The 1983 baseball team was coached by Barry Deist and led by seniors Shawn Bates, Randy Williams, and Doug Yarnik. Williams went on to play one season at Lewis & Clark Community College, setting a school record for home runs his freshman year.

Basketball (Boys)

Coming off an outstanding season that saw the program graduate most of its production, coach Mike Stivers had to rebuild for the 1982-83 season. Despite the heavy losses, seniors Jim Coyne, Morris Treadway, and Doug Yarnik led the team to a respectable 9-15 overall record, including 6-8 in the South Central Conference. After the season, Coyne was named Team MVP and 1st Team All-Conference. Don Johnson took home the Free Throw Award (76%), while Deron Stein was named Defensive MVP.

Basketball (Girls)

Larry Kuba's 1982-83 basketball team finished the year 12-10 overall and 8-6 in the South Central Conference. After dropping the first three games of the season, SHS roared back with nine wins in its next ten games. Junior Sharon Bodi, a 1st Team All-Conference selection, paced the unit by averaging 15 points and 9 rebounds per game. Fellow junior Mary Hering averaged 10 points per game and won the team's Free Throw Award (83%). She was also named 1st Team All-County and was an Honorable Mention All-Conference selection. Senior Lynn Yakos averaged 8 points and a team-leading 10 rebounds per game for the Lady Bulldogs. After the season, Bodi, Yakos, and senior Kim Pickerill shared Team MVP honors. Additional seniors on the team were Tammy Dooley and Debbie Jones.

Football

Coach Barry Deist's 1982 football team finished the season 5-4 overall and 4-3 in the South Central Conference, which was won by Carlinville for the first of five straight titles. Staunton's campaign began in fine fashion, with the Bulldogs shutting out Hillsboro by a score of 12-0. Unfortunately, a three-game losing streak ensued, as SHS dropped games to Greenville (30-7), Carlinville (30-6), and North Greene (8-2). The Dogs jumped back on the winning track in convincing fashion with a Week 5 pounding of Virden (40-0), and they followed up that win with a 27-6 defeat of Nokomis. After losing to Gillespie (13-0) in Week 7, Staunton wrapped up the season with consecutive victories over Litchfield (41-29) and Southwestern (26-15).

Seniors on the team included Shawn Bates, Russ Best, Joe Bloemker, Damian Dobrinich, Jim Hemp, Mike Holeschek, Jeff Kilduff, Fitz Musick, John Rabida, Brian Scrianko, Rick Wall, Randy Williams, and Doug Yarnik. After the season, Scrianko and Williams were named 1st Team All-Conference. Dobrinich and Rabida were 2nd Team All-SCC selections, as were juniors Larry Caldieraro and Tom Scherff. Finally, Best and Musick were awarded Honorable Mention status.

Golf (Boys)

The 1982 golf team finished the season 6-5 in match play. SHS was led by seniors Mike Cipriano, Jim Coyne, Scott Graves, and Morris Treadway, but the Dogs featured Team MVP Kevin Schulmeister, a junior. Schulmeister had a strong regular season for coach Larry Kuba's crew, and he later advanced to Sectional play.

Track (Boys)

The 1983 Staunton track team was coached by Dave Martin and featured seniors Mike Cipriano, Jim Coyne, Damian Dobrinich, Fitz Musick, Rick Wall, and Doug Yarnik. Tom Scherff, a junior, was voted Team MVP.

Track (Girls)

Donna Ruehrup's 1983 track team finished 2nd at the Macoupin County Meet and 4th at both the South Central Conference and Sectional track meets. Three Lady Bulldogs advanced to State, including senior Lynn Yakos (high jump), sophomore Lee Karl (shot put), and freshman Darla Sievers (400 meters). Both Yakos and Karl were Sectional champions in their respective events, while Sievers set a school record on her way to a 2nd place finish at the meet. Seniors on the squad included Deanne Coalson, Dori Hartman, Jamie Seketa, Debbie Tuey, and Yakos. After the season, Yakos was named Team MVP for the second consecutive year.

Volleyball

Though the 1982 volleyball team was unable to duplicate its overall success from previous seasons, Donna Ruehrup's club was still able to capture a Regional title, thus giving the program six straight years with a postseason championship. The Lady Bulldogs finished the season with a record of 19-10. Interestingly enough, half of the squad's losses came to Virden, as SHS dropped all five matchups with VHS.

The Lady Bulldogs were relatively young in 1982, with juniors Sharon Bodi, Carol Hughes, and Kim Mueller filling major roles on the team. Bodi was the team's Offensive MVP, and she also took home All-County and All-Conference 1st Team honors. Hughes was named Defensive MVP, while Mueller took home 2nd Team All-SCC honors. Senior Lynn Yakos was an All-Conference Honorable Mention selection. Additional seniors on the team were Connie Greeling and Debbie Jones.

Class of 1984

Baseball

The 1984 baseball team captured its third South Central Conference championship in five years, as the Dogs finished 12-2 in the SCC and 15-6 overall. Seniors Roger Banovz, Mike Bekeske, Larry Caldieraro, Randy Harbison, and Kevin Schulmeister were instrumental in the team's success. In fact, Banovz and Caldieraro were named to the All-Conference 1st Team, while Bekeske and Harbison were Honorable Mention selections. Juniors Rich Garde (Honorable Mention) and Dave Jones (1st Team) were also named to the All-SCC squad.

Caldieraro later returned to his alma mater to lead the baseball team. During his tenure, one of his teams made a trip to State, while another set a school record for victories in a season.

Basketball (Boys)

The 1983-84 basketball team finished the season 20-6 overall, marking the first time in nearly three decades that the program had produced a 20-game winner. The season sparked the best four-year run in SHS basketball history, as the Dogs also hit the 20-win mark in each of the next three years. Furthermore, Mike Stivers' squad captured the South Central Conference championship with a 13-1 mark in the league, with the lone loss coming to Litchfield. The SCC title was also the first of four straight for the program.

The season began in fine fashion for SHS, as the Bulldogs took home the championship of the Metro East Lutheran Turkey Tipoff with wins over Livingston (63-46), Chicago Lutheran East (97-47), and Edwardsville Metro East Lutheran (68-58) behind the play of tournament MVP Tom Scherff. However, Bunker Hill served as the team's nemesis during the year, as the Minutemen accounted for half of Staunton's losses that season. Not only did Bunker Hill defeat SHS in the regular season, but the Minutemen also defeated the Bulldogs in the title games of both the Macoupin County and Regional tournaments.

Tom Scherff and John Karl were the lone seniors on the squad, and thus many underclassmen had a significant effect on the season. For instance, junior Deron Stein received All-Conference and All-County recognition, and he also took home Team MVP and the Free Throw Award (82%). Defensive MVP Jeff Paitz was also a junior, and he also garnered All-Conference (1st Team) and All-County (2nd Team) honors. Scherff and junior Kevin Goebel were each named All-SCC Honorable Mention.

Basketball (Girls)

Larry Kuba's 1983-84 basketball team featured seniors Denise Brown, Mary Hering, Carol Hughes, and Kim Mueller. The veteran squad finished the year with a record of 10-11 overall. The Lady Bulldogs began the campaign with three wins in their first four games, and they ended the season in similar fashion. However, a five-game losing streak halfway through the schedule led to the average overall finish. After the season, Hering was named to the South Central Conference All-Conference squad as a 2nd Team member, as was junior Lisa Kasubke. Hering (1st Team) and Kasubke (2nd Team) were also named to the Macoupin County All-Tournament team.

Football

The 1983 football team was directed by Barry Deist and finished the season with an overall record of 6-3, including 5-2 in the South Central Conference. The year began with a 26-6 victory over Hillsboro in Week 1, but unfortunately SHS dropped two straight games to Greenville (21-6) and eventual SCC champion Carlinville (28-0). A four-game winning streak ensued, including victories over North Greene (28-0), Virden (14-7), Nokomis (24-7), and Gillespie (13-7). A loss to Litchfield (20-6) in Week 8 preceded a 31-0 shutout of Southwestern to close out the season.

Seniors on the team included Roger Banovz, Mike Bekeske, Tony Bianco, Larry Caldieraro, Phil Evans, Randy Harbison, John Karl, Steve Knop, and Tom Scherff. Bianco and Scherff were honored with 1st Team All-Conference status, while Caldieraro and Karl took home 2nd Team accolades. Banovz, Bekeske, Evans, and Harbison joined them on the All-SCC team as Honorable Mention members, as did juniors Don DeVries and Deron Stein. After the season, Caldieraro enrolled at Southern Illinois University where he played football for the Salukis for two seasons. He eventually returned to SHS to coach football in addition to his duties as head baseball coach. Meanwhile, Scherff continued his football career for one season at Kansas State University.

Golf (Boys)

The 1983 golf squad featured experience behind seniors Mark Biznek, Tim Fischer, Mike Lane, Don Miller, and Kevin Schulmeister. Unfortunately, Larry Kuba's team was unable to gain momentum through the season, eventually finishing with an overall record of 3-7-1. Following the season, Schulmeister was named Team MVP by his peers.

Track (Boys)

Seniors Randy Harbison, Steve Knop, Don Miller, and Tom Scherff paced the 1984 track team, which was coached by Dave Martin.

Track (Girls)

Coach Donna Ruehrup's 1984 track team featured seniors Nikki Coyne, Mary Hering, Laura Marandat, and Kim Mueller.

Volleyball

Donna Ruehrup's volleyball team experienced yet another magical season in 1983. The Lady Bulldogs finished 22-5 and captured South Central Conference, Macoupin County, Regional, and Sectional titles before losing in the Super-Sectional to Riverton. Seniors Sharon Bodi, Denise Brown, Mary Hering, Carol Hughes, Kim Mueller, and Dimitria Sies served as anchors of the team. After the season, Bodi, Mueller, and junior Lee Karl shared Offensive MVP honors, while Karl captured Defensive MVP recognition. At County, both Bodi and Karl were named to the All-Tournament team, and Bodi and Mueller were both named to the All-SCC 1st Team. Also garnering All-SCC recognition were Sies (2nd Team), Brown (Honorable Mention), and Hering (Honorable Mention). Finally, after the season Bodi was named to the All-State team, taking home Honorable Mention accolades. Bodi and Mueller continued their playing careers at McKendree University.

Class of 1985

Baseball

The baseball team was unable to repeat as South Central Conference champions in 1985, as the Bulldogs finished with a record of 12-8 on the season, including 8-6 in SCC play. The Dogs were a streaky bunch, as they opened the year with four straight losses before winning four straight games. The squad eventually won six out of seven contests before being knocked out of the Regional Tournament by Litchfield. Coach Barry Deist's team featured seniors Brian Banovz, John Isaacks, Dave Jones, Don Coalson, Rich Garde, Jeff Paitz, and Deron Stein. Sophomore Kevin Gockel won the Hitting Award (.373), though Banovz (.500) and Coalson (.405) did have success at the plate in limited at-bats. On the mound, Jones and Garde shared the

Pitching Award. After defeating Hillsboro (4-3) and Gillespie (4-0) to reach the Regional final, the Dogs fell to Litchfield (7-2) in the championship game.

Basketball (Boys)

The 1984-85 basketball team had an outstanding season, posting the highest winning percentage (.926) in school history. The Bulldogs finished 25-2 on the season, including 13-1 in the South Central Conference. Along the way, Staunton captured its second straight SCC title, as well as the first of three straight Macoupin County championships. The Bulldogs also defended their title at the Metro East Lutheran Turkey Tipoff. Unfortunately, both of Staunton's losses on the year came at the hands of Litchfield. After the two teams split games in the regular season, the rivals matched up in the title game of the Regional Tournament where Litchfield defeated SHS by a score of 63-51.

The Bulldogs were coached by Mike Stivers, and the team included seniors Kevin Goebel, Jeff Paitz, Deron Stein, and Mark Stierwalt. Stein had an exceptional year, taking home MVP honors of the Metro East Lutheran Turkey Tipoff to begin the campaign. He was also named to the All-SCC 2nd Team and All-County 1st Team. Paitz also fared well on the year. He was named to the All-Conference 1st Team and also voted Defensive MVP. Junior Roman Meckles won the Free Throw Award by knocking down 78% of his tries from the line. Finally, junior Rick Landrem had a breakout season for the Dogs. He was honored with 1st Team All-Conference recognition and was also the MVP of the County Tournament. After the season, Landrem and Stein shared Team MVP honors.

Basketball (Girls)

Larry Kuba's 1984-85 basketball team finished just 11-14 on the season, including 7-7 in the South Central Conference. However, the squad was able to capture the championship at the Macoupin County Tournament for the first time in program history. The unit was led by seniors Janette Hughes, Susan Dustmann, and Lisa Kasubke. Kasubke was chosen as Team MVP, while Hughes won the Free Throw Award by hitting 64% of her attempts from the charity stripe. Meanwhile, junior Darla Sievers led the Lady Bulldogs in scoring. After the season, Hughes moved on to Blackburn College where she competed in both basketball and volleyball for the institution.

Football

The 1984 football team had a very good year under the leadership of Barry Deist. The team ended 7-2 overall, including a 2nd place finish in the South Central Conference with a 5-2 record. Week 1 saw SHS defeat Hillsboro by a score of 32-6, and the team grabbed a second win with a 14-7 victory over Greenville in Week 2. Unfortunately, Southwestern ruined any conference championship hopes by edging out the Bulldogs in Week 3 by a score of 3-0. A tough win over Carlinville (20-14) ensued, as did a forfeit victory over North Greene due to a teacher's strike. Virden hung a 26-14 loss on the Bulldogs in Week 6, but Staunton finished strong with consecutive victories over Nokomis (19-6), Gillespie (27-19), and Litchfield (10-0). Despite the Staunton victory over Carlinville, the Cavaliers moved on to their third straight league title.

The senior group was a deep and talented bunch that season. Brian Banovz, Tim Bruhn, Rich Deal, Don DeVries, Brian Evans, Rich Garde, Kevin Goebel, Al Hanner, John Isaacks, Dave Jones, Ray Rantanen, Joe Seketa, Deron Stein, Mark Stierwalt, Karl Tallman, and Adrian

Vesper comprised the group. Bruhn and Stein were the lone Bulldogs on the All-SCC 1st Team, though fellow seniors Deal, DeVries, Garde, Goebel, Isaacks, Jones, and Vesper were honored with 2nd Team accolades. Junior Tim Gusewelle also made 2nd Team All-Conference, while Rantanen and Seketa were named Honorable Mention. Team awards were given to Offensive MVP's Deal and Stein, as well as Defensive MVP's Bruhn and Garde.

Golf (Boys)

Larry Kuba's 1984 golf team featured just one senior in the form of Team MVP Eric Hutchins. The squad finished 3-13 overall. Additional lettermen for the team included juniors Bruce Cozart and Wes Horstmeyer, as well as freshmen Jason Kramer and Brian Young.

Track (Boys)

The 1985 track team included seniors Rich Deal and Jeff Paitz. The unit was coached by Dave Martin.

Track (Girls)

Though the Lady Bulldogs did not capture any team titles, the 1985 track season was one of the most important campaigns in school history. For the first time ever, Staunton High School produced a state champion when freshman Becky Coyne won the 100 meter low hurdles at the Illinois State Track Meet. To date, only one individual (Ryan Brown, 2002 boy's golf) and one team (1993 boy's basketball) have matched her accomplishment, though it is worth mentioning that she duplicated the feat her senior year. Donna Ruehrup coached the 1985 team, which featured seniors Janette Hughes, Lee Karl, and Erika Miller.

Volleyball

Donna Ruehrup's 1984 Bulldogs had yet another spectacular year behind the performance of seniors Donna Coalson, Susan Dustmann, Janette Hughes, Lee Karl, Lisa Kasubke, and Pam Poeling. Staunton finished the year 24-7 overall and undefeated in South Central Conference play. The win total marked the sixth time in seven years that the program eclipsed the 20-win mark. In addition to winning the SCC for the second straight season, the Dogs also repeated as Macoupin County, Regional, and Sectional champions. The team also won its own tournament, the Staunton Invitational.

Individual standouts for SHS included Karl and Kasubke, who were both named 1st Team All-Conference and All-County. Karl was also chosen as the team's Offensive MVP, while Kasubke was honored as the Defensive MVP. Fellow senior Hughes took home 2nd Team All-SCC honors, and sophomore Dana Sievers was an Honorable Mention recipient. After the season, Karl was named 1st Team All-State. She continued her volleyball career for two seasons at Saint Xavier University in Chicago. While there, Karl also competed in softball for the Cougars. Meanwhile, Hughes played volleyball and basketball for Blackburn College.

Class of 1986

Baseball

Barry Deist's 1986 baseball team finished the season with a record of 13-9 overall, including 4-6 in the South Central Conference. The Bulldogs were led by seniors Greg Deist, Tim Gusewelle, Roman Meckles, and Al Schwartz. At the conclusion of the season, juniors Bart Caldieraro and Kevin Gockel were named to the All-Conference team.

Basketball (Boys)

Mike Stivers' 1985-86 basketball team continued a dominant run that included the program's third straight South Central Conference title, its second straight Macoupin County championship, and the first of two straight Regional titles. The team finished the season with an overall record of 22-6, including 8-2 in the SCC. The year got off to a great start with seven straight wins. At County, SHS played three exhilarating games to capture the title. After knocking off Girard (70-56) in the opening round, the Bulldogs defeated Carlinville (49-48) in overtime to advance to the title game. Waiting for SHS was Bunker Hill. In a classic game, Staunton defeated the Minutemen by a score of 40-39 to capture the tournament championship. At Regionals, SHS defeated Raymond Lincolnwood (77-48), Hillsboro (77-62), and Gillespie (64-43) to easily take the title. However, the Bulldogs fell to Venice in the Sectional Tournament by a score of 52-49, effectively ending the outstanding season.

Seniors on the team included Greg Deist, Tim Gusewelle, Rick Landrem, and Roman Meckles. They were aided by juniors Kevin Gockel and Bret Kasubke. Landrem capped off a brilliant career with 1st Team All-SCC and All-County honors, while Meckles garnered 2nd Team All-Conference and All-County recognition. Kasubke won the first of two straight County MVP awards, and he was also named 1st Team All-SCC, while Gockel took home Honorable Mention status.

Basketball (Girls)

The 1985-86 basketball team finished the season 7-14 overall, including 2-8 in the South Central Conference. Coach Larry Kuba's squad included seniors Dana Anschutz, Alison Kuba, and Darla Sievers. Junior Dana Sievers had an outstanding season for the Lady Bulldogs. In addition to leading the team in scoring, she captured All-Conference 2nd Team honors and was a member of the All-County 1st Team. Darla Sievers took home All-SCC Honorable Mention status, as well as All-County 2nd Team honors. She also won the Free Throw Award (61%) and was the team's leading rebounder. Dana and Darla Sievers shared Team MVP honors.

Football

Coach Barry Deist's football team finished 4-5 during the 1985 campaign, including 3-2 in the South Central Conference. The season began with a shutout loss to Hillsboro (39-0) and continued with a Week 2 loss to Greenville (20-10). In Week 3, the Bulldogs squeaked into the win column with a 21-20 victory over Nokomis. Staunton rode the momentum to three more wins, including defeats of Litchfield (21-6), Southwestern (19-8), and Gillespie (26-0). Unfortunately, the Dogs ended the season with three successive losses. Week 7 saw SHS lose to Triad by a score of 17-7. In Week 8, Staunton was defeated by rival and eventual SCC champion Carlinville (14-6), and the Dogs followed up that game with a loss to Bethalto Civic Memorial (19-8) to close out the season.

Despite the lackluster showing in the SCC, Staunton was able to place several members on the All-Conference team. Junior Bart Caldieraro took home 1st Team honors, as did seniors Greg Deist, Tim Gusewelle, Jim Kinder, and Joe Randle. Seniors Roman Meckles and Ron Philips were chosen for the All-Conference 2nd Team, while Honorable Mention status was awarded to seniors Rick Miller and Jeff Ries, as well as juniors Kevin Gockel and Ryan Ocepek. Additional seniors on the squad included Terry Feldmann, Al Schwartz, Bill Willows, and Wally Yeager. As for team awards, Gockel, Gusewelle, and Meckles shared Offensive MVP honors, while Caldieraro, Kinder, and Randle shared the team's Defensive MVP award.

Golf (Boys)

The 1985 golf team finished with an overall record of 6-8 under Larry Kuba. Letter winners included juniors Brett Kasubke, Danny Ray, Bill Scherff, sophomore Brett Ahring, and freshman Jim Williamson. Wes Horstmeyer was the lone senior on the squad. Scherff was named Team MVP at the conclusion of the season.

Track (Boys)

In his sixth and final season as track coach, Dave Martin witnessed his athletes turn in excellent individual performances throughout the 1986 season. Along the way, several school records were broken, some of which still stand to this day. One of the greatest seasons in school history was turned in by junior Bill Scherff, culminating in a 5th place finish at State in the pole vault. He also won the South Central Conference, Macoupin County, and Sectional track meets in the pole vault, breaking the event record at all three meets. Additionally, he set school marks in both hurdle events and was a member of the 400 meter relay team that broke an SHS record. Joining Scherff on the 400 meter relay team were seniors Greg Deist and Tim Gusewelle, as well as junior Bret Kasubke. The 800 meter relay team also set a school record, and it featured Scherff, Deist, Gusewelle, and junior Mike LaRosa. Both relay teams qualified for the State Meet. Finally, Gusewelle and Kasubke also set school marks during the season in the triple jump and high jump, respectively. Additional senior track members in 1986 were Jim Kinder, Joe Randle, and Glen Tebbe.

Track (Girls)

Coach Donna Ruehrup's 1986 track team depended on seniors Dana Anschutz, Lisa Lindsay, Jane Marcuzzo, and Darla Sievers. Anschutz, in particular, had an excellent campaign, capping it off with an appearance at State in the shot put.

Volleyball

Having graduated a phenomenal senior class the prior season, the Staunton volleyball team found itself in rebuilding mode for the 1985 campaign. With nine losses in its last ten games, SHS finished with a record of 5-21 overall, including 3-7 in the South Central Conference. The losing record was the first in a decade for the program, and it also represented the first time since her rookie season that Donna Ruehrup's crew was unable to capture a conference or tournament championship. Seniors on the squad included Dana Anschutz, Mary Foster, Alison Kuba, and Darla Sievers.

Class of 1987

Baseball

Barry Deist welcomed back a solid senior class for the 1987 campaign, including Bart Caldieraro, Kevin Gockel, Jeff Gusewelle, Bret Kasubke, and Danny Ray. The Bulldogs posted a 9-9 record overall, including a 5-5 mark in the South Central Conference. Though the team got off to a slow start, the Dogs rebounded with five wins in six games before losing to Hillsboro in the Regional. Sophomore Fred Harbison won the Pitching Award (4-2, 4.10 ERA). Caldieraro (.383) and Gockel (.378) shared the team's Hitting Award, while Ray (.342), and junior John Rae (.340) also performed well at the plate. Gockel continued his baseball career at Illinois State University.

Basketball (Boys)

The 1986-87 basketball team capped off the best four-year run in the program's history. The Dogs finished the season with a record of 21-7 overall and 7-3 in the South Central Conference. Along the way, SHS clinched its fourth straight 20-win season, fourth straight SCC title, third straight Macoupin County crown, and second straight Regional championship. Also, by reaching the Sectional final, the Dogs advanced as far as any basketball team in school history, excluding the 1993 state championship team.

The Dogs began the season with three straight wins before succumbing to Southwestern, a team that prevailed over Staunton in the other SCC matchup as well. However, at County, SHS exacted revenge on the Piasa Birds, easily defeating them in the championship by a score of 63-48. Staunton defeated Girard (60-39) and Gillespie (59-51) to reach the title game. In the Regional, the Bulldogs defeated Edwardsville Metro East Lutheran (77-53) before narrowly getting by Greenville (62-59) for the right to advance to the Sectional. At the Sectional Tournament, the Bulldogs knocked off Kinmundy (68-59) before falling to Venice (51-45) in the title game.

With the loss, one of the greatest basketball players in school history saw his high school career come to an end. Bret Kasubke capped off his senior season with several honors, including County MVP, 1st Team All-Conference, *State Journal-Register* 1st Team All-Area, and Team MVP. He also joined his father in the 1000 Point Club after finishing his career with 1341 points scored, a total that is believed to be the second-most in school history. Following the season, Kasubke was chosen to participate in the Illinois Basketball Coaches Association (IBCA) All-Star game. He was a member of the Class 1A All-Stars, a team directed by legendary Bunker Hill coach Jim Hlafka. Kasubke's own coach, Mike Stivers, served as an assistant to Hlafka. Following graduation, Kasubke enrolled at Quincy University where he played four years of basketball for the Hawks.

Kasubke was not alone in earning individual accolades, as senior Kevin Gockel and junior Jeff Windau both captured 2nd Team All-Conference and All-County honors. Windau and senior Jeff Gusewelle shared the Free Throw Award, as each player hit 67% of his shots from the charity stripe. Bill Scherff rounded out the seniors on the squad. Gockel later returned to SHS and directed the basketball program for twelve seasons.

Basketball (Girls)

The 1986-87 basketball team was very young and, in fact, did not have a senior on the roster. However, the youthful Lady Bulldogs mirrored the success of the 1985 season, winning the Macoupin County Tournament despite a losing record. SHS followed an early six-game losing streak with six straight wins and eventually finished 11-14 overall and 4-6 in the South Central Conference. The Lady Bulldogs featured juniors and co-MVP's Gayle Gusewelle and Tracy Kuba. Gusewelle was a 1st Team All-County and All-Conference performer, and she also led the team in scoring and rebounding and won the Free Throw Award (53%). Kuba captured 2nd Team All-SCC honors while leading the team in assists. Larry Kuba directed the squad.

Football

The 1986 football team finished the season with an overall record of 3-6, including 2-3 in the South Central Conference. Seniors on the squad included Dave Bierbaum, Bart Caldieraro, Phil Callovini, Matt Dawson, Kevin Gockel, Jeff Gusewelle, Darren Hanner, Mike LaRosa, Harry Mengelkamp, Ryan Ocepek, Rob VanDeHey, and George Wisnasky. The unit was directed by Barry Deist.

The Bulldogs started off the season with a loss to Hillsboro (28-7) in Week 1, but the team rebounded with a Week 2 defeat of Greenville by a score of 32-27. The Dogs responded to a loss to Nokomis (28-12) by shutting out Litchfield (20-0) in Week 4. Two straight losses ensued, including an 18-0 setback to Southwestern and a heartbreaking defeat to Gillespie on Homecoming by a score of 20-14. After defeating Triad (7-3) on Senior Night, the year ended with consecutive losses to Carlinville (16-6) and Bethalto Civic Memorial (14-0). Carlinville once again won the SCC in 1986, the school's fifth straight league crown. After the season, several Bulldogs were honored with All-Conference accolades. Caldieraro, Gockel, LaRosa, and junior John Rae all took home 1st Team honors, while Wisnasky (2nd Team) and Callovini (Honorable Mention) were also recognized by SCC coaches.

Golf (Boys)

Coach Larry Kuba's 1986 golf team was led by seniors Bret Kasubke, Danny Ray, and Bill Scherff. The unit finished with a record of 4-7, with Kasubke taking home Team MVP honors.

Track (Boys)

The 1987 track team welcomed a new coach in the form of Ron Sturomski for the first of his five seasons directing the program. He inherited a solid group of performers, including letter winners Phil Deist, Brad Hemann, Jason Kramer, Ryan Ocepek, Bill Scherff, and Brad Young. Among the best track athletes to ever walk the halls of Staunton High School, Scherff continued his career at Southern Illinois University.

Track (Girls)

Coach Donna Ruehrup's 1987 track team featured letter winners Kim Becker, Krissy Kleeman, Kim Leaser, Amy Orr, Julie Seketa, and Tracy Spencer. Unfortunately, the Lady Bulldogs finished last at the South Central Conference Meet for the first of two straight seasons.

Volleyball

Coming off its first losing season in ten years, the volleyball program looked to get back to its winning ways in 1986. Donna Ruehrup's team did just that by finishing the season with an overall record of 19-6 and capturing South Central Conference and Regional championships along the way. The team featured just two seniors, Shelia Banovz and Dana Sievers. Sievers was named as the team's Offensive MVP, and she also captured All-County and All-Conference 1st Team honors. Banovz also made the All-SCC team as an Honorable Mention pick. Finally, junior and Defensive MVP Tracy Kuba (1st Team) and sophomore Jerri Hochmuth (2nd Team) also captured All-Conference honors.

Class of 1988

Baseball

Seniors Kevin Dal Pozzo and John Rae led the baseball team to a successful season in 1988. Barry Deist's crew finished the year 11-6 overall, including 6-4 in the South Central Conference. SHS began the regular season with four straight victories and ended it with five consecutive wins before losing to Gillespie in the Regional Tournament. The Dogs posted some impressive offensive numbers during the season, specifically in wins over Bunker Hill (18-3), Litchfield (25-10), Edwardsville Metro East Lutheran (18-4), and Worden (32-1). Rae was particularly impressive, posting some of the best offensive numbers in school history and taking home the team's Hitting Award (.509, 30 RBI) in the process. The Pitching Award went to sophomore Darik Jones (6-2). At the conclusion of the season, Rae and junior Fred Harbison were named to the All-Conference 1st Team, while Dal Pozzo, Jones, and junior Brian Barks took home Honorable Mention status.

Basketball (Boys)

Coming off the best four-year run in school history, the 1987-88 basketball team had to reload after losing most of its production from the previous season to graduation. The Bulldogs responded with a competitive year that saw the team finish with a record of 11-13 overall and 3-7 in the South Central Conference. The Dogs got off to a surprisingly fast start to the season but, unfortunately, dropped seven of their final eight games. Coach Mike Stivers' team was led by senior Jeff Windau, a 1st Team All-Conference and All-County selection. Fellow senior Kelly Brown was named All-SCC Honorable Mention. Windau took home Team MVP honors, as well as the Free Throw Award, while senior Kevin Dal Pozzo received Defensive MVP honors.

Basketball (Girls)

Having not graduated any players from the previous season's Macoupin County championship team, the 1987-88 Lady Bulldogs had cause for optimism entering the year. SHS responded with its first winning season in five years, though the 13-12 mark was somewhat disappointing given preseason expectations. The Lady Bulldogs finished 3-7 in the South Central Conference under the direction of Larry Kuba.

Seniors Gayle Gusewelle, Tracy Kuba, and Kim Winslow provided outstanding leadership for the team over the course of the year. Gusewelle turned in one of the best seasons in school history, and she was rewarded for her efforts with 1st Team All-Conference and County MVP honors. At County, the Lady Bulldogs reached the championship game by defeating Bunker Hill (60-37) and Southwestern (45-43) before falling to Carlinville (50-42). Winslow thrived in her last year in red and white, and she was named All-SCC Honorable Mention and 2nd Team All-

County. Kuba also starred for SHS, taking home 2nd Team All-Conference and All-County awards. Kuba and Gusewelle shared Team MVP honors, with Gusewelle capturing the Free Throw Award (66%). Gusewelle went on to play basketball at Blackburn College. After concluding an excellent college career, she returned to SHS to run the basketball program, staying in the position for four years.

Football

Barry Deist's football program experienced a down year in 1987, as the Bulldogs finished just 2-7 overall and 1-4 in the South Central Conference. However, despite the record, the losses that SHS incurred during the season occurred in very competitive games. For instance, in Week 1 the Bulldogs fell to Hillsboro by a score of 13-12. SHS followed that game up with another tough loss, this time to Greenville (14-7). The team's first win came in Week 3, as Staunton soundly defeated Nokomis by a score of 47-13. The heartbreaking losses continued into Week 4, as SHS was narrowly defeated by Carlinville (8-6). The second win of the season came in Week 5 against Litchfield (22-6). Unfortunately, the year ended with consecutive setbacks to Southwestern (23-0), Gillespie (22-12), Triad (15-0), and Columbia (48-6). Triad won the SCC for the first time in school history that season.

One bright spot for the Bulldogs was the play of senior John Rae. Not only was the Defensive MVP selected as an All-SCC 1st Team member, but he was also invited to participate in the exclusive Shriner's All-Star game. Fellow seniors Jeff Windau (Honorable Mention) and Kelly Yeager (2nd Team) were also honored by conference coaches, and Yeager also captured the team's Offensive MVP award. Additional seniors included Kelly Brown, Bob Bruhn, Dennis Foster, Doyle Ivey, Jason Kramer, Tim Margaritis, Eric Schuette, John Scroggins, and Gene Sternes.

Golf (Boys)

Coach Larry Kuba's golf team featured just two seniors in 1987, and Brett Ahring and John Knowles were looked upon to provide leadership for the young team. The Dogs ended the season 6-9 overall and finished 3rd at the South Central Conference Meet, with Ahring taking home All-Conference honors at the event. The 1987 SCC Meet was the league's initial golf tournament, and Litchfield captured 1st place at the four-team event that also included Carlinville and Triad. After the season, junior Jim Williamson was named Team MVP.

Golf (Girls)

The 1987 golf team featured just two players in the form of senior Gayle Gusewelle and junior Julie Seketa. Larry Kuba coached the players during the season.

Track (Boys)

Ron Sturomski's second season leading the track program saw the Bulldogs finish in 3rd at the Macoupin County Meet and 4th at the South Central Conference Meet in 1988. Seniors Rick Ficker, John Knowles, Jason Kramer, E.J. McNaughton, and Scott Slemer paced the team.

Track (Girls)

The track team as a whole did not fare well in 1988, as the Lady Bulldogs finished in last place at the South Central Conference Meet. However, the season was special because senior Becky Coyne won a state title for the second time in her career. Coyne, who also captured a championship in the 100 meter low hurdles as a freshman, won that same event her senior year. In fact, her time of 13.9 seconds was a Class A state record. Interestingly enough, it was the last year for the event in girl's track, as the 100 meter high hurdles replaced it the next season. Coyne also placed 3rd at State in the 300 meter hurdles as a senior. Additionally, she won the South Central Conference Meet in the 200 meters and the 100 meter hurdles, while also taking home Macoupin County crowns in both hurdle events. Coyne continued her running career at Southern Illinois University. Additional seniors on the team included Kris Goebel, Tracy Harbaugh, and Tricia Spencer. The unit was coached by Donna Ruehrup.

Volleyball

The 1987 volleyball team finished the season with a record of 8-16 overall and 5-5 in the South Central Conference under the leadership of Donna Ruehrup. Seniors Kris Goebel and Kim Winslow led the Lady Bulldogs, with Goebel taking home 1st Team All-Conference status. Though the club dropped eight of its first ten games, improvements were made throughout the campaign. However, the losing record did represent just the second time in twelve years that one of Coach Ruehrup's volleyball teams finished below .500.

Class of 1989

Baseball

Seniors Brian Barks, Simon Hannig, Fred Harbison, and Jim Williamson led the baseball team during the 1989 season. The Dogs were coached by Barry Deist and finished the schedule with a record of 3-11 overall, including 2-8 in the South Central Conference. Unfortunately, the worst season in Deist's long tenure as baseball coach also accounted for the lowest win total in the program's documented history. Victories on the year came against Carlinville, Gillespie, and Litchfield. At the conclusion of the season, juniors Phil Deist (Honorable Mention) and Ed Fletcher (1st Team) were named to the All-Conference team. Hannig continued playing the sport for two seasons at Blackburn College, and he also participated in football for the school.

Basketball (Boys)

Coach Mike Stivers' 1988-89 basketball team finished the season with a record of 14-12 overall, including 4-6 in the South Central Conference. The squad started the year in fine fashion, capturing the Metro East Lutheran Turkey Tipoff championship with wins over Livingston (71-41), Mt. Olive (68-38), and the host school (70-57). The Bulldogs were well-rounded, as all five starters were major contributors. Senior Simon Hannig was a 1st Team All-Conference and All-County member, while junior Brad Hemann was named All-Conference Honorable Mention and 1st Team All-County. Sophomore Brad Best had an outstanding season on his way to becoming the school's all-time leading scorer. Best posted 18.5 points and 7.8 rebounds on the year while taking home 2nd Team All-Conference honors. Seniors Steve Bahn and Fred Brauer contributed excellent defense, and Bahn was rewarded with Defensive MVP honors. Junior Phil Deist captured the Free Throw Award after hitting 77% of his tries from the charity stripe.

Basketball (Girls)

Having lost most of its firepower from the previous season, the 1988-89 basketball team struggled to a 2-21 record, including a winless 0-10 in the South Central Conference. The lone wins came over Auburn (38-22) and Kincaid South Fork (46-31). Despite the team's struggles, seniors Angie Hainaut and Jerri Hochmuth did their best to keep Staunton in games. In particular, Hochmuth had a fine campaign, capturing Team MVP and the Free Throw Award while also being named All-SCC Honorable Mention. Larry Kuba served as the team's head coach.

Football

The 1988 football team finished the season with an overall record of 4-5, including 2-3 in the South Central Conference, which was won by Triad for the second straight year. The Dogs began the campaign with a loss to Hillsboro (14-6) in Week 1 but followed with consecutive wins over Greenville (19-14) and Nokomis (12-6). After a Week 4 loss to Carlinville (27-7), the Dogs took care of Litchfield (33-16) and Southwestern (29-6) in convincing fashion. Unfortunately, SHS finished the season on a three-game losing streak, which included losses to Gillespie (22-12), Triad (28-12), and Columbia (35-8).

The Dogs were coached by Barry Deist and featured seniors Bart Albrecht, Steve Bahn, Brian Barks, Fred Brauer, Ray Cline, Keith Dal Pozzo, Simon Hannig, Fred Harbison, Mike Masinelli, Jeff Miller, Jeff Ocepek, Bob Pelt, Mark Sievers, and Chris Weidler. The Offensive MVP award was shared by Barks, Cline, and Hannig, while Harbison was named Defensive MVP. At the All-Conference meeting, Barks, Cline, and junior Phil Deist were named 1st Team All-SCC. All-Conference 2nd Team accolades went to Hannig and Harbison, as well as juniors Ed Fletcher, Dave Gerdes, and Brad Hemann. After the season, Barks was named 1st Team All-Area by the *Telegraph*, while Deist and Hannig took home 3rd Team honors. Hannig continued his football career for four seasons at Blackburn College while also competing in baseball for the Beavers.

Golf (Boys)

The 1988 golf team featured just one senior, but he was a standout in the form of Jim Williamson. Not only did Williamson take home medalist honors at the South Central Conference Tournament, but he eventually advanced to State. As a team, Larry Kuba's club finished the season at 7-7 overall. After the year ended, Williamson moved on to Spoon River College where he competed in golf for one season.

Track (Boys)

Coach Ron Sturomski's track program continued to improve during the 1989 season, paving the way for the following year's historic campaign. Seniors Simon Hannig, Mike Masinelli, and Scott Miller paced the team, though all the State-qualifiers were underclassmen. The Dogs sent two relay teams and one individual to the State Meet that season. Sophomore Tim Straub qualified in the 800 meters, as did the 400 meter and 800 meter relay teams consisting of juniors Greg Best, Phil Deist, Brian Dustman, and Chris Knowles.

Track (Girls)

Donna Ruehrup's 1989 track team placed 5th at the South Central Conference Meet and 4th at the Macoupin County Meet behind seniors Krissy Kleeman and Julie Seketa. However, the

Lady Bulldogs turned in several school records during the year. Freshman Shayne Isbell set a new mark in the 100 meter hurdles, while her twin sister Crystal advanced to State in the high jump. Another freshman, Melissa Heidke, broke the school record in the 3200 meters. Finally, the 3200 meter relay team of Kleeman and sophomores Ann Little and Jeanene and Jodi Oberto also shattered the previous school record.

Volleyball

The 1988 volleyball team finished the season with a 7-3 mark in the South Central Conference. Unfortunately, with an overall record of 10-15, the Lady Bulldogs experienced back-to-back losing seasons for the first time in the program's documented history. SHS began the year with seven straight losses and ended it with three straight defeats. In between, the Lady Bulldogs were very competitive with ten wins in fifteen games. Coach Donna Ruehrup had to say goodbye to a large senior class made up of Susan Haase, Angie Hainaut, Jerri Hochmuth, Stefanie Mansholt, and Mindy Ott. Hochmuth, the team's Offensive MVP, captured 1st Team All-SCC honors. Defensive MVP Hainaut was a 2nd Team All-Conference selection, as was sophomore Becky Miller.

CHAPTER 9

Classes of 1990 – 1999

Overview

The 1990s saw Staunton High School capture its first-ever Illinois team championship when the 1993 basketball Bulldogs won the IHSA Class 1A State Tournament. Unfortunately for the program, the title ended a run of basketball dominance at the school, as the Bulldogs enjoyed just one winning season in the next fifteen years. The 1994 baseball team also made an appearance at State, and the program overall enjoyed a very strong decade, including setting a school record for victories in 1998. Regrettably, like the basketball program, baseball too later suffered, eventually faltering to ten straight losing seasons. While the football program did not have a great decade by SHS standards, the last three years of the era did see the Bulldogs return to the IHSA Playoffs. Included in the run was an undefeated regular season in 1997. Arguably the best sport of the decade was boy's golf. Not only did SHS golf win eight conference championships in a nine-year span, but the program also qualified for the State Tournament on four separate occasions.

Softball was introduced as a sport at SHS in 1993, and soccer became an option for girls in the school just one year later. Unfortunately, neither program has enjoyed much success since its introduction. The new offerings came at the expense of the track program, which the school dropped as a sport for girls after the 1992 season. While the school did allow girls to compete as individuals and practice with the boy's team, the days of separate track coaches for the two genders were over. Finally, girl's bowling was added as a sport in 1998-99, and a boy's team followed one year later. The school itself also experienced a structural change during the decade, as a fire in the cafeteria destroyed a portion of the high school, resulting in a new multipurpose building in 1994. The added space was a blessing for the district's indoor sports teams.

One of the biggest changes of the decade dealt with the realignment of the South Central Conference. Beginning with the 1997-98 school year, the South Central Conference was totally revamped into a superconference that included twelve teams. Joining current SCC schools Alton Marquette, Carlinville, Gillespie, Litchfield, Southwestern, and Staunton were East Alton-Wood River and Roxana out of the Mississippi Valley Conference and Greenville, Hillsboro, Pana, and Vandalia out of the now defunct Mid-State Conference. Concerning sports such as cross country, golf, soccer, tennis, and track, the league operated as a twelve-team conference. However, the league was split into two six-team divisions, the SCC East and SCC West for baseball, basketball, football, softball, and volleyball. Though each division played crossover games against the other in order to ease scheduling concerns, those contests did not count as conference games in the standings. Unfortunately, when the divisions were set, Staunton was placed in the SCC East, apart from traditional rivals Carlinville and Gillespie. From a competitive standpoint, the Bulldogs had their work cut out for them. Not only was SHS the smallest school in its division, but over time the SCC East proved to be much tougher than the SCC West in nearly every sport. While the Dogs continued to hold their own in contests pitted against SCC West opponents, most sports programs at the school struggled to consistently compete in the SCC East.

Class of 1990

Baseball

Barry Deist's 1990 baseball team finished the year with a record of 6-9 overall and 3-6 in the South Central Conference. After a 3-0 start, the schedule was marred by rainouts, and the Dogs never found a groove during the season. The Bulldogs were eventually eliminated by Ramsey in the Regional. SHS featured a solid senior class that included Greg Best, Phil Deist, Brian Dustman, Ed Fletcher, and Jeff Schwartz. Fletcher captured both the Pitching Award (3.32 ERA) and Hitting Award (.456), and he was also named 1st Team All-Conference. Fletcher eventually returned to SHS and served as the district's high school principal for six years.

Basketball (Boys)

Despite starting the year off with four consecutive losses, the 1989-90 basketball team finished the season with a record of 14-11, including 6-4 in the South Central Conference. Mike Stivers' squad took 2nd place in the SCC and at the Macoupin County Tournament despite having only one senior, Jeff Yarnik, on the team. In addition to Yarnik, the team featured Brad Best, a junior standout who solidified himself as one of the best basketball players in school history. Best averaged a double-double for the season by scoring 25.2 points and snaring 11.8 rebounds per game. In fact, it is believed that his scoring average is the best single-season mark in school history, and his rebounding average is also high on the list. After the season, Best took home Team MVP honors and the Free Throw Award (72%) to go along with 1st Team All-SCC and 1st Team All-County accolades. Additionally, he was a 2nd Team All-Area pick by the *Telegraph* and *State Journal-Register*. Yarnik also had an outstanding season, capturing 2nd Team All-County honors as well as being named All-SCC Honorable Mention.

Basketball (Girls)

Kim Leaser was the lone senior on the 1989-90 basketball team, a squad that set a program record for victories by finishing 14-10 overall and 5-5 in the South Central Conference. The Lady Bulldogs were coached by Larry Kuba and featured outstanding offensive balance with Leaser, juniors Glenda Kleeman and Debra Sievers, and sophomore Shayne Isbell sharing the load. Leaser captured Team MVP honors in addition to All-Conference Honorable Mention recognition. Kleeman (2nd Team), Sievers (Honorable Mention), and Isbell (Honorable Mention) were also named to the All-Conference team. The latter three captured All-County recognition as well, with Sievers taking home 1st Team accolades and Kleeman and Isbell each capturing 2nd Team honors. Isbell won the Free Throw Award by hitting 66% of her attempts from the charity stripe. After the season, Kleeman was named All-Area by WSMI Radio.

Football

The 1989 season saw a coaching legacy come to an end as Barry Deist directed his last football game at Staunton High School after fifteen years as the head coach and seven years as an assistant. Leaving with the former SHS standout were seniors Greg Best, Dave Cox, Phil Deist, Brian Dustman, Ed Fletcher, Gary Fuller, Dave Gerdes, Brad Hemann, Tony Masinelli, Bronson Painter, and Brad Young.

Though Deist's teams finished with nine winning seasons overall, the 1989 campaign ended with a record of 3-6 and 2-3 in the South Central Conference. The campaign got off to a rough start for the Dogs with consecutive losses to Hillsboro (15-10) and Greenville (15-0). A Week 3 shutout of Nokomis (42-0) preceded losses to Triad (33-7) and Carlinville (43-6). The Bulldogs got back on track with two straight wins over Litchfield (14-7) and Southwestern (17-6), but the year ended with defeats to Gillespie (35-0) and Columbia (39-14). Carlinville won the SCC title that season.

After the season, several Bulldogs were honored for their accomplishments on the field. Deist and Fletcher both took home 1st Team All-SCC honors. Gerdes was named 2nd Team All-Conference, and Hemann and Painter received Honorable Mention status. Best (Offensive MVP) and Fletcher (Defensive MVP) won team awards, and Fletcher was also named 1st Team All-Area by the *Telegraph*. Meanwhile, Deist was named 2nd Team All-Area. Fletcher later returned to his alma mater and served as high school principal for six years.

Golf (Boys)

Larry Kuba's 1989 golf squad included just one senior, Mike Ficker. However, the team was composed of some very talented underclassmen who helped set a program record for victories the following season. The Dogs ended the year with a mark of 12-7, including a 2nd place finish at the South Central Conference Tournament. The team featured sophomore and Team MVP Jason Przymuzala. Not only did he lead the squad with a 40.8 scoring average, but Przymuzala put together rounds of 79 (Regional) and 83 (Sectional) to qualify for State. Przymuzala was also an All-Conference honoree, as were sophomore Nathan Spudich and freshman Andy Kuba.

Track (Boys)

The 1990 track team is considered the finest squad in modern school history. Coach Ron Sturomski's crew won the program's first Sectional championship behind seniors Greg Best, Phil Deist, Brian Dustman, Dave Gerdes, Chris Knowles, Tony Masinelli, and Brad Young. In addition, the team won every track meet that it entered during the season, including titles at the South Central Conference and Macoupin County events.

At Conference, Gerdes won both the discus and shot put competitions, while juniors Tim Straub (800 meters, 1600 meters) and Kevin Boeckenstedt (300 meter hurdles) also took gold. Additionally, Best, Deist, Dustman, and Knowles teamed up to capture championships in both the 400 meter and 800 meter relays. At County, Gerdes won the shot put competition, and the aforementioned individuals also captured gold in their respective events. Additionally, the Bulldogs received championship performances out of the 1600 meter relay team of Boeckenstedt, junior Matt Bracht, and freshmen Brad Best and Dan Burgard. Finally, the 400 meter and 800 meter relay teams qualified for State, as did Gerdes (shot put) and Straub (800 meters, 1600 meters). In fact, Straub took 6th place overall in the 800 meters, while Gerdes captured 7th place in the shot put to wrap up the magical season.

Track (Girls)

Coach Donna Ruehrup's 1990 track team featured a strong group of sixteen participants. The squad was mostly made up of underclassmen and featured just one senior, Kristy LaRosa.

Volleyball

Donna Ruehrup's 1989 volleyball team was filled with underclassmen, as the squad's roster included just two seniors, Tammy Garde and Melanie Ureta. Though inexperienced, the youthful club finished with a record of 16-11 on the year, including 7-3 in the South Central Conference. The mark was good for the program's first winning season in three years and touched off a string of five consecutive winning seasons. The highlight of the year came at the Macoupin County Tournament when the Lady Bulldogs captured the championship for the first of three straight titles. After the season, junior Sherry Masinelli captured 1st Team All-SCC honors, while fellow classmates Janelle Franke, Glenda Kleeman, and Becky Miller were all named Honorable Mention winners. Masinelli took home Offensive MVP honors, while Garde received the Defensive MVP award.

Class of 1991

Baseball

Barry Deist's 1991 baseball team finished the season with an overall record of 13-10, including 7-3 in the South Central Conference. Senior Jason Huhsman and freshman Jeremy May each hit .351 to share the team's Hitting Award, while junior Nathan Spudich (7-2, 2 saves, 2.37 ERA) took home the Pitching Award. All-Conference 1st Team members included seniors Scott Bremer, Huhsman, and Dan Lyday, while Spudich and sophomore Andy Kuba captured Honorable Mention accolades. John Mitchelar joined Bremer, Huhsman, and Lyday in the senior class. After the season, Huhsman took his talents to Lewis & Clark Community College. After competing for two years for the Trailblazers, he moved on to Southern Illinois University-Edwardsville and played two additional seasons for the Cougars.

Basketball (Boys)

The 1990-91 basketball season was a very exciting one for Staunton High School. After starting the year off by splitting their first six games, the Bulldogs ran off fifteen straight wins and eventually finished with a record of 21-5 overall and 9-1 in the South Central Conference. The SCC mark was good for a league title, and the Dogs also captured the Macoupin County Tournament championship. Unfortunately, coach Mike Stivers had to say goodbye to an excellent senior class made up of Brad Best, Kevin Klein, Jason Huhsman, Dave Legendre, Dan Lyday, and Doug Stevens. Best took home Team MVP honors, while Stevens and junior Nathan Calcari shared the Free Throw Award. Junior Kevin Hemken averaged 16.1 points and 7.3 rebounds for the Dogs, and he was named 1st Team All-Conference and All-County for his efforts. Additionally, Hemken was chosen for the *Telegraph's* All-Area 2nd Team. Klein took home 2nd Team All-Conference and All-County distinction, while Lyday was named All-SCC Honorable Mention.

With Best's departure from the program, SHS saw its all-time leading scorer graduate with a total of 1681 points. Best, who averaged 22.6 points and 8.9 rebounds, was named 1st Team All-SCC for the second straight season and also captured County MVP honors. He also took home 1st Team All-Area honors from the *Telegraph*, the *State Journal-Register*, and WSMI Radio. Finally, Best was named All-State Honorable Mention by the Associated Press. After graduating from SHS, he continued his basketball career for three seasons at Monmouth College.

Leaving with the Class of 1991 was the coach of the Bulldogs, Mike Stivers. In his thirteen seasons at the helm, SHS won 213 games, making Stivers the program's all-time wins leader by a large margin. During that span, his teams claimed seven conference titles, six county crowns, three Regional titles, and eclipsed the 20-win mark on five occasions.

Basketball (Girls)

Coach Larry Kuba's 1990-91 basketball team duplicated its record from the previous season and matched a school mark for wins by finishing 14-10 overall and 5-5 in the South Central Conference. The achievement marked the first time that the program experienced back-to-back winning seasons and the only instance during its time in the SCC.

Senior Glenda Kleeman had an outstanding season for the Lady Bulldogs, capturing 1st Team All-SCC, All-County, and WSMI Radio All-Area honors. She was also a finalist for the *Telegraph's* Athlete of the Year award. Seniors Becky Miller and Debra Sievers were named Honorable Mention All-Conference and All-County, while Jeanene Oberto rounded out the senior class. At the end-of-year sports banquet, Sievers was awarded Defensive MVP and the Free Throw Award (61%), while Kleeman took home Offensive MVP honors.

Football

The 1990 football team found itself under new leadership for the first time in sixteen years when Dave Martin took over the program. Unfortunately, Coach Martin inherited a huge rebuilding project, and the Dogs faltered to their first winless campaign since 1955, the program's sixth such season on record. The result was an 0-9 campaign, including 0-5 in the South Central Conference.

Week 1 saw SHS lose to Hillsboro by a score of 20-6. The loss was followed by two more non-conference setbacks to Greenville (55-0) and Nokomis (9-6). In the SCC slate, Staunton fell to Triad (42-6), Carlinville (44-6), Litchfield (20-0), Southwestern (24-7), and Gillespie (43-7). Week 9 saw Staunton's season end with a non-conference loss to Columbia by a score of 34-14. Gillespie went on to win the SCC, riding the momentum all the way to a 2nd place finish at State.

SHS featured just five seniors in the Class of 1991, including Dave Legendre, John Mitchelar, Craig Nolan, Bill Privette, and Matt Ray. Legendre and Nolan each received 2nd Team All-SCC honors, and Ray was given Honorable Mention status. Nolan was the team's Defensive MVP, while Ray took home Offensive MVP honors. Due to the lack of seniors on the squad, many underclassmen gained valuable time on the field, and the experience went a long way toward Martin's quest to turn the program around.

Golf (Boys)

The 1990 golf team set a school record for wins. In fact, the squad dropped just one matchup the entire regular season, finishing with an overall record of 22-1. Larry Kuba's team won the South Central Conference Tournament for the first time in school history and advanced to State for the second time after finishing 2nd at the Regional and 3rd at the Sectional. The Bulldogs placed 14th at State.

Although the team featured four seniors in the form of Brad Best, Kevin Boeckenstedt, Brad Cool, and Larry Miller, the State-qualifiers were made up entirely of underclassmen. Junior and Team MVP Jason Przymuzala paced the squad, and he was joined at State by classmates Nathan Calcari, Chris Schaefer, and Nathan Spudich. Sophomore Andy Kuba and freshman Jeremy May rounded out the superb group of golfers. May took home medalist honors at the SCC Meet, and Calcari, Przymuzala, Schaefer, and Spudich also earned All-Conference accolades.

Track (Boys)

Coming off one of the best seasons in school history, Ron Sturomski's 1991 track team was ready to build upon the success from the previous year. Although the squad did not match the success of the prior season, SHS did have several individuals qualify for State. Included in the bunch was senior Tim Straub, a 3rd place finisher in the 800 meters. Straub also qualified for State in the 1600 meters and was a member of the 3200 meter relay team that included fellow seniors Mark Rantanen and Blake Schuette, as well as junior Nathan Calcari. Finally, senior Darrell Buffington also qualified for State in his specialty, the shot put. Additional seniors on the team included Kevin Boeckenstedt, Matt Bracht, Kevin Klein, Bill Privette, and Jason Schuette.

Track (Girls)

Although Donna Ruehrup's 1991 track team did not experience much team success, several competitors established new school records during the campaign. Freshman Alena Michuda set a new school record in the 1600 meters, and the 400 meter and 800 meter relay teams also set new school marks for the Lady Bulldogs. The 400 meter relay team was composed of seniors Tricia Banovz and Jeannie Best, as well as juniors Patricia Bohlen and Sherry Masinelli. The 800 meter team included Banovz, Bohlen, Masinelli, and sophomore Jenny Mundy. Joining Banovz and Best in the senior class were Nicole Best and Ann McLean.

Volleyball

The 1990 volleyball team had an outstanding season, advancing to the Super-Sectional for the first of two straight seasons. Donna Ruehrup's club ended the year with an overall record of 25-5, including a spotless 10-0 in the South Central Conference. In addition to the SCC title, the Lady Bulldogs also captured championships at the Macoupin County, Regional, and Sectional tournaments. Staunton's road to postseason success began with Regional victories over Livingston, Gillespie, and Carlinville. After disposing of Pittsfield and Raymond Lincolnwood to take the Sectional crown, SHS fell to Auburn in the Super-Sectional, narrowly missing the program's second appearance at State.

Class of 1991 volleyball participants included Janelle Franke, Glenda Kleeman, Becky Miller, Jeanene Oberto, Jodi Oberto, and Debra Sievers. Franke, Miller, and junior Sherry Masinelli were each named to the All-SCC 1st Team, while Kleeman, Sievers, and sophomore Sam Cooper took home Honorable Mention status. Masinelli (1st Team) and Miller (2nd Team) were also named All-Area by the *Telegraph*, and Ruehrup was the publication's Coach of the Year. For her all-around performance in athletics, Kleeman was named as a finalist for the *Telegraph's* Athlete of the Year award. Upon graduation, Miller moved on to Augustana College to continue her volleyball career for the Vikings.

Class of 1992

Baseball

The 1992 baseball season was the final one for Barry Deist as head baseball coach at Staunton High School. Effectively wrapping up a career that saw him lead the program for twenty-two seasons, Deist won approximately 200 games over that time period. His coaching tenure is the longest in SHS baseball history, and his win total likely is as well, though records are incomplete.

The 1992 team included seniors Kevin Hemken, Vince Hughes, Nathan Spudich, and Rob Taylor. However, the year belonged to the underclassmen, as junior Andy Kuba and sophomore Jeremy May were both honored with 1st Team All-Conference accolades in a season that saw SHS finish 11-11 overall and 4-6 in the South Central Conference. Though the season in general was uneventful, one game does deserve mention. In an 11-5 victory over Southwestern, Kuba displayed perhaps the greatest individual hitting display in school history. He finished the game 4-5 at the plate, including three home runs, a double, and all eleven of the team's RBI's. The team's Hitting Award winner, Kuba finished the year with a batting average of .430. Meanwhile, May won the Pitching Award with a record of 5-2 on the mound. Upon graduation, Hughes went on to Blackburn College where he continued his baseball career in addition to participating in golf for the Beavers.

Basketball (Boys)

The 1991-92 basketball team found itself with a new leader, though it was not his first time coaching basketball at Staunton High School. Randy Legendre, who led the program for three years from 1973-76, and had most recently been serving as an assistant, took over for his second stint as varsity basketball coach at SHS. Though the team graduated plenty of firepower from the previous season, Legendre did welcome back a strong senior class that included Nathan Calcari, Kevin Hemken, Jason Przymuzala, Chris Schaefer, and Dan Strohkirch.

Legendre's squad continued where the previous team left off, capturing the South Central Conference title, as well as the championship of the Macoupin County Tournament. However, things did not look good early for the Bulldogs, as the club started off the year by dropping four straight games. Fortunately, SHS righted the ship, rolling to six straight wins and later enjoying two separate five-game winning streaks. The campaign ended at the Bunker Hill Class A Regional when SHS fell to the host school 66-63 in an exciting game. The loss ended Staunton's season at 17-9 overall and 8-2 in the SCC.

Several individuals had outstanding seasons for the Bulldogs but none bigger than Hemken (18.4 points, 8.7 rebounds), the team's Offensive MVP. Hemken was named 1st Team All-Conference, All-County, *Telegraph* All-Area, and WSMI Radio All-Area. He was also named to the exclusive Associated Press All-State team as an Honorable Mention selection. However, Hemken was not alone in earning accolades that season, as fellow classmate Calcari was named MVP at the Macoupin County Tournament and was an All-SCC Honorable Mention choice. Junior Kevin Meyer was on the All-SCC and All-County 1st Team, while fellow junior Andy Kuba took home 2nd Team All-Conference accolades. Kuba was also named Defensive MVP and won the team's Free Throw Award (86%). Upon graduation, Schaefer played one season at Fontbonne University in Clayton, Missouri. While there, he also competed in golf for the school.

Basketball (Girls)

Coach Larry Kuba's basketball squad featured just two seniors in 1991-92, with Michelle Kirkwood and Sherry Masinelli leading the charge for the Lady Bulldogs. Masinelli earned Team MVP honors for SHS, and she and junior Angie Sievers were also honored with All-Conference Honorable Mention status. Mary Morgan earned the Free Throw Award after hitting

64% of her tries from the charity stripe. Staunton finished the season with a record of 6-16 overall but failed to win a game in the South Central Conference, finishing 0-10 in league play.

Football

The 1991 football team made big strides in the second year of Dave Martin's tenure with the program. Coming off a winless campaign from the previous season, the Bulldogs finished 3-6 overall and 2-3 in the South Central Conference, which was won by Triad. Staunton began the year with a 19-7 win over Hillsboro, the first victory for the program in twelve outings. Unfortunately, a 15-6 loss to Greenville in Week 2 prompted a five-game slide that included losses to Nokomis, Gillespie, Triad, and Carlinville. SHS got back on track in Week 7 with a shutout victory over Litchfield (21-0), and the Dogs followed up that win by defeating Southwestern by a score of 29-21. The season ended with a loss to Columbia.

Staunton football seniors included Jeff Dal Pozzo, Ryan Kilduff, Bryan King, Ron Maedge, Bill Mosser, Tim Ott, and Dan Strohkirch. Kilduff, Mosser, and Ott were all honored with All-Conference 2nd Team accolades, while Dal Pozzo was named Honorable Mention. Dal Pozzo and Ott shared the Offensive MVP award, while Kilduff was named the team's Defensive MVP.

Golf (Boys)

Coming off a 14th place finish at the State Tournament and having returned each participant from that squad, Larry Kuba's 1991 golf team expected success on the links. The team made good on its goals, finishing 17-3 in match play and winning the program's only Regional crown along the way. The Bulldogs, winners of the Greenville Invitational, also captured their second straight South Central Conference title. The team eventually placed 6th at State.

Seniors Nathan Calcari, Jason Przymuzala, Chris Schaefer, and Nathan Spudich provided leadership for a squad that also featured sophomores Brian Hughes and Jeremy May. As stated, the Bulldogs captured the title at the Greenville Invitational, as Przymuzala led the way in taking home medalist honors. At the SCC Tournament, an amazing feat was witnessed when all six golfers earned All-Conference distinction, with May capturing medalist honors. Calcari, Przymuzala, and May shared the Team MVP award, and each was also honored by both the *Telegraph* and Metro East Golf Coaches Association (MEGCA). The *Telegraph* honored May as its Player of the Year, while Przymuzala was named 1st Team All-Area and Calcari was a 2nd Team selection. The MEGCA awarded May with 1st Team All-Area accolades, while Przymuzala (2nd Team) and Calcari (3rd Team) were also noted by the publication. Przymuzala continued his career at Lincoln College before moving on to the University of Tennessee–Martin. Meanwhile, Calcari played four seasons collegiately at Millikin University, while Schaefer competed for two years at Fontbonne University.

Track (Boys)

The track program welcomed a new coach in 1992, as Larry Caldieraro led the squad in his one and only season at the helm. Caldieraro welcomed seniors Nathan Calcari and Don McNaughton to the team, not to mention a group of talented underclassmen. The result was a 3rd place finish in the South Central Conference, a 2nd place showing at the Macoupin County Meet, and 2nd place at Sectionals. Additionally, several school records were broken during the season. Calcari tied the school mark in the 400 meters, while sophomore Dennis Bohlen set a new record in the 300 meter hurdles. The school record in the 1600 meter relay was actually broken on two occasions. Initially, McNaughton teamed with juniors Shannon Campbell and Jason Sternickle and sophomore John Sharp to break the old mark. Later in the season the team of Calcari, McNaughton, Campbell, and Sharp once again set a new school record in the event.

Track (Girls)

After twenty seasons as an activity at Staunton High School, with eighteen of them coming under the leadership of Donna Ruehrup, the track program was disbanded as a female sport after the 1992 season. Although a few girls continued to compete as individuals in track, it was nearly fifteen years before the program enjoyed the level of participation that it had initially experienced. Patricia Bohlen, Denise Boston, Sherry Masinelli, and Jennifer Oberto comprised the senior track members in the Class of 1992.

Volleyball

Donna Ruehrup's 1991 volleyball team duplicated the success of the previous season, winning South Central Conference, Macoupin County, Regional, and Sectional championships before losing in the Super-Sectional. The Sectional title was the team's second straight and sixth overall, by far the most of any team sport at Staunton High School. The Lady Bulldogs also took gold at the Staunton Invitational on their way to a record of 22-5.

SHS had a deep and talented class of senior girls in the form of Kris Ahring, Angie Bertolino, Tisha Colley, Melissa Heidke, Michelle Kirkwood, Sherry Masinelli, Sara Scheller, and Daphne Ureta. Ahring and Offensive MVP Masinelli were both honored with 1st Team All-Conference recognition, while Bertolino received All-SCC 2nd Team status. Junior and Defensive MVP Sam Cooper, as well as sophomore Alena Michuda, were named 1st Team All-Conference by league coaches.

Class of 1993

Baseball

For the first time in more than two decades, the baseball program welcomed a new manager. Larry Caldieraro, a Staunton alum, had served as an assistant for a couple of years prior to taking the reins of the team. He welcomed seniors Brad Best, Chris Geisler, Mark Johnson, Andy Kuba, George Moore, Matt Popovich, Tim Scheller, and Brad Skertich in his first year on the job. The Bulldogs played .500 ball for most of the year, ending the season with a record of 10-11 overall, including 6-3 in the South Central Conference. Staunton placed five members on the All-Conference squad, led by 1st Team selections Kuba and Scheller. Johnson joined junior Jeremy May and sophomore Chad Neuhaus as Honorable Mention honorees. Kuba (.500) and May (.448) led the offensive attack for the Bulldogs. After the season, Kuba was named as a finalist for the *Telegraph's* Athlete of the Year award.

Basketball (Boys)

Much has been written about the 1992-93 state championship basketball team, and the squad must certainly be considered in the same breath as the 1923 football team as the greatest in school history. However, what is so remarkable about the season is that it was a true Cinderella story, and the squad is still considered by many as the last great underdog state championship team in Illinois. The club was coached by Randy Legendre and assistant Dave Lamore, and consisted of seniors Brad Best, Andy Kuba, Kevin Meyer, Matt Popovich, and Brad Skertich, juniors Ron Hampton, Jeremy May, and Corey Painter, and sophomores Derek Brauer, Lucas Calcari, Tony Dal Pozzo, and Mike Kovaly. The team finished 27-4 overall and 9-1 in the South Central Conference. The win total matched a school record in basketball, and the SCC mark was good for the program's third successive league title.

Although a state title may not have been on the radar, the team did have high goals in mind for the campaign. Coming off a 17-9 season that saw the Bulldogs win South Central Conference and Macoupin County championships, SHS returned three starters in Kuba, Meyer, and Skertich. However, what was missing from the squad was a true point guard. Hampton, a transfer from Livingston High School, filled the void to perfection. With May rounding out the starting lineup, the Bulldogs were a formidable force for any opponent.

The Bulldogs faced a brutal early season schedule that saw them falter to a 2-2 record to begin the year, including losses to Breese Central and Bethalto Civic Memorial. Remarkably, the state champions did not even win the Macoupin County championship, as Virden nipped SHS in the title game by a score of 55-51. The other loss on the year came in a game at Southwestern when the Piasa Birds soundly defeated SHS by a score of 66-49. However, that loss was the last of the season for Staunton, as the Bulldogs rode a six game winning streak into postseason play. The Dogs easily captured the Greenville Regional, defeating Roxana (72-51) and Bunker Hill (92-54) to take the title. At the Vandalia Sectional, the Bulldogs survived in overtime to defeat St. Elmo (70-66), thus setting up a showdown with SCC foe Litchfield in the championship game. The Dogs took care of business against the Purple Panthers for the third time on the season, winning 71-55 to advance to the Super-Sectional at Eastern Illinois University. In the Super-Sectional, Staunton faced a favored Bridgeport Red Hill team in what became one of the most exciting games in Illinois history.

Going into the Super-Sectional against Bridgeport Red Hill, SHS was ranked 15th in the Sweet 16, meaning that the Dogs were basically going to be underdogs from that game forward. The contest itself was a back-and-forth affair from the opening tip, but with just seconds remaining the Bulldogs found themselves down six points with Red Hill at the line to seal the game. However, the Salukis missed the front end of a one-and-one opportunity, and Kuba hit a quick 3-pointer to bring SHS to within one possession of tying the game. Amazingly, after another missed front-end free throw, Kuba hit yet another 3-pointer to send the game into overtime. In the first overtime, the Bulldogs once again had their backs to the wall, down by three with just seconds remaining. This time it was May's turn to play the hero, as he hit a 3-pointer at the buzzer to send the game into a second overtime. Finally, in that frame, with the Bulldogs down one point, Kuba tipped in his own miss at the buzzer to send Staunton to State for the first time in SHS basketball history.

In the early 1990's, March Madness was still being played at the University of Illinois, and so the Bulldogs and their fans invaded Champaign to face the Riverton Hawks. The Dogs looked nervous from the opening tip, falling behind 11-0 before recording a single point. However, it was all Staunton from that juncture, as the Dogs captured a 52-43 victory to advance to the Class 1A semifinals. Next up for the Dogs were the Cardinals of Hamilton High School. After once again falling behind early, SHS fought back and won 52-42 to advance to the championship game.

Most experts believed that the state championship had already been decided when Chicago Hales Franciscan defeated Cairo and future NBA player Tyrone Nesby in the other semifinal. Hales Franciscan is a perennial championship contender that regularly has several Division 1 athletes on its roster, and 1992-93 was no different in that regard. However, the Bulldogs were unfazed, and the unit used a strong team defense and some timely scoring to take home a 66-62 victory, thus securing the school's first and only state championship in any team sport.

After the season ended, several SHS players received numerous individual awards. Kuba and Meyer were both named to the All-Conference 1st Team, WSMI Radio All-Area 1st Team, and Associated Press All-State Honorable Mention. Kuba, who led the team in scoring (20.4) and rebounding (9.9), captured Player of the Year honors by the *Telegraph*, 1st Team All-Area status by the *State Journal-Register*, *Sun-Times* All-State 1st Team honors, and was also named to the All-Tournament 1st Team at State. At the end of the school year, he was also a finalist for the *Telegraph's* Athlete of the Year award. Meyer put up similar numbers (17.6 points, 8.5 rebounds) and also received recognition by the *Telegraph* (1st Team), *State Journal-Register* (Special Mention), and was All-Tournament (2nd Team) at State. After high school, he played one season at Blackburn College. Hampton, a 2nd Team All-Area pick by the *Telegraph*, captured the Free Throw Award (75%) and, along with Skertich, was named All-Conference Honorable Mention. Finally, Kovaly was fortunate enough to advance to State in the IHSA's 3-Point Shootout, becoming the first of three Bulldogs to accomplish the feat.

Basketball (Girls)

The 1992-93 basketball team got off to a nice start by winning two straight games to open the season. However, SHS faltered the rest of the way, eventually finishing with a record of 5-16 overall and 1-9 in the South Central Conference. Senior Janna Streif had a nice year for SHS, taking home All-Conference Honorable Mention status. However, the key cog for Staunton was senior Angie Sievers, the Team MVP, Free Throw Award winner (68%), and 1st Team All-Area honoree by WSMI Radio. Sievers also captured 2nd Team All-Conference and 2nd Team All-County accolades. Joining Streif and Sievers in the senior class were Robin Campbell, Mary Morgan, and Kristina Struebig. The Lady Bulldogs were directed by Larry Kuba.

Football

Dave Martin led the 1992 football team to the program's first winning season in eight years. The squad finished the campaign with an overall record of 5-4, including 2-3 in the South Central Conference. Unfortunately, the team fell short of its goal of making the playoffs, as it took at least six wins to qualify for the postseason in those days. The year began in excellent fashion, as the Bulldogs won three straight games, defeating Hillsboro (26-7), Greenville (19-7), and Nokomis (33-0) to begin the schedule. Though the Dogs fell short in their first SCC game, a 12-7 loss to eventual champion Gillespie, SHS improved to 4-1 overall with a Week 5 victory over Triad (21-13). Unfortunately, two straight losses ensued, including a Week 6 shutout loss to Carlinville (34-0), as well as a heartbreaking loss to Litchfield (26-25). The Bulldogs gave themselves a legitimate shot at the postseason with a Week 8 victory over Southwestern, but Columbia quickly dashed Staunton's playoff aspirations in a 42-6 romp of the Dogs.

The Class of 1993 football players included Terry Albrecht, Shannon Campbell, Ryan Gusewelle, Mark Johnson, Andy Kuba, Kevin Meyer, George Moore, Matt Popovich, Randy Rogers, Tim Scheller, Brad Skertich, and Jason Sternickle. Albrecht and Gusewelle secured 1st Team All-Conference accolades, while Kuba, Meyer, Popovich, and Skertich joined juniors

Corey Painter and John Sharp on the 2nd Team. Moore was recognized by SCC coaches as a Special Mention All-Conference football player. Finally, Albrecht (2nd Team) and Gusewelle (3rd Team) were both honored by the *Telegraph* as All-Area football players. After the school year, Kuba was named as a finalist for the *Telegraph's* Athlete of the Year award based on his outstanding play in baseball, basketball, football, and golf.

Golf (Boys)

Larry Kuba's 1992 golf team finished the season 15-6 in match play and, more importantly, captured the program's third straight South Central Conference championship. Seniors Brad Best, Andy Fritz, and Andy Kuba provided leadership, though the play of juniors Brian Hughes and Jeremy May sparked the team's success. Hughes attained medalist honors at the SCC Tournament, while Kuba and May were also All-SCC performers. May, the team's scoring leader (38.2) and MVP, advanced all the way to the State Tournament that season. Kuba, who split his time between the golf and football teams, was a finalist in the *Telegraph's* Athlete of the Year competition.

Softball

Jim Mathis became Staunton's first-ever softball coach in 1993, as the school commissioned the sport as an official activity for the first time. The program's first game was against Litchfield, and the Lady Bulldogs emerged with a 13-7 victory. Though he directed the team for just two seasons, Mathis was instrumental in getting the softball program off the ground. His first group of seniors included Robin Campbell, Sam Cooper, Monica Scheller, and Angie Sievers. Scheller won the Hitting Award with a .415 batting average for a team that finished 6-11 overall and 4-3 in the South Central Conference.

Track (Boys)

The 1993 track team had a phenomenal end to the season, as SHS won the Sectional for just the second time in school history. Interestingly enough, the Bulldogs actually experienced only mild team success early in the year, most likely due to a lack of numbers in the program. In fact, Staunton won the Sectional with only six individuals competing. Among the competitors were seniors Brad Best and Shannon Campbell, juniors Dennis Bohlen and James Castelli, and sophomores Dean Heidke and Josh Schuette.

The Bulldogs finished 3rd at both the South Central Conference and Macoupin County track meets. At the SCC Meet, Bohlen showed off his diverse skill set by winning gold in both throwing events (discus, shot put) and setting a new SCC record in the hurdles. Other conference champions included Best in the 200 meters and Schuette in the 1600 meters. At County, Bohlen took 1st place in the hurdles, with Best and Schuette once again capturing gold in their respective events. Bohlen placed in the top three in all four of his events at the Sectional Meet, including a title in the discus. Other Sectional champions were Heidke in the 200 meters and Schuette in the 3200 meters. Additionally, Best qualified for State in the 100 meters, Bohlen in the hurdles and shot put, and Schuette in the 1600 meters. After the season, it was determined that Bohlen had broken a school record in the discus.

Volleyball

Seniors Robin Campbell, Sam Cooper, Angie Sievers, and Kristina Struebig led the 1992 volleyball squad into battle. After overcoming an early five-game losing streak, the team finished 16-12 overall and 7-3 in the South Central Conference. In addition to the strong SCC finish, the Lady Bulldogs reached the title game of both the Macoupin County and Regional tournaments for coach Donna Ruehrup. After the season, Cooper and junior Alena Michuda were named to the All-Conference 1st Team, while junior Adrienne Spudich and sophomore Sara Zuber captured 2nd Team All-SCC honors.

Class of 1994

Baseball

Based on how the regular season unfolded, nobody could have known 1994 baseball season would end up as one of the best in school history. Coach Larry Caldieraro entered his second season on the job by welcoming seniors Tim Crainick, Ron Hampton, Brad LaRosa, Jeremy May, Kevin Mitchell, and Scott Williams to the fold. Despite a strong group of upperclassmen, the Bulldogs entered postseason action with a record of just 9-9 overall and 6-4 in the South Central Conference. However, SHS caught fire at the right time, riding the arms of Hampton and May all the way to the State Tournament. The Bulldogs defeated Pana, Litchfield, and Alton Marquette to win the Regional before knocking off Southwestern and Raymond Lincolnwood to win the Sectional. At State, the Bulldogs were stopped by Kankakee McNamara, effectively ending the Cinderella run through the postseason.

Interestingly enough, the State-qualifying squad barely made it out of the first round of Regionals. In a 3-1 victory over Pana, the Bulldogs escaped with the help of two home runs by junior Brian Murphy. Another close game followed, with the Dogs holding off Litchfield by a score of 4-2. Finally, the Regional title could be celebrated after a 9-6 victory over Alton Marquette. The Bulldogs entered Sectional action as a decisive underdog. Their first game was against SCC foe Southwestern, a team that defeated Staunton twice during the regular season by scores of 14-4 and 5-0. Southwestern took a 2-1 lead into the seventh inning of the third matchup, and in fact the Piasa Birds had a no-hitter going with two outs in the frame. However, the Bulldogs had a no-quit attitude in them. Junior Derek Brauer drew a walk, LaRosa was hit by a pitch, and junior Derek Allen also walked to load the bases. Murphy again played hero in one of the most dramatic at-bats in school history. With two outs and two strikes, Murphy launched a bases-clearing double to give SHS a 4-2 lead. Hampton finished out a spectacular game on the mound by setting Southwestern down in the bottom of the seventh to send the Bulldogs to the Sectional final. In the final, May threw a one-hitter to help the Bulldogs defeat the Lancers of Raymond Lincolnwood by a score of 3-1. A key defensive play occurred in the sixth inning, as junior Tony Dal Pozzo made a diving stop in the hole and gunned down a runner at the plate to help preserve the Staunton victory.

The Sectional title sent SHS to State for the third time in school history. Unfortunately, the Bulldogs ran into a tough squad from Kankakee McNamara, losing 6-0. The team thus finished with an overall record of 14-10. In addition to the aforementioned players, other team members included juniors Vic Buehler, Tom Lane, and Chad Neuhaus, as well as sophomore Joe Odorizzi. After the season, Caldieraro was named Coach of the Year by the *Telegraph*. Additionally, Hampton, Murphy, and Neuhaus took home All-Conference Honorable Mention accolades, while May was named 1st Team All-SCC. May, who ended up his senior season with a .466 batting average, was also named to the *Telegraph* All-Area 1st Team. Finally, he was named Athlete of the Year by the *Telegraph*. Although it has since been discontinued, the newspaper used to honor the best all-around athletes from the Riverbend Area, including large schools Alton and Edwardsville. Though other SHS athletes have been finalists for the award, in 1994 May became the only person in school history to win it. When considering team success across multiple sports, it is easy to see why May was pegged as the winner. Not only was he on the State-qualifying baseball team, but he was also a member of three golf teams that advanced to State. Finally, he was a starter on the 1993 basketball team that captured the only state championship in school history.

Although LaRosa did not continue his playing career after high school, he did stick with baseball, serving as an athletic trainer for several Major League Baseball teams. In fact, LaRosa accumulated two World Series rings early in his career. He was with the Florida Marlins' AA organization, the Carolina Mudcats, during the big league squad's 2003 championship season. He also received a ring in 2006 while serving with the AA Springfield Cardinals, an affiliate of the St. Louis Cardinals. It is also worth noting that LaRosa completed his internship with the St. Louis Cardinals in 1998 during Mark McGwire's record-setting home run season.

Basketball (Boys)

Coming off the school's only state title in any team sport, the 1993-94 basketball squad had a huge target on its back, receiving every opponent's best shot each night out. Despite returning two starters and a successful JV team from the previous season, the pressure took its toll on a squad that finished 9-18 overall and 4-6 in the South Central Conference. The Dogs began the season with five straight losses and took a four-game losing streak into Regional action. However, the Bulldogs came alive in postseason play, defeating Alton Marquette (76-65) and upsetting top seed Bunker Hill (50-46) to advance to the program's fourth straight Regional title game. Awaiting Staunton in the title game was the host school, Roxana. Though SHS forced the championship game into overtime, the Shells were too much in the end, winning by a score of 65-63.

Ron Hampton capped off a solid senior season by being named 2nd Team All-SCC, 2nd Team All-County, and 1st Team All-Area by WSMI Radio. He was also named to the Associated Press All-State team as an Honorable Mention choice. Hampton continued his playing career at Blackburn College. Junior Mike Kovaly was the only other player to receive a basketball honor, taking home 2nd Team All-Conference accolades. However, after the school year was over, senior Jeremy May was named Athlete of the Year by the *Telegraph* for his outstanding career success across all three of his sporting activities (baseball, basketball, golf). Brad LaRosa and Corey Painter joined Hampton and May in the Class of 1994. The end of the year also marked Randy Legendre's last full season directing the program, as he resigned his post halfway through the following year.

Basketball (Girls)

Though the 1993-94 basketball team finished just 3-18 overall and 0-10 in the South Central Conference, some context is required when analyzing the season. The squad featured just one senior in the form of Laura Witt, but unfortunately she went down with a knee injury and was unable to play most of the year. Additional injuries and medical conditions led to three other main contributors being sidelined, forcing the Lady Bulldogs to play mostly underclassmen on the varsity squad. Junior Sara Zuber did her best to keep Staunton competitive. Zuber provided leadership for the youthful squad and was also a 2nd Team All-Conference selection for coach Larry Kuba. The experience gained by the underclassmen paid dividends later on, however, as the squad broke the school record for wins the following year.

Football

In his fourth and final year at the helm of the football program, coach Dave Martin led the 1993 team to a 5-4 record for the second consecutive year. The Bulldogs finished 3-2 in the South Central Conference behind seniors Dennis Bohlen, Mark Bruhn, Scott Colley, Tim Crainick, Brian Herbeck, Travis King, Brad LaRosa, Tim Miller, Corey Painter, Jon Rondi, John Sharp, Jeremy Streeb, and Scott Williams.

The season began very well for SHS, as the Dogs raced off to a 4-1 start. Week 1 saw SHS easily handle Hillsboro by a score of 38-7. A Week 2 setback to Greenville (27-7) preceded shutout victories over Nokomis (19-0) and Southwestern (24-0). The Bulldogs stayed hot with a 21-14 win over Gillespie in Week 5, but the momentum stopped there. Consecutive losses to Alton Marquette (19-0) and Carlinville (42-8) put a playoff appearance in jeopardy, though the Dogs did respond with a Week 8 win over Litchfield (32-8). With six victories needed to secure a postseason berth, SHS faced a tall task in Week 9 when Hardin Calhoun came to town. The Warriors were fresh off an undefeated campaign that saw them win the Class 1A state championship the prior season. In one of the hardest-hitting football games ever witnessed at Staunton High School, the Warriors pulled away with a 34-20 victory on their way to a second straight state title. Though SHS wound up with a winning record for the second straight year, the team once again fell short of the IHSA Playoffs. It is worth mentioning that SCC champion Carlinville made a deep postseason run, eventually finishing 2nd at State.

After the season, the Bulldogs had to say goodbye to Bohlen, one of the best running backs to ever wear a Staunton uniform. Using an unbelievable mix of speed and power, he rushed for 1072 yards on the season. Bohlen was named 1st Team All-SCC and *Telegraph* All-Area, joining Colley on both squads. All-SCC 2nd Team members included Bruhn and Herbeck, with LaRosa, Painter, Rondi, Sharp, and junior Derek Brauer taking home Honorable Mention status. After the season, Sharp continued his football career for two seasons at Monmouth College.

Golf (Boys)

The 1993 golf team had another outstanding season, capturing the South Central Conference championship for the fourth consecutive year and eventually finishing in 5th place at the State Tournament. SHS made it to State by placing 4th at both the Regional and Sectional golf tournaments. The Bulldogs were led by seniors Ron Hampton, Brian Hughes, Jeremy May, and Kevin Mitchell, a group that guided the team to a 16-3 record in match play.

At the SCC Meet, five Bulldogs finished with All-Conference honors, including May, the conference medalist. Hampton, Hughes, Mitchell, and freshman B.J. Brown rounded out the All-SCC group. May (38.1) and Brown (38.9) both had excellent scoring averages for the Dogs, and were subsequently honored with All-Area status by the *Telegraph* and the Metro East Golf Coaches Association. May received 1st Team honors by both parties, while Brown took home 2nd Team accolades. At the end of the year, May was named *Telegraph* Athlete of the Year for all sports. He continued his golf career at Rend Lake, achieving National Junior College All-American status as a sophomore. May later competed for one season at Western Illinois University. Meanwhile, Hughes moved on to Blackburn College where he competed for two seasons for the Beavers.

Golf (Girls)

Freshman Amanda Conroy represented the lone female on the 1993 golf team. Conroy, who was coached by Larry Kuba, was the first female to compete for SHS in six years.

Soccer (Girls)

A new sport was introduced to SHS in 1994, as girls were allowed to participate in soccer for the first time in school history. Playing a schedule that included some of the biggest schools in the area (Chatham Glenwood, Granite City, O'Fallon, Triad), the inaugural squad finished with a record of 5-6-1 under the direction of Jennifer Dutko. The first seniors in the program's history were Alena Michuda and Adrienne Spudich.

Softball

The 1994 softball season represented the last one for coach Jim Mathis. Just like the program itself, the Lady Bulldogs were a young team with no seniors on the roster. Not only did SHS graduate a solid senior class from the previous season, but the introduction of soccer as a female sport also hurt the program from a numbers standpoint. The Lady Bulldogs finished the season 4-14 overall, with each win coming in South Central Conference play (4-6). The squad was led by a solid sophomore group, including All-SCC Honorable Mention winners Emily Henry and Heather Kirkwood. The Team MVP award went to Kirkwood, while fellow sophomore Stefanie Kershaw led the squad with a .302 batting average. Although Mathis was at the helm for just two seasons, he must be given credit as a driving force behind the implementation of softball as a sport at SHS.

Track (Boys)

Dave Williams' 1994 track team had a solid season, placing 3rd at the Macoupin County and Sectional meets. Additionally, the Bulldogs took 4th place at the South Central Conference Meet. Though the squad was unable to duplicate the previous year's success, three individuals did have outstanding seasons. Senior Dennis Bohlen cemented his place as one of the best track athletes in school history by capturing SCC, County, and Sectional titles in the discus and the shot put, while also competing well in the hurdles. Junior Josh Schuette won conference (3200 meters) and county (1600 meters) gold and also advanced to State in the 1600 meters. Finally junior Dean Heidke advanced to State in the 100 meters.

Volleyball

Seniors Alena Michuda, Adrienne Spudich, Lisa Taylor, and Laura Witt led the 1993 volleyball team into action. The squad, coached by Donna Ruehrup, wound up 14-11 overall and 7-3 in the South Central Conference. During the year, the Lady Bulldogs won their own Staunton Invitational. Unfortunately, the end of the season brought to a close the illustrious coaching career of Donna Ruehrup. Arguably the most successful coach in school history, Ruehrup directed the volleyball program for nineteen years and finished with a career record of 328-155 (.679). During her tenure the program captured nine SCC titles, eight Macoupin County championships, five District titles, six Regional and Sectional crowns, and made one appearance at State. Upon graduation, Michuda continued her volleyball career at Lewis & Clark Community College for two seasons before moving on to the University of Illinois-Springfield. At UIS, Michuda competed in volleyball for two seasons and also played tennis for one year.

Classes of 1990 - 1999

Class of 1995

Baseball

Despite finishing the season 12-9 overall and 5-5 in the South Central Conference, the 1995 baseball season was somewhat of a disappointment given the fact that SHS returned several key contributors from the previous year's State-qualifier. SHS started off just 3-3 but won six of seven games to gain momentum during the middle portion of the schedule. However, the Bulldogs struggled down the stretch, dropping three of four before entering Regionals. After a 5-4 victory over Ramsey, SHS lost an 8-0 decision to Alton Marquette to end the year.

Coach Larry Caldieraro's team featured seniors Derek Allen, Derek Brauer, Vic Buehler, Tony Dal Pozzo, Mike Kovaly, Tom Lane, Chris Loeh, Brian Murphy, and Chad Neuhaus. Allen and Brauer took home All-SCC 1st Team accolades, while sophomore Steve Moore was an Honorable Mention selection. After the season, Allen and Buehler continued their careers at Lewis & Clark Community College, and Buehler played an additional season at Missouri University of Science & Technology.

Basketball (Boys)

The 1994-95 basketball season started off with promise but, unfortunately, ended in disappointment. The Bulldogs darted off to a 6-2 start, including a championship in the Staunton Thanksgiving Tournament to begin the year. SHS defeated Greenville (61-50), Bethalto Civic Memorial (79-65), and Nokomis (66-55) to win the round-robin affair. However, the Dogs dropped eight straight games and eventually wound up with a record of 8-16 overall, including 2-8 in the South Central Conference.

After the aforementioned 6-2 start, the Bulldogs fell to 6-6 after an upset loss to Northwestern in the first round of the Macoupin County Tournament. At that point, beloved coach and former state champion, Randy Legendre, resigned his position as leader of the basketball program. Assistant Dave Lamore, who experienced tremendous success as head coach of Livingston High School before coming to SHS, took the reins for three games (0-3) before he too decided to step down. Kevin Gockel, who began the season as the program's freshmen coach, finished out the campaign in the lead position, with Lamore serving as his assistant. Though the team finished just 2-7 down the stretch, Gockel solidified the post by staying on as head coach for the next twelve years.

Seniors in the Class of 1995 included Derek Brauer, Vic Buehler, Lucas Calcari, Tony Dal Pozzo, Mike Kovaly, Jon Legendre, and Brian Murphy. Kovaly was named Offensive MVP, while Calcari took home Defensive MVP honors. Brauer won the Free Throw Award in addition to being named 2nd Team All-SCC. Kovaly and junior Joe Odorizzi were named All-Conference Honorable Mention by league coaches.

Basketball (Girls)

The 1994-95 basketball team set a school record for wins that was not broken for sixteen years. The 16-8 Lady Bulldogs finished 7-3 in the South Central Conference, the program's best-ever finish in SCC play. Included in the run was a middle portion of the schedule that saw the Lady Bulldogs win eight of nine games. The squad was coached by Larry Kuba and led by seniors Angie Klein and Sara Zuber, an All-Conference Honorable Mention selection. The Lady Bulldogs also featured a strong junior class that included standouts Stefanie Kershaw, Marcy

Molinar, and Pam Wieseman. Kershaw won the Free Throw Award (71%) and was named All-Conference Honorable Mention. Molinar (2nd Team) and Wieseman (1st Team) were both members of the All-Conference team, and both also captured All-Area 1st Team honors from WSMI Radio. Additionally, each received All-Tournament 1st Team status at the Macoupin County Tournament.

Football

The 1994 football team welcomed a new coach to lead the program when Scott Tonsor took over the reins at Staunton High School. Though the Bulldogs completed the season with a record of 4-5 overall, including 3-2 in the South Central Conference, on paper the team finished just six points shy of making the playoffs. A Week 3 loss to Nokomis (15-14) and a Week 9 loss to two-time defending state champion Hardin Calhoun (22-19) put a damper on what was otherwise a successful season for the Bulldogs.

The year began with a Week 1 victory over Hillsboro (19-13). However, consecutive losses to Greenville (21-0) and Nokomis (15-14) hurt the playoff push. SHS recovered by destroying Southwestern (44-0) in Week 4 but dropped a close game to rival Gillespie (28-19) the very next week. Once again, the Bulldogs rebounded with a hard-fought win over Alton Marquette by a score of 14-7. However, a blowout loss to SCC champion Carlinville (52-6) ended the team's postseason hopes, though the Dogs did respond with a victory over Litchfield (22-19) before dropping the aforementioned game to Hardin Calhoun.

Coach Tonsor was blessed to have a deep and talented senior class in his first season on the job, led by Offensive MVP Vic Buehler and Defensive MVP Lucas Calcari. Additional seniors included Steve Ahrens, Derek Allen, Derek Brauer, Tony Dal Pozzo, Jason Foulk, Jeff Hebenstreit, Dean Heidke, Pete Knapp, Mike Kovaly, Jon Legendre, Chad Neuhaus, Artie Partridge, Scott Schmitt, Josh Schuette, Jim Sharp, and Matt Sievers. Brauer, Buehler, Calcari, Hebenstreit, and Kovaly were all named to the All-Conference 1st Team, while Sievers was 2nd Team selection. Dal Pozzo and Sharp took home 3rd Team honors, and Heidke rounded out the award winners with Honorable Mention accolades. *Telegraph* All-Area performers included 2nd Team members Brauer and Kovaly, as well as 3rd Team members Buehler, Calcari, and Hebenstreit. Kovaly later took his talents to Augustana College where he continued his football career for one season.

Golf (Boys)

Despite having graduated an outstanding senior class from a team that finished 5th at State, the 1994 version of coach Larry Kuba's golf team also enjoyed an amazing season. In fact, the Bulldogs finished 18-2 in match play and captured the South Central Conference championship for the fifth straight year. The team's leadership came from the lone senior on the squad, Kevin Dustmann. Amazingly, other than Dustmann, each travelling member of the team was a sophomore or freshman. Sophomore and Team MVP B.J. Brown posted the lowest scoring average on the club. He advanced all the way to State and finished in 6th place overall. SHS placed five members on the All-Conference team, including Brown, the medalist, and fellow sophomore Brad Rizzi. Freshmen Elliot Kolkovich, Brett Tevini, and Donnie Vazzi also captured All-SCC honors. After the season, Brown was named 1st Team All-Area by the *Telegraph*, *News-Democrat*, and the Metro East Golf Coaches Association.

Golf (Girls)

Sophomore Amanda Conroy once again served as the lone female golfer in 1994, with Larry Kuba serving as her coach.

Soccer (Girls)

The 1995 soccer team was coached by Jennifer Dutko in her second and final season leading the team. The squad featured just two seniors, Angie Klein and Shannen Thomas, but included a talented group of underclassmen who sparked the program to eight consecutive non-losing seasons. The Lady Bulldogs began the year with five wins in their first seven games but went on to lose four straight, eventually finishing with an overall record of 6-7-1.

Softball

Despite having just one senior on the roster in the form of Jamie Schmidt, the 1995 softball season was considered a successful one for the fledgling team and program. The Lady Bulldogs finished 9-9 overall and 4-6 in the South Central Conference under new mentor Kyle Freeman. The season included a win over Edwardsville and a five-game winning streak that ended with a postseason loss to Bunker Hill. The youthful Lady Bulldogs had five players recognized as All-Conference Honorable Mention, including juniors Emily Henry and Heather Kirkwood, sophomore Maria Garbin, and freshmen Susan Fletcher and Becky Roddick. Freeman stayed on as head coach for seven seasons and still holds the program's all-time marks for years of service, wins, and winning percentage.

Track (Boys)

Dave Williams welcomed seniors Jason Foulk and Josh Schuette to the 1995 track team, a squad that placed 3rd in the South Central Conference and 4th at the Macoupin County Meet. Foulk had an outstanding senior year that was capped off with an appearance at State in both the 100 meters and 200 meters.

Volleyball

The 1994 volleyball team welcomed a new coach for the first time in nearly two decades when Kim Murray took over the program for the first of two seasons at the helm. She welcomed three seniors to the team in the form of Jamie Schmidt, Shannen Thomas, and Sara Zuber. Unfortunately, the campaign ended with a losing record, as the Lady Bulldogs finished 10-17 overall and 5-5 in the South Central Conference. Thomas and Zuber capped off their senior seasons in impressive fashion, as both were named All-Area by the *Telegraph*. Additionally, each was named to the All-Conference team, with Zuber taking home 1st Team honors and Thomas being named to the 2nd Team. Junior Andrea Williamson also landed a spot on the squad as an Honorable Mention performer. Finally, Zuber was a member of the All-Tournament 1st Team at the Macoupin County Tournament. After the season, Thomas was named Offensive MVP, while junior Stefanie Kershaw took home Defensive MVP honors.

Class of 1996

Baseball

Seniors Brian Bequette, Charlie Best, Cory Callovini, Jeremy Molinar, Joe Odorizzi, and T.J. Trettenero led coach Larry Caldieraro's baseball team to a solid season in 1996. The club finished 11-7 overall, including 4-5 in the South Central Conference. SHS played .500 baseball for most of the year before winning seven of eight heading into the postseason. Alton Marquette, a team that SHS had defeated earlier in the year, ended Staunton's season in the Regional with a 16-6 rout of the Bulldogs.

While Callovini had an outstanding year for SHS, resulting in All-SCC 1st Team honors, most of the team's production came from underclassmen. Sophomores Ben Frank and Luke Melm, both All-SCC Honorable Mention choices, had outstanding years in their first season at the varsity level. Melm also captured Team MVP honors and the Hitting Award (.458). Junior Steve Moore won the Pitching Award (4-3, 2.87 ERA) in addition to All-Conference 1st Team honors. Moore was also named to the *Telegraph's* All-Area 2nd Team and finished the season as a finalist for the publication's Athlete of the Year award.

Basketball (Boys)

Kevin Gockel began his first full year as SHS basketball coach during the 1995-96 campaign. Though the squad started off slowly (0-5), the Bulldogs finished the regular season with very competitive play down the stretch, eventually bowing out of the Regional with a 69-68 loss to Roxana. The postseason setback left the Dogs with a 9-16 record overall, including 5-5 in the South Central Conference.

Senior Bulldogs included Brian Bequette, Joe Odorizzi (15.7 points, 7.9 rebounds), Shane Semanek, and Todd Wall. At the end of the season, Wall took home Defensive MVP honors, while junior Steve Moore was named Offensive MVP (22.5 points, 7.0 rebounds) and the Free Throw Award winner (85%). Moore (1st Team) and Odorizzi (2nd Team) were both named All-SCC and All-County, and Moore was also a 1st Team All-Area pick by the *Telegraph* and WSMI Radio. At the end of the school year, Moore was a finalist for the *Telegraph's* Athlete of the Year award.

Basketball (Girls)

Coach Larry Kuba's Lady Bulldogs finished the 1995-96 basketball season with a record of 11-11 overall, including 3-7 in the South Central Conference. Coming off a record-breaking season, SHS rode early momentum to a 5-1 start. After stumbling in the middle portion of the schedule, the Lady Bulldogs closed with four straight victories before losing in the Regional to Greenville in overtime (51-48).

Staunton featured a large senior group that included Amber Brinson, Dawn Colley, Tiffany Hemann, Stefanie Kershaw, Marcy Molinar, Amber Taylor, and Pam Wieseman. Brinson and Kershaw shared Defensive MVP honors, Wieseman took home Offensive MVP honors, and Hemann won the Free Throw Award after hitting 75% of her attempts from the line. Wieseman, who averaged 16 points per game, was named 2nd Team All-Conference and 1st Team All-Area by WSMI Radio. Molinar, who pumped in 14.5 points per game, also took home WSMI 1st Team All-Area honors. Joining Wieseman on the All-Conference squad were Honorable

Mention picks Brinson and Kershaw. Upon graduation, Wieseman continued her basketball career at Missouri Baptist University.

Football

Scott Tonsor's second season directing the Staunton football program saw the 1995 Bulldogs bring home a record of 3-6 overall, including 2-3 in the South Central Conference. Despite the record, SHS continued to play competitive football under Tonsor, setting a foundation for successful future seasons. The year began with a 28-14 setback to Hillsboro, but the Bulldogs rebounded with a close win over Greenville (25-18). The next two games were blowouts, with the Dogs coming out on the wrong end of a 38-14 game with Nokomis and the right end of a 46-0 shutout of Litchfield. A close loss to Southwestern (20-13) preceded a tight win over Gillespie (7-0). Unfortunately, the Gillespie win marked Staunton's last victory of the season, as the team ended with three straight losses to Alton Marquette (42-0), Carlinville (62-29), and Hardin Calhoun (23-15). Carlinville won the SCC in 1995 for the third straight season.

Seniors on the team included Charlie Best, Cory Callovini, Mike Callovini, Jason Hebenstreit, Brad Legendre, Jeremy Molinar, Joe Odorizzi, Josh Rantanen, Greg Sievers, and T.J. Trettenero. Callovini was a standout player for the Dogs, serving as the team's lone representative on the All-Conference 1st Team. He also captured 2nd Team All-Area honors by the *Telegraph* and *State Journal-Register*. Molinar, Odorizzi, Rantanen, and junior Greg Wittman took home 2nd Team All-SCC accolades, while Best, Hebenstreit, Legendre, Sievers, and juniors Ryan Machota and Harley Williams garnered Honorable Mention status. After the season, Odorizzi was accepted to the United States Military Academy at West Point based on his academic, athletic, and leadership qualities.

Golf (Boys)

For the first time in six seasons, the 1995 golf team failed to win the South Central Conference Tournament. The Bulldogs instead brought home 2nd place after losing to Alton Marquette by a single stroke. SHS finished 17-4 on the season and qualified for the Sectional Tournament after finishing in 3rd place at the Regional. Seniors Jim Lentz, Pat Schaefer, and Stephen Struebig provided stability for coach Larry Kuba's unit, but the bulk of the contribution came from underclassmen. In particular, Team MVP B.J. Brown, a junior, had an outstanding season. Brown led the team in scoring average (37.2) and captured SCC medalist honors. Additionally, the *Telegraph* tabbed Brown as its Player of the Year for the first of two consecutive seasons. Sophomores Elliot Kolkovich and Brett Tevini also performed at an All-Conference level for SHS. Finally, the *News-Democrat* named Brown (1st Team), junior Brad Rizzi (3rd Team), Kolkovich (3rd Team), and Tevini (3rd Team) to its All-Area squad.

Golf (Girls)

Coach Larry Kuba welcomed one girl, junior Amanda Conroy, to the team for the 1995 golf season. Conroy had a solid year overall, setting the stage for an outstanding senior campaign.

Soccer (Girls)

After initially serving as an assistant coach, Tim Smiddy's first season as head coach of the soccer program saw the team finish 9-4-3 in 1996. Though the mark was broken within a year, the win total was a school record for the young program. Included in the final record was a win over powerhouse Alton Marquette during a stretch that saw the Lady Bulldogs go without a loss for nine games, including a championship at the Metro East Lutheran Shootout. After defeating the host school 1-0, SHS beat Gillespie 4-3 to win the title. The Lady Bulldogs were led by seniors Amber Brinson, Tiffany Hemann, Tracy Straub, Elena Tallman, and Andrea Williamson. Hemann took home Team MVP honors at the conclusion of the season. Williamson later returned to SHS and ran the soccer program for seven years, the longest tenure in program history.

Softball

Kyle Freeman's second season directing the softball program saw the 1996 team finish with a record of 9-10 overall, including 5-5 in the South Central Conference. The Lady Bulldogs enjoyed three separate three-game winning streaks during the season, but the club ended the year on a four-game slide. The team was led by seniors Dawn Colley, Emily Henry, and Heather Kirkwood. Kirkwood moved on to Lewis & Clark Community College where she played two seasons for the Trailblazers. She later returned to SHS and succeeded Freeman as softball coach.

Track (Boys)

Coach Dave Williams' 1996 track team did not include a senior, though the squad still fared well despite being inexperienced. Junior and Team MVP John Masinelli paced the squad, which finished 4th at the South Central Conference Meet and 5th at the Macoupin County Meet. The lone SCC champion for Staunton was sophomore Dustin Bramley in the discus.

Track (Girls)

For the first time in a few years, Staunton High School witnessed female athletes participate in track during the 1996 season. Nearly every competitor was a freshman, and Team MVP Megan Sievers paced the rookie group, which included fellow freshmen Christin Cavoretto, Tara Lorenz, Wendy Machota, Beth Wesbrook, and Nicole Ziglar. Sophomores Marci Kolkovich and Jennifer Snell rounded out the squad, which finished 5th in the South Central Conference and 7th at the Macoupin County Meet. The Lady Bulldogs were coached by Dave Williams.

Volleyball

The 1995 volleyball season represented the second and final one for coach Kim Murray. The Lady Bulldogs were very streaky during the campaign and eventually finished with an overall record of 15-14, including 7-3 in the South Central Conference. After a stretch of seven wins in eight games, with the only loss coming to Carlinville in the Macoupin County Tournament, the Lady Bulldogs turned around and dropped six of seven heading into Regionals. After wins over Livingston and Morrisonville, the season ended with a setback to Raymond Lincolnwood.

Departing with Murray was a deep and talented senior class that included Amber Brinson (Offensive MVP), Kaycia Crosslin, Emily Henry (Defensive MVP), Stefanie Kershaw, Elena Tallman, Pam Wieseman, and Andrea Williamson. Brinson had an outstanding year, taking home 1st Team All-Conference, All-County, and *Telegraph* All-Area honors. Additional All-Conference members were Kershaw (Honorable Mention), Tallman (1st Team), and Williamson (2nd Team), with Williamson also gathering All-County accolades. Upon graduation, Brinson took her talents to Missouri Baptist University.

Class of 1997

Baseball

Coach Larry Caldieraro's 1997 baseball team had a fine season, accumulating a 16-9 overall record. Unfortunately, the team narrowly missed out on a South Central Conference championship after finishing 7-3 in league play. Also, despite taking the #1 seed into Regionals, SHS lost 1-0 on a no-hitter to Litchfield, effectively ending the season. Seniors in the Class of 1997 included Matt Bruhn, Bill Cleveland, Daron Kapp, Aaron Klenke, Ryan Machota, Steve Moore, and Beau Sievers.

The Dogs started out of the gate quickly and eventually put their 13-4 record on the line against Carlinville in the final game of the SCC slate. Unfortunately, a 3-2 upset loss cost SHS a share of the conference title. Additionally, the loss started a three-game slide from which the Bulldogs never recovered. After the season, Moore and Sievers joined juniors Ben Frank and Luke Melm, as well as sophomore Ted Frank, on the All-Conference 1st Team. Additionally, Machota overcame an injury-laden senior year to capture All-SCC Honorable Mention status. At the annual sports banquet, Sievers took home the Hitting Award (.340), while Moore captured the Pitching Award (5-4, 0.79 ERA). After the season, Moore was named to the *Telegraph* All-Area 2nd Team and was a finalist for the publication's Athlete of the Year award. He later returned to his alma mater and coached the baseball team for four years in addition to his similar role with the basketball and soccer programs.

Basketball (Boys)

Nathan Buerkett, Ryan Machota, John Masinelli, Steve Moore, and Beau Sievers comprised the senior class for the 1996-97 basketball season. On paper, the campaign was fairly uneventful, as the Bulldogs finished 13-13 overall and 6-4 in the South Central Conference under coach Kevin Gockel. However, the team played several exciting games, including three overtime contests that resulted in victories for the Bulldogs. The Dogs started the season with five consecutive losses before winning five of seven entering the Macoupin County Tournament. After easily disposing of Northwestern (83-61), the Bulldogs were all but on their way to the championship game after jumping ahead of Carlinville by a score of 24-2 after one quarter of play. However, the Cavaliers chipped away at the Staunton lead and amazingly beat the Bulldogs by a score of 52-46. The Cavaliers moved on to upset Southwestern for the title. After the tough loss, SHS dropped the 3rd place game to Bunker Hill (72-60). Following the tournament, Moore was named 1st Team All-County, while junior Ben Frank was named to the 2nd Team.

In a game at Gillespie late in the season, the Miners, winners of only one game that season, seemingly had the Bulldogs beat. GHS was up by three points and shooting a free throw with only three seconds remaining on the clock. However, after the Miners missed the charity toss, junior Brian Coalson hit perhaps the longest shot in school history. After grabbing the rebound in the lane, Coalson took one dribble and heaved an attempt from the opposite free throw line that somehow connected to send the game into overtime. In the extra period, the Bulldogs pulled away for a 67-62 victory. Interestingly enough, Gillespie was coached by Troy Redfern, who later served as a coach and athletic director at Staunton High School. Further heroics were witnessed on Senior Night against Carlinville, as Frank hit a 3-pointer at the buzzer to send the game into overtime in a contest eventually won by the Bulldogs (60-59). Finally, in the first game of Regionals, junior Sam Miller stole the ball and scored with only seconds remaining to propel the Dogs to a 55-54 win over Roxana. Unfortunately, the season ended in the semifinals of the tournament with a 64-60 setback to eventual champion Greenville.

Midway through the season, a unique opportunity occurred in which Moore was able to shoot in a 3-point competition at halftime of a Chicago Bulls game. The event pitted three boys and three girls from across the state against each other in the contest, which was eventually won by the girls. Back to the local scene, after the season Frank (2nd Team), Masinelli (Honorable Mention), and Moore (1st Team) were named All-SCC, and Moore was also named 1st Team All-Area by the *Telegraph*, *State Journal-Register*, and WSMI Radio. Frank was also named All-Area by the *Telegraph*, garnering Honorable Mention status. At the sports banquet, Masinelli took home Defensive MVP honors, while Moore was named Offensive MVP (21.2 points, 9.7 rebounds) and the Free Throw Award winner (89%). A *Telegraph* Athlete of the Year finalist, Moore finished his career with 1208 points. He later returned to SHS and served as head basketball coach while also spending time in the same capacity with the baseball and soccer programs.

Basketball (Girls)

The 1996-97 basketball team labored to a 4-17 record overall, including 2-8 in the South Central Conference. The Lady Bulldogs defeated Bunker Hill, Carlinville (twice), and Mt. Olive during the season. Seniors and All-Conference Honorable Mention choices Becky Baum and Jacki Fritz did their best to spur the squad, which also included seniors Maria Garbin, Krissy Meyer, and Tiffany Spudich. Team MVP Fritz took home the Free Throw Award (60%) for coach Larry Kuba's team.

Football

Scott Tonsor's 1996 football team accomplished something that had not been done in nineteen seasons, as the Bulldogs made the IHSA Playoffs for just the second time in school history. The Dogs eventually finished with a record of 6-4 overall and 4-1 in the South Central Conference, good for 2nd place behind champion Southwestern.

The postseason berth looked doubtful early in the year, as the team started off with a record of 2-3 after five games. After beginning the season with a 21-0 shutout of Hillsboro, Staunton dropped consecutive games to Greenville (27-6) and Rushville Industry (30-0). After opening SCC play by defeating Litchfield (29-6), the Bulldogs lost a close game to Southwestern (27-24) in what ended up deciding the conference championship. In fact, the SCC football title was the first in school history for Southwestern High School. Staunton ended the regular season with league victories over Gillespie (28-0), Alton Marquette (24-0), and Carlinville (32-18). However, entering the team's Week 9 game at undefeated Hardin Calhoun, the Bulldogs had to pull an upset in order to attain the six wins needed to qualify for the playoffs. In an epic battle, the game went into overtime before SHS emerged with a 33-32 win. Staunton drew a tough opponent in the first round of IHSA Playoffs, as the Bulldogs had to travel to Decatur to take on St. Teresa. The Bulldogs fought hard but were simply outmatched in suffering a 54-8 loss.

Seniors Matt Bruhn, Mike Grabruck, Keith Gregory, Tim Klein, Jarrod Leckrone, Ryan Machota, Josh Marquis, Danny Mosser, Harley Williams, and Greg Wittman led the team into battle during the season. Bruhn (2nd Team), Gregory (1st Team), Leckrone (Honorable Mention), Marquis (Honorable Mention), and Wittman (2nd Team) were each named to the All-Conference squad. Joining the aforementioned players as All-SCC were juniors Dustin Bramley (2nd Team),

Ben Frank (1st Team), Alex Rigoni (1st Team), and Jason Steinmeyer (1st Team), as well as sophomores Brett Herbeck (2nd Team) and Billy Schuette (Honorable Mention). Frank was also named 1st Team All-Area by the *Telegraph* and *State Journal-Register*, while Gregory was a 2nd Team choice by the *Telegraph*. After high school, Gregory continued his football career at Central Methodist University in Fayette, Missouri for two seasons before moving on to Southern Illinois University where he played an additional two years for the Salukis.

Golf (Boys)

The 1996 golf team is considered among the greatest in school history. In addition to winning the Greenville Invitational, the Bulldogs won the program's sixth South Central Conference championship in seven seasons. Furthermore, SHS finished the regular season with a perfect 20-0 record in match play. The Dogs ended the season at the State Tournament, taking home a 5th place trophy for the school. The 5th place finish at State matched the best result in program history, as the 1993 team also finished 5th overall. Due to his team's success, Larry Kuba was named Coach of the Year by the *Telegraph* at the conclusion of the season.

Seniors on the team included B.J. Brown, Daron Kapp, Andy Renner, and Brad Rizzi. Brown and Rizzi teamed up with juniors Denny Conroy, Elliot Kolkovich and Brett Tevini, as well as freshman John Caldieraro, to form the championship squad. Amazingly, each Staunton golfer at the SCC Tournament came away with All-Conference honors. Additionally, Brown (Player of the Year), Kolkovich (1st Team), Tevini (2nd Team), and Caldieraro (2nd Team) were named All-Area by the *Telegraph*. Brown took home 1st Team All-Area honors by the *News-Democrat*, while Rizzi (Honorable Mention), Conroy (Honorable Mention), Kolkovich (2nd Team), Tevini (3rd Team), and Caldieraro (2nd Team) were also honored by the publication. Finally, Brown (1st Team), Kolkovich (2nd Team), Tevini (Honorable Mention), and Caldieraro (3rd Team) were chosen as All-Area performers by the Metro East Golf Coaches Association. The end of the season brought to a close the stellar career of Brown, the Team MVP. After finishing 6th in the state as a sophomore, Brown finished 2nd overall as a senior. After graduation, he continued his golf career for four seasons at Illinois State University.

Golf (Girls)

Senior Amanda Conroy finished out her golf career in outstanding fashion during the 1996 season. Conroy advanced to the Sectional Tournament under the tutelage of Larry Kuba. After the season, she was honored as an All-Area golfer by the *Telegraph* (1st Team), the *News-Democrat* (2nd Team), and the Metro East Golf Coaches Association (2nd Team).

Soccer (Girls)

The 1997 soccer team set a school record for wins, as coach Tim Smiddy's club finished 10-5-2 on the season, including 4-1-1 in the South Central Conference. After beginning the season with a victory, the Lady Bulldogs dropped four straight games. However, the team responded by playing eleven straight contests without a loss before being knocked out of the postseason by Triad (4-0). Seniors Carrie Bivens and Laila Hochmuth provided leadership for a squad that featured Team MVP and *Telegraph* All-Area selection Leslie Bono, a junior. Offensive MVP honors went to sophomore Mickey Schutzenhofer, while Bivens took home the Defensive MVP award. Bivens continued her playing career for three seasons at McKendree University.

Softball

Kyle Freeman's 1997 softball team set a school record for victories in a season, though the mark was shattered the following year. The Lady Bulldogs finished the campaign 12-13 overall, including 6-4 in the South Central Conference, the best league finish in the young program's history. The squad started off hot but closed with eight losses in nine games, with five of those setbacks coming by just one run. Junior standouts Becky Roddick (Hitting Award, .513) and Susan Fletcher (Pitching Award) paced the Lady Bulldogs, while seniors Becky Baum, Jamie Broderick, Maria Garbin, and Tiffany Spudich contributed to the cause.

Track (Boys)

Coach Dave Williams welcomed five seniors to the 1997 track team, including Cory Buffington, Dennis Dawson, Mike Grabruck, Keith Gregory, and John Masinelli. The Bulldogs finished 4th at the South Central Conference Meet and 5th at the Macoupin County Meet. Masinelli, Team MVP for the second straight season, won the SCC championship in the high jump, and he also teamed up with Buffington and juniors Brian Schaefer and Luke Schuette on the 1600 meter relay team that at one time held the school record.

Track (Girls)

Dave Williams welcomed just one athlete to the 1997 track team, as freshman Lisa Phifer was the lone competitor for the Lady Bulldogs. Phifer finished 4th at the South Central Conference Meet in the 400 meters and 5th in the 200 meters. At the Macoupin County Meet, she placed 5th in the 400 meters.

Volleyball

Seniors Jamie Broderick, Kara Meyer, and Krissy Meyer welcomed a new coach to the fold for the 1996 volleyball season, as Becky Pepper served as the program's leader for the first of two seasons at the helm. The club experienced a solid season by finishing 15-11 overall and 7-3 in the South Central Conference. Included in the mark was a run of five straight victories in the middle portion of the schedule, not to mention a three-game winning streak to end the regular season. At the end of the campaign, twin sisters Kara and Krissy Meyer shared Offensive MVP honors, while Broderick was named Defensive MVP.

Class of 1998

Baseball

Despite the success that Staunton baseball has experienced throughout its history, the program never enjoyed a 20-win season. However, that changed in 1998 when coach Larry Caldieraro's squad set a school record for wins by finishing 20-6 overall. Seniors in the Class of 1998 included Brian Coalson, Denny Conroy, Ben Frank, Luke Melm, Alex Rigoni, Jason Steinmeyer, and Brett Tevini.

The season started off very well, as the Bulldogs shot off to a 10-1 record that included wins in the team's first two South Central Conference East games. Unfortunately, the Dogs cooled off a bit, dropping four of their next six SCC East games and eventually finishing 6-4 in league play. However, SHS responded by winning its final four games of the regular season, including a 3-0 shutout of SCC East champion Greenville, a team that went on to take 3rd place at State. Taking a four-game winning streak into the postseason, the Bulldogs easily handled Livingston (11-0), Gillespie (14-4), and Hillsboro (7-2) in taking home the Regional title. At Sectionals, SHS defeated Jacksonville Routt (10-8) to advance to the finals. The game took place on a very windy day, and Staunton hitters took advantage of the conditions, as both Coalson and junior Vinnie Sanvi belted two home runs for the Dogs. However, the biggest hit came in the seventh inning with Staunton trailing 8-6. With the bases loaded and one out, Frank hit a walk-off grand slam to clinch a berth in the Sectional final. Unfortunately, the team's eight-game winning streak and the season itself came to an end with a 3-1 setback to Rochester.

Frank wrapped up an impressive senior year by taking home 1st Team All-Conference and *Telegraph* All-Area honors. He was also named as a finalist for the publication's exclusive Athlete of the Year award for his success in baseball, basketball, and football. Frank was joined on the All-SCCE team by fellow seniors Coalson and Melm. Juniors Scott Billings, Ted Frank, Darren Ott, and Sanvi were also awarded All-Conference distinction. After the season, Frank landed at Missouri University of Science & Technology and competed for the Miners for four years.

Basketball (Boys)

Coach Kevin Gockel and seniors Brian Coalson, Ben Frank, Sam Miller, and Luke Schuette entered the 1997-98 basketball season as new members of the South Central Conference East. The SCC East was traditionally much tougher than the SCC West in most sports, but especially in basketball. The inaugural season of league play highlighted the discrepancy, as the Dogs finished just 3-7 in the SCC East, yet 7-1 in crossover games against the SCC West. Overall, with a record of 12-12, the Bulldogs finished at .500 for the second straight year.

Coalson (15.7 points, 7.6 rebounds), Frank (18.9 points), and Miller (15.2 points) formed one of the best scoring trios in school history. Though the team finished 3rd at the Macoupin County Tournament, Coalson turned in one of the most memorable performances in school history. In three games that included a victory over Northwestern (81-61), a loss to Virden (84-75), and a win over Southwestern (77-61), Coalson averaged 27 points and 11 rebounds in capturing 1st Team All-County honors, and he was also a member of the All-SCCE 2nd Team. In addition to being a 1st Team All-Conference and All-County selection, Frank was also a *Telegraph* 2nd Team All-Area performer. After the school year, he was named a finalist for the publication's Athlete of the Year award, cementing his place as one of the best all-around athletes in the area. Miller, a prolific 3-point shooter (57 makes in twenty games played) captured 2nd Team All-County honors. At the annual sports banquet, Frank was named Offensive MVP, and he shared Defensive MVP honors with Miller. Meanwhile, junior Ted Frank won the Free Throw Award by making 71% of his attempts from the charity stripe.

Basketball (Girls)

The 1997-98 basketball team struggled in its first year in the South Central Conference East, finishing 0-10 in division play. Overall, coach Larry Kuba's Lady Bulldogs finished 4-17 for the second consecutive season. Much like the previous campaign, wins on the year came at the expense of Bunker Hill, Carlinville, and Mt. Olive (twice). Seniors Leslie Bono and

Meaghan Calcari led a team that featured juniors Beth Moore (2nd Team All-County) and Megan Sievers (Free Throw Award) and sophomore Christie Partridge (All-SCCE Honorable Mention).

Football

The 1997 football season was quite simply one of the finest in school history. Not only did the Bulldogs win the program's first conference championship in twenty-six years, but they also tied a school record for wins with a 10-1 mark overall. Furthermore, by finishing undefeated (9-0) in the regular season, the Dogs turned in the program's fifth such season on record.

Coach Scott Tonsor returned several starters from the previous year's playoff team, and thus the Bulldogs got out of the gate quickly, easily disposing of Gillespie (28-0) and Carlinville (36-6) to begin the year. It is worth noting that, due to the new SCC alignment, the games against Carlinville and Gillespie were non-conference affairs for the first time since the 1920s. Week 3 saw the Dogs battle with Southwestern, the eventual SCC West champion. The game was close throughout, but eventually SHS hung on for a 20-13 victory over the Piasa Birds in a matchup between division champions. Staunton began SCC East play with lopsided wins over Hillsboro (41-7) and Litchfield (54-6) before winning closer games against Pana (28-9), Greenville (35-21), and Vandalia (28-13) to finish 5-0 in league action. Week 9 saw SHS wrap up its fifth undefeated regular season in school history with a 36-14 victory over Alton Marquette.

In that era, the IHSA Playoffs consisted of six classes, and Staunton's enrollment usually bordered on the dividing line between Class 2A and Class 3A. Unfortunately for SHS, the Bulldogs were placed in the much tougher Class 3A in 1997. Thus, despite taking a #1 seed into the postseason, the Dogs had a tough road ahead of them. Week 10 began the postseason with Staunton hosting its first playoff game in school history, as the Bridgeport Red Hill Salukis came to town. The last time the two schools met in any sport was during the 1993 basketball season when the Dogs, en route to a state title, defeated the Salukis in one of the greatest games in Illinois history. The two schools also conducted a tough battle on the gridiron, and SHS came out on top by a score of 13-7. The win sent the Bulldogs to DuQuoin for the second round of the playoffs. The Indians have one of the best football traditions in Illinois and, in fact, own a record for qualifying for the postseason twenty-seven straight times. Thus, despite being the top seed, Staunton was arguably a slight underdog in the game. The two teams battled to a 7-7 tie at the half, but a late touchdown by the Indians proved to be the difference in a 14-7 victory.

The playoff loss meant the end of high school football for seniors Dustin Bramley, Cory Buse, Ben Frank, John Lentz, Eric Lievers, Luke Melm, Alex Rigoni, Luke Schuette, Scott Skertich, and Jason Steinmeyer. Many of the seniors were awarded All-Conference honors, as Bramley, Frank, Melm, Rigoni, Schuette, and Steinmeyer all took home 1st Team accolades. Joining them on the All-SCCE 1st Team were juniors Ted Frank, Brett Herbeck, and Billy Schuette, while Nathan Sievers was awarded Honorable Mention status. The *Telegraph* honored Tonsor as its Coach of the Year, and Ben Frank was a finalist for the publication's Athlete of the Year award at the end of the school year. Ben Frank also made the *Telegraph's* 1st Team All-Area football team, as did Rigoni and Steinmeyer. Fullback Billy Schuette rushed for 1371 yards on the season, one of the highest single-season totals in school history. For his efforts, he was named 2nd Team All-Area. Finally, Steinmeyer was recognized as an All-State football player by the Illinois High School Football Coaches Association, and he continued his career at Washington University. Rigoni also continued his football career, playing one season at Missouri University of Science & Technology.

Golf (Boys)

Larry Kuba's 1997 golf squad enjoyed another outstanding regular season, finishing 17-1 in match play and repeating as South Central Conference champions. The team finished 2nd at the Regional Tournament, thus advancing to Sectionals for the third straight season. Senior golfers included Denny Conroy, Mike Kellebrew, Elliot Kolkovich, Brett Tevini, and Brandon Young. Kolkovich shared Team MVP honors with sophomore John Caldieraro. As stated, the squad won the SCC, and Kolkovich, Young, and Caldieraro each earned All-Conference honors. Each was also named to the *Telegraph's* All-Area squad, as Kolkovich (2nd Team), Young (Honorable Mention), and Caldieraro (1st Team) joined Tevini (Honorable Mention) in garnering recognition. Kolkovich (2nd Team), Tevini (Honorable Mention), Young (3rd Team), and Caldieraro (2nd Team) were also honored by the Metro East Golf Coaches Association as All-Area selections.

Soccer (Girls)

In his last season directing the program, Tim Smiddy led the 1998 soccer team to an overall record of 8-8-1, including 7-3-1 in the South Central Conference. During the year, the Lady Bulldogs emerged as champions of the Metro East Lutheran Shootout. After disposing of Columbia (2-1), SHS faced off against the host team and defeated the Knights (2-0) to capture the title. The team was better than the overall record indicated, as the Lady Bulldogs dropped close matchups to powerhouse programs Alton Marquette, Chatham Glenwood, Edwardsville, Rochester, and Triad. Senior soccer players included Jamie Banovz, Leslie Bono, Meghan Calcari, Tara Semanek, Crista Straub, and Rachel Streeb. Bono (1st Team), Calcari (2nd Team), Straub (2nd Team), and Streeb (2nd Team) captured All-Conference honors, and they were joined by juniors Kristi Brown (Honorable Mention) and Mickey Schutzenhofer (1st Team). At the sports banquet, Bono took home the Team MVP award.

Softball

The 1998 softball season was by far the best in school history. By finishing the year 16-3, the Lady Bulldogs and coach Kyle Freeman set a school record for wins. Furthermore, by finishing a perfect 8-0 in the South Central Conference East, SHS captured its only championship of any sort in the softball program's history. The team's losses were to Carrollton (13-4) and Bunker Hill (twice by the score of 6-4). Unfortunately, the second loss to Bunker Hill ended Staunton's season in the Regional.

The Lady Bulldogs were led by seniors Janey Best, Susan Fletcher, Becky Lockhart, and Becky Roddick. Best (1st Team), Fletcher (Honorable Mention), and Roddick (1st Team) were each named to the All-Conference squad, as were juniors Laura Bruhn (1st Team), Stacey Fletcher (1st Team), and freshman Natalie Laurent (1st Team). Susan Fletcher won the Pitching Award (5-3, 1.65 ERA), while Laurent (.469), Best (.442), and Stacey Fletcher (.413) led the team offensively.

Track (Boys)

Coach Scott Tonsor took over the track program for the 1998 season, his first of two years on the job. He welcomed six seniors to the team in the form of Dustin Bramley, Zach Cooper, John Jascur, John Lentz, Josh Meade, and Sam Miller. Bramley, the team's top point scorer, captured gold in the shot put at the Macoupin County Meet. The squad finished 8th at the South Central Conference Meet.

Volleyball

Coach Becky Pepper began her final volleyball campaign by leading the program to its second straight 15-11 season in 1997, which included a 6-4 finish in the South Central Conference East. Coach Pepper's squad included seniors Leslie Bono, Meaghan Calcari, Malinda Eller, Susan Fletcher, Tara Semanek, Jennifer Snell, and Beth Zuber.

Although the transition to the SCC East was not an easy one, the Lady Bulldogs did accomplish quite a feat by knocking off league champion Pana in one of the regular season meetings. The Lady Bulldogs rode the momentum of that matchup into the Macoupin County Tournament, defeating Southwestern and Mt. Olive before losing to Carlinville. SHS responded with a victory over Virden to capture 3rd place at the event. At County, Bono and sophomore Katie Bequette were chosen as 1st Team members of the All-Tournament team. Bono (1st Team) and Bequette (2nd Team) were also named All-Conference, as were Eller (Honorable Mention) and sophomore Christie Partridge (2nd Team). After the season, Bono was chosen as the team's Offensive MVP, while Bequette took home Defensive MVP honors.

Class of 1999

Baseball

Although Larry Caldieraro's 1999 baseball team did not experience postseason success, the club is still considered as one of the best in school history. SHS finished the year with a record of 18-5, including 7-2 in the South Central Conference East. The Bulldogs returned several key contributors from the previous season's record-setting squad, and they used that experience to shoot off to a 7-0 start to begin the year. After dropping both games of a doubleheader to Bethalto Civic Memorial, the Bulldogs reeled off six more wins before matching up against Greenville, a perennial SCC East contender. Unfortunately, SHS dropped the contest by a score of 6-5 and later in the season once again lost to the Comets by just one run (8-7). In fact, all five of Staunton's losses came by just one run, as SHS outscored opponents by a tally of 208-90 on the year. Unfortunately, the season ended in heartbreaking fashion, as the top-seeded Bulldogs dropped a Regional semifinal matchup to Carlinville by a score of 10-9.

The loss ended the high school baseball careers of a very talented group of seniors, including Scott Billings, Ted Frank, Brett Herbeck, Terry Murphy, Darren Ott, Mike Pirok, Vinnie Sanvi, Billy Schuette, and Mike Tranter. Billings, Frank, Herbeck, Murphy, Ott, and Sanvi were each be named to the All-Conference 1st Team, and Ott (2nd Team) and Sanvi (1st Team) were also *Telegraph* All-Area performers. Three individuals continued their careers after high school. Tranter went on to play four seasons at Rose-Hulman Institute of Technology. Ott, the recipient of the team's Pitching Award (7-2, 2.85 ERA), moved on to McKendree University where he was an All-Conference performer for the Bearcats. Meanwhile, Sanvi completed four seasons at Missouri University of Science & Technology. Sanvi, the Team MVP and Hitting Award winner, finished his senior year in fine fashion, posting unbelievable offensive numbers (.508, 14 HR, 38 RBI). Although records are incomplete, Sanvi's single-season and career offensive numbers are likely among the best in school history.

Classes of 1990 - 1999

Basketball (Boys)

Having graduated three prolific scorers from the previous season, the 1998-99 basketball team featured a young squad with only two seniors, Ted Frank and Mike Tranter. However, the team was loaded with underclass talent, including junior Aaron Hainaut (13.9 points) and sophomores Zack Rigoni (Offensive MVP, Free Throw Award at 83%) and Mark Sievers (Defensive MVP). Coach Kevin Gockel's squad eventually finished the year with a record of 10-17 overall, including 4-6 in the South Central Conference East. A bright spot in the season came during and after the Macoupin County Tournament. After a loss in the first round, SHS went on to win four of its next five games. After the season, Frank was named All-Conference Honorable Mention, while Rigoni took home 2nd Team honors. Both were named to the All-County 2nd Team.

Basketball (Girls)

Larry Kuba's 1998-99 basketball team made significant strides from the previous two seasons. The Lady Bulldogs finished the year 12-14 overall and 5-5 in the South Central East. The .500 record in SCC East play tied for the program's best finish since the league split into two divisions. Although SHS struggled in the early portion of the schedule, the team won four of five games down the stretch before falling in the Regional.

The Staunton roster consisted of three seniors, as Beth Moore, Robyn Painter, and Megan Sievers provided leadership for the squad. A strong group of juniors that included Katie Bequette, Elaine Imhoff, and Christie Partridge provided most of the firepower for the Lady Bulldogs. Partridge, in particular, had an outstanding season, taking home 1st Team All-Conference and All-County honors. Painter was also a 2nd Team All-County selection and, along with Imhoff, was named All-SCCE Honorable Mention. Bequette was also named All-Conference, taking home 2nd Team honors. At the annual sports banquet, Bequette and Imhoff shared Defensive MVP honors, while Partridge was named Offensive MVP and the Free Throw Award winner (65%).

Bowling (Girls)

For the first time in school history, SHS offered bowling for students beginning in 1998-99. The first season featured only female participants, though a boy's team was introduced the following year. Sarah Gregory served as the lone senior for the Lady Bulldogs in their inaugural season, while junior Jessica Cochran sported the highest average for a team that finished 8-4 under coach Dave Williams. Additional members of the historic team were juniors Lacey Albrecht, Heather Colley, Sarah Fritz, Elisabeth Johnson, and Christy Kilduff, sophomores Heidi Hubert, Stacee Meyer, and Jessica Straub, and freshmen Renee Henson, Danielle Stein, and Erin Wilhoit.

Football

Coming off one of the greatest campaigns in school history, the 1998 football team looked to continue the program's run of successful seasons. While coach Scott Tonsor's team did not match the previous year's win total, the Dogs did advance to the second round of the IHSA Playoffs for the second straight season. Overall, the Bulldogs finished 7-4 on the year, including 3-2 in the South Central Conference East.

The season began in fine fashion, as the Dogs ran their streak of consecutive regular season wins to fifteen with victories over Gillespie (41-6) and Carlinville (25-6). Unfortunately, eventual SCC West champion Southwestern ended the Staunton's streak with a 41-12 thrashing of the Bulldogs. SHS rebounded well from the defeat and began SCC East play by easily defeating Hillsboro (42-12) and Litchfield (50-12). Regrettably, any aspirations for back-to-back SCC East titles ended with a 38-6 loss to eventual champion Pana. Another defeat ensued, this time to Greenville by a score of 21-12. Victories over Vandalia (50-0) and Alton Marquette (29-12) wrapped up a successful regular season.

Having qualified for postseason play for the third consecutive season, SHS was experienced enough to handle being an underdog on the road in the first round of the IHSA Playoffs. The LeRoy Panthers, state champions two years prior, came into the contest with a record of 8-1. However, SHS played disciplined football and eventually came away with a 19-16 upset. Unfortunately, the season ended the very next week when SHS hosted and lost to Stillman Valley by a score of 27-15. The Cardinals advanced on to the state semifinals before bowing out at 11-2. However, the stage was set for one of the best programs in Illinois, as Stillman Valley went on to win back-to-back state titles and eventually secured championships in three of the following five seasons.

The Bulldogs were led onto the field in 1998 by seniors Tyler Atwood, Ted Frank, Brett Herbeck, Ed Hirschl, Tim Kershaw, Brett Luster, Bryan Ondes, Vinnie Sanvi, Billy Schuette, and Nathan Sievers. Herbeck, the team's Defensive MVP, was selected as All-State Honorable Mention by the Illinois High School Football Coaches Association. He eventually moved on to play for Augustana College for two seasons. Meanwhile, Schuette capped off a brilliant rushing career, finishing with 1247 yards on the season. Though exact totals are unknown, with nearly 3400 yards rushing, Schuette is likely near the top of the school's all-time yardage list. When the All-Conference team was announced, Frank, Herbeck, Luster, Sanvi, and Schuette were each honored by SCC East coaches.

Golf (Boys)

The 1998 golf team finished the season with a 17-2 record in match play. More importantly, the Bulldogs captured the program's eighth South Central Conference title in nine years, one of the greatest runs in SHS sports history. Though coach Larry Kuba's team featured just one senior in the form of Mike Pirok, the Dogs were stacked with younger talent, including junior and Team MVP John Caldieraro. Not only did Caldieraro take home medalist honors at the SCC Tournament, but he was also named to the Metro East Golf Coaches Association 1st Team All-Area. Freshmen Ryan Brown and Mark Pirok were also All-Conference performers, while sophomores Andrew Caldieraro (2nd Team) and Mike Rizzi (3rd Team) were named MEGCA All-Area.

Soccer (Girls)

Coach Rob Werden took over the soccer program for the 1999 season, his first of four years at the helm. Werden welcomed a solid senior class that included Kristi Brown, Christin Cavoretto, Jeanie DeVries, Robyn Painter, Mickey Schutzenhofer, and Megan Sievers. The Lady Bulldogs proved to be a streaky team, as they put together three-game winning streaks on three separate occasions. The Lady Bulldogs finished with an overall record of 9-7-2, including 7-3-2 in the South Central Conference. The league mark was good for a 2nd place finish, the best in the program's history.

Arguably one of the best players in program history, Schutzenhofer was a 1st Team All-Area pick by the *Telegraph*. A four-year letter winner, she was also named Team MVP at the conclusion of the season. Schutzenhofer moved on to McKendree University and played four seasons for the Bearcats. Painter also continued her soccer career at the collegiate level, competing for one season at Eastern Illinois University.

Softball

Kyle Freeman's 1999 softball team struggled early in the season but caught fire late by winning five straight games and seven of nine before falling to Hillsboro (2-0) in the Regional. Overall, the Lady Bulldogs finished with a record of 9-9, including a 5-3 mark in the South Central Conference East. Seniors Laura Bruhn, Stacey Fletcher, Wendy Machota, Beth Moore, and Heather Washburn provided leadership for the team. Fletcher and Moore had outstanding seasons for the Lady Bulldogs, and each was named to the All-SCCE 1st Team. Moore won the team's Hitting Award, while Fletcher captured the Pitching Award. One of the best players to ever compete for the program, Fletcher continued her career for four seasons at Missouri University of Science & Technology.

Track (Boys)

Scott Tonsor welcomed just one senior to the track team in 1999, as Ed Hirschl provided leadership for the squad. Though the Bulldogs had solid depth, the team faltered to a last place finish at the South Central Conference Meet. However, two juniors provided a spark for the Dogs, as Aaron Hainaut captured gold in the discus at the Macoupin County Meet, and distance runner Michael Williams led the team in points scored.

Volleyball

The volleyball program welcomed its fourth coach in six years when Don Schaefer took over the program in 1998. Schaefer welcomed seniors Laura Bruhn, Christin Cavoretto, Robyn Painter, and Megan Sievers to a squad that eventually finished 16-9 overall, including 6-4 in the South Central Conference East. The Lady Bulldogs got off to a blistering start by beginning the year with five straight wins. Though the team did not capture a championship during the campaign, the Lady Bulldogs did take home 2nd place in the SCC East, Macoupin County Tournament, and Regional Tournament. Katie Bequette, a junior standout, captured Team MVP honors for SHS and also took home 1st Team All-Conference and All-County accolades. Christie Partridge, also a junior, was named to the All-SCCE 2nd Team and was a 1st Team All-County selection. Finally, Painter took home 2nd Team All-Conference honors at the conclusion of the season.

CHAPTER 10

Classes of 2000 – 2009

Overview

The decade of the 2000s saw SHS add four new programs to its menu of sports offerings, as boy's bowling, boy's soccer, and boy's and girl's cross country were sanctioned by the district. While the female cross country team experienced success right away, the other three sports were less fortunate. First, due to cost considerations, bowling was discontinued following the 2002-03 season. Although boy's soccer has generally enjoyed high player turnout, the program has struggled from a competitive standpoint, experiencing just two winning seasons in its history. Finally, although various individuals have experienced success, the boy's cross country program has yet to field a full team since its reintroduction in 2006.

Much like the fledgling programs at the school, nearly every established activity also struggled during the 2000s, making it one of the worst sporting decades in SHS history. There were few positive moments during the era, as baseball endured ten straight losing seasons, softball posted just one winning campaign, and boy's basketball, girl's basketball, and football enjoyed just two winning years each. The volleyball team did have three winning seasons but, given the historical success of that sport at SHS, the 2000s were considered a disappointment for the program. While girl's soccer and boy's track were much more successful than the aforementioned programs, by far the best sport of the decade was girl's golf. Since its inception as a program, girl's golf has only suffered one losing season and holds the highest historic winning percentage of any sport in the school. Although the boy's golf program mostly struggled during the decade, Ryan Brown became just the second individual state champion at SHS, as he captured a share of the title at the 2001 IHSA State Tournament in a rain-shortened event.

Although there were no changes to the South Central Conference during the 2000s, during the decade the Staunton Board of Education voted to leave the SCC for the Prairie State Conference (PSC). While the move was supported by the school board, administration, and coaches in the district, it was a controversial decision in the community. However, the school's time in the new league was limited, as the Bulldogs switched back to a revamped SCC after just three years in the PSC. Finally, a noteworthy development occurred in 2004-05, as the Staunton school district annexed the Livingston school district in a move that was supported overwhelmingly by voters in both communities.

Class of 2000

Baseball

Having graduated an excellent group of players from the previous season, coach Larry Caldieraro's 2000 baseball team found itself in rebuilding mode. With just one senior, Joe Klein, on the roster, the Dogs were a youthful squad looking to gain experience. SHS played solid baseball early, starting off the season by splitting its first eight games. Unfortunately, just one win in the next ten games led to a record of 8-16 overall and 2-7 in the South Central Conference East. Junior Larry Senaldi had an excellent season, taking home Team MVP honors after leading the Dogs at the plate (.358 batting average) and on the mound (1.96 ERA). Senaldi was rewarded for his efforts with a spot on the All-SCCE 1st Team.

Basketball (Boys)

Kevin Gockel's 1999-2000 basketball team was a youthful squad led by junior Zack Rigoni. A 1st Team All-Conference selection, Rigoni was also named to the All-County 2nd Team. Additionally, he received Honorable Mention All-Area from the *State Journal-Register* after leading the Bulldogs in scoring (12.6) and winning the team's Free Throw Award (80%). Fellow junior Mark Sievers was an All-SCCE Honorable Mention pick for a team that included seniors Aaron Hainaut, Dave Hirschl, and Mike Popovich. After playing competitive basketball early in the season, the Bulldogs faltered down the stretch, ending the year with a five-game losing streak. SHS eventually finished with a record of 9-18 overall, including 5-5 in the South Central Conference East.

Basketball (Girls)

After starting out the season with a 6-2 record, coach Larry Kuba's 1999-2000 basketball team finished the year with a respectable 11-15 mark but stumbled to a 1-9 in the South Central Conference East. The roster included just two seniors, but they were standouts in the form of Katie Bequette and Christie Partridge. Bequette, the team's Defensive MVP, was an Honorable Mention All-SCCE selection. Partridge, the team's Free Throw Award winner, was a 2nd Team All-Conference pick. Partridge also captured 1st Team All-County honors at the Macoupin County Tournament, and after the season she moved on to Blackburn College to play basketball for one season before switching to volleyball.

Bowling (Boys)

Though girls in the district had already been competing in bowling for one season, the 1999-2000 school year was the first for a boy's bowling team at SHS. Coach Dave Williams welcomed a young squad that had no seniors on the roster. However, freshman Nick Jones had an outstanding campaign, leading the Bulldogs in scoring average. SHS finished the inaugural season with a 3-9 record overall.

Bowling (Girls)

The 1999-2000 bowling team enjoyed a successful season under the direction of Dave Williams. The Lady Bulldogs finished the year with a record of 9-2-1 behind the performance of seniors Jessica Cochran, Heather Colley, Sarah Fritz, and Christy Kilduff. Cochran sported the team's highest scoring average for the second consecutive season.

Cross Country (Boys)

Though SHS did not officially field a cross country team, senior Michael Williams participated in the sport as an individual during the 1999 season. Not only did he advance to the Sectional Meet, but Williams also turned in one of the top times at the South Central Conference Meet, thus earning him All-Conference honors. He continued his cross country career at Oral Roberts University. While there, he also participated in track for the school.

Classes of 2000 - 2009

Football

After making the playoffs for three consecutive seasons, the youthful 1999 football team took a small step back by finishing 4-5 overall, including 2-3 in the South Central Conference East. Although the season started off in fine fashion with a shutout of Carlinville (26-0), the Dogs dropped three straight games to East Alton-Wood River (34-21), Gillespie (43-12), and Hillsboro (28-26). The loss to the Hiltoppers was especially heartbreaking since Hillsboro went on to win the SCC East that season. Meanwhile, Southwestern captured the SCC West for its fourth title in as many years. The Dogs got back on the winning track with a Week 5 shutout of Litchfield (35-0), but Pana ended Staunton's postseason aspirations with a 28-6 victory over SHS. The Bulldogs responded with strong play in wins over Greenville (27-13) and Vandalia (44-6). However, a tough loss to Roxana (20-13) ended the campaign.

Coach Scott Tonsor fielded a fairly young team comprised mostly of juniors, as Jason Dugger, Aaron Hainaut, and Mike Popovich were the only seniors to suit up for Staunton that season. Five underclassmen were 1st Team All-SCCE choices, including juniors Danny Feldmann, Cory McCunney (Defensive MVP), Lance Semanek, Mark Sievers, and sophomore Tyler Washburn. Junior Brandon Fletcher was an Honorable Mention selection, as were Hainaut and Popovich. Additionally, Feldmann and Semanek were both honored with 2nd Team All-Area status by the *Telegraph*. After the season, Semanek was chosen All-State Honorable Mention by the Illinois High School Football Coaches Association.

Golf (Boys)

Larry Kuba's 1999 golf team once again had an outstanding season, finishing 20-3-1 overall, with two of the team's three losses coming at the hands of large school powers Edwardsville and O'Fallon. The record wrapped up a ten-year period that saw SHS golf win nearly 90% of its matches, as the program compiled a 179-25-1 mark overall, not to mention tremendous success in conference and postseason tournaments. The 1999 team did qualify for the Sectional Tournament at the end of the season after finishing 4th at the Regional. However, a 3rd place finish at the South Central Conference Tournament ended a run of eight titles in the previous nine years.

The Bulldogs were led by seniors John Caldieraro and Ben Clark in 1999. Caldieraro capped off his career in fine fashion by capturing All-Conference accolades for the fourth consecutive season. He was also a Metro East Golf Coaches Association 1st Team All-Area performer, and the team's low scorer also captured medalist honors at the Greenville Invitational. Sophomore Ryan Brown joined Caldieraro on the All-Conference team and was a 2nd Team MEGCA selection. Finally, junior Andrew Caldieraro was named to the MEGCA 3rd Team.

Soccer (Boys)

Soccer was offered to males at Staunton High School beginning in 1999. Though the inaugural season produced just a 4-12 record overall, including 1-7 in the South Central Conference, the program made big strides under coach Tim Smiddy. The Dogs were led by seniors Dave Hirschl, Joe Klein, G.T. Prante, and Ian Schaefer. Klein took home Team MVP honors and was named to the All-SCC 1st Team. Meanwhile, Prante was listed on the All-Conference 2nd Team, and Hirschl took home Honorable Mention status. Upon graduation, Schaefer continued his career at Lewis & Clark Community College for one season.

Soccer (Girls)

Rob Werden's second season leading the soccer program saw the 2000 team finish 8-8-5 overall and 4-3-1 in the South Central Conference. The Lady Bulldogs were led by seniors Heather Colley, Lisa Phifer, Stephanie Stoverink, and Amanda Williamson. Stoverink was named to the 2nd Team All-Conference squad, and she also took home Offensive MVP honors, while junior Amber Watters and sophomore Jennifer Wyatt shared the Defensive MVP award. Additional All-SCC performers included sophomores Melissa Newbold (2nd Team) and Danielle Stein (Honorable Mention) and freshman Bethany Stoverink (Honorable Mention).

Softball

Kyle Freeman's 2000 softball team recorded an overall mark of 9-16, including 4-4 in the South Central Conference East. After beginning the year by splitting its first two games, SHS went 2-13 in its next fifteen contests. However, the Lady Bulldogs caught fire late, finishing with six wins in their final seven games before losing to Alton Marquette in the postseason. Beth Wieseman, the lone senior on the team, was a 1st Team All-Conference selection, as was junior Natalie Laurent. Additionally, Laurent earned the team's Hitting Award and Pitching Award for her stellar performance during the season.

Track (Boys)

Seniors Aaron Hainaut, Mike Popovich, and Michael Williams provided leadership for the 2000 track team. Though the Bulldogs finished in 9th place at the South Central Conference Meet, Williams captured gold in the 1600 meters. At the Macoupin County Meet, Hainaut took 1st place in the discus. Hainaut also won his event at the Sectional, and he was joined at State by Williams (1600 meters) and sophomore Craig Phifer (800 meters). At the sports banquet, Hainaut and Williams shared Team MVP honors. The Bulldogs were coached by Dave Williams. Michael Williams, Dave's son, continued his track career at Oral Roberts University where he also ran cross country for the Golden Eagles.

Volleyball

The 1999 volleyball team had an outstanding year and nearly matched the school record for victories in a season along the way. Coach Don Schaefer's squad ended up 27-6 overall against a very difficult schedule, and the Lady Bulldogs also finished 8-2 in the South Central Conference East. The conference record was good for a share of the league crown, the program's last SCC title. However, the Lady Bulldogs did not settle for just one championship in 1999, as the club also secured titles at both the Macoupin County and Regional tournaments. Unfortunately, the magical season ended in the Sectionals with a loss to traditional powerhouse Breese Central.

The Lady Bulldogs featured senior standouts Katie Bequette and Christie Partridge. Both Bequette (1st Team) and Partridge (2nd Team) were *Telegraph* All-Area performers, while Schaefer took home the publication's Coach of the Year award. Both seniors also captured All-Conference and All-County 1st Team accolades, while juniors Andrea Snell and Leticia Tevini were named 2nd Team All-SCCE. Bequette was chosen as the team's Offensive MVP, and Partridge took home Defensive MVP honors. They were joined in the senior class by Lisa Phifer and Becky Eller. Upon graduation, Bequette competed for four seasons at Elmhurst College. Meanwhile, Partridge enrolled at Blackburn College where she played three years of volleyball in addition to one season of basketball.

Classes of 2000 - 2009

Class of 2001

Baseball

Larry Caldieraro welcomed back a large group of seniors for the 2001 baseball season, including R.C. Belair, Mike Coalson, Brandon Fletcher, John Moore, Donny Nicholas, Mike Rizzi, Lance Semanek, and Larry Senaldi. Unfortunately, the squad struggled throughout most of the year, ending with a record of 9-22 overall, including 2-8 in the South Central Conference East. The Bulldogs started off a respectable 4-5 early in the schedule but faltered to just two wins in their next sixteen games. Fletcher (Team MVP), Moore, Rizzi (Hitting Award), and Senaldi were each honored with All-Conference accolades after the season. Meanwhile, Coalson took his talents to Maryville University in St. Louis and competed for the Saints for four seasons.

Basketball (Boys)

With seven straight non-winning seasons since the 1993 state championship team, the Staunton basketball program looked to rebound during the 2000-01 season with an excellent group of seniors leading the way. The Class of 2001 was one of the deepest and most athletic groups in program history. Included in the mix were Mike Coalson, Chad Dugger, Danny Feldmann, Joe Miller, Zack Rigoni, Mike Rizzi, and Mark Sievers. The Bulldogs were coached by Kevin Gockel.

The Dogs started off the season just 1-3 but quickly rebounded and gained momentum heading into the Macoupin County Tournament. At County, SHS defeated Southwestern (71-59), Gillespie (60-51), and Carlinville (62-47) to win the tournament championship. The squad stayed hot, eventually winning ten of eleven heading into postseason play. The only loss in that span came to Pana, a team that went on to finish 2nd at State that season. However, on the last night of the regular season, SHS avenged the Pana defeat with a 66-63 victory over the Panthers. The Bulldogs entered the difficult Hillsboro Regional as the #3 seed. After defeating Mt. Olive (81-25) in the opening round, the Bulldogs played an instant classic against Litchfield, winning 94-91 in double overtime. The victory placed SHS in the Regional final against Hillsboro, a team that had defeated top-seeded Gillespie earlier in the week. The Bulldogs defeated Hillsboro for the third time on the season by a score of 76-64, capturing the program's eighth Regional title. Unfortunately, SHS fell to Rochester by a score of 94-83 in the Sectional semifinal, effectively ending the campaign at 22-9, including 8-2 in the South Central Conference East. The league record represents the best finish for the program in conference play since the 1992-93 season.

Rigoni capped off an excellent career by leading the team in scoring with 17.6 points per game. He ended his career with 1070 points, one of the highest totals in school history. For his accomplishments, Rigoni was named 1st Team All-SCCE, County MVP, *Telegraph* Player of the Year, and All-Area by the *State Journal-Register* (1st Team), WSMI Radio (1st Team), and the *Post-Dispatch* (Honorable Mention). The standout also took home the team's Offensive MVP and Free Throw Award (81%). Adding to his list of accomplishments, during the season Rigoni was selected as one of six student-athletes (three boys, three girls) from across the state to shoot 3-pointers at halftime of a Chicago Bulls game. Junior and Defensive MVP Craig Phifer led the team in rebounding (6.6) and was a 2nd Team All-Conference and 1st Team All-County selection. Dugger and Sievers were both named Honorable Mention All-SCCE, and Dugger (11.4 points) also took home 2nd Team All-County honors. Miller, an excellent all-around player for the team, continued his career at Lewis & Clark Community College for two seasons before playing two additional years at the University of Illinois-Springfield.

Basketball (Girls)

After more than two decades leading the basketball team, coach Larry Kuba retired after the 2000-01 season with 192 victories, by far the most in program history. Leaving with him were seniors Carrie Frank, Lamanda Heltsley, Natalie Laurent, Kristina Schmidt, and Amber Watters. Kuba's last season at the helm produced a record of 7-20 overall and 1-9 in the South Central Conference East. After beginning the year a respectable 4-6, SHS suffered through a 3-14 finish. Laurent and sophomore Heather Caldieraro shared Team MVP honors, and each was also named 2nd Team All-Conference. Caldieraro was a 1st Team All-County selection, and she took home the Free Throw Award with a 68% clip from the charity stripe.

Bowling (Boys)

Coach Dave Williams and senior Nathan Brashears led the 2000-01 bowling team to a 4-7 record overall. Sophomore Nick Jones paced the team with a 191 average.

Bowling (Girls)

Senior Jessica Straub and junior Danielle Stein led the 2000-01 bowling team to a 5-8 record on the season. Stein paced the Lady Bulldogs with a 152 scoring average. The team was coached by Dave Williams.

Football

Scott Tonsor's 2000 football team was a senior-laden squad that produced a South Central Conference East championship and advanced to the second round of the Playoffs. With most of the seniors starting both ways, amazingly, each position on both sides of the ball was filled by Class of 2001 graduates. The outstanding group included Aaron Beisner, R.C. Belair, Nathan Brashears, Chad Dugger, Danny Feldmann, Brandon Fletcher, Roger Large, Cory McCunney, John Moore, Donny Nicholas, Zack Rigoni, Lance Semanek, Larry Senaldi, Mark Sievers, and Justin Winslow. The Bulldogs ended the season with a record of 8-3 overall, including a perfect 5-0 in the SCC East.

Though the campaign ended well, the Bulldogs started off slowly, suffering losses to Carlinville (13-0) and eventual SCC West champion East Alton-Wood River (26-12) to begin the year. However, SHS went on to win eight consecutive games, beginning with a 41-0 shutout of Gillespie in Week 3. Next up was defending SCC East champion Hillsboro. The Bulldogs played a remarkable game against the Hilltoppers, eventually handing HHS its only regular season loss in a 27-20 upset victory. The loss to Staunton was Hillsboro's lone SCC blemish in a five-year period that saw the Hilltoppers win four conference titles beginning in 1999. After a Week 5 victory over Litchfield (56-6), the Bulldogs welcomed Pana on Homecoming with a share of the league title on the line. Down 21-7 at the half, SHS fought back and took the lead, only to see Pana tie the game 27-27 with under a minute to go in the contest. However, SHS blocked the extra point attempt and eventually drove the ball to the Pana ten yard line with four seconds left in the game. In dramatic fashion, Semanek kicked a field goal as time expired to defeat the Panthers by a score of 30-27. Shutout victories over Greenville (17-0) and Vandalia (38-0) ensued, giving the Bulldogs their second SCC East title in four years. The Dogs wrapped up the season with another thrilling victory, this time defeating Roxana by a score of 10-7.

Classes of 2000 - 2009

Much like the Pana game, the Bulldogs drove deep into Roxana territory with only seconds left on the clock before Semanek again split the uprights for the victory.

The fine regular season put Coach Tonsor's program in the IHSA Playoffs for the fourth time in five seasons. The Bulldogs were cast in Class 2A as a #10 seed, and thus they were on the road in the first round against #7 seed Albion Edwards County. Though the Lions came into the game with an 8-1 record, they had not played the level of competition that the Bulldogs had faced during the season. Staunton's strength of schedule proved to be important, and the Bulldogs eventually prevailed by a score of 24-14. SHS faced a much tougher opponent in the second round of the postseason, as Tolono Unity ventured to Staunton. Though the Bulldogs were decided underdogs, SHS hung tough throughout the game. In fact, the Bulldogs took a 26-21 lead into the fourth quarter before the Rockets scored twice late to go ahead 34-26. SHS eventually drove down into Tolono Unity territory before the drive stalled at about the twenty yard line, ending the game and the season for the Bulldogs. The Rockets pushed on to the Class 2A championship game before finishing 12-2 and earning 2nd place in the state.

Several Staunton players garnered postseason accolades for their fine play throughout the year. Feldmann, Fletcher, McCunney, Nicholas, Rigoni, Semanek, and Sievers all were named to the All-Conference 1st Team, while Belair took home Honorable Mention status. The *Telegraph* awarded All-Area 1st Team recognition to Nicholas, Rigoni, and Semanek, while Fletcher was named Honorable Mention. Rigoni was also named to the *State Journal-Register* (1st Team) and *Post-Dispatch* (2nd Team) All-Area teams. Finally, the elusive running back was rewarded for his school-record 1445 yards rushing with 1st Team All-State status by the Illinois High School Football Coaches Association. Despite missing most of his junior campaign with an injury, Rigoni still finished with 2523 career yards and 31 touchdowns, including an average of 7.2 yards per attempt.

Golf (Boys)

Larry Kuba wrapped up a brilliant coaching career during the 2000 season, guiding the golf team for the twenty-sixth and final time. Ironically, though Kuba made a name for himself on the gridiron as a prep athlete, his coaching career is remembered for the nearly three hundred victories that he directed on the links. The 2000 season produced a respectable 13-13 record in match play, though the campaign did represent the first time in twelve years that the program did not produce a winning season. The Bulldogs finished in 8th place at the South Central Conference Meet, with junior Ryan Brown capturing All-SCC honors. Brown was also the team's low scorer on the season for a unit that featured only one senior, Dustin Scheller.

Golf (Girls)

Junior Ashley Goodman was the lone female golfer during the 2000 season. However, she enjoyed a productive campaign, taking home All-Conference honors and advancing to Sectional play. Goodman was mentored by Larry Kuba in his final season as golf coach.

Soccer (Boys)

The second season of soccer at Staunton High School resulted in a 3-14-2 record for coach Tim Smiddy's 2000 squad, including 1-7 in the South Central Conference. After getting off to a decent start, SHS won just once in its final ten games. Seniors Brandon Kuba, Jonas Manka, and Jason Meade paced the club, with Kuba taking home Team MVP honors. A 2nd Team All-SCC selection, Kuba was also named Honorable Mention All-Area by the *Telegraph*. Manka also received 2nd Team All-SCC, while junior Craig Phifer took home Honorable Mention status.

Soccer (Girls)

The 2001 soccer team was very streaky, as it went through periods of three, five, and four games without a loss on its way to a 12-7-2 record overall, including 4-3 in the South Central Conference. In fact, the win total was a school record for coach Rob Werden's crew, though the mark was reestablished in each of the next two years. Karen Best, Kristina Schmidt, Buffy Struebig, and Amber Watters comprised the senior class for the Lady Bulldogs. The Offensive MVP was shared by junior Danielle Stein and sophomore Bethany Stoverink, while Watters and sophomore Jennifer Wyatt shared Defensive MVP honors.

Softball

The 2001 softball team finished the season with a record of 7-15 in Kyle Freeman's seventh and final year leading the program. The Lady Bulldogs suffered through stretches of 1-5 at both the beginning and end of the season, but the squad played solid ball in the middle portion of the schedule. Though Freeman's last year coaching softball produced the lowest victory total of his career, he still stands as the program's all-time wins and winning percentage leader. Freeman also led the Lady Bulldogs to their only softball championship, a South Central Conference East title in 1998. Leaving the program with Freeman were seniors Carrie Frank, Natalie Laurent, Stacee Meyer, and Nicole Wieseman.

Track (Boys)

The 2001 track program welcomed its third coach in as many years when Tim Smiddy took the reins for one season. With no seniors on the squad, Smiddy counted on the lower levels to stabilize a team that finished 10th at the South Central Conference Meet. One individual who stepped up to the challenge was sophomore Doug Watters, a State-qualifier in the 1600 meters.

Volleyball

The 2000 volleyball season represented Don Schaefer's third and final year leading the program. The result was a 13-17 season for the Lady Bulldogs, including a 4-6 finish in the South Central Conference East. The season started off very well, as the team won its first four contests, with each victory coming against SCC West opponents. Included in the 4-0 slate was a victory over local power Carlinville. The team's overall record itself is somewhat deceiving considering the Lady Bulldogs finished 0-8 in tournaments at Jacksonville and Belleville. At those events, the club competed well but lost to Peoria Richwoods, Champaign Centennial, Champaign Central, Freeburg, Mt. Vernon, Highland, Centralia, and Trenton Wesclin.

The Lady Bulldogs had three seniors on their roster, including Andrea Snell, Leticia Tevini, and Amber Watters. Snell, the team's Offensive MVP, was a 1st Team All-County selection at the Macoupin County Tournament, at which the Lady Bulldogs finished in 3rd place. Snell was also an All-Conference selection, as she was honored with 2nd Team status. Junior Andrea Prante was named 1st Team All-SCCE, and she was also named Defensive MVP at the awards banquet. Finally, Tevini garnered All-Conference Honorable Mention status for SHS.

Classes of 2000 - 2009

Class of 2002

Baseball

Larry Caldieraro's 2002 baseball team finished the season 7-14 overall and 1-7 in the South Central Conference East. Seniors Nathan Doherty, Troy Horman, Danny Scroggins, Josh Tranter, and Tyler Washburn paced the squad. Following the season, Doherty was named All-SCCE Honorable Mention. Meanwhile, Tranter moved on to play one season for Rose-Hulman Institute of Technology.

Basketball (Boys)

The 2001-02 basketball team had to reload after losing seven outstanding seniors from the previous season's Macoupin County and Regional championship squad. However, the Dogs did return one key player in the form of Craig Phifer. Teaming up with fellow senior Tim Sievers, Phifer paced the Bulldogs with 19.1 points and 9.6 rebounds per game. He also won the Free Throw Award by knocking down 69% of his attempts from the charity stripe. Despite Phifer's efforts, SHS finished with a record of 10-18 overall and 3-7 in the South Central Conference East for coach Kevin Gockel. Following the season, junior Mike Brown was named to the All-SCCE 2nd Team after averaging 10.9 points per game for the Dogs. Phifer was a 1st Team All-Conference, All-County, and *Telegraph* All-Area selection. After scoring 979 points in high school, he continued his basketball career at the University of Evansville.

Basketball (Girls)

For the first time in more than twenty years, the 2001-02 basketball season began with a new head coach. Gayle Gusewelle, one of the best players in SHS history, returned to her alma mater to become the third head coach at the school. She welcomed just one senior to the fold, Rebecca Nathan. The youthful Lady Bulldogs played very competitive basketball during the season, eventually finishing with a record of 13-14 overall and 3-7 in the South Central Conference East. Juniors Heather Caldieraro and Jennifer Wyatt paced the squad, with Caldieraro taking home 1st Team All-Conference and All-County honors, while Wyatt was named All-SCCE 2nd Team. Caldieraro was also a 2nd Team All-Area selection by the *Telegraph*.

Bowling (Boys)

The 2001-02 bowling team included seniors Chris Cabaness and Dan Lesko. The Bulldogs were led by junior Nick Jones, and the squad was coached by Dave Williams.

Bowling (Girls)

Coach Dave Williams welcomed a large group of seniors for the 2001-02 bowling season. The group included Melissa Bowen, Ashley Stein, Danielle Stein, Megan Straub, and Erin Willhoit. Danielle Stein was the unit's top performer on the season.

Football

The 2001 football team suffered through the program's seventh winless season after finishing 0-9 overall, including 0-5 in the South Central Conference East. With Scott Tonsor having moved on to become SHS principal, the program was left in the hands of former SHS standout Larry Caldieraro. Unfortunately, SHS had to replace each starting position on both sides of the ball, and thus Caldieraro inherited a huge rebuilding project in his first season at the helm.

SHS opened the campaign with three non-conference rivals, first losing to Gillespie (31-14) before suffering a crushing loss to eventual SCC West champion Carlinville (60-6). In Week 3, SHS suffered a close loss to Southwestern by a score of 16-7. SCC East champion Hillsboro defeated the Bulldogs 47-7 to open league action, and the Dogs went on to lose conference games to Litchfield (23-14), Pana (50-12), Greenville (34-20), and Vandalia (31-12). The year concluded with a Week 9 setback to Alton Marquette (45-31), which ended the careers of seniors Rich Barber, Nick Bruhn, Mike Cerentano, Chris Maddalon, Jeff Metrick, Jared Roddick, Hunter Smith, and Jeff Tevini. Postseason accolades were dominated by underclassmen, as sophomores Nick Baker, Richie Fletcher, and John Molinar were each named to the All-SCCE 1st Team.

Golf (Boys)

The 2001 golf team welcomed a new coach in the form of Dave Williams. Though Williams directed the program for just one season, it was a magical year for Staunton High School. Ryan Brown, a senior, cemented his place in SHS history by becoming just the second athlete to win an individual state title for the school. The golf team in general had a successful campaign, as Brown and fellow seniors Bob Pirok and Ray Trost led the unit to a 5th place finish at the South Central Conference Tournament, as well as an overall match play record of 18-7. In addition to winning State, Brown was named 1st Team All-SCC and 1st Team All-Area by the *Telegraph*. The state title itself came in interesting fashion, as weather played havoc on the tournament from the beginning. Eventually, the event was cancelled after the first day with Brown holding a share of the lead with five other golfers. He used the momentum of his title run to secure a golf scholarship to Illinois State University where he played four years for the Redbirds.

Golf (Girls)

Senior Ashley Goodman was the lone female golfer in 2001 for coach Dave Williams. Goodman enjoyed an outstanding senior season that included All-Conference accolades for the second straight year.

Soccer (Boys)

Tim Smiddy's third season at the helm of the soccer program produced a 4-12 record in 2001. The Bulldogs finished 3-6 in the South Central Conference behind seniors Dan Lesko, Mike Mansholt, and Justin Wilhelm. Mansholt and Wilhelm wrapped up their careers with All-Conference Honorable Mention honors, and sophomore Zac Bianco and freshman Cody Gerdes were also named All-SCC Honorable Mention.

Soccer (Girls)

The 2002 soccer team set a school record for wins for the second straight season under coach Rob Werden. The club finished 13-6-2 overall and 3-4 in the South Central Conference. The team got off to a great start, as the Lady Bulldogs dropped just one match in their first nine games. Unfortunately, the campaign ended in the postseason at the hands of powerhouse Chatham Glenwood (1-0). The end of the campaign also brought an end to Werden's coaching tenure after four successful years at the helm. Seniors Renee Henson, Michelle Mayfield,

Melissa Newbold, Andrea Prante, Jennifer Rosenthal, Danielle Stein, and Jennifer Wall paced the squad. All-SCC members included Stein (1st Team), Newbold (2nd Team), and sophomore Jessica Wieseman (Honorable Mention).

Softball

The 2002 softball season brought a change in leadership, as Heather Ondes became the program's third head coach. Ondes, a Staunton alum and former softball player, welcomed seniors Laura Fritz, Rita Kirksey, Jamie Mansholt, and Danielle Robeza to the fold. Behind the play of junior Kati Krivi and freshman Ashleigh Ries, the Lady Bulldogs finished the year with a record of 11-12 overall and 4-3 in the South Central Conference East. Krivi was named to the 1st Team All-SCCE squad, and she was joined by Ries, who also won the Hitting Award with a .466 batting average.

Track (Boys)

The track team welcomed its fourth coach in as many years when B.J. Ogata took over the program in 2002. The revolving coaching door ended with Ogata, as he solidified the position and turned the program into one of the most consistent in the area. Though his first unit finished last at the South Central Conference Meet, continuing a five-year struggle near the bottom of the league, SHS finished no worse than 4th in its conference over the next decade. Freshman standout Josh Ohlinger captured Team MVP honors after winning the 200 meters at the Macoupin County Meet. Seniors on the team included Mike Cerentano and Jeff Metrick.

Volleyball

The 2001 volleyball team welcomed a new coach in the form of Lana Odorizzi. While the Lady Bulldogs finished just 15-17 overall, including 3-7 in the South Central Conference East, the team got hot at the right time, eventually capturing the program's second Regional championship in three seasons. The squad took a #5 ranking into the six-team Bunker Hill Regional. However, SHS pulled three straight upsets, defeating #4 East Alton-Wood River, #1 Southwestern, and #2 Bunker Hill to take the crown. Unfortunately, Staunton ran into eventual state champion Breese Mater Dei in the semifinals of the Sectional, and the loss ended the careers of seniors Andrea Prante, Rebecca Nathan, Melissa Newbold, and Danielle Robeza. Prante had an outstanding senior campaign, taking home 1st Team All-Conference status as well as *Telegraph* All-Area 2nd Team honors. Robeza was a 2nd Team All-SCCE selection, as well as Honorable Mention All-Area. Finally, Newbold was awarded All-Conference Honorable Mention status.

Class of 2003

Baseball

Coach Larry Caldieraro's 2003 baseball team fielded just one senior, Nick Jones. Though the hitting and pitching were adequate for such a young team, the Bulldogs showed their inexperience in the field, as defensive miscues eventually led to a 3-21 season overall, including a winless 0-10 campaign in the South Central Conference East. Unfortunately, the win total stands as the lowest in the program's documented history. Jones accounted for all three SHS victories on the mound, and he received All-Conference Honorable Mention status for his performance. Sophomore Joe Scroggins took home All-SCCE 1st Team honors, and freshman Kyle Pirok was an Honorable Mention selection.

Basketball (Boys)

Kevin Gockel began his eighth season as head basketball coach in 2002-03 with just one senior, Mike Brown, on the roster. Brown had an excellent campaign, pacing the Bulldogs in scoring at 15.8 points per game. Sophomore Doug Stiegemeier also had a fine year, averaging 12.1 points and 7.0 rebounds for the Dogs, while also taking home the squad's Free Throw Award (78%). Unfortunately, the Bulldogs as a team had a rough campaign, finishing 5-24 overall and 1-9 in the South Central Conference East. A fifteen-game losing streak in the middle portion of the schedule sealed the team's fate. At the end of the year, Brown was named 2nd Team All-Conference, while Stiegemeier was an Honorable Mention selection.

Basketball (Girls)

Gayle Gusewelle's 2002-03 basketball team tied a school record for wins by finishing 16-11 overall. The Lady Bulldogs got off to a sizzling start, beginning the year with nine straight wins before cooling off in South Central Conference East play (3-7). However, Staunton regained form heading into the Macoupin County Tournament. At County, the Lady Bulldogs defeated Mt. Olive (50-28) and Gillespie (40-31) before succumbing to Southwestern by a score of 48-29 in the championship game. The County title was the first of five straight for Southwestern.

Unfortunately, Gusewelle had to say goodbye to an excellent senior class that included Dominique Bianco, Heather Caldieraro, Kelli Mueller, and Jennifer Wyatt. Caldieraro (1st Team) was named to the All-Conference team for the third straight year, while Wyatt (Honorable Mention) was an All-SCCE selection for the second time in as many years. Caldieraro was also a WSMI Radio All-Area selection, and she wrapped up her career with over 1000 points scored, perhaps becoming the first female in school history to accomplish the feat.

Bowling (Boys)

Seniors Joe Hemphill and Nick Jones provided leadership for the 2002-03 bowling team, which was coached by Dave Williams. Jones, the team's scoring leader, capped off a fine career that resulted in a 12th place finish at the State Tournament. Unfortunately, the SHS bowling program was disbanded at the end of the season.

Bowling (Girls)

Coach Dave Williams welcomed just one senior for the 2002-03 season, Kendra Kuethe. After a relatively successful five years, the campaign served as the last for bowling at SHS.

Football

Coming off a winless season, the football program looked to make improvements in 2002. Larry Caldieraro entered his second year as head coach by welcoming seniors Mike Brown, Kevin Gregory, Robert Handegan, and Zac Henske to the team. Though the Dogs struggled overall, SHS did break into the win column with a 16-13 victory over Vandalia in Week 8 of the season. Staunton finished the year 1-8 overall and 1-4 in the South Central Conference East.

Classes of 2000 - 2009

The season began with losses to SCC West foes Gillespie (30-13), Carlinville (58-6), and Southwestern (41-0). In Week 4, eventual SCC East champion Hillsboro shut out the Dogs by a score of 41-0. Conference losses to Litchfield (36-7), Pana (23-13), and Greenville (42-16) followed. The program's losing streak had reached seventeen games spanning three seasons before the aforementioned Week 8 contest against Vandalia. The game was close throughout but, in the end, the Dogs were able to bring home a victory by a score of 16-13. Week 9 saw the Bulldogs take on an Alton Marquette team that had just secured its first-ever SCC West championship. The Staunton group competed well but fell by a score of 32-6. Following the season, junior Luke Pirok was named 1st Team All-SCCE, while fellow junior and Defensive MVP Thomas Scroggins was an Honorable Mention selection.

Golf (Boys)

The 2002 golf team found itself under new leadership for the third time in as many years when Troy Redfern took over the program. Redfern welcomed a quality group of seniors in his first year as head coach, including Chris Euler, Joe Hemphill, Kyle Masinelli, and Drew Stiegemeier. The unit finished 12-14 in match play and took 7th place at the South Central Conference Tournament. Stiegemeier finished out his career in fine fashion by advancing to Sectional play.

Golf (Girls)

Freshman Heidi Caldieraro was the lone female participant on the 2002 golf team. The experience served her well, and she eventually became one of the best female golfers in school history. Caldieraro was guided during the season by coach Troy Redfern.

Soccer (Boys)

Tim Smiddy began his fourth and final season leading the soccer program by welcoming seniors Dan Dietiker, Derek Fey, Walter Hull, and Doug Watters to the 2002 team. The Bulldogs began the year by winning three of their first six games but faltered down the stretch, eventually finishing 5-12 overall and 2-7 in the South Central Conference. Fey and Watters were All-Conference 2nd Team selections for the Dogs, and junior Nino Cavataio took home Honorable Mention honors.

Soccer (Girls)

Having established a school record for wins in each of the previous two seasons, the 2003 soccer team looked to once again break the mark. However, the Lady Bulldogs would have to do so with a new coach, as Darrin Bonney took over the program for his one and only year at the helm. The season was a fantastic one, with the Lady Bulldogs finishing 15-5-1 on the year and once again breaking the school record for wins. Seniors Sarah Brodie, Barbara Deist, Jennifer Kuck, Theresa Mucelli, Bethany Stoverink, and Jennifer Wyatt paced the unit. Brodie and Stoverink each garnered All-Conference Honorable Mention honors, as did junior Jessica Wieseman and freshman Julie Hainaut. Wyatt wrapped up an outstanding career by being named 1st Team All-SCC. In fact, Wyatt was named All-Conference in each sport her senior year and was also a member of two teams that set a school record for wins.

Softball

Seniors Dominique Bianco, Carrie Brackman, Heather Caldieraro, Ashly Colley, Kati Krivi, and Kelly Nicholas led the 2003 softball team to a record of 11-13 overall and 5-4 in the South Central Conference East. Krivi, an Honorable Mention selection, represented Staunton on the All-Conference team. The club was coached by Heather Ondes.

Track (Boys)

After several seasons of subpar track teams, the 2003 Bulldogs were able to finish 3rd at both the South Central Conference and Macoupin County track meets. In doing so, the Dogs touched off a streak of ten straight years where they legitimately competed for conference and county crowns under the leadership of B.J. Ogata. Kevin Gregory and Doug Watters were the lone seniors on a team that featured some outstanding underclassmen. Sophomore Josh Ohlinger won the SCC in both the 100 meters and 200 meters and also took gold at County in the 100 meters. He was joined in the winner's circle by sophomore Doug Stiegemeier, a conference champion in the 400 meters and a county champion in the high jump and 400 meters. Stiegemeier eventually qualified for State in the 400 meters. The 3200 meter relay team of Watters, Stiegemeier, junior Nino Cavataio, and freshman Aaron Brashears not only won the SCC but also advanced to State. In addition to his role on the relay team, Watters also won a conference title, and competed at State, in the 1600 meters. Finally, sophomore Brad Pirok was a Macoupin County champion and State-qualifier in the 3200 meters.

Track (Girls)

After several years without a female track team, the 2003 season saw freshmen Laci Fletcher and Jennie Satterlee participate for the Lady Bulldogs under the leadership of coach B.J. Ogata. Both individuals scored points for the team at the South Central Conference and Macoupin County track meets, and Satterlee also advanced to State in the discus.

Volleyball

Fresh off a Regional championship, the 2002 volleyball team rode the momentum of the previous season into a successful 16-12 campaign that included a 6-4 record in the South Central Conference East. The Lady Bulldogs played a very difficult schedule that included losses to Chatham Glenwood, Normal Community, Peoria Richwoods, and Freeburg. Seniors Dominque Bianco, Barbara Deist, Tiffany Eller, Kelli Mueller, Kelly Nicholas, and Jennifer Wyatt led the charge for coach Lana Odorizzi's crew. Wyatt turned in an outstanding final season, and she was rewarded for her efforts with 1st Team All-Conference honors. Nicholas was an All-SCCE 2nd Team selection, while Mueller took home Honorable Mention status.

Class of 2004

Baseball

After twelve years and 135 wins, the 2004 baseball season served as Larry Caldieraro's last as head coach of the sport at SHS. Caldieraro's last team finished with a record of 6-18 overall, including 3-7 in the South Central Conference East. The year started off well, as the

Bulldogs won their first two games of the season. However, the Dogs lost twelve straight contests before playing better ball down the stretch. Senior Luke Pirok did his best to provide a spark for the Bulldogs, collecting Team MVP honors as well as All-SCCE Honorable Mention status. Juniors Mike Corby (1st Team) and Ricky Moulton (Honorable Mention) were also named All-Conference, while sophomore Kyle Pirok collected the Hitting Award. Joining Luke Pirok in the senior class were Richie Fletcher, Thomas Scroggins, and Nathan Tatum.

Basketball (Boys)

Though the 2003-04 basketball team finished just 6-24 overall, including a winless 0-10 in the South Central Conference East, the campaign itself offered plenty of intrigue, as half of Staunton's victories were major upsets. After beginning the year with nine straight defeats, the Bulldogs jumped into the win column with a 47-45 victory over Carrollton, one of the top teams in the area. The Dogs faltered to seven more defeats in a row before heading into the Macoupin County Tournament at Mt. Olive. After recording a win in the play-in game over Bunker Hill (52-46), the Dogs were pitted against #1 seed Girard. Amazingly, the Bulldogs became the first #8 seed in county history to defeat the top-ranked team when they upset GHS by a score of 62-52. SHS eventually finished 4th in the tournament after losing to Southwestern (79-39) and Carlinville (72-46). Mt. Olive went on to defeat Southwestern in the title game, taking home its first Macoupin County title since 1949. After losing seven more games in succession, SHS won three straight near the end of the year, including an upset win over Mt. Olive. The year ended in the Regionals with a 53-47 setback to Litchfield.

Junior Doug Stiegemeier, the team's Free Throw Award (74%) winner, paced the squad with 14.9 points and 7.0 rebounds per game. Senior Luke Pirok was also a major contributor (13.8 points) for the Bulldogs. Joining Pirok in the senior class were Tyler Easter, Richie Fletcher, Brian Hastings, Jason Ray, and Cory Rodriguez. Both Pirok (2nd Team) and Stiegemeier (Honorable Mention) were named to the All-Conference team, and Stiegemeier also took home 1st Team All-County honors and Special Mention All-Area accolades from the *Telegraph*. After the season, Stiegemeier was named Offensive MVP, and Pirok captured Defensive MVP honors.

Basketball (Girls)

Gayle Gusewelle's 2003-04 basketball team finished 10-17 overall and 2-8 in the South Central Conference East. Other than a six-game losing streak halfway through the year, the Lady Bulldogs played .500 basketball for most of the season. The Lady Bulldogs placed 3rd at the Macoupin County Tournament and were led by junior Ashleigh Ries and sophomore Kim Phifer. Both players were 2nd Team All-Conference selections, while Ries also took home 1st Team All-County and 1st Team All-Area honors from WSMI Radio. The roster included just two seniors in the form of Darcy Bruhn and Jessica Wieseman.

Football

Larry Caldieraro's 2003 football team finished the season 1-8 overall and 0-5 in the South Central Conference East. The Dogs began the year with a competitive game against Carlinville but, unfortunately, fell by a score of 21-6. Week 2 saw the Bulldogs suffer a 33-14 setback to East Alton-Wood River. SHS moved into the win column with a Week 3 victory over Gillespie (33-22). Unfortunately, the SCC East slate was not kind to the Dogs. Hillsboro, which went on to win its third straight league title, easily defeated the Bulldogs by a score of 55-8 in Week 4.

While the team also struggled in a loss to Litchfield (57-18), SHS was very competitive in setbacks to Pana (12-8), Greenville (42-38), and Vandalia (78-41). The loss to Vandalia was a particularly interesting affair, as the two teams combined to score 119 points, one of the highest scoring games in IHSA history. The Bulldogs fell to SCC West champion Roxana (48-0) in Week 9 to close out the season.

Despite the team's record, junior Josh Ohlinger had an outstanding year, rushing for 1189 yards and taking home 1st Team All-Conference honors. Senior Luke Pirok also captured 1st Team honors for the Bulldogs. At the athletic banquet, Ohlinger took home Offensive MVP honors, while senior Thomas Scroggins captured Defensive MVP honors. Joining Pirok and Scroggins in the senior class were Nick Baker, Casey Best, Steve Clark, Jeromy Embry, Richie Fletcher, Randy Hamilton, Jason Ray, Cory Rodriguez, Nathan Tatum, and Fletcher Werner.

Golf (Boys)

Seniors Jeff Coalson, Brian Hastings, and Lucas Hemp led the golf team into action during the 2003 season. The Bulldogs finished 6-20 overall and in 7th place at the South Central Conference Tournament under coach Troy Redfern. Hemp was the most effective SHS player during the year, as he led the team in scoring average and advanced to Sectionals.

Golf (Girls)

Sophomore Heidi Caldieraro once again served as the lone female golfer for coach Troy Redfern. Caldieraro enjoyed a fine 2003 season, taking home All-Conference honors at the South Central Conference Tournament.

Soccer (Boys)

After five years as a sport at Staunton High School, the soccer program attained its best season on record in 2003. The Bulldogs finished 10-6-2 on the year, setting a school record for wins in the process. By finishing 7-2 in the South Central Conference, the Dogs also achieved their best-ever finish in league play, taking home 3rd place. After beginning the year with a 1-3 record, SHS lost just two of its next thirteen games before ending the season with 2-1 defeat at the hands of Edwardsville Metro East Lutheran in the Regionals.

First-year coach Steve Moore had to say goodbye to a large and quality group of seniors, including Jimmy Blum, Nino Cavataio, Shawn DeLeonyPena, Wes Freezeland, Matt Hainaut, Shane Heigert, Andrew Morgan, and Kevin Staake. Team MVP Hainaut captured 2nd Team All-SCC honors, and he was joined on the squad by juniors Cody Gerdes (1st Team), Mike Moseley (1st Team), and Brad Pirok (Honorable Mention). During the season, Gerdes set a school record with 14 goals, a mark that stood for eight years.

Soccer (Girls)

Having graduated an excellent senior class from the previous season, the 2004 soccer team struggled to a record of 2-16-1 overall and 2-4 in the South Central Conference. Unfortunately, the win total represents the lowest in program history. The rebuilding project was placed on Andrea Williamson in her first season on the job. Though her first season was challenging, Williamson went on to serve seven years and win 50 games, both of which are program records. Amanda Bond, Holly Hunsinger, Annie James, Jessica Wieseman, and Alisabeth Young comprised the senior class in 2004. Wieseman was an All-SCC Honorable Mention selection, as was sophomore Julie Hainaut. Additionally, sophomore Melissa Vitiello was a 1st Team All-Conference selection for the Lady Bulldogs.

Softball

The 2004 softball team struggled to a 1-21 season, the lowest win total in program history. The Lady Bulldogs captured their lone victory in a 3-1 South Central Conference East affair against Vandalia, and thus the team finished 1-9 in conference play. Coach Heather Ondes' team included only one senior, as Angie Best provided leadership for the club. The Lady Bulldogs were led by Team MVP Cassie Huff, a junior, and Hitting Award winner Dana Rigor, a sophomore. Rigor also captured All-Conference 1st Team honors, as did freshman Brittani Kreger. In fact, Kreger went on to capture All-Conference accolades in each of her four seasons of high school softball.

Track (Boys)

The 2004 track team experienced one of its best seasons in recent history, and B.J. Ogata was recognized as the *Telegraph's* Coach of the Year based on his squad's exploits. The Dogs placed 3rd in the South Central Conference and finished 2nd at both the Macoupin County and Sectional track meets. With only one senior, Nino Cavataio, on the roster, the Dogs gained valuable experience and confidence that eventually contributed to another outstanding campaign the following year. Cavataio continued his running career by taking up cross country at Blackburn College.

At the SCC Meet, juniors Josh Ohlinger (100 meters, 200 meters), Brad Pirok (3200 meters), and Doug Stiegemeier (400 meters) each repeated as conference champions in their respective events. The 3200 meter relay team consisting of Cavataio, Stiegemeier, and sophomores Aaron Brashears and Justin Embry was also victorious. Each individual and the relay team were also county champions, with Pirok picking up a title in the 1600 meters as well. Pirok ran both distance events at State and, in fact, took 6th place overall in the 3200 meters. His finish was the best individual performance at State since 1991, though he fared even better the following season. Joining Pirok in Charleston were Ohlinger (100 meters, 200 meters) and Stiegemeier (high jump, 400 meters). Three relay teams also qualified for State, including the 400 meter (Ohlinger, junior Mike Moseley, junior Joe Stranimeier, sophomore Mike Jurgess), 1600 meter (Cavataio, Stiegemeier, Moseley, Brashears), and 3200 meter (Cavataio, Stiegemeier, Brashears, Embry) relay units. Sectional champions included Ohlinger in both sprints, as well as the 400 meter and 3200 meter relay teams.

Track (Girls)

Although Jennie Satterlee was unable to make a return appearance to State in 2004, the sophomore did finish 3rd at the South Central Conference, Macoupin County, and Sectional track meets. She was coached by B.J. Ogata.

Volleyball

The volleyball landscape changed for the 2003 season, as the IHSA adopted rally scoring, thus replacing the traditional method of side-out scoring in which a team could only record a point when serving. Unfortunately, the change was fairly insignificant for Staunton volleyball, as the program was in rebuilding mode after having graduated a quality senior class the prior season. The year actually began fairly well, as SHS recorded wins in four of its first five nontournament games. However, Lady Bulldogs struggled down the stretch, and eventually coach Lana Odorizzi's crew slipped to a record of 5-23 overall, including 2-8 in the South Central Conference East. The lone seniors on the team included Kayla Brown and Darcy Bruhn. Brown took home 2nd Team All-SCCE honors, as did junior Ashleigh Ries.

Class of 2005

Baseball

The 2005 baseball season welcomed a new coach, as SHS alum Steve Moore took over the program. Unfortunately, a new manager and philosophy brought similar results, as the Bulldogs suffered through their sixth straight losing season. Despite a 3-3 start, including a signature win over then-undefeated Columbia, the top-ranked team in the St. Louis area, the Bulldogs ended the year with a 6-19 overall record. Though the Dogs were competitive in nearly every league game, SHS finished a winless 0-9 in the South Central Conference East.

One bright spot for the Bulldogs during the year was the play of junior Ben Atwood. Atwood, a product of Staunton's annexation of the Livingston school district that same year, captured the Pitching Award (3.78 ERA), Hitting Award (.363 average), and Team MVP. Additionally, he was named to the All-Conference 1st Team. Senior Joe Scroggins, an Honorable Mention selection, joined Atwood on the All-SCCE team. Additional seniors on the Staunton club included Kyle Bruhn, Mike Corby, Matt McCann, Ricky Moulton, and Josh Ziegler. Ziegler moved on to play baseball at Blackburn College for two seasons.

Basketball (Boys)

Kevin Gockel's 2004-05 basketball team got off to a nice start to the season, winning three of the first five games on the schedule. However, the team dropped ten of its next eleven contests, a slide that was not helped by the loss of four-year starter Doug Stiegemeier to injury. The Dogs rebounded for the Macoupin County Tournament, which was hosted by Staunton. After disposing of Southwestern (52-46) in the first round, the Bulldogs lost a tough game to eventual champion Carlinville (59-50). SHS responded in the 3rd place game by downing Gillespie by a score of 62-60. At the conclusion of the tournament, Stiegemeier and fellow senior Scott Meyer were named to the All-County team. The Bulldogs eventually ended the season with a loss in the Regional to Southwestern (72-65), finishing the year with an overall record of 9-18, including 1-9 in the South Central Conference East.

Meyer and Stiegemeier were joined in the senior class by Brad Pirok and Joe Scroggins. In addition to All-County honors, both Meyer and Stiegemeier were named 2nd Team All-Conference. Stiegemeier led the squad with 14.5 points per game and took home the Free Throw Award (69%), while Meyer pumped in 13.8 points per game. An All-Area pick by the *Telegraph* (2nd Team), *State Journal-Register* (Honorable Mention), and WSMI Radio (1st Team), Stiegemeier finished his high school career with 1130 total points. He advanced on to play four years at Webster University in St. Louis.

Basketball (Girls)

Gayle Gusewelle's final season directing the basketball program saw the Lady Bulldogs finish 10-17 overall and 2-8 in the South Central Conference East in 2004-05. The team competed well in the Macoupin County Tournament, which was hosted by Staunton. After beginning tournament play by downing Mt. Olive (52-40) and Virden (58-33), the Lady Bulldogs succumbed to Southwestern by a score of 45-39 in the championship game. The title was the third in succession for Southwestern, which went on to win five straight county crowns. Despite the loss, junior Kim Phifer was named County MVP, and senior Ashleigh Ries took home 1st Team honors. The only other senior on the team was Mallory Nathan, and she and Ries were both named All-SCCE Honorable Mention. Phifer, meanwhile, was a 1st Team selection, and she wrapped up her excellent junior season by being named to the *Telegraph* (2nd Team), *State Journal-Register* (Special Mention), and WSMI Radio (1st Team) All-Area teams.

Cross Country (Boys)

The 2004 cross country season was an interesting one at Staunton High School. Though the district did not officially sponsor the sport, runners were allowed to compete individually, and senior Brad Pirok did just that in 2004. However, since he was also a member of the soccer team, and because the district has a policy forbidding students to play two sports during the same athletic season, Pirok had to wait until soccer was over to begin his cross country campaign. Therefore, he missed the whole regular season of the cross country schedule, including the South Central Conference Meet.

Running his first career race at Regionals, Pirok wasted no time in making his mark by capturing the event title in impressive fashion. He then moved on to the Sectional, finishing in 2nd place and securing a spot in the State finals. In Peoria, Pirok competed exceptionally well and took home All-State honors after finishing in 7th place overall (the top twenty-five finishers are considered All-State). At the conclusion of the season, Pirok was a 1st Team All-Area selection by the *State Journal-Register* and was named Runner of the Year by the *Telegraph*. He continued his career at Southern Illinois University where he also competed in track for the Salukis.

Football

In Larry Caldieraro's fourth and final season leading the program, the 2004 football team finished 1-8 overall and 0-5 in the South Central Conference East. Also saying goodbye to the program that season was senior Josh Ohlinger, one of the most gifted running backs in school history. Despite the team's overall record, Ohlinger, the team's Offensive MVP, was a 1st Team All-SCCE selection. Ohlinger was joined on the All-Conference team by junior Randy Large. Additional seniors in the program included Kyle Bruhn, Josh Manley, Matt Mitchelar, and Josh Ziegler. Though he continued to teach at Staunton High School, Coach Caldieraro moved on to serve as defensive coordinator for a Mt. Olive program that made several deep postseason runs.

The year started out with five very difficult games, as SHS was outscored 250-30 in the early part of the schedule. Losses to Carlinville (61-12), East Alton-Wood River (50-6), Gillespie (27-0), Hillsboro (63-6), and Litchfield (49-6) began the season in dire fashion, though the Dogs were very competitive in the latter portion of the campaign. Close losses to Pana (29-20) in Week 6 and Vandalia (18-13) in Week 8 showed the team was making progress, though a 47-0 defeat to Greenville in Week 7 was a setback. However, Week 9 against Roxana saw the Bulldogs grab a victory in a battle of winless teams by a score of 26-19. The SCC East was won by Greenville in 2004 for the first time in the school's history. However, the title set off an amazing run that included seven league championships in a span of eight years. Meanwhile,

East Alton-Wood River took home the SCC West crown on its way to an undefeated regular season.

Golf (Boys)

Doug Stiegemeier was the lone senior on the 2004 golf team, a squad coached by Troy Redfern. The Bulldogs finished 14-18 in match play and placed 6th at the South Central Conference Tournament. A bright spot for the Dogs was the play of sophomore Chris Redfern, who advanced to Sectional competition.

Golf (Girls)

Though there were not enough participants to field a team, the 2004 golf season featured quality play from junior Heidi Caldieraro and sophomore Christina Geisler. Caldieraro took home All-Conference accolades for the second straight season, and both golfers qualified for Sectional play. The girls were coached by Troy Redfern.

Soccer (Boys)

The 2004 soccer team won ten games for the second straight season, thus tying the school record for victories. In the end, the Dogs finished 10-8 overall and 5-4 in the South Central Conference under the direction of Steve Moore. SHS started off the season with two straight wins and stood at 6-3 on the year before dropping four of its next five games. However, the Bulldogs responded with three straight wins to close out the regular season, including impressive victories over Breese Central (3-0) and Carlinville (4-2). Unfortunately, the season ended in a loss to Jerseyville (1-0) in the Regional.

After the season, Coach Moore had to say goodbye to arguably the best senior class in program history, as Shane Baker, Shawn Brodie, Kevin Euler, Cody Gerdes, Tom McDowell, Scott Miller, Mike Moseley, Brad Pirok, Dan Podwojski, and Tony Seganfredo all wrapped up their high school careers. Euler continued his career at Illinois College where he participated in soccer for three seasons. Gerdes and Moseley repeated as 1st Team All-Conference selections, while Podwojski and junior Tyler Bianco received Honorable Mention accolades. Named to the *Telegraph* All-Area team were Brodie, Bianco, and Gerdes, as each was an Honorable Mention selection. After the season, Moseley was voted by his peers as Team MVP. The Bulldogs featured a well-rounded attack led by Bianco (12 goals), Brodie (11 goals), and Gerdes (10 goals). Gerdes' season total gave him 24 goals for his career, briefly making him the school's all-time leading scorer.

Soccer (Girls)

Seniors Kendra Meyer, Danielle Milkovich, and Megan Thomas suited up for the 2005 soccer team during coach Andrea Williamson's second year with the program. Coming off the worst season in program history, the Lady Bulldogs showed promise by winning two of their first three games. Unfortunately, the team went nine straight contests without a victory, finishing 5-14-1 overall, including a 2-5 mark in the South Central Conference. Leading the charge were junior Julie Hainaut and sophomore Jackie DeVries. Hainaut was an All-SCC Honorable Mention award winner, while DeVries was named to the All-Conference 2nd Team.

Classes of 2000 - 2009

Softball

Heather Ondes' 2005 softball team finished the season with an overall record of 5-15. However, the Lady Bulldogs competed fairly well in the South Central Conference East, finishing 4-6 in league play. Ondes welcomed seniors Charley Barlow, Brittany Floyd, and Hilary Odorizzi to the fold, with Barlow taking home Team MVP honors. Barlow was also an Honorable Mention All-SCCE choice, while sophomore and Hitting Award winner Brittani Kreger took home 1st Team honors.

Tennis (Boys)

In 2005, sophomore Andy Beswick became what is believed to be the first tennis participant at Staunton High School in more than seventy years. Though Beswick was unable to capture any awards during the season, he did advance out of the first round in both South Central Conference and Sectional action.

Track (Boys)

The 2005 track team was arguably the best at the school since the 1990 squad that won South Central Conference, Macoupin County, and Sectional titles. The 2005 version nearly duplicated those feats by taking gold at County and finishing 2nd at the other two events. Furthermore, behind the efforts of seniors Josh Ohlinger and Brad Pirok, the Dogs finished in 15th place at State, the school's best showing since 1929. In Charleston, Ohlinger placed 5th in the 200 meters and 7th in the 100 meters, while Pirok captured 2nd in the 3200 meters to account for Staunton's scoring at State.

Coach B.J. Ogata's squad was a deep and talented one led by seniors Robbie Albrecht, Mike Moseley, Ohlinger, Pirok, Dan Podwojski, Doug Stiegemeier, and Brandon Ziegler. In fact, during the year the seniors alone set four school records. The county championship was made possible with 1st place finishes by Ohlinger (100 meters, 200 meters), Pirok (1600 meters, 3200 meters), Stiegemeier (high jump, 400 meters), and junior Aaron Brashears (800 meters). Additionally, the 800 meter relay team (Moseley, junior Mike Jurgess, sophomore Joe Stranimeier, freshman Kevin Tucker) and 3200 meter relay team (Stiegemeier, Brashears, junior Justin Embry, freshman Randall Hoehn) also captured gold. At the SCC Meet, winners included Ohlinger (long jump, 100 meters, 200 meters), Pirok (1600 meters, 3200 meters), Stiegemeier (400 meters), and the 3200 meter relay team (Stiegemeier, Brashears, Embry, Hoehn).

At the Sectional Meet in Nashville, Ohlinger (100 meters, 200 meters), Pirok (3200 meters), the 800 meter relay team (Moseley, Ohlinger, Jurgess, Stranimeier), and the 3200 meter relay team (Stiegemeier, Brashears, Embry, Hoehn) emerged as champions. In addition to those winners, Staunton sent Brashears (800 meters), Stiegemeier (400 meters), and the 400 meter relay team (Moseley, Ohlinger, Jurgess, Stranimeier) to Charleston. Due to Ohlinger's heavy workload, freshman Dean Sheffer ran in his place on the 3200 meter relay team at State. After the season, Pirok continued his career at Southern Illinois University, competing four years for the Salukis.

Track (Girls)

After several years with zero, one, or two participants, coach B.J. Ogata finally had an ample number of athletes come out for the 2005 track team. With twelve girls competing, the Lady Bulldogs had a successful season that included two athletes qualifying for State. Though the team finished just 8th at the South Central Conference Meet, the result was the program's best finish in ten years. The squad also posted strong points at the Macoupin County Meet, with juniors Kim Phifer (800 meters) and Jennie Satterlee (discus) both taking gold at that event. Though they did not place in Charleston, both girls advanced to State in their respective events.

Volleyball

Lana Odorizzi wrapped up her four-year coaching tenure at the end of the 2004 volleyball season. The Lady Bulldogs settled for a 6-15 record in Coach Odorizzi's final year behind the play of seniors Danielle Milkovich, Mallory Nathan, Hilary Odorizzi, Ashleigh Ries, Brittany Robeza, and Lisa Turner. SHS fared well at the Macoupin County Tournament, finishing 2nd overall with Hilary Odorizzi and Ries taking home All-County 1st Team honors. However, the Lady Bulldogs struggled in South Central Conference East play, though Hilary Odorizzi (2nd Team), Ries (Honorable Mention), Robeza (2nd Team), and junior Kim Phifer (2nd Team) were honored with All-Conference accolades. Though Lana Odorizzi's tenure at Staunton came to a close, she later took on coaching duties at Gillespie where she enjoyed several successful seasons in the lead position. Unfortunately, her departure from SHS volleyball touched off an era of high coaching turnover for the program, as it would be led by six different head coaches in seven seasons.

Class of 2006

Baseball

The 2006 baseball team featured a senior class that included Ben Atwood, Eric Baum, Dusty Brooke, Kyle Pirok, Darrin Prigmore, Justin Revisky, David Rucker, and Shaun Thomas. The Bulldogs finished the year with a record of 6-13 overall, including 2-8 in the South Central Conference East. Along the way, coach Steve Moore's squad dropped several close games, including three by the score of 1-0. However, the Bulldogs came alive against rival Gillespie. After defeating the Miners early in the season by a score of 16-3 in six innings at GCS Stadium, the Bulldogs once again had Gillespie's number with a 16-0 shutout in five innings in the Regional. Unfortunately, the Dogs dropped a 1-0 decision to Edwardsville Metro East Lutheran, the top-seeded team in the Sectional complex. After the season, Atwood, Pirok, and Revisky were each named to the All-Conference 1st Team. Atwood was also named Team MVP and the Hitting Award winner, while Revisky captured the Pitching Award.

Basketball (Boys)

Kevin Gockel's 2005-06 basketball team finished 8-19 overall, including 1-9 in the South Central Conference East. Though the team struggled throughout most of the season, one portion of the schedule proved fruitful for SHS. After capturing their final two games to take the consolation title at the Macoupin County Tournament, the Bulldogs lost by just one point to Litchfield before knocking off Pana for the team's lone SCC East win. The Dogs featured excellent guard play that year, as seniors Ben Atwood, Tyler Bianco, and Randy Henrion provided leadership for the squad. Atwood, the team's Offensive MVP, paced the Bulldogs with 14.8 points per game. Bianco pumped in 11.2 points per game and also took home Defensive MVP honors, while junior Chris Redfern won the Free Throw Award (71%). Atwood wrapped up his senior season with 2nd Team All-Conference honors, and he was also named 2nd Team All-Tournament at the Macoupin County Tournament.

Basketball (Girls)

The 2005-06 basketball season brought a change to the program as Rob Corso took over the reins. Corso's inaugural season was extremely successful, as the Lady Bulldogs tied a school record by finishing 16-11 behind the play of seniors Julie Hainaut, Kim Phifer, Jenny Satterlee, and Melissa Vitiello. The team started the year with five wins in its first six games and later won four straight before falling to Nokomis (64-51) in the championship game of the Carlinville Holiday Tournament. The Lady Bulldogs had high hopes entering the Macoupin County Tournament. But, after defeating Girard (45-40), SHS fell to a Bunker Hill team that it had beaten twice previously during the season. The 39-38 heartbreaker dropped the Lady Bulldogs into the 3rd place game, which they won over Carlinville by a score of 44-38.

With elite competition in the South Central Conference East, including eventual state champion Hillsboro, the Lady Bulldogs finished just 3-7 in league play. However, the strength of schedule did earn the team a #1 rank heading into the Bunker Hill Regional. Unfortunately, the club had dropped two straight contests heading into postseason play, and the trend continued with a loss to Alton Marquette in the semifinals of the tournament. Following the season, Hainaut was recognized as an Honorable Mention All-SCCE selection. Meanwhile, Phifer cemented her place as one of the top players in school history by going over 1000 points in her career. As a result, she garnered 1st Team All-Conference, All-County, and WSMI Radio All-Area recognition.

Cross Country (Girls)

Though there was no official team, freshman Alex Senaldi competed as an individual runner during the 2005 cross country season. Senaldi captured All-Conference recognition at the South Central Conference Meet and, in fact, she garnered All-SCC accolades in each of her four years of high school, including two individual conference championships. However, 2005 was her only year running alone, as the next season saw SHS field the first female cross country team in school history.

Football

The Staunton football program welcomed a new coach for the 2005 season in the form of Mike Parmentier. A former standout at Southwestern, Parmentier had assisted at Bethalto Civic Memorial and Edwardsville before experiencing success as a head coach at Girard. Parmentier's first game leading SHS ended in improbable fashion, as Staunton went to Gillespie in Week 1 and shocked the Miners by a score of 8-7. Staunton scored late in the game and, instead of playing for the tie, elected to go for the win. The two-point conversion was successful and the Dogs knocked off a Miners team that went on to win the South Central Conference West and advanced to the second round of the playoffs.

As for the Dogs, the season opener was the lone win on the year, as the team finished 1-8, including 0-5 in the SCC East. However, looking at the scores, improvement was evident throughout the season, especially considering SHS faced six teams that went on to make the playoffs. In Week 2, the Dogs fell to Carlinville (29-12) and followed up with a loss to Southwestern (24-14) in Week 3. The conference portion of the schedule saw the team go down to defeat against Hillsboro (34-0), Litchfield (34-13), Pana (14-13), Greenville (41-6), and

Vandalia (28-27). The year ended with a loss to Alton Marquette (29-14). Greenville and Hillsboro tied for the SCC East title that season.

One of Parmentier's goals before the campaign started was to increase the number of participants in the program, and seniors Aaron Brashears, Justin Embry, Todd Gray, David Hamilton, James Horne, Mike Jurgess, Jason Knop, John Krivi, Randy Large, Tim Long, Jason Morgan, Brent Muenstermann, Kyle Pirok, Justin Revisky, David Rucker, and Shaun Thomas answered the call. Three seniors were honored with All-Conference accolades, with Hamilton and Pirok being named to the 1st Team and Thomas receiving Honorable Mention. Hamilton continued his football career at McKendree University.

Golf (Boys)

The 2005 golf team finished 16-18 in match play and 8th at the South Central Conference Tournament. Seniors Eric Baum, Dusty Brooke, and Tyler Zirges paced the squad, with Zirges taking home All-SCC honors. Zirges also qualified for Sectional play, as did junior Chris Redfern. The Bulldogs were coached by Troy Redfern.

Golf (Girls)

Although several participants had competed as individuals, SHS never before had enough members to field a female golf team. However, that changed with the start of the 2005 season, as senior Heidi Caldieraro, junior Christina Geisler, sophomores Katie Hitz and Angela Meade, and freshmen Carmi Cioni, Stormy Dufrain, and Anna Kroeger comprised the first squad in school history. Interestingly enough, while most fledgling programs tend to undergo a rough start before enjoying stability, the girl's golf program was successful from day one. In fact, it holds the highest winning percentage of any team sport at Staunton High School.

Coach Troy Redfern's unit finished its inaugural campaign with a 17-10 record in match play, including a 3rd place showing at the South Central Conference Tournament. Though Geisler was an All-SCC performer, the club was paced by Caldieraro, who took home All-Conference honors for the third straight season. Caldieraro, the team's low scorer on the season, eventually advanced to State, placing 46th overall. She went on to play golf for one season at Southern Illinois University-Edwardsville.

Soccer (Boys)

Having graduated the most talented class in program history, the 2005 soccer team got off to a slow start, winning just one time in its first six matches. However, seniors Brett Allen, Tyler Bianco, Brendan Clark, Randy Henrion, Anthony McKay, and Ben Rhodes righted the ship, helping the Bulldogs to a respectable 8-9-3 record, the third best season in program history. The mark included a 5-4 record in South Central Conference play, with Bianco (1st Team) and juniors David Podwojski (2nd Team) and Dan Mathenia (Honorable Mention) each being named to the All-Conference team. With 13 goals as a senior, Team MVP Bianco established an overall program record with 25 tallies for his career. The Bulldogs were coached by Steve Moore in his final season with the program.

Soccer (Girls)

Andrea Williamson's third season leading the soccer program once again saw the team make strides, as the 2006 Lady Bulldogs finished 8-12-2 overall and 3-4 in the South Central Conference. After winning two of its first three contests, SHS dropped five straight games before rebounding with a three-game winning streak. The season ended with a postseason loss (2-1) to Springfield Lutheran. Seniors Kari Cerentano, Julie Hainaut, Ashleigh Nurdin, Vanessa Stout, and Courtney Stoverink fueled the turnaround, with Hainaut taking home Team MVP honors.

Softball

Heather Ondes' 2006 softball team finished the year 4-17 overall, including 2-8 in the South Central Conference East. Both league wins came against Litchfield, though SHS dropped eight straight games to end the season after the second win over the Purple Panthers. The Lady Bulldogs were led by seniors Danielle Lancaster, Britni Nicholson, Dana Rigor, and Megan Wieseman. Rigor was an All-SCCE 1st Team honoree, as was junior Brittani Kreger. Meanwhile, freshman Lauren Newbold was an All-Conference Honorable Mention selection. After the season, Wieseman was voted Team MVP by her peers.

Tennis (Boys)

Junior Andy Beswick competed as an individual for Staunton High School during the 2006 tennis season. Interestingly enough, he likely became the last individual in SHS history to compete in a non-sanctioned school sport. According to district policy, athletes can no longer participate as individuals in sports that are not endorsed by the school. Thus, barring a policy change or the addition of tennis as a team sport, Beswick is officially the last tennis participant in school history.

Track (Boys)

Despite having graduated an excellent class of seniors from the previous season, coach B.J. Ogata's track program continued to experience success in 2006. The unit, led by seniors Aaron Brashears, Brendan Clark, Justin Embry, Mike Jurgess, and Chris Lapolice, placed 3rd in the South Central Conference, 2nd in Macoupin County, and 4th at the Sectional. At the SCC Meet, Brashears teamed up with sophomores Aaron Foster and Randall Hoehn, as well as freshman Lucas Loots to win the 3200 meter relay. At County, Brashears (800 meters), Embry (1600 meters), Jurgess (100 meters, 200 meters), and junior Brett Miller (3200 meters) each captured gold for the Bulldogs. Additionally, the 1600 meter relay team of Brashears, Hoehn, and sophomores Dean Sheffer and Kevin Tucker took 1st place, as did the 3200 meter relay team of Brashears, Foster, Hoehn, and Loots. Finally, Brashears, Embry, Hoehn, and Loots teamed up in the 3200 meter relay to claim a Sectional title, thus moving on to State in the event. Brashears (800 meters) and Jurgess (200 meters) also competed as individuals in Charleston. Brashears, the Team MVP, moved on to Illinois College where he competed in cross country and track for one season.

Track (Girls)

Coach B.J. Ogata's 2006 track program experienced a successful season, especially concerning individual accomplishments. The Lady Bulldogs finished in 5th place at the South Central Conference Meet and in 2nd place at the Macoupin County Meet. At Conference, senior Jennie Satterlee captured gold in the discus. At County, Satterlee won both the discus and the shot put, while freshman Alex Senaldi entered the winner's circle in the 800 meters. At the Sectional Meet, Satterlee won the discus, and she went on to finish in 4th place in that event at State. Additionally, senior Kim Phifer was the Sectional champion in the 800 meters, while

Senaldi posted State-qualifying times in both the 800 meters and 1600 meters. Satterlee, the Team MVP, continued her career at Southern Illinois University-Edwardsville. She and Phifer were joined in the senior class by Keely Meyer.

Volleyball

Despite a large contingent of seniors in 2005, the outlook for the volleyball program was cloudy, as the school district had trouble filling the head coaching vacancy. Luckily, Bill Hanks, who had experienced success as a long-time coach at Bunker Hill, stepped up to the plate in volunteering to take on the task for one season. Though SHS got off to a hot start with early victories over Gillespie, Roxana, and Litchfield, the Lady Bulldogs struggled the rest of the way. The campaign concluded with a 3-18 overall record, the worst result in program history. Included in the mark was a 1-9 finish in the South Central Conference East. Seniors Frannie Combs, Vanessa Dobrinich, Julie Hainaut, Sandy Nicholas, Kim Phifer, Nikki Prost, Dana Rigor, Jennie Satterlee, Kelly Scroggins, and Courtney Stoverink paced the squad, with Phifer receiving All-Conference Honorable Mention recognition.

Class of 2007

Baseball

Steve Moore's 2007 baseball team struggled to a 5-16 overall record, including 2-7 in the South Central Conference East. After starting the year at 2-2, the Dogs suffered through nine straight losses before rebounding with better play down the stretch. One bright spot during the season was the play of sophomore and Team MVP Zack Arnett. Arnett hit .388 and finished with a 3.09 ERA, both of which led the team. For his efforts, he was named All-Conference (1st Team) and *State Journal-Register* All-Area (Special Mention). Kyle Billings, Josh Bruhn, Ryan Elliott, Josh Odorizzi, David Podwojski, Josh Revisky, and Kyle Whitlock were seniors on the squad.

Basketball (Boys)

The 2006-07 basketball team finished 5-21 overall and 0-10 in the South Central Conference East under coach Kevin Gockel. After twelve years at the helm, the season served as Gockel's last with the program. The Dogs started the year slowly, dropping their first six games before defeating Alton Marquette. The team continued to struggle through most of the schedule, though an upset win over Bunker Hill on the road was a season highlight. Senior Bulldogs included Adam Brackman, David Podwojski, and Chris Redfern, with Redfern being named All-Conference Honorable Mention and Offensive MVP. Podwojski captured Defensive MVP honors at the postseason awards banquet, with sophomore Lucas Loots winning the Free Throw Award (61%). Brackman led the team in scoring (8.2) and rebounding (6.7).

Basketball (Girls)

Rob Corso's 2006-07 basketball team finished 7-18 overall and 2-8 in the South Central Conference East. Despite winning the first two games of the season in blowout fashion, the Lady Bulldogs were unable to sustain the momentum, as untimely injuries reduced the effectiveness of several players. Jackie DeVries served as the lone senior on the team in Coach Corso's final season with the program.

Cross Country (Boys)

While several individuals had been competing individually throughout the years, for the first time since 1978, Staunton High School made cross country a formal team sport in 2006. Though the program lacked enough participants to compete as a team since its reintroduction, coach Dave Williams was fortunate enough to mentor several outstanding runners over the years. He welcomed three such competitors in 2006, including senior John Mihelcic and sophomores Lucas Loots and Jake Rhodes. Amazingly, in his only year participating in the sport, Mihelcic won the South Central Conference championship, advanced to State (65th place), and was named 1st Team All-Area by the *Telegraph*. Loots began a remarkable career by capturing All-SCC honors and qualifying for the Sectional.

Cross Country (Girls)

Much like the situation on the boy's team, coach Dave Williams welcomed just three female cross country participants in 2006, the school's initial season offering the sport to students in the district. Though there were not enough runners to officially field a team, junior Diondra Horner, sophomore Alex Senaldi, and freshman Kadambari Jain competed well for the Lady Bulldogs. Senaldi and Jain qualified for the Sectional, and Senaldi also captured the individual championship at the South Central Conference Meet. The lack of numbers in the program was not an enduring problem, and in fact the Lady Bulldogs enjoyed tremendous team success in the upcoming seasons.

Football

The football team took a step forward in 2006, finishing 3-6 overall and 2-3 in the South Central Conference East. The win total represented the most victories the program had experienced in six seasons, as well as the first time the team had won a conference game in four years. Mike Parmentier's crew got off to a good start in Week 1 by shutting out Gillespie (26-0). Unfortunately, SHS went scoreless in the next three games, losing to Carlinville (17-0), Southwestern (25-0), and Hillsboro (31-0). Consecutive wins over Litchfield (12-6) and Pana (24-21) gave the upstart team postseason aspirations, but those were dispelled with three straight losses to end the season, as the Bulldogs fell to Greenville (34-10), Vandalia (28-7), and Alton Marquette (44-12). Eventual champions in the SCC included Hillsboro (East) and East Alton-Wood River (West).

Seniors Zach Bertels, Josh Bruhn, Josh Revisky, and sophomore Josh Teeske were all named 1st Team All-Conference for their outstanding play on the field in 2006. Bertels was also awarded All-Area by the *Telegraph* (1st Team) and the *State Journal-Register* (2nd Team). Joining Bertels, Bruhn, and Revisky in the senior class were Kyle Billings, Logan Billings, Steve Boster, Matt Collins, Kyle DeVries, Justin Haustein, Stewart Heim, David Patzius, Justin Potillo, and Kyle Whitlock.

Golf (Boys)

The 2006 golf team experienced one of its most successful seasons in years as the squad finished 21-17 and advanced to Sectional play. Coach Troy Redfern's Bulldogs finished in 3rd place at the South Central Conference Tournament, the program's best finish in seven years.

Senior Chris Redfern was the team's low scorer on the season, and also captured All-Conference honors at the SCC event. Sophomore Mike Mihelcic was also an All-Conference performer and was later named All-Area by the *Telegraph*. Senior Bulldogs included Andrew Brown, Ryan Elliott, and Chris Redfern.

Golf (Girls)

The 2006 golf program, in just its second year as a team sport, enjoyed another successful season under coach Troy Redfern. The Lady Bulldogs finished 21-12 overall and in 3rd place at the South Central Conference Tournament. The team was led by its lone senior, Christina Geisler. An All-Conference performer, Geisler had an outstanding regular season and eventually advanced to the State Tournament. At State, she finished in 28th place overall. Along with Geisler, sophomore Stormy Dufrain and freshman Elyse Banovic also advanced to Sectional play. Banovic also attained All-Conference status to begin an illustrious career that eventually saw her become the most decorated female golfer in school history.

Soccer (Boys)

The 2006 version of the soccer team found itself under new leadership, as Ken Pelletier took over the program. The club finished with a record of 8-11-2, including a 3-4 mark in the South Central Conference. After a rocky start, the Dogs finished on a terror, winning three consecutive games via shutout before falling in the Regional to Trenton Wesclin on penalty kicks. Seniors on the team included Adam Brackman, Andy Gai, Matt Lesko, Dan Mathenia, Brett Miller, Josh Odorizzi, David Podwojski, and Nick Rekart. Podwojski was named Team MVP, and he also captured 2nd Team All-SCC honors. Meanwhile, Brackman received Honorable Mention status. Miller moved on to compete in soccer for one season at Illinois College.

Soccer (Girls)

Andrea Williamson's 2007 soccer team finished 8-11-1 overall and 4-3 in the South Central Conference. The Lady Bulldogs got off to a slow start but finished the year with just one loss in their final six regular season contests. Seniors included Ashley Brummett, Jackie DeVries, Megan Lilley, Ali Neuhaus, Dana Snell, and Meghan Williamson, with Neuhaus capturing 1st Team All-SCC honors as well as being named Defensive MVP. The program also received a spark from Sophia Roedel, a foreign exchange student from Germany. Roedel garnered All-Conference 2nd Team honors, and she was also named Offensive MVP at the postseason awards banquet.

Softball

The 2007 softball team finished with a 4-16 overall record, including 2-8 in the South Central Conference East. The year got off to a bad start when the Lady Bulldogs were shut out in their first four games. However, the team rebounded to play .500 ball over the middle portion of the schedule before once again struggling to score runs down the stretch. After six seasons leading the program, 2007 marked the end of Heather Ondes' tenure, and she departed with seniors Natalie Albrecht, Whitney Conroy, Ashleigh Fiori, and Brittani Kreger. Kreger was named Team MVP and received All-SCCE Honorable Mention status. By making the All-Conference team as a senior, Kreger pulled off the rare feat of being named All-Conference in all four years of her high school career.

Track (Boys)

Coach B.J. Ogata's 2007 track team finished 4th at the South Central Conference Meet, with senior Joe Stranimeier (200 meters) capturing the lone conference title for the Dogs. Stranimeier took gold in the 200 meters at the Macoupin County Meet, and he was joined in the winner's circle by fellow senior Brett Miller (3200 meters) and junior Randall Hoehn (1600 meters). In addition to capturing Team MVP honors, Hoehn qualified for State in the 800 meters, with Miller (3200 meters) and sophomore Lucas Loots (1600 meters) joining him in Charleston. Seniors on the track team included Zach Bertels, Steve Boster, John Mihelcic, Miller, Justin Potillo, and Stranimeier. Upon graduation, Miller moved on to compete at Illinois College for four seasons. While there, he also participated in cross country for three seasons and played soccer for one year.

Track (Girls)

The 2007 track team was coached by B.J. Ogata and included seniors Rachel Crouch and Susan Thomas. Team MVP Alex Senaldi set school marks in both the 1600 meters and 3200 meters that year, qualifying for State in both events. Sophomore Sam Feldmann also set a school record (100 meter high hurdles) for a team that finished 7th in the South Central Conference.

Volleyball

Marvin Hayden coached the 2006 volleyball team in his one and only year leading the program. The Lady Bulldogs finished with a record of 6-15 overall, including 2-8 in the South Central Conference East, behind seniors Rachel Crouch, Jessica James, Brittani Kreger, and Dana Snell. Sophomores Lika Hindi and Lauren Newbold were both named All-SCCE Honorable Mention at the conclusion of the year.

Class of 2008

Baseball

The 2008 baseball team played just three games at home during the season, finishing with two victories in those contests. However, coach Steve Moore's squad struggled on the road and eventually finished with an overall record of 5-13, including 2-6 in the South Central Conference East. The Dogs actually started the season 4-4 behind the play of seniors Nick Coyne, Andrew Foster, Tim Homeier, Brandon Margaritis, Andrew Milkovich, Phil Rhodes, and Cody Rigor. Unfortunately, SHS dropped nine of ten games to close out the season, including a 2-1 loss to Roxana in the Regional. Margaritis captured the Pitching Award with a 3.18 ERA on the mound, while sophomore and Team MVP Jake Langley won the Hitting Award with a .360 batting average. After the season, Langley was named to the All-Conference 1st Team, and he was also an All-Area Special Mention choice by the *State Journal-Register*.

Basketball (Boys)

The 2007-08 basketball team welcomed back just one starter from the previous season, and the Dogs also welcomed a new coach in the form of Steve Moore, a former SHS basketball player. Coach Moore's initial senior class included Nick Coyne, Tim Homeier, Phil Rhodes,

Ryan Stroup, and Brad Wright. Though the Bulldogs finished the year below .500 with a 14-15 record, the mark actually represented the second most wins for the program in fifteen years. The Bulldogs also played in the program's first championship game in seven years and, in fact, made three title game appearances that season. At the Metro East Lutheran Turkey Tipoff, the Bulldogs defeated East Alton-Wood River (53-24) and Dupo (63-53) before pulling an upset of Roxana (53-52) to advance to the title game. Unfortunately, the Dogs fell to Litchfield by a score of 60-53 in the championship. At the Macoupin County Tournament, SHS bested Southwestern (64-50) before upsetting Bunker Hill (60-57) to reach the title match. In the championship contest, Girard defeated the Dogs 59-51 for the Macoupin County crown. Finally, in the Regional, SHS pulled a semifinal game upset of Hillsboro (50-43) before dropping a thrilling game to Pana (68-61) to close out the season.

Though Staunton played well in tournament action, the team finished just 1-9 in the South Central Conference East, finishing in last place for the sixth consecutive season. Oddly enough, SHS likely would have won the SCC West that season after going 9-0 in crossover games. The Dogs were led during the year by Rhodes and junior Cody Best. Rhodes, the Team MVP, was also the Free Throw Award winner (73%). Meanwhile, Best led the team in scoring with an average of 10.3 points per game. Rhodes and Best were both named to the All-County 1st Team. Best was also honored by the Southern Illinois high school basketball website, A Baseline View, with All-Area Honorable Mention status. Rhodes was a 2nd Team All-Conference honoree, and he also took home All-Area accolades from the *State Journal-Register* (Honorable Mention) and WSMI Radio (1st Team). After the season, Rhodes became just the second of three Bulldogs in school history to advance to State in the IHSA's 3-Point Shootout.

Basketball (Girls)

The 2007-08 basketball team welcomed a new coach, as Troy Redfern took over the program. The Lady Bulldogs got off to a rough start, beginning the season with just one win in their first eleven games, including an eventual 0-9 record in the South Central Conference East. However, the team was very competitive down the stretch and eventually finished with an overall mark of 7-18. Redfern later served as the leader of two record-setting teams at SHS, and he left the program as its all-time winning percentage leader.

Coach Redfern's first seniors were Bethany Banovz, Paige Buffington, and Stephanie Darrah. While Darrah won Defensive MVP honors, the team's featured player was junior Lauren Newbold. The Offensive MVP led the Lady Bulldogs in scoring and rebounding, and at the conclusion of the season she was named All-SCCE Honorable Mention for her efforts in league play. Newbold was also named to the Macoupin County All-Tournament 1st Team after leading the Bulldogs to the consolation championship. At County, the Lady Bulldogs lost in the first round to Bunker Hill (41-36) before defeating Mt. Olive (72-22) and Gillespie (54-35). Finally, Newbold was an Honorable Mention All-Area choice by the *State Journal-Register*.

Cross Country (Boys)

The 2007 cross country program saw only one runner sign up for the sport, but he was a standout participant in the form Lucas Loots, a junior. Loots, under the tutelage of coach Dave Williams, emerged as the champion of both the South Central Conference and Regional cross country meets. He eventually advanced to State and took 22nd place overall, thus capturing All-State accolades. For his efforts, he was named the *Telegraph's* Runner of the Year.

Classes of 2000 - 2009

Cross Country (Girls)

The 2007 cross country season represented the first time that SHS had enough female participants to field an entire team. The depth proved to be vital, as the Lady Bulldogs won the South Central Conference championship for the first of two straight seasons. Staunton also placed 2nd in the Regional, thus advancing to Sectional action for the first of three straight appearances. The squad was led by junior Alex Senaldi and freshman Katie Trettenero. Senaldi and Trettenero finished 2nd and 3rd, respectively, at both the SCC and Regional meets. Both were All-Conference runners, and Trettenero eventually qualified for State, finishing 79th overall. For her efforts, she was named to the *Telegraph's* All-Area 1st Team. The Lady Bulldogs were coached by Dave Williams and included senior Diondra Horner. After the season, Senaldi was named Team MVP.

Football

Coach Mike Parmentier's football program continued to make strides during the 2007 campaign, and in fact that season the Bulldogs qualified for the IHSA Playoffs for the first time in seven years. After a close loss in the first round of the postseason, the team finished with a 5-5 overall record, including 2-3 in the South Central Conference East. The seniors responsible for the turnaround were Dustin Barrett, Nick Cerentano, Todd Collins, Aaron Foster, Guy Hackworth, Wes Hindi, Justin Ladendorf, John McMahon, Tyler Muenstermann, Neal Parker, Cody Rigor, Dean Sheffer, David Trost, Zach Wisnasky, and Brad Wright. Five seniors continued their playing careers after high school, including Barrett, Muenstermann, and Wright at McKendree University. Foster continued his career at Culver-Stockton College, while Ladendorf ended up at Millikin University.

SHS was tested right out of the gate against a Carlinville squad that went on to win the SCC West. However, Staunton was up to the challenge, defeating the Cavaliers by a score of 12-10. Week 2 saw the Dogs drop a close game to East Alton-Wood River (20-12) before defeating Gillespie (35-0) in Week 3. The SCC East portion of the schedule saw SHS play several close games after a Week 4 loss to Hillsboro (30-6). In those games, Staunton defeated Litchfield (20-14) and Pana (18-7) before succumbing to Greenville (29-18) and Vandalia (7-6). Greenville eventually won the SCC East, the first of five straight titles for the Comets. With a 4-4 record heading into the final regular season game, the Dogs needed a victory over Roxana to clinch the program's first postseason appearance since the 2000 season. SHS responded to the situation favorably, walloping Roxana by a score of 55-6 to secure the postseason berth. Staunton's opponent in the IHSA Class 3A Playoffs was top-ranked and undefeated Carterville. However, the Dogs were not intimidated, and they gave the Lions a tough game before falling by a score of 26-20. Carterville ended up advancing to the quarterfinals before ending its season at 11-1.

While the Bulldogs owed much of their success to a stout defense, the introduction of a lethal passing attack also contributed to the turnaround. Josh Teeske, a junior quarterback, set a school record at the time with 1380 yards passing. On the receiving end of most of Teeske's passes were junior Cody Best (30 catches for 465 yards) and Ladendorf (25 catches for 301 yards). On the defensive side of the ball, Wright set a school record with 8 interceptions.

At the conclusion of the season, Best, Collins, McMahon, Muenstermann, Teeske, and Wright were each named 1st Team All-Conference, while Ladendorf and Wisnasky took home Honorable Mention accolades. The *Telegraph* named Best, Collins, Muenstermann, Teeske, and Wright to its All-Area 1st Team, and Wright was also named All-Area by the *State Journal-Register* (1st Team) and *Post-Dispatch* (Honorable Mention). Finally, Wright was honored as a

1st Team All-State football player by the *News-Gazette*, Illinois High School Football Coaches, and Maxpreps.

Golf (Boys)

The 2007 golf team finished 9-26 overall, including a 6th place finish at the South Central Conference Tournament. Seniors Nick Coyne, Logan Hemp, Brandon Margaritis, and Phil Rhodes provided leadership for the squad, with Rhodes taking home All-Conference accolades. Mike Mihelcic, a junior, led the team in scoring average and eventually advanced to Sectional competition. Mihelcic was an All-SCC and *Telegraph* All-Area performer for the second straight season for coach Troy Redfern's club.

Golf (Girls)

The 2007 golf team finished the year with a 20-3 record in match play, giving the program its highest season winning percentage (.870) in its brief history. The Lady Bulldogs also competed well at the South Central Conference Tournament, finishing in 3rd place. The squad later qualified for the Sectional Tournament. Interestingly enough, despite other sports programs at SHS being on the rise, the golf team was the only one during the 2007-08 school year to finish with a winning record. Coach Troy Redfern's team was led by seniors Katie Hitz, Andrea Kuttin, and Angela Meade but featured the standout play of sophomore Elyse Banovic. A 1st Team All-SCC and *Telegraph* All-Area performer, Banovic eventually placed 18th at State, the highest finish ever by a female golfer at Staunton High School.

Soccer (Boys)

After four straight solid seasons, the 2007 soccer team took a step back by finishing 3-15-1 overall and 2-7 in the South Central Conference. After a 2-2 start that included victories over Roxana and Springfield Lutheran, the Bulldogs went on to win just one (against Vandalia) of their next fifteen matches. Seniors Randall Hoehn, Tim Homeier, Fritz Hull, Andrew Milkovich, and Ryan Stroup did their best to keep the Bulldogs competitive, and Hoehn was awarded Team MVP honors for his work on the field. After the season, Hoehn and Milkovich were both named to the All-SCC 2nd Team. The club was coached by Ken Pelletier.

Soccer (Girls)

The 2008 soccer team finished the year with a record of 4-11-1, including a 2-4 mark in the South Central Conference. However, the Lady Bulldogs performed much better than their record indicated, as nine of the eleven losses came by just one goal. Unfortunately, the program had to say goodbye to seniors Julie Collman, Stephanie Darrah, Cindy Gregory, Kelsey Morris, Keli Plenske, and Ashley Slifka. After the season, Morris was selected as Team MVP, while Darrah was an All-Conference 2nd Team selection. The Lady Bulldogs were coached by Andrea Williamson.

Softball

The softball program welcomed the fourth coach in its history when Doug Zehr took over in 2008. The season began with a 3-4 record before the Lady Bulldogs dropped their next nine games. Though Zehr's first squad finished just 5-16 overall, including 1-9 in the South Central Conference East, he eventually directed the program to successive winning campaigns. Zehr's team included seniors Paige Buffington, Mindy Graves, and Marissa Huff. However, the Lady

Bulldogs were led by the outstanding play of underclassmen Lauren Newbold, a junior, and Rachel Hadjan, a sophomore. Both individuals were honored with All-Conference 1st Team accolades, and each was also an All-Area Special Mention choice by the *State Journal-Register*.

Track (Boys)

Coach B.J. Ogata welcomed more than thirty participants to the 2008 track team. With outstanding depth on the squad, the Bulldogs finished in 3rd place at both the South Central Conference and Sectional track meets. Seniors included Aaron Byrne, Todd Collins, Aaron Foster, Wes Hindi, Randall Hoehn, Tyler Muenstermann, Dean Sheffer, Ryan Stroup, Cory Tucker, and Brad Wright. Though the Bulldogs scored well at the SCC Meet, the team recorded a championship in just one event, the 3200 meter relay. The winning unit was comprised of Foster, Hoehn, and juniors Evan Allison and Lucas Loots. The Bulldogs also won the event at the Macoupin County Meet, though sophomore Scott Prost ran in place of Loots, who was busy winning the 1600 meters and 3200 meters. The 3200 meter relay team of Foster, Hoehn, Allison, and Loots captured the Sectional championship later that season, thus securing a trip to State. Loots also competed in the 1600 meters in Charleston, and Team MVP Sheffer ran the 200 meters at State. After the season, Loots was named All-Area by the *Telegraph*.

Track (Girls)

The 2008 track team included seniors Jordan Chappell, Katie Hitz, Diondra Horner, Stephanie Semanik, and Katharine Volle. Though coach B.J. Ogata's squad finished just 8th at both the South Central Conference and Sectional track meets, several underclassmen did fare well as individuals. Junior Kelsey Henke captured gold in the 200 meters at the Macoupin County Meet, and fellow junior Alex Senaldi took home titles in both the 800 meters and 1600 meters. Meanwhile, freshman Katie Trettenero won the 3200 meters at County. Senaldi, the Team MVP, eventually qualified for State in the 3200 meters.

Volleyball

The 2007 volleyball team finished 5-21 overall and 2-8 in the South Central Conference East under coach Amber Scruton in her one and only season leading the program. The Lady Bulldogs featured a young roster, though seniors Cindy Gregory and Ashley Slifka provided leadership for the team. Juniors Lauren Newbold (2nd Team) and Lika Hindi (Honorable Mention) were named All-Conference for the Lady Bulldogs, with Hindi taking home Team MVP honors.

Class of 2009

Baseball

The 2009 baseball team, in its last season in the South Central Conference East, welcomed a new coach, Ryan McGowen, to lead the club. Though the Bulldogs made some overall improvements, a 7-13 record (including 3-6 in the SCC East), guaranteed the program its tenth straight losing season. The Bulldogs dropped their first five games of the year before pulling out a huge upset win over Bethalto Civic Memorial in the second game of a doubleheader. The victory sparked a three-game winning streak that led to five wins in six outings. However, the

Dogs ended the season with seven losses in their final nine games, including a 2-1 setback to East Alton-Wood River in the Regional.

Seniors Zack Arnett, John Bryan, Dakota Kreger, Jake Rhodes, Chris Taylor, Matt Tranter, and Taylor Wright led Staunton attack in 2009. Arnett, the Team MVP, completed an outstanding career with All-Conference Honorable Mention honors. He later moved on to MacMurray College and competed for the Highlanders for two seasons. Junior Jake Langley also enjoyed an outstanding campaign, winning the Hitting Award (.450) and capturing All-SCCE Honorable Mention status. Langley was also an All-Area selection by the *Telegraph* (1st Team) and *State Journal-Register* (Honorable Mention).

Basketball (Boys)

Steve Moore's second season at the helm of the basketball program saw the Bulldogs finish 21-10 overall, including 5-5 in the South Central Conference East. Interestingly enough, the overall record represented just the second winning season since the 1993 state championship squad, a period of sixteen years. Furthermore, the conference record ended a six-year string of last place finishes in the league, a span that saw SHS go 4-56 overall in the SCC East. For the second straight season, SHS fared very well in crossover games, finishing 8-1 against SCC West opponents.

The Bulldogs got off to a hot start in 2009-10, beginning the season 12-2, including winning the championship of the Carlinville Holiday Tournament for the first time in school history. At Carlinville, the Bulldogs won all four of their games by defeating Mt. Olive (70-47), Bunker Hill (51-34), Riverton (50-43), and top-seeded Raymond Lincolnwood (62-59). SHS also captured the Macoupin County championship for the first time since 2001, knocking off Virden (67-31), Carlinville (63-42), and Girard (49-44) to take the title. Unfortunately, untimely injuries took their toll on SHS, and the team limped into postseason play having lost five of eight games. However, staunch defense and home-court advantage during the Regional helped SHS defeat Alton Marquette (50-38) and Southwestern (40-36) to take the crown. The team's season ended at the Sectional with a loss to Greenville (67-50) for the third time on the year.

SHS had to say goodbye to the best senior class of basketball players since 2001, as Cody Best, Tyler Brauer, Lucas Loots, Mike Mihelcic, Daryl Podwojski, Jake Rhodes, Chris Taylor, and Taylor Wright all graduated in 2009. Best, in particular, had an outstanding season, leading the team in scoring (10.4 points) and sharing Team MVP honors with Mihelcic. Best was named County MVP, All-SCCE 1st Team, and All-State Honorable Mention by both the Illinois Basketball Coaches Association and Illinois Basketball Services. Furthermore, he was an All-Area selection by the *Telegraph* (1st Team), *State Journal-Register* (2nd Team), WSMI Radio (1st Team), and A Baseline View (Special Mention). In addition to Team MVP honors, Mihelcic captured All-Conference Honorable Mention status and was also named All-Area by the *State Journal-Register* (Honorable Mention) and WSMI (1st Team). Junior Kevin Fuller had an outstanding season for the Bulldogs, particularly in the Macoupin County championship game, and he was listed on the All-Tournament 1st Team for his efforts. Finally, Podwojski took home the squad's Free Throw Award by hitting 78% of his attempts from the line. In fact, in a late-season game at Carlinville, Podwojski drained 20-22 from the line. After the season, Moore was named Coach of Year by the Carlinville Rotary Club at the organization's annual All-Star event. Meanwhile, Best continued playing basketball for one season at Lewis & Clark Community College before moving on to compete for MacMurray College.

Classes of 2000 - 2009

Basketball (Girls)

Troy Redfern's second season leading the basketball program saw the team make big improvements in 2008-09. The Lady Bulldogs finished 12-14 overall and 5-5 in the South Central Conference East behind seniors Lika Hindi, Lauren Newbold, and Devin Painter. The highlight of the campaign was a stretch of close wins over Hillsboro (54-52), Litchfield (57-55), and Pana (48-46), three teams that had traditionally dominated SHS on the hardcourt. Both Newbold (1st Team) and Painter (Honorable Mention) captured All-SCCE honors, and each was also named to the All-County team. Newbold also took home 1st Team All-Area recognition by the *Telegraph* and WSMI Radio. Finally, with 1093 points and 798 rebounds, Newbold wrapped up her career as one of the all-time scoring and rebounding leaders in SHS history. Given her accomplishments across all sports, Newbold is rightly considered one of the best female athletes to ever compete at Staunton High School.

Cross Country (Boys)

Senior Lucas Loots was back for the 2008 cross country season and looking to add to his accomplishments from the previous campaign. Not only did Loots finish the year with All-Conference and *Telegraph* All-Area honors for the second consecutive season, but he once again received All-State status by finishing 13th overall in Peoria. Loots, who was coached by Dave Williams, continued his cross country career in college at the University of Chicago.

Cross Country (Girls)

The 2008 cross country team enjoyed another successful season by winning the South Central Conference title for the second consecutive year, as well as advancing to Sectional competition for the second of three straight trips. At the SCC Meet, freshman Mia Stefani and sophomore Katie Trettenero each captured All-Conference honors. However, the day belonged to senior Alex Senaldi. Not only did Senaldi win the event, but she finished out a great career by capturing All-Conference status for the fourth consecutive season, including two conference titles. At State, Senaldi finished 82nd overall. For her efforts, she was named the *Telegraph's* Runner of the Year. She continued her running career at McKendree University.

Football

The 2008 football team qualified for the IHSA Playoffs for the second straight year after finishing 6-4 overall and 2-3 in the South Central Conference East. The Dogs started off the campaign 5-0, as they would the next three seasons as well. The year began with a 38-7 victory over Carlinville in which SHS dominated both sides of the football against its long-time rival. After easily disposing of East Alton-Wood River (36-13) in Week 2, the Bulldogs welcomed a contest with arch-rival Gillespie. Although the Miners kept it close, the Staunton defense earned its first shutout of the season (12-0). SCC East victories in Week 4 and Week 5 over Hillsboro (18-6) and Litchfield (28-0), respectively, set the stage for a matchup with Pana. Unfortunately, the Panthers came away with a 23-18 victory, prompting a three-game losing streak that included losses to Greenville (16-6) and Vandalia (7-0). SHS got back to its winning ways in a Week 9 blowout of Roxana (48-0) to end the regular season. The three close SCC East losses came back to haunt the Dogs when postseason pairings were announced. Not only was Staunton cast as one of the smallest schools in Class 3A, but a low seed meant the Bulldogs had to embark on a trip to traditional powerhouse Anna-Jonesboro. The Dogs competed hard but were no match for the Wildcats, suffering a shutout by a score of 52-0.

On a side note, the SCC East title was captured by Greenville in 2008, while the SCC West crown was shared by Alton Marquette, Carlinville, and Southwestern. Many Bulldogs were honored at the end of the season with 1st Team All-Conference accolades, including seniors Kevin Ahrens, Cody Best, Gary Fuller, Dakota Kreger, and Josh Teeske. Junior Mike Ebersohl joined them on the 1st Team, while sophomore Adam Boston received Honorable Mention status. Ahrens, Best, and Teeske were each named to the *Telegraph* All-Area 1st Team, and Ahrens was also honored by the *State Journal-Register* as a 2nd Team award winner. Teeske threw for 1105 yards, breaking the one thousand yard mark for the second consecutive season. Best caught 27 balls for 458 yards, making him one of the top receivers in school history. Additionally, Boston ran for 734 yards, while junior Blake Steele ran for 546. Seniors on the team included Ahrens, Zack Arnett, Best, Tyler Brauer, John Bryan, Devin Clark, Chris Ebersohl, Fuller, Kreger, K.T. Lancaster, Alex Medd, Tony Rowell, Tyler Schneck, Teeske, Luke Wisnasky, and Taylor Wright. The Bulldogs were coached by Mike Parmentier.

Golf (Boys)

Troy Redfern's 2008 golf team finished the season 11-23 overall, including a 10th place finish at the South Central Conference Tournament. Seniors on the squad included Mike Barkoviak, Mike Mihelcic, and Jake Rhodes. Despite the down season, Mihelcic closed out his career in fine fashion, taking home All-Conference honors for the third consecutive season. He continued his playing career for two years at Lewis & Clark Community College.

Golf (Girls)

The 2008 golf team made program history by capturing the unit's first-ever Regional championship behind the leadership of coach Troy Redfern. The squad finished 20-4 overall and in 2nd place at the South Central Conference Tournament, representing the program's best-ever finish at that event. Seniors Carmi Cioni, Stormy Dufrain, and Anna Kroeger sparked the squad, with Cioni and Dufrain taking home All-Conference honors. Dufrain was also named to the *Telegraph's* All-Area 1st Team. However, the season belonged to junior Elyse Banovic. Banovic not only took home All-Conference and All-Area 1st Team honors, but she also advanced to the State Tournament for the second straight year, finishing in 28th place overall.

Soccer (Boys)

Ken Pelletier's third season leading the soccer program saw the 2008 Bulldogs finish 3-14-2 overall and 2-7 in the South Central Conference. The Dogs started the season slowly, going nine games without a win before an 8-0 triumph over East Alton-Wood River. The highlight of the year came in a 4-2 upset of Litchfield. However, the Purple Panthers exacted their revenge in the Regional, defeating SHS by the score of 8-0 to end Staunton's season. Class of 2009 soccer players included Evan Allison, Cody Drennan, Mitch Glisson, Steve Hokhold, Daryl Podwojski, Chris Taylor, Tyler Wall, and Eric Yarnik. Yarnik was voted Team MVP, and he and junior Anthony Fairman also captured All-Conference 2nd Team honors.

Soccer (Girls)

After struggling the previous season, the 2009 soccer team rebounded with an excellent year, finishing 13-6-1 overall and 6-2 in the South Central Conference. The Lady Bulldogs played very well down the stretch and, at one point, went eight straight games without a loss. In fact, the strong play jolted Staunton into the Regional championship game for the first time in

SHS soccer history. Unfortunately, an awkward bounce on a shot from near mid-field reached the back of Staunton's net, giving Carlinville a 1-0 victory that ended a successful campaign for the Lady Bulldogs.

Senior squad members in 2009 included Tara Allen, Carmi Cioni, Devin Painter, Kellie Rucker, and Kelsey Sczurek. Allen captured Team MVP honors and 1st Team All-Conference accolades for coach Andrea Williamson's unit. Painter was named to the All-SCC 2nd Team, as was sophomore Courtney Darrah. Junior Devon Bennett and sophomore Lindsey Mathenia were each awarded Honorable Mention status. Upon graduation, Allen continued her soccer career at Blackburn College, and Painter moved on to Kaskaskia College.

Softball

The 2009 softball team enjoyed its first winning season in eleven years behind the leadership of Doug Zehr. The squad ended the campaign with an overall record of 13-8, including 7-3 in the South Central Conference East. A key stretch of the season came when the Lady Bulldogs reeled off seven consecutive wins near the midpoint of the schedule. Seniors Kayla Brown, Anna Kroeger, Lauren Newbold, and Ashley Rensing all had solid seasons for the squad, as did junior Rachel Hadjan. In fact, Newbold and Kroeger were each named All-SCCE 1st Team, while Brown and Hadjan enjoyed 2nd Team honors. Additionally, all four players were honored by the *State Journal-Register* with All-Area Special Mention status. Hadjan and Newbold shared Team MVP honors. Hadjan won the Pitching Award (1.81 ERA) for SHS, and Newbold took home the team's Hitting Award (.429).

Track (Boys)

The 2009 track team, directed by B.J. Ogata, finished in 4th place at the South Central Conference Meet. Lucas Loots was the lone conference champion for the Bulldogs, as he took 1st place in the 1600 meters. He also was the lone Staunton champion at the Macoupin County Meet. At County, Loots had an incredible day, taking gold in the 800 meters, 1600 meters, and 3200 meters. Loots qualified for State in 1600 meters and 3200 meters, and he also helped the 3200 meter relay team advance to State. At State, Loots' classmates, fellow seniors Evan Allison, Cody Drennan, Mitch Glisson, and Eric Yarnik, comprised the relay team. Additional seniors on the track team included Mike Barkoviak, K.T. Lancaster, and Tony Rowell. Loots was named Team MVP for his efforts during the season, and he was also named Track Athlete of the Year by the *Telegraph*. Loots continued his track career at the University of Chicago for two years in addition to the three seasons he spent with the institution's cross country squad.

Track (Girls)

B.J. Ogata's 2009 track team finished 7th at the South Central Conference Meet behind the efforts of freshman Mia Stefani, the SCC champion in the 800 meters. At the Macoupin County Meet, senior Alex Senaldi capped off an impressive career with a victory in the 3200 meters. Senaldi and Stefani teamed up with senior Lika Hindi and junior Jessica Jarman in the 3200 meter relay that qualified for State, while sophomore Kristen McDowell joined them in Charleston after qualifying in the high jump. Hindi and Senaldi shared Team MVP honors, and they were joined in the Class of 2009 by Kelsey Henke and Andrea Rothgangel. After the season, Senaldi moved on to McKendree University where she competed in cross country and track.

Volleyball

The 2008 volleyball team welcomed its fifth coach in as many years. The coaching turnover was beginning to take its toll on the once-proud program, as the Lady Bulldogs had not experienced a winning season in six years. However, former SHS standout Andrea Prante was hired to change the culture of volleyball at Staunton, and she succeeded with a successful season of 15-11 overall, including 6-4 in the South Central Conference East.

SHS featured just two seniors in 2008, but they were solid players and leaders in the form of Lika Hindi and Lauren Newbold. Newbold served as the focal point of the team, capturing All-Conference honors for the third consecutive season, as well as being named Offensive MVP. Lindsey Mathenia, a sophomore, took home Defensive MVP honors and All-Conference 2nd Team recognition. Fellow sophomore Kristen McDowell was named All-SCCE Honorable Mention. Though Hindi and Newbold moved on after the season, the Lady Bulldogs had a solid corps of underclassmen who gained valuable experience, setting the stage for two phenomenal seasons to follow.

CHAPTER 11

Classes of 2010 – 2012

Overview

The 2010s witnessed a monumental move by the Staunton school district, as the decision was made to switch from the South Central Conference to the Prairie State Conference. While the change was supported within the district by the school board, administration, and coaches, it sparked controversy in the community. Regardless of one's opinion on the ruling, leaving the SCC East (in which SHS was the smallest school) for the less competitive PSC (in which SHS was the biggest school initially) was no doubt good for the trophy cases at Staunton High School. After having won just eight conference titles in twelve years in the restructured SCC, the Bulldogs captured nine titles in only three years of PSC competition. The PSC championship total occurred despite the fact that there were fewer sports offered by the conference, as the league did not provide for male or female competition in cross country, golf, or soccer. In fact, four of the eight aforementioned SCC titles were awarded in boy's golf and girl's cross country (two each).

Although SHS competed well against teams from the SCC West (Alton Marquette, Carlinville, East Alton-Wood River, Gillespie, Roxana, and Southwestern) after the conference split in 1997, the Bulldogs struggled mightily within their own division, the SCC East (Greenville, Hillsboro, Litchfield, Pana, Vandalia). In its final years in the conference, SHS finished near the bottom of the SCC East in virtually every sport. On the other hand, the first year in the PSC saw each sport offered at Staunton High School finish either first or second in the final standings. Although a general improvement in talent at SHS cannot be ignored, there is no doubt that switching to the PSC was a huge boon to Staunton's sports programs in regard to wins and losses.

It is worth noting the changes that took place in the South Central Conference after Staunton and Gillespie departed for the Prairie State Conference. Though the organization still kept its divisional format, there were three major changes to the setup. First, with no new schools invited to replace Staunton and Gillespie, the SCC East and SCC West included only five teams each. Second, divisional play in football was scrapped, and the SCC became a closed conference, meaning that each of the nine regular season football games was now a conference affair. Finally, though both the SCC East and SCC West continued to award separate conference championships in baseball, basketball, softball, and volleyball, crossover games between the divisions now counted in the standings for the first time. Thus, each team now played thirteen conference games. Included in the total was a home-and-home matchup with each divisional opponent (eight games), as well as one crossover game against schools in the other division (five games).

The Prairie State Conference itself experienced notable change in just the short time that Staunton was a member, and the foggy future of the league played a part in the district's decision to return to the South Central Conference. Beginning in 2009-10, the PSC was made up of nine schools, including Gillespie, Girard, Kincaid South Fork, Mt. Olive, New Berlin, Nokomis, Pawnee, Staunton, and Virden. It is worth noting that New Berlin did not compete in the PSC in football, and instead it was a member of the Sangamo Conference for that sport only. By changing affiliations just for football, the Pretzels allowed the two leagues to have a balanced schedule, allowing Week 1 and Week 9 matchups between the PSC and Sangamo. Following the school year, however, New Berlin voted to join the Sangamo for all sports. 2010-11 also saw the formation of the North Mac school district, a consolidation between Girard and Virden. Thus, the PSC needed to add a school to remain at eight members, and Bunker Hill eventually left the Western Illinois Valley Conference to fill the void.

In 2012-13, Staunton and Gillespie were set to rejoin the South Central Conference. Shortly after Girard and Virden consolidated to form the North Mac, the new district elected to leave the Prairie State Conference for the Sangamo Conference. The departure left the PSC in limbo, and thus Staunton, Gillespie, and Nokomis accepted an offer to join the SCC, which had just voted to remove the Metro East schools of Alton Marquette, East Alton-Wood River, and Roxana. However, at the last moment Nokomis chose to stay in the PSC, and thus Roxana was invited back into the fold. Thus, in 2012-13, the new South Central Conference will feature Carlinville, Gillespie, Greenville, Hillsboro, Litchfield, Pana, Roxana, Southwestern, Staunton, and Vandalia. The SCC will operate as one league without divisions, with conference members competing against each other one time each in baseball, basketball, football, soccer, softball, and volleyball. On a side note, the new Prairie State Conference will feature Alton Marquette, Bunker Hill, Decatur Lutheran (football only), Edwardsville Metro East Lutheran, Kincaid South Fork, Mt. Olive, and Nokomis. East Alton-Wood River was unable to land in a new conference and will therefore become an independent, and Pawnee will join North Mac in the Sangamo Conference.

In addition to the changes in conference affiliation, there were other notable happenings during the early 2010s. First, a new all-weather track was built for the 2009-10 school year. The facility improvement allowed SHS to host large meets that were impossible to put on before the addition. Also, after a dreadful 2000s that saw SHS experience very few winning seasons, the 2010s showed early promise, as most programs in the district enjoyed success in the first years of the decade. In particular, three achievements deserve mention. First, the 2010 football team tied a school record for victories and advanced to the IHSA Quarterfinals, the deepest advancement in SHS football history. Additionally, the 2012 girl's soccer team won a Regional championship, accounting for the only title in SHS soccer history. Finally, the boy's track team was able to win the Prairie State Conference in each of the three seasons in which Staunton was a member of the league.

Class of 2010

Baseball

Ryan McGowen's second season leading the baseball program saw the Bulldogs post a record of 15-6 overall, including 5-1 in the Prairie State Conference. The winning record was the first in eleven seasons for the once-proud program, and the league mark actually gave the Dogs a share of the PSC title with Nokomis. The title represented the program's first conference championship since 1984. The Bulldogs began the season by winning six straight and eleven of thirteen, with the only losses in that span coming to Bethalto Civic Memorial in a doubleheader. SHS eventually took a three-game winning streak into Regionals before losing to Edwardsville Metro East Lutheran by a score of 9-6 to end the year.

The 2010 season was the last for Coach McGowen and seniors Kevin Billings, Charlie Clark, Jake Langley, and Tyler Lapolice. Langley won the Hitting Award with a .540 average, one of the highest marks in school history. Clark also had an amazing season, posting a .523 batting average while also winning the Pitching Award (6-3, 1.49 ERA). Langley and Clark shared Team MVP honors, and they were both named to the *Telegraph* (1st Team) and *State Journal-Register* (Honorable Mention) All-Area teams. Meanwhile, Billings joined Langley and Clark as a 1st Team All-PSC selection, while freshmen Austin Hollaway and A.J. Sitko began excellent careers with All-Conference Honorable Mention accolades. After leaving SHS, Clark continued his career at MacMurray College.

Basketball (Boys)

Coach Steve Moore had to replace an abundance of talent for the 2009-10 basketball season, as the Bulldogs graduated eight excellent seniors from the previous year. However, the Class of 2010 that included Kevin Fuller, Andy Goebel, and Scott Prost did their best to minimize the effects of the lost production. In fact, Fuller provided the program one of the most dominate statistical seasons in several years, as he posted 17.6 points and 9.4 rebounds per game while also winning the Free Throw Award (68%). Additionally, he drew 28 charges on the season, one of the highest totals in school history. Goebel was also very impressive in his final campaign, posting 12.9 points and knocking down 60 shots from the 3-point line. In fact, he eventually advanced to State in the IHSA's 3-Point Shootout, becoming just the third player in school history to achieve such a feat. Upon graduation, Fuller and Goebel continued to compete at Illinois College and Webster University, respectively.

The Bulldogs as a team posted an 18-11 record overall, including a 6-2 mark in their first season in the Prairie State Conference, good for a 2nd place tie. One highlight of the season came at the Carlinville Holiday Tournament where the Bulldogs won the championship for the second straight year. At Carlinville, the Dogs defeated Gillespie (50-31) before losing to Litchfield (57-56) in pool play. However, after the Dogs downed Riverton by a score of 48-40, it was determined that SHS won the pool tiebreaker, with free throw percentage being the deciding factor. Staunton took advantage of the opportunity and defeated Raymond Lincolnwood (59-52) to win the title. Unfortunately, there were several missed opportunities as well. In fact, eight of Staunton's eleven losses came in the closing minutes of the game. One such loss was at the Macoupin County Tournament. The Dogs began tournament action with a 54-40 win over Virden but fell to Southwestern (47-44) in an upset loss. The Bulldogs rebounded to take 3rd place when Goebel hit a 3-pointer at the buzzer to defeat Bunker Hill (46-44). SHS also missed an opportunity to repeat as Regional champions. The Dogs avenged the loss to Southwestern, defeating the Piasa Birds by a count of 47-42 to begin postseason action. Unfortunately, Staunton played one of its worst games of the year in a 59-53 setback to an upstart Alton Marquette squad in the Regional final.

After the season, both Fuller and Goebel were highly decorated for their outstanding senior campaigns. In addition to sharing Team MVP honors, both were 1st Team All-Conference winners, as well as All-Area selections by the *State Journal-Register*. A 1st Team All-County performer, Fuller also took home All-Area awards from the *Telegraph* (1st Team) and A Baseline View (Special Mention). Finally, he was a Special Mention All-State choice by the Illinois Basketball Coaches Association.

Basketball (Girls)

For the first time in program history, the 2009-10 basketball team won a league championship after finishing 7-0 in its initial season in the Prairie State Conference. The Lady

Bulldogs actually got off to a slow start on the year, beginning just 3-7 after ten games. However, the Lady Bulldogs continued to compete and eventually went 13-4 down the stretch before losing to Hillsboro in the Regional championship game. Coach Troy Redfern's squad tied the school record for wins after finishing 16-12 overall, though his team shattered the mark the very next season. Rachel Hadjan and Kaitlin Schrader were the lone seniors on the club that season, and they teamed up with juniors Briana Rae and Sam Senaldi to spur the unit's success. Schrader and Rae shared Offensive MVP honors, while Senaldi captured the Defensive MVP award. Both Schrader and Rae were named 1st Team All-PSC, and each was also named to the *State Journal-Register* All-Area team.

Cross Country (Girls)

Coach Dave Williams' 2009 cross country team qualified for the Sectional for the third straight season behind the leadership of seniors Jessica Banovz, Sara Hall, Kadambari Jain, and Jessica Jarman. Unfortunately, due to the change in conferences, SHS was unable to defend its South Central Conference crown, which it had won for two consecutive seasons. Team MVP Katie Trettenero, a junior, paced the Lady Bulldogs.

Football

In terms of scheduling, the switch from the South Central Conference to the Prairie State Conference affected football more than any other sport at Staunton High School. In fact, eight of Staunton's nine regular season games came against new opponents, as only Gillespie, which also made the switch from the SCC to the PSC, was retained from the previous season's schedule. In addition to facing new conference foes, the PSC had a scheduling agreement with the Sangamo Conference in order to fill Week 1 and Week 9 of the schedule. As such, 2009 saw SHS face off against several schools that the Bulldogs had never before competed against on the gridiron. Additionally, the Bulldogs had a chance to renew old rivalries, as the PSC was made up of several schools that were once members of the SCC.

The year began with a game against Riverton, one of three teams (along with Auburn and Williamsville), that exited the Prairie State Conference for the Sangamo Conference, thus opening up spots in the PSC for Gillespie and Staunton. The Bulldogs were sharp in the contest, defeating the Hawks by a score of 32-13. SHS followed up that victory with easy league wins over Gillespie (48-14) and Girard (60-6). Week 4 of the season saw the Bulldogs renew their football rivalry with Mt. Olive in the first meeting between the schools since 1979. In an exciting game at Mt. Olive, the Dogs held on to beat the Wildcats by a score of 20-12. Pawnee gave SHS yet another tough game in Week 5, but the Bulldogs held on for a 15-12 victory. In the first meeting between Staunton and Kincaid South Fork, the Bulldogs easily handled the Ponies to the tune of 48-13. Victories over Virden (16-6) and Nokomis (49-6) closed out an undefeated PSC campaign at 7-0, thus crowning SHS as Prairie State Conference champions in the school's first year in the league.

The last game of the regular season saw the Bulldogs take on Petersburg PORTA for the first time in school history. The Dogs were playing for an undefeated regular season, but PORTA did not comply, as the Bluejays easily defeated Staunton by a score of 37-14. Regardless, SHS still secured a high seed and a first round playoff game against Bismarck-Henning. The Bulldogs played poorly in the game, yet still had an opportunity to win the contest after it went into overtime. After scoring on their first possession of the extra frame, the Blue Devils elected to kick the extra point, which was successful. The Dogs responded by also scoring a touchdown in overtime. However, due to an inconsistent kicking game, SHS decided to go for the two-point conversion and a chance to win the game. Unfortunately, in a controversial decision, the pass attempt for the conversion was ruled incomplete and Bismarck-Henning escaped with a 21-20 victory.

Despite the postseason upset, coach Mike Parmentier and his players experienced an amazing season. In addition to the conference championship, the Dogs finished 8-2 overall, the program's highest win total in nine years. Leading the charge were seniors Kevin Billings, Alex Braden, Andrew Braden, Charlie Clark, Mike Ebersohl, Kevin Fuller, Adam Hamilton, Ken Helfer, Kevin Kozemczak, Tyler Lapolice, Matt Miller, Wes Mitchell, Scott Prost, Blake Steele, and Nathan Ward. Ebersohl continued his football career for one season at Washington University. Fuller went on to Illinois College to compete in both football and basketball, whereas Clark played both football and baseball at MacMurray College.

The PSC employs a less-stringent All-Conference policy than the SCC, and as many as thirteen Bulldogs were honored after the season. Billings, Ebersohl, Fuller, Prost, and Steele were each 1st Team selections for SHS, as were juniors Adam Boston and Brady Moore. Clark joined juniors Kyle Brauer and Dylan Caldieraro, as well as sophomore Zack Ward, on the 2nd Team, while Nathan Ward and junior Dusty Graves were Honorable Mention choices. Ebersohl took home All-Area 1st Team honors from the *State Journal-Register*, and he was also named 1st Team All-Area by the *Telegraph* where he was joined by Fuller, Prost, and Steele. The Bulldogs featured an extremely impressive stable of running backs in 2009, as Steele rushed for 1081 yards, and Boston and Graves totaled 613 yards and 605 yards, respectively.

Golf (Boys)

The 2009 golf team finished the season with a match play record of 10-22. Troy Redfern's group of golfers included just two seniors, Quinn Fiori and Stephen Hagan, and was led by low scorer Austin Billings, a freshman.

Golf (Girls)

Seniors Elyse Banovic and Caroline Cavallo led the 2009 golf team to a 26-6 record, the highest win total in SHS golf history. The Lady Bulldogs captured the Regional championship for the second straight year, thus advancing to Sectional play for the last of three straight trips. Banovic capped off an impressive career that saw her win the Regional and finish 19th at State. For her efforts she was named to the *Telegraph's* All-Area 1st Team. The best female golfer in SHS history, Banovic moved on to Eastern Illinois University to continue her golf career with the Panthers. The Lady Bulldogs were coached by Troy Redfern.

Soccer (Boys)

The soccer team struggled to a 2-16 record in 2009, the lowest win total in the program's history. The record can partially be attributed to a lack of depth, as the Bulldogs were barely able to field a team on several occasions due to injuries. Coach Ken Pelletier and seniors Anthony Fairman, Ben McDowell, and Aaron Slifka did their best to piece the team together, and they were aided by the play of junior Brett Kinder and sophomore Devin Gerdes. Kinder was named Team MVP, while Gerdes was a 1st Team All-Area selection by the *Telegraph*.

Soccer (Girls)

Andrea Williamson's seventh and final season as coach of the soccer program saw the 2010 team finish with a record of 10-8-2. SHS played .500 ball for most of the year. However, the team got hot late, winning four consecutive games before falling to Girard (1-0) in the Regionals. Seniors Devon Bennett, Lindsay Felchner, and Alicia Snyder fueled the successful season, and they were aided by the outstanding play of several underclassmen. Among the standouts was junior and Team MVP Sam Senaldi.

Softball

The 2010 softball team finished the season at 11-10 overall and 5-1 in the Prairie State Conference. The Lady Bulldogs played several close games in league play and nearly won the PSC in their first season in the new conference. Unfortunately, a 1-0 loss to New Berlin ruined any championship aspirations. After the season, coach Doug Zehr had to say goodbye to seniors Rachel Hadjan and Sam Ray. Hadjan was a 1st Team All-Conference selection, as was freshman Kerstin Brown. Meanwhile, sophomore Marissa Zirges and freshman Kim Machuga were Honorable Mention selections. Hadjan finished her senior season as Team MVP after leading the squad with a .414 batting average and a 1.53 ERA on the mound. The *State Journal-Register* All-Area Honorable Mention selection continued her career at McKendree University for one season.

Track (Boys)

Coach B.J. Ogata's 2010 track team won the Prairie State Conference in its first year in the new league. The Dogs were paced by the exploits of seniors Anthony Fairman and Andy Goebel. Fairman won the PSC in the high jump, triple jump, and the 400 meters, while Goebel captured gold in the 800 meters. Goebel also teamed up with junior Dylan Rooney, sophomore Nick Banovz, and freshman Sam Allison to win the 3200 meter relay. Other PSC champions included Allison in the 1600 meters and freshman Tom Homeier in the 3200 meters. At the Macoupin County Meet, Team MVP Fairman again captured titles in the high jump and triple jump to lead the Bulldogs to a 5th place finish. Fairman eventually qualified for State in both events after winning the high jump at Sectionals and placing 2nd in the triple jump. Junior Brett Kinder also qualified for State in 2010 in the high jump, as SHS made a clean sweep of the event at Sectionals. Fairman, who set a school record in the high jump, was a 1st Team All-Area selection by the *Telegraph*.

Track (Girls)

The 2010 track program made a clean sweep of the Prairie State Conference Meet, as the girls joined the boys in the winner's circle. Coach B.J. Ogata and seniors Claire Cioni, Sara Hall, Jessica Jarman, Ashley Rettig, Kaitlin Schrader, and Brittany Staake led the squad. The Lady Bulldogs owed the conference title to wins in three relay events. Cioni teamed with juniors Stephanie Becker and Deirdra Fey and sophomore Jordan Frye to win the 400 meter relay. Cioni, Becker, junior Kristen McDowell, and freshman Sophie Fairman won the 800 meter relay, while Jarman, Rettig, junior Katie Trettenero, and sophomore Amanda Cornell teamed up to win the 3200 meter relay. Also victorious at the PSC Meet were Cioni in the 100 meters and Fairman in the 200 meters.

The Lady Bulldogs placed 3rd at the Macoupin County Meet, as Fairman (400 meters), Fey (long jump), and McDowell (high jump) placed 1st for the team. Fairman was the lone Sectional champion for the Lady Bulldogs, as she won the 400 meters at that event. Fairman, the Team MVP, eventually placed 6th at State in the triple jump and 8th at State in the 400 meters. Several competitors broke school records in 2010, including Cioni (pole vault), McDowell (high jump), Fairman (triple jump, 400 meters), the 400 meter relay team (Cioni, Fey, Becker, Frye), and the 800 meter relay team (Cioni, Becker, McDowell, Fairman). At the conclusion of the season, both Fairman and McDowell were named 1st Team All-Area by the *Telegraph*.

Volleyball

The 2009 volleyball team featured just one senior, as Alicia Snyder was the lone veteran on coach Andrea Prante's squad. However, the unit included an excellent group of juniors who helped lead the Lady Bulldogs to a share of the Prairie State Conference championship in their first year in the league. More importantly, SHS won its first Regional in eight years and accumulated its most wins in ten years by finishing 23-6 overall and 7-1 in the PSC. The campaign started off with five straight victories and eventually included six more wins in succession before a loss in the Macoupin County Tournament, at which SHS finished in 3rd place. The victory in their final game at County sprung an eight-game winning streak for the Lady Bulldogs that included a championship at the Jerseyville Tournament. The team began Regionals with an easy win over Southwestern before being pushed to three games in a tight win over Vandalia. At Sectionals, SHS disposed of Greenville in two games before succumbing to eventual state champion Freeburg.

Several individuals obtained postseason recognition for SHS, including All-Conference performers Yana Fairman (1st Team), Kristen McDowell (1st Team), Briana Rae (2nd Team), and Sam Senaldi (Honorable Mention), all juniors. Fairman was selected 1st Team All-Area by the *State Journal-Register*, and McDowell and Rae were also noted with Honorable Mention status. The *Telegraph* listed McDowell as a 1st Team performer in its All-Area selections. Meanwhile, Fairman was selected as the team's Offensive MVP, while fellow junior Lindsey Mathenia captured the Defensive MVP award.

Class of 2011

Baseball

The SHS baseball team had to fight the weather in 2011, as record rains kept the team to just fifteen games played on the year. However, the Dogs, under first-year coach Kyle McBrain, made the most of their time in the field, posting a 10-5 record that included a 4-2 mark in the Prairie State Conference. The Bulldogs dropped two of their first three games, but SHS finished the regular season with just two losses in its last eleven regular contests before losing to Hillsboro (3-0) in the first round of Regionals. The team consisted mostly of underclassmen, though seniors Adam Boston, Dusty Graves, and Brady Moore played an integral role in the fine season. Moore was named to the All-Conference 2nd Team, joining sophomores Austin Hollaway (1st Team), A.J. Sitko (1st Team), Dillon Diesselhorst (2nd Team), and Larry Caldieraro (Honorable Mention) as All-PSC honorees. Hollaway and Sitko were also named 1st Team All-Area by the *Telegraph*, and Sitko was named All-Area Honorable Mention by the *State Journal-Register*. Diesselhorst took home Team MVP honors, while Sitko garnered the Pitching Award.

Finally, Hollaway and Moore shared the Hitting Award, as each finished the season with a .490 batting average.

Basketball (Boys)

Despite having lost most of its production from the previous season, the 2010-11 basketball team saw seniors Kyle Brauer, Jordan Johnson, Brett Kinder, and Brady Moore lead the squad to its second consecutive 18-11 record, which included a 4-3 mark in the Prairie State Conference. In addition to the successful regular season, the Bulldogs made a push to the title game of both the Macoupin County Tournament and Regional Tournament before falling to favorites North Mac and Alton Marquette, respectively. The Dogs featured a balanced attack led by junior Devin Gerdes (11.6 points). Gerdes earned 1st Team All-PSC honors, and he was also an All-Area selection by the *State Journal-Register* (Honorable Mention) and A Baseline View (Special Mention). Kinder and sophomore Austin Hollaway shared Team MVP honors, and each was also named All-Conference Honorable Mention. Kinder also captured All-County accolades as well as All-Area Special Mention from A Baseline View. Brauer capped off his senior season with an outstanding Macoupin County Tournament, joining Kinder on the All-Tournament team. Meanwhile, Moore won the Free Throw Award by hitting 76% of his tosses from the charity stripe. The Bulldogs were coached by Steve Moore.

Basketball (Girls)

The 2010-11 basketball team entered the record books as the best in school history. The Lady Bulldogs shattered the previous season record of 16 wins by finishing 20-7 overall. The team also captured the Prairie State Conference championship, finishing 7-0 for the second consecutive season. The Macoupin County Tournament witnessed a change in 2011, as the event switched to pool play for the first time in its history. The move was made as a result of the consolidation between Girard and Virden that left just seven Macoupin County schools offering girl's basketball. After #1 seed and heavy favorite Southwestern was upset early in the tournament by North Mac in pool play, SHS went on to capture its first county title since 1987. In the process, the Lady Bulldogs easily defeated Mt. Olive (70-25), Carlinville (55-36), Bunker Hill (50-18), and North Mac (47-33) on their way to the crown. Unfortunately, Staunton saw its season end in the Regional final for the second time in as many years, as Litchfield defeated SHS on its way to a Super-Sectional appearance.

Seniors Briana Rae, Sam Senaldi, and sophomore Sophie Fairman were each named 1st Team All-Conference for the Lady Bulldogs. Rae and Senaldi also captured All-County honors, with Rae securing the MVP for her efforts in leading her team to the championship. Rae was also named to the *Telegraph* All-Area 1st Team, and she (3rd Team) and Fairman (Honorable Mention) were both honored by the *State Journal-Register* as well. Fairman (11.2 points, 9.0 rebounds) and senior Courtney Darrah shared Defensive MVP honors, while Rae (11.9 points, 8.8 rebounds) took home the Offensive MVP trophy. Junior Katie Yakos won the Free Throw Award. Upon graduation, Darrah continued her playing career at the St. Louis College of Pharmacy, whereas Rae landed at Blackburn College.

Cross Country (Boys)

Although the 2010 cross country program did not have enough members to compete as a full team, seniors Matt Bononi, Tristan Coan, and Dillon Parker participated as individuals under the tutelage of Dave Williams. After the season ended, Coan was presented Team MVP honors.

Cross Country (Girls)

Coming off three straight Sectional appearances, the 2010 cross country team was unable to duplicate the success of previous years. Team MVP Katie Trettenero did her best to spark the squad by qualifying for Sectional competition, and she was named 1st Team All-Area by the *Telegraph* for her efforts. Dave Williams coached the unit, which included seniors Surbhi Jain and Trettenero. In addition to running track for the institution, Trettenero also continued her cross country career at Southern Illinois University-Edwardsville.

Football

Mike Parmentier's sixth season directing the SHS football team resulted in a year for the record books. Although the Dogs failed to win the Prairie State Conference (6-1), SHS advanced to the quarterfinals of the IHSA Playoffs for the first time in school history. Furthermore, by finishing 10-2 overall, the Bulldogs tied the school record for wins. The season started off with relative ease, as the Dogs defeated Riverton (42-14), Gillespie (36-0), Bunker Hill (49-0), and Mt. Olive (62-0) by a combined score of 189-14, with both opponent touchdowns being scored against the second unit. However, Week 5 saw Staunton face off against a staunch Pawnee squad. The Bulldogs were actually outplayed in the contest, losing the battle in almost every statistical category. However, the only number that mattered was on the scoreboard, and somehow SHS found a way to win the game by a count of 6-5. After defeating Kincaid South Fork (48-7) in Week 6, Staunton faced another tough PSC team in the North Mac Panthers. North Mac was established in the 2010-11 school year after the Girard and Virden school districts consolidated. While both schools had been struggling in various sports at the time, North Mac was a force to be reckoned with, and in fact the Panthers captured several championships in their inaugural year in the Prairie State Conference. Unfortunately for Staunton, one of those titles came in football, as SHS dropped a heartbreaker (27-21) to the Panthers. The game was reminiscent of the Pawnee matchup, but this time Staunton won almost every meaningful statistical category. However, the Panthers made key plays on special teams and defense to win the game and, eventually, the Prairie State Conference championship. Though disappointed with the loss, the Dogs had higher aspirations for the year and, after soundly defeating Nokomis (41-7) and Petersburg PORTA (49-7), made good on those goals in the postseason.

Due to low playoff points (total opponent wins on the season), Staunton received a #5 seed in its quadrant and had to hit the road in the opening round of the postseason, a rare occurrence for an 8-1 team. SHS headed south to take on the Red Bud Musketeers, champions of the Cahokia Conference. Despite a huge size advantage on the line, Red Bud could not contain Staunton's ground attack, and the Bulldogs won easily by a score of 61-36. The first round road game proved to be a blessing in disguise, as Staunton received a home game in the second round. Despite being the lower seed, SHS was favored in its game against #1 Johnston City, representing the Black Diamond Conference in a very weak year for the league. The Bulldogs left no doubt who the better team was after destroying the Indians by a score of 42-7. Although the area was hoping for a Macoupin County showdown with Carlinville in the quarterfinals, the Cavaliers were unable to hold up their end of the bargain, as they fell to traditional powerhouse Casey-Westfield in the second round. The Warriors have one of the best fan bases of any program in the state, and their faithful came to Staunton in masses to see their team take on the upstart Staunton squad. SHS started strong, but Casey-Westfield's massive line eventually wore down the Dogs en route to a 34-20 victory.

With team success comes individual accolades, and several Bulldogs were honored for their outstanding 2010 season. Seniors Adam Boston, Dylan Caldieraro, Dusty Graves, and Brady Moore all earned 1st Team All-Conference honors. Seniors Bryan Rucker and Nick Dobrinich made the All-PSC 2nd Team, as did juniors Kory Sczurek and Austin Sherfy and sophomore David Vaughn. Junior Brad Seketa led the passing attack with 911 yards, and fellow junior Zack Ward finished with 502 rushing yards on the season. Both were also named to the All-Conference 2nd Team for their fine play. Finally, seniors Kyle Brauer and Andrew Slifka were named All-PSC Honorable Mention. Junior placekicker Kole Billings had an outstanding season in an area that had been a weakness for SHS in previous years, and he was named to the *Telegraph's* All-Area 1st Team for his efforts on the field. Billings was joined on the All-Area team by Boston, Caldieraro, and Moore. Additionally, Boston (1st Team) and Moore (2nd Team) were *State Journal-Register* All-Area picks. After the season, Boston was chosen for the exclusive Shriner's All-Star game in Peoria. Finally, with his outstanding season at fullback (1186 yards rushing) and linebacker, Boston was chosen for the Illinois High School Football Coaches Association All-State 1st Team, cementing his place as one of the finest players to ever put on the pads for the Bulldogs. Unfortunately, the Dogs graduated an excellent senior class, including Boston, Tyler Braden, Brauer, Caldieraro, Brad Clark, Dobrinich, Graves, Corey Harbison, Jordan Johnson, Levi Ladendorf, Moore, Rucker, Slifka, and Matt White.

Golf (Boys)

Troy Redfern's golf team finished the 2010 season with a record of 7-15 in match play. The team featured just one senior in the form of Mason Fraser. Freshman Ryan Fretz finished with the lowest scoring average on the team, and he eventually advanced to Sectional competition.

Golf (Girls)

The 2010 golf team, under the leadership of Troy Redfern, finished with its sixth straight winning season since the program's inception, compiling a 15-9 record. Seniors Deirdra Fey and Cecily Haase provided leadership for the team, while junior Courtney Redfern finished with the lowest scoring average. Haase and Redfern both advanced to Sectional play that season.

Soccer (Boys)

The 2010 SHS soccer team welcomed the fourth coach in the program's twelve-year history, as Brad Fulk was promoted to the lead position after previously serving as an assistant coach for the team. Despite competitive play throughout the year, the Dogs finished with a record of 3-13-2, the program's sixth straight losing season. The team started off slow, winning just once in its first ten games. However, two wins in the final three regular season matchups showed promise, though the Dogs eventually fell to Carlyle in the Regional by a score of 2-1. Senior soccer players included Christian Anglin, Seth Anglin, Brett Kinder, Matt Rich, Dylan Rooney, Lee Snead, Phil Trettenero, Mike Volle, and Sam Young. Team MVP Kinder led the club in assists with 6, while junior Devin Gerdes tallied 8 goals to lead the Dogs in scoring.

Soccer (Girls)

The SHS soccer team found itself under new leadership in 2011, as Julie Tyler took over the program. The Lady Bulldogs got off to an excellent start, winning their first four games and five of six. Unfortunately, the club lost its next five games and eventually finished with a record of 9-10 overall. Senior soccer players included Courtney Darrah, Lacie Davis, Jody DeVries, Ashley Foster, Lindsey Mathenia, Briana Rae, and Sam Senaldi. All-Sectional Honorable Mention from the Illinois High School Soccer Coaches Association went to Senaldi, who also took home Team MVP honors.

Softball

The Staunton softball team got off to a rocky start in 2011 but finished strong down the stretch. The Lady Bulldogs were coached by Doug Zehr, who retired from his teaching and coaching posts after the season. After winning just once in its first nine games, SHS rebounded to finish the year 6-13 overall, including 3-3 in the Prairie State Conference. All-PSC members included seniors Melissa Heigert (1st Team) and Sarah Caldieraro (Honorable Mention), sophomores Kim Machuga (1st Team) and Kerstin Brown (2nd Team), and freshman Dianna Highlander (2nd Team). Heigert and Machuga were both named All-Area Honorable Mention by the *State Journal-Register*, while Machuga also grabbed a spot on the *Telegraph* All-Area 1st Team. Caldieraro and Team MVP Heigert were the only seniors on the squad. Heigert continued her softball career at Lewis & Clark Community College.

Track (Boys)

The 2011 track team enjoyed a successful season behind the performance of junior Jake Mahin. Mahin was the Prairie State Conference, Macoupin County, and Sectional shot put champion, while also winning conference and county titles in the discus. He eventually advanced to State in both events, finishing 7th overall in the shot put. Coach B.J. Ogata's squad took 2nd place at County and won the PSC for the second consecutive season, though in an odd way. After the PSC Meet, the team trophy was originally handed to North Mac. However, it was later discovered that points scored by SHS in the long jump were accidentally awarded to Mt. Olive. The correction was not made until the next day, but the end result was a tie between the Bulldogs and Panthers.

Joining Mahin as PSC champions were seniors Jordan Johnson (triple jump), Brett Kinder (1600 meter relay), Dylan Rooney (1600 meter relay), and sophomores Sam Allison (800 meters, 1600 meter relay) and David Vaughn (1600 meter relay). The group of Kinder, Rooney, Allison, and Vaughn went on to win the Sectional in their relay, thus advancing to State. Mahin (discus, shot put) and the 1600 meter relay team broke school records during the year, and they were honored by the *Telegraph* with 1st Team All-Area accolades. Seniors on the squad included Matt Bononi, Brad Clark, Nick Dobrinich, Johnson, Kinder, Thomas Kloss, Rooney, and Mike Volle. Following the season, Kinder was voted Team MVP by his peers.

Track (Girls)

Coach B.J. Ogata's 2011 track team was paced by the efforts of Sophie Fairman, a sophomore. Fairman was a champion in multiple events at the Prairie State Conference Meet (triple jump, 100 meters, 200 meters), Macoupin County Meet (triple jump, 200 meters, 400 meters), and Sectional Meet (400 meters, 3200 meter relay). She eventually capped off the season by qualifying for State in the maximum four events, capturing 3rd overall in the triple jump and 4th in the 400 meters. Senior Kristen McDowell qualified for State in the high jump while also winning conference and county titles in her event. Amanda Cornell, a junior, won the PSC crown in the 800 meters, while the 1600 meter relay team won the PSC (senior Yana Fairman, senior Katie Trettenero, junior Mia Stefani, sophomore Brooke Buffington) and

Sectional (Cornell, Stefani, Buffington, Sophie Fairman) titles before competing at State (Yana Fairman, Cornell, Stefani, Buffington). The Lady Bulldogs finished 2nd overall in the PSC and 3rd at County.

After the season, Sophie Fairman and relay teammates Cornell, Stefani, and Buffington were all named to the *Telegraph* All-Area 1st Team. Also, by the end of the year several athletes had shattered school records, including Sophie Fairman (triple jump, 100 meters, 400 meters), McDowell (high jump), and the 3200 meter relay team of Buffington, Cornell, Sophie Fairman, and Stefani. Seniors on the team included Yana Fairman, Deirdra Fey, McDowell, and Trettenero. Upon graduation, Trettenero continued her track career at Southern Illinois University-Edwardsville where she also ran cross country.

Volleyball

The 2010 volleyball season was eagerly anticipated, as SHS returned the bulk of its lineup from a very successful 2009 campaign. However, a major change took place in the leadership ranks, as long-time junior high coach Mike Korte was asked to take on high school coaching duties as well. Fortunately, Korte's success at the lower levels carried over to the varsity ranks, as the Dogs finished the season 25-5 overall. Included in the excellent record was a championship at the Jerseyville Tournament. However, the Lady Bulldogs were unable to defend their Prairie State Conference crown, instead finishing 6-1 in league play and in 2nd place to North Mac. SHS exacted revenge on the Panthers at the Macoupin County Tournament, as the Lady Bulldogs went on to defeat the new Girard-Virden consolidation to win their first county title in more than a decade. Unfortunately, Staunton was placed in a very difficult Regional and eventually fell to top-seeded Carlyle in the title game.

Team MVP Kristen McDowell capped off an amazing career by being named 1st Team All-Conference and All-County her senior year, as well as *State Journal-Register* All-Area Honorable Mention. McDowell was also honored by the *Telegraph* when she was named Player of the Year for the circulation area. Also of note, Korte was named Coach of the Year by the *Telegraph* for the team's success in his inaugural season at the helm. Senior Briana Rae joined McDowell as 1st Team All-Conference and All-County, and she was also named 1st Team All-Area by the *Telegraph*. Sophie Fairman had a breakout sophomore season, capturing 2nd Team All-PSC honors and *Telegraph* (1st Team) and *State Journal-Register* (Honorable Mention) All-Area awards. Finally, seniors Yana Fairman and Lindsey Mathenia were named to the All-Conference 2nd Team. Following graduation, McDowell continued her volleyball career at Webster University. Meanwhile, the elder Fairman was accepted to the United States Air Force Academy, quite an accomplishment given its strict admission policy based on academics, athletics, and leadership ability. Joining Fairman, Mathenia, McDowell, and Rae in the Class of 2011 were Lauren Gaudette and Sam Senaldi.

Class of 2012

Baseball

With nearly every key contributor set to return from the previous season, the 2012 baseball campaign looked promising on paper. Unfortunately, injuries decimated coach Kyle McBrain's pitching staff, as Staunton's top three hurlers were unable to throw for the Bulldogs. The result was an 8-11 finish that included a 1-5 mark in the Prairie State Conference. The Bulldogs were once again a fairly young team with only two seniors, Kole Billings and Tylor McBride, on the roster. Sophomore and Team MVP Sean Abernathy was a 2nd Team All-PSC selection for the Dogs, as was fellow sophomore Ryan Fretz. The Hitting Award (.397) and 1st Team All-Conference distinction went to junior A.J. Sitko. Meanwhile, junior Sam Trettenero took home the Pitching Award (3-3, 5.56 ERA).

Basketball (Boys)

The 2011-12 basketball team was short on experience, as the squad featured just two seniors in the form of Nate Colley and Devin Gerdes. As such, coach Steve Moore's unit experienced an up-and-down season that ended with a 17-14 record overall, including a 3-4 mark in the Prairie State Conference. However, the Bulldogs caught fire in the Macoupin County Tournament, downing Gillespie (46-34), Mt. Olive (54-52), Southwestern (47-33), and Bunker Hill (46-37) to capture the school's fifteenth county title. The Bulldogs played four games at the tournament due to a switch from brackets to pool play. With Northwestern having entered into a co-op with Greenfield, the tournament included just seven teams, thus prompting event administrators to make the change. After the tournament, Gerdes and junior Austin Hollaway were named to the All-County team.

For the first time in five seasons, the Bulldogs failed to make the Regional championship game. The Dogs began postseason play with a 60-42 victory over East Alton-Wood River before falling to Roxana (55-51) to end the year. Following the season, Team MVP Hollaway and fellow junior Billy Bartle were honored as 1st Team All-Conference selections. Hollaway was also an All-Area choice by the *State Journal-Register* (Honorable Mention) and A Baseline View (Special Mention). Gerdes led the team in scoring with 13.6 points per contest, while the Free Throw Award was won by A.J. Sitko (71%).

Basketball (Girls)

The 2011-12 basketball team was coached by Troy Redfern and included seniors Monica McMahon, Katie Yakos, and Marissa Zirges. However, the year was highlighted by the play of junior Sophie Fairman, the most decorated female basketball player in program history. Fairman put up 14.3 points, 12.2 rebounds, and 7.5 blocks per game on the season, including several triple-doubles throughout the year. One such game came against Kincaid South Fork when she posted 27 points, 25 rebounds, and 14 blocks to spur the Lady Bulldogs to victory. Fairman's 173 blocks on the season represents one of the highest totals in state history. In addition to being named 1st Team All-Conference and All-County, Fairman also took home 1st Team All-Area honors from the *Telegraph* and *State Journal-Register*. Finally, she was named to three All-State teams. The *News-Gazette* and Illinois Basketball Services awarded Fairman Honorable Mention status, while the Illinois Basketball Coaches Association named her Special Mention. Fellow junior Kerstin Brown was also recognized for the Lady Bulldogs, as she took home All-Conference Honorable Mention accolades.

The season itself did not match the individual exploits, as the Lady Bulldogs struggled early before winning four of their last five regular season games. The campaign ended with a loss to eventual Regional champion Gillespie in the opening round of the postseason. Overall, SHS finished 11-13, including 5-2 in the Prairie State Conference. Unfortunately, the season served as the last for Coach Redfern, who left the program as its winning percentage leader.

Cross Country (Girls)

Coach Dave Williams' 2011 cross country roster included seniors Katie Bowen, Amanda Cornell, Rachael Hoehn, and Mia Stefani. The Lady Bulldogs enjoyed a solid campaign, with Hoehn eventually qualifying for Sectional competition.

Football

Coach Mike Parmentier's 2011 Bulldogs ended the year with a 7-4 record overall and a 5-2 mark in the Prairie State Conference. The Dogs once again began the year hot, turning in a Week 1 victory over Pleasant Plains (19-9) in the first-ever matchup between the two schools. Week 2 saw SHS begin conference play with a shutout victory over Nokomis (48-0), and the Dogs stayed undefeated in the league with a hard-fought 19-15 victory over Gillespie in Week 3. After two easy wins over Bunker Hill (42-0) and Mt. Olive (56-6), SHS lost a heartbreaker to eventual PSC champion Pawnee (24-21) in Week 6. Staunton easily handled Kincaid South Fork (63-26) in Week 7 but lost to North Mac (45-22) on Senior Night and Auburn (26-14) in Week 9. Despite just a 6-3 regular season, SHS landed a very favorable postseason draw, as the Bulldogs were scheduled to host fellow Prairie State Conference school Nokomis in the opening round of the playoffs. Though it was not as easy as the first matchup, the Dogs eventually prevailed with a 56-39 victory to set up a rematch with North Mac. Unfortunately, the Panthers once again had Staunton's number, defeating the Dogs by a score of 26-12.

Coach Parmentier had to say goodbye to seniors Josh Barnes, Dillon Bertels, Kole Billings, Kyle Castaldi, Cody Gonterman, Jake Mahin, Tylor McBride, Dan Nafziger, Alex Ocepek, Brandon Saffel, Kory Sczurek, Austin Sherfy, and Zack Ward. Barnes (Honorable Mention), Billings (1st Team), Mahin (2nd Team), Sczurek (1st Team), Sherfy (1st Team), and Ward (1st Team) all captured All-PSC honors for the Bulldogs. They were joined on the All-Conference team by juniors Larry Caldieraro (2nd Team), Austin Hollaway (1st Team), Chaz Johnson (2nd Team), David Vaughn (Honorable Mention), and sophomore Jake Bruhn (2nd Team). In fact, Bruhn set a school record with 1815 yards passing. His favorite target was Hollaway, who caught 27 balls for 517 yards. Meanwhile, Ward led the team in rushing with 446 yards. The Bulldogs also had several All-Area performers, including *Telegraph* 1st Team selections Sczurek, Sherfy, Ward, and Hollaway. Sherfy (2nd Team) and Ward (1st Team) also captured *State Journal-Register* All-Area honors, and Ward was named Honorable Mention All-State by the Illinois High School Football Coaches Association.

Golf (Boys)

With no seniors in the program, coach Troy Redfern's 2011 golf team included juniors Zach Augustine, Zach Hadjan, and Brad Mongold, sophomores Andrew Cisler and Zach Garde, and freshman Blake Kolesa. The inexperience hurt the Bulldogs, as the club finished the year with a 6-23 record in match play.

Golf (Girls)

Since its inception in 2005, the golf program has been the most successful in school history when considering winning percentage. In fact, Troy Redfern's crew had never experienced a losing season until 2011, as the Lady Bulldogs turned in an 8-16 overall record. However, down seasons for the golf program could be considered successful by other standards, as the team finished 3rd at Regionals and thus advanced to Sectional competition for the fourth time in five years. Seniors Courtney Redfern and Marissa Zirges sparked the squad, with Redfern taking home 1st Team All-Area status from the *Telegraph*.

Soccer (Boys)

Coach Brad Fulk continued to attract a large number of athletes to the soccer program, and in fact the 2011 squad featured the biggest senior class in SHS soccer history. Tanner Aljets, Nick Banovz, Dylan Barrett, Tyler Boston, Eric Brown, Nate Colley, A.J. Cozart, Devin Gerdes, Tim McVey, Alex Odom, Nate Price, and Ryan Wall formed the group. The Bulldogs struggled early in the campaign, winning just one time in their first twelve games. However, Coach Fulk refocused the group, leading the Dogs to a 3-3-1 record down the stretch before ending the season with a loss to Carlinville in the Regional. The Bulldogs finished the year with an overall record of 4-14-2. Though the year was disappointing from a team perspective, junior standout Tyler Finnegan had an outstanding season for the Bulldogs. By scoring 17 goals, Finnegan set a school record for tallies in a single year.

Soccer (Girls)

By all accounts, the 2012 soccer season was supposed to be a rebuilding one for the Lady Bulldogs. Having graduated most of its firepower from the previous season, the team struggled in the early part of the schedule. In fact, the year began with five successive losses and a 2-9 record halfway through the campaign. However, coach Julie Tyler and seniors Rachael Hoehn, Kaitlyn Jensen, and Erin Massey continued to plug away. The work ethic and determination eventually culminated in the first postseason title in SHS soccer history after the Lady Bulldogs captured the Regional championship. Seeded last in the four-team Regional Tournament, the Lady Bulldogs upset top-ranked Carlinville (2-1) to advance to the title game. Awaiting the club was rival Gillespie, a team that had already defeated SHS three times on the season. However, the fourth matchup between the schools resulted in a 2-0 victory and Regional title for the Lady Bulldogs. At the Class 1A Warrensburg-Latham Sectional, Staunton fell to Mt. Zion (3-0) to end the magical postseason run. The Lady Bulldogs wrapped up the year with an overall record of 7-13-2. After the season, sophomore and Team MVP Lindsay Allen was named to the Illinois High School Soccer Coaches Association's All-Sectional team as an Honorable Mention selection. Allen was also chosen by the *Telegraph* as a 1st Team All-Area performer.

Softball

The 2012 softball program welcomed a new coach to the helm in the form of Jennifer Brooke. Previously an assistant coach in the program, Brooke inherited a small but solid senior class that included All-Conference performers Monica McMahon (1st Team), Katie Yakos (Honorable Mention), and Marissa Zirges (Honorable Mention). McMahon captured the team's Hitting Award, and she capped off an impressive senior campaign by blasting three home runs in her final two games, which were postseason affairs with Hillsboro (won 3-1) and Gillespie (lost 12-2). The Team MVP award went to sophomore pitcher Hannah McEnery, while fellow sophomore Kayla Rettig was an All-PSC 1st Team selection. The highlight of the season for SHS was a 3-2 win over a Carrollton team that brought a sparkling 17-1 record into the game and finished 24-5 overall. The Lady Bulldogs played their best game of the year in pulling the upset, and the victory sparked a three-game winning streak. SHS eventually finished with a 10-13 mark overall, including 3-3 in the Prairie State Conference.

Track (Boys)

B.J. Ogata's 2012 track team enjoyed another outstanding season, as the Dogs finished 1st in the Prairie State Conference, 2nd at the Macoupin County Meet, and 3rd at the Sectional Meet. The PSC championship was the program's third straight title, meaning that the Bulldogs took home conference gold in every season as league members. Individual PSC champions included senior Jake Mahin (discus, shot put), junior Sam Allison (pole vault, 400 meters), freshman Marcus Sitko (triple jump), and the 400 meter relay team consisting of seniors Dylan Bertels and Kyle Castaldi, sophomore Blake Kinder, and Sitko. Mahin, Sitko, and the relay team also captured gold at the Macoupin County Meet in their respective events.

The Sectional Meet was hosted by SHS for the first time in decades, and the host school did not disappoint its fans. The Bulldogs saw two competitors enter the winner's circle at Sectionals, as Allison won the 400 meters and Mahin broke his own school records in both the discus and shot put to advance to State. At State, Mahin turned in one of the most impressive performances in school history by taking home 2nd overall in the discus and 5th in the shot put. For his efforts, Mahin was recognized by the *Telegraph* as its Track Athlete of the Year. Seniors on the 2012 track team included Nick Banovz, Bertels, Castaldi, Mahin, Alex Murday, and Shane Nalezyte.

Track (Girls)

Seniors Amanda Cornell and Mia Stefani led the 2012 track team into action. The unit was coached by B.J. Ogata and paced by the exploits of Team MVP Sophie Fairman, a junior. The Lady Bulldogs placed 4th in their last season in the Prairie State Conference and 3rd at the Macoupin County Meet. Fairman set four of her seven school records during the season, and she duplicated her success from the previous year by taking 3rd place overall in the triple jump and 4th place in the 400 meters at State. She also competed in the 200 meters at the event. Earlier in the season, Fairman was a multiple champion at the PSC Meet (long jump, triple jump), the Macoupin County Meet (long jump, triple jump, 200 meters, 400 meters), and the Sectional Meet (triple jump, 400 meters). After the season, Fairman was named to the *Telegraph's* All-Area 1st Team.

Volleyball

Coming off its best season in more than a decade, coach Mike Korte's volleyball program had to rebuild in 2011 following the graduation of an outstanding senior class. However, the Lady Bulldogs reloaded instead, finishing the year 16-8 overall and 5-2 in the Prairie State Conference. SHS got off to a hot start on the season and never looked back, though an upset loss to Pawnee did cost the team a share of the PSC crown, which was won by Gillespie. The Macoupin County Tournament was considered wide open, and Carlinville took advantage of the parity to capture yet another title. Staunton, which lost to CHS in pool play, went on to finish 3rd. Interestingly enough, since 1988, no team other than Carlinville or Staunton has won the Macoupin County Tournament.

SHS was led by junior Sophie Fairman. A 1st Team All-Conference and All-County performer, Fairman was also a *State Journal-Register* All-Area Honorable Mention selection. Fairman, the team's Offensive MVP, was joined in a strong junior class by Kerstin Brown and Kim Machuga. Brown, the team's Defensive MVP, was a 2nd Team All-PSC choice, while Machuga took home Honorable Mention status. The lone seniors on the team, Kassie Elliott (2nd Team) and Katie Yakos (Honorable Mention), were also All-Conference selections. At the end of the season, Fairman was chosen as the *Telegraph's* Player of the Year, giving SHS its second winner of the award in as many years. Given her success in basketball, track, and volleyball, Fairman cemented her place as one of the best female athletes in school history.

ATTACHMENT 1

Team Accomplishments

Baseball

YEAR	W	L	T	COACH	TEAM NOTES / PERCENTAGE
1922-23	9	0	0	Paul Miller	
Total	**9**	**0**	**0**	**Paul Miller (1)**	100.0%
1923-24	8	0	0	Gilbert Lane	
1924-25*	0	0	0	Gilbert Lane	
Total*	**8**	**0**	**0**	**Gilbert Lane (2)**	100.0%
1925-41	N/A	N/A	N/A	N/A	No Team
1941-42	4	3	0	Carl Mendenhall	District Champions
Total	**4**	**3**	**0**	**Carl Mendenhall (1)**	57.1%
1942-43*	2	1	0	B.H. Gibbons	District Champions
1943-44*	4	1	0	B.H. Gibbons	District, Sectional Champions, State (Quarterfinals)
1944-45*	3	1	0	B.H. Gibbons	
1945-46*	0	1	0	B.H. Gibbons	
1946-47*	0	1	0	B.H. Gibbons	
Total*	**9**	**5**	**0**	**B.H. Gibbons (5)**	64.3%
1947-48*	0	1	0	Joe Jurkanin	
1948-49*	0	1	0	Joe Jurkanin	
1949-50*	0	1	0	Joe Jurkanin	
1950-51*	1	1	0	Joe Jurkanin	SCC, District Champions
1951-52*	1	1	0	Joe Jurkanin	SCC, District Champions
Total*	**2**	**5**	**0**	**Joe Jurkanin (5)**	28.6%
1952-53*	0	1	0	Bill Edwards	
1953-54	12	3	0	Bill Edwards	SCC Champions
Total*	**12**	**4**	**0**	**Bill Edwards (2)**	75.0%
1954-55	11	6	0	Fred Brenzel	SCC Champions
1955-56	7	7	0	Fred Brenzel	SCC Champions
1956-57	16	3	0	Fred Brenzel	SCC, District, Regional, Sectional Champions, State (Quarterfinals)
1957-58	13	2	0	Fred Brenzel	SCC Champions
1958-59	16	6	0	Fred Brenzel	SCC, District, Regional Champions
1959-60	11	7	0	Fred Brenzel	SCC Champions
1960-61	8	3	0	Fred Brenzel	SCC Champions
1961-62	13	6	0	Fred Brenzel	SCC Champions
1962-63	15	6	0	Fred Brenzel	SCC, District, Regional Champions
1963-64	11	7	0	Fred Brenzel	
1964-65	18	2	0	Fred Brenzel	SCC, District Champions
1965-66	12	2	0	Fred Brenzel	SCC Champions
1966-67	9	3	0	Fred Brenzel	SCC Champions
1967-68*	2	1	0	Fred Brenzel	District Champions
1968-69*	0	1	0	Fred Brenzel	
1969-70	16	4	0	Fred Brenzel	SCC, Regional Champions
Total*	**178**	**66**	**0**	**Fred Brenzel (16)**	73.0%
1970-71*	0	1	0	Barry Deist	
1971-72*	0	1	0	Barry Deist	
1972-73*	9	2	0	Barry Deist	SCC Champions
1973-74	8	6	0	Barry Deist	
1974-75	4	7	0	Barry Deist	
1975-76	11	9	0	Barry Deist	
1976-77	9	9	0	Barry Deist	

Year	W	L	T	Coach	Notes
1977-78	6	7	0	Barry Deist	
1978-79	6	7	0	Barry Deist	
1979-80	16	4	0	Barry Deist	SCC Champions
1980-81	4	13	0	Barry Deist	
1981-82	9	7	0	Barry Deist	SCC Champions
1982-83*	0	1	0	Barry Deist	
1983-84	15	6	0	Barry Deist	SCC Champions
1984-85	12	8	0	Barry Deist	
1985-86	13	9	0	Barry Deist	
1986-87	9	9	0	Barry Deist	
1987-88	11	6	0	Barry Deist	
1988-89	3	11	0	Barry Deist	
1989-90	6	9	0	Barry Deist	
1990-91	13	10	0	Barry Deist	
1991-92	11	11	0	Barry Deist	
Total*	**175**	**153**	**0**	**Barry Deist (22)**	**53.4%**
1992-93	10	11	0	Larry Caldieraro	
1993-94	14	10	0	Larry Caldieraro	Regional, Sectional Champions, State (Quarterfinals)
1994-95	12	9	0	Larry Caldieraro	
1995-96	11	7	0	Larry Caldieraro	
1996-97	16	9	0	Larry Caldieraro	
1997-98	20	6	0	Larry Caldieraro	Regional Champions
1998-99	18	5	0	Larry Caldieraro	
1999-00	8	16	0	Larry Caldieraro	
2000-01	9	22	0	Larry Caldieraro	
2001-02	7	14	0	Larry Caldieraro	
2002-03	3	21	0	Larry Caldieraro	
2003-04	6	18	0	Larry Caldieraro	
Total	**134**	**148**	**0**	**Larry Caldieraro (12)**	**47.5%**
2004-05	6	19	0	Steve Moore	
2005-06	6	13	0	Steve Moore	
2006-07	5	16	0	Steve Moore	
2007-08	5	13	0	Steve Moore	
Total	**22**	**61**	**0**	**Steve Moore (4)**	**26.5%**
2008-09	7	13	0	Ryan McGowen	
2009-10	15	6	0	Ryan McGowen	PSC Champions
Total	**22**	**19**	**0**	**Ryan McGowen (2)**	**53.7%**
2010-11	10	5	0	Kyle McBrain	
2011-12	8	11	0	Kyle McBrain	
Total	**18**	**16**	**0**	**Kyle McBrain (2)**	**52.9%**
TOTAL*	**593**	**480**	**0**	**BASEBALL**	**55.3%**

Basketball (Boys)

YEAR	W	L	T	COACH	TEAM NOTES / PERCENTAGE
1920-21	7	9	0	Noble Newsum	
1921-22*	6	3	0	Noble Newsum	
Total*	**13**	**12**	**0**	**Noble Newsum (2)**	**52.0%**
1922-23*	3	1	0	Paul Miller	

Team Accompishments

Total*	3	1	0	Paul Miller (1)	75.0%
1923-24	11	7	0	Gilbert Lane	
1924-25	7	8	0	Gilbert Lane	
Total	18	15	0	Gilbert Lane (2)	54.5%
1925-26*	5	4	0	Byron Bozarth	
Total*	5	4	0	Byron Bozarth (1)	55.6%
1926-27	15	10	0	Carroll McBride	
1927-28	21	6	0	Carroll McBride	County, District Champions
Total	36	16	0	Carroll McBride (2)	69.2%
1928-29	7	14	0	A.R. Pruitt	
Total	7	14	0	A.R. Pruitt (1)	33.3%
1929-30	4	18	0	Judson Jones	
1930-31	7	8	1	Judson Jones	
1931-32*	0	4	0	Judson Jones	
1932-33*	2	8	0	Judson Jones	
Total*	13	38	1	Judson Jones (4)	26.0%
1933-34	13	14	0	Cliff Stiegemeier	
1934-35	21	5	0	Cliff Stiegemeier	SCC, County Champions
1935-36	24	6	0	Cliff Stiegemeier	Regional Champions
1936-37*	4	14	0	Cliff Stiegemeier	
Total*	62	39	0	Cliff Stiegemeier (4)	61.4%
1937-38	11	14	0	Hubert Pierce	Regional Champions
1938-39	10	14	0	Hubert Pierce	
Total	21	28	0	Hubert Pierce (2)	42.9%
1939-40	10	12	0	Carl Mendenhall	
1940-41	10	17	0	Carl Mendenhall	
1941-42	11	15	0	Carl Mendenhall	
Total	31	44	0	Carl Mendenhall (3)	41.3%
1942-43	15	11	0	B.H. Gibbons	
1943-44	21	6	0	B.H. Gibbons	
1944-45	27	5	0	B.H. Gibbons	SCC, Regional Champions
1945-46	17	11	0	B.H. Gibbons	County Champions
1946-47	11	15	0	B.H. Gibbons	
Total	91	48	0	B.H. Gibbons (5)	65.5%
1947-48	4	19	0	Joe Jurkanin	
1948-49	11	13	0	Joe Jurkanin	
1949-50	12	14	0	Joe Jurkanin	
1950-51	19	10	0	Joe Jurkanin	
1951-52	23	4	0	Joe Jurkanin	SCC, County Champions
Total	69	60	0	Joe Jurkanin (5)	53.5%
1952-53	8	17	0	Bill Edwards	
1953-54	12	14	0	Bill Edwards	
1954-55	7	17	0	Bill Edwards	
1955-56	4	20	0	Bill Edwards	
Total	31	68	0	Bill Edwards (4)	31.3%
1956-57	5	18	0	Wayne Beach	
Total	5	18	0	Wayne Beach (1)	21.7%
1957-58	20	9	0	Enno Lietz	SCC, County Champions
1958-59	13	13	0	Enno Lietz	

1959-60	12	16	0	Enno Lietz	
1960-61	9	12	0	Enno Lietz	
1961-62	8	12	0	Enno Lietz	
1962-63	11	16	0	Enno Lietz	
Total	**73**	**78**	**0**	**Enno Lietz (6)**	48.3%
1963-64	5	17	0	Bill McCullough	
1964-65	7	15	0	Bill McCullough	
1965-66	9	13	0	Bill McCullough	
Total	**21**	**45**	**0**	**Bill McCullough (3)**	31.8%
1966-67	11	13	0	Dave Davison	
1967-68	6	17	0	Dave Davison	
1968-69	9	15	0	Dave Davison	
1969-70	8	16	0	Dave Davison	
Total	**34**	**61**	**0**	**Dave Davison (4)**	35.8%
1970-71	5	17	0	Don Miller	
1971-72	2	20	0	Don Miller	
1972-73	3	21	0	Don Miller	
Total	**10**	**58**	**0**	**Don Miller (3)**	14.7%
1973-74	14	11	0	Randy Legendre	SCC Champions
1974-75	12	14	0	Randy Legendre	
1975-76	4	18	0	Randy Legendre	
Total	**30**	**43**	**0**	**Randy Legendre (3)**	41.1%
1976-77	6	17	0	Jerry Landrem	
Total	**6**	**17**	**0**	**Jerry Landrem (1)**	26.1%
1977-78	5	15	0	Larry Lux	
Total	**5**	**15**	**0**	**Larry Lux (1)**	25.0%
1978-79	7	22	0	Mike Stivers	
1979-80	19	7	0	Mike Stivers	SCC, County Champions
1980-81	11	12	0	Mike Stivers	
1981-82	19	8	0	Mike Stivers	SCC, County, Regional Champions
1982-83	9	15	0	Mike Stivers	
1983-84	20	6	0	Mike Stivers	SCC Champions
1984-85	25	2	0	Mike Stivers	SCC, County Champions
1985-86	22	6	0	Mike Stivers	SCC, County, Regional Champions
1986-87	21	7	0	Mike Stivers	SCC, County, Regional Champions
1987-88	11	13	0	Mike Stivers	
1988-89	14	12	0	Mike Stivers	
1989-90	14	11	0	Mike Stivers	
1990-91	21	5	0	Mike Stivers	SCC, County Champions
Total	**213**	**126**	**0**	**Mike Stivers (13)**	62.8%
1991-92	17	9	0	Randy Legendre	SCC, County Champions
1992-93	27	4	0	Randy Legendre	SCC, Regional, Sectional, State Champions
1993-94	9	18	0	Randy Legendre	
1994-95	8	16	0	Randy Legendre	
Total	**61**	**47**	**0**	**Randy Legendre (4)**	56.5%
1995-96	9	16	0	Kevin Gockel	
1996-97	13	13	0	Kevin Gockel	
1997-98	12	12	0	Kevin Gockel	
1998-99	10	17	0	Kevin Gockel	
1999-00	9	18	0	Kevin Gockel	

Year	W	L	T	Coach	Team Notes / Percentage
2000-01	22	9	0	Kevin Gockel	County, Regional Champions
2001-02	10	18	0	Kevin Gockel	
2002-03	5	24	0	Kevin Gockel	
2003-04	6	24	0	Kevin Gockel	
2004-05	9	18	0	Kevin Gockel	
2005-06	8	19	0	Kevin Gockel	
2006-07	5	21	0	Kevin Gockel	
Total	118	209	0	Kevin Gockel (12)	36.1%
2007-08	14	15	0	Steve Moore	
2008-09	21	10	0	Steve Moore	County, Regional Champions
2009-10	18	11	0	Steve Moore	
2010-11	18	11	0	Steve Moore	
2011-12	17	14	0	Steve Moore	County Champions
Total	88	61	0	Steve Moore (5)	59.1%
TOTAL*	1064	1165	1	BASKETBALL	47.7%

Basketball (Girls)

YEAR	W	L	T	COACH	TEAM NOTES / PERCENTAGE
1978-79	1	10	0	Joe Dugan	
1979-80	6	11	0	Joe Dugan	
Total	7	21	0	Joe Dugan (2)	25.0%
1980-81	13	8	0	Larry Kuba	
1981-82	6	12	0	Larry Kuba	
1982-83	12	10	0	Larry Kuba	
1983-84	10	11	0	Larry Kuba	
1984-85	11	14	0	Larry Kuba	County Champions
1985-86	7	14	0	Larry Kuba	
1986-87	11	14	0	Larry Kuba	County Champions
1987-88	13	12	0	Larry Kuba	
1988-89	2	21	0	Larry Kuba	
1989-90	14	10	0	Larry Kuba	
1990-91	14	10	0	Larry Kuba	
1991-92	6	16	0	Larry Kuba	
1992-93	5	16	0	Larry Kuba	
1993-94	3	18	0	Larry Kuba	
1994-95	16	8	0	Larry Kuba	
1995-96	11	11	0	Larry Kuba	
1996-97	4	17	0	Larry Kuba	
1997-98	4	17	0	Larry Kuba	
1998-99	12	14	0	Larry Kuba	
1999-00	11	15	0	Larry Kuba	
2000-01	7	20	0	Larry Kuba	
Total	192	288	0	Larry Kuba (21)	40.0%
2001-02	13	14	0	Gayle Gusewelle	
2002-03	16	11	0	Gayle Gusewelle	
2003-04	10	17	0	Gayle Gusewelle	
2004-05	10	17	0	Gayle Gusewelle	
Total	49	59	0	Gayle Gusewelle (4)	45.4%

YEAR	W	L	T	COACH	TEAM NOTES / PERCENTAGE
2005-06	16	11	0	Rob Corso	
2006-07	7	18	0	Rob Corso	
Total	**23**	**29**	**0**	**Rob Corso (2)**	**44.2%**
2007-08	7	18	0	Troy Redfern	
2008-09	12	14	0	Troy Redfern	
2009-10	16	12	0	Troy Redfern	PSC Champions
2010-11	20	7	0	Troy Redfern	PSC, County Champions
2011-12	11	13	0	Troy Redfern	
Total	**66**	**64**	**0**	**Troy Redfern (5)**	**50.8%**
TOTAL	**337**	**461**	**0**	**BASKETBALL**	**42.2%**

Bowling (Boys)

YEAR	W	L	T	COACH	TEAM NOTES / PERCENTAGE
1999-00	3	9	0	Dave Williams	
2000-01	4	7	0	Dave Williams	
2001-02*	0	0	0	Dave Williams	
2002-03*	0	0	0	Dave Williams	
Total*	**7**	**16**	**0**	**Dave Williams (4)**	**30.4%**
TOTAL*	**7**	**16**	**0**	**BOWLING**	**30.4%**

Bowling (Girls)

YEAR	W	L	T	COACH	TEAM NOTES / PERCENTAGE
1998-99	8	4	0	Dave Williams	
1999-00	9	2	1	Dave Williams	
2000-01	5	8	0	Dave Williams	
2001-02*	0	0	0	Dave Williams	
2002-03*	0	0	0	Dave Williams	
Total*	**22**	**14**	**1**	**Dave Williams (5)**	**60.8%**
TOTAL*	**22**	**14**	**1**	**BOWLING**	**60.8%**

Cross Country (Boys)

YEAR	W	L	T	COACH	TEAM NOTES / PERCENTAGE
1975-76	N/A	N/A	N/A	Gale Bryan	
1976-77	N/A	N/A	N/A	Gale Bryan	
1977-78	N/A	N/A	N/A	Gary Baxter	Sectional
1978-79	N/A	N/A	N/A	Gary Baxter	

Cross Country (Girls)

YEAR	W	L	T	COACH	TEAM NOTES / PERCENTAGE
2007-08	N/A	N/A	N/A	Dave Williams	SCC Champions, Sectional
2008-09	N/A	N/A	N/A	Dave Williams	SCC Champions, Sectional
2009-10	N/A	N/A	N/A	Dave Williams	Sectional

Team Accomplishments

2010-11	N/A	N/A	N/A	Dave Williams	
2011-12	N/A	N/A	N/A	Dave Williams	

Football

YEAR	W	L	T	COACH	TEAM NOTES / PERCENTAGE
1911-12	1	3	1	Bill Eccles	
1912-13	3	2	0	Bill Eccles	
1913-14	5	2	0	Bill Eccles	
1914-15	5	2	1	Bill Eccles	
1915-16	6	1	0	Bill Eccles	
1916-17	1	2	0	Bill Eccles	
1917-18	0	3	0	Bill Eccles	
1918-19	N/A	N/A	N/A	N/A	No Team
1919-20	5	1	1	Bill Eccles	
1920-21	7	1	1	Bill Eccles	
1921-22	7	3	0	Bill Eccles	
Total	**40**	**20**	**4**	**Bill Eccles (10)**	**65.6%**
1922-23	9	1	0	Paul Miller	
1923-24	10	0	0	Paul Miller	Central/Southern District Champions, IHSA Points/TD Records
Total	**19**	**1**	**0**	**Paul Miller (2)**	**95.0%**
1924-25	6	1	2	Byron Bozarth	
1925-26	7	1	0	Byron Bozarth	
Total	**13**	**2**	**2**	**Byron Bozarth (2)**	**82.4%**
1926-27	5	4	0	Carroll McBride	
1927-28	8	0	1	Carroll McBride	SCC Champions
Total	**13**	**4**	**1**	**Carroll McBride (2)**	**75.0%**
1928-29	8	2	0	A.R. Pruitt	SCC Champions
Total	**8**	**2**	**0**	**A.R. Pruitt (1)**	**80.0%**
1929-30	1	6	1	Judson Jones	
1930-31	4	4	1	Judson Jones	
1931-32	6	3	0	Judson Jones	
1932-33	0	5	4	Judson Jones	
Total	**11**	**18**	**6**	**Judson Jones (4)**	**40.0%**
1933-34	4	5	0	Cliff Stiegemeier	
1934-35	6	2	2	Cliff Stiegemeier	
1935-36	7	2	0	Cliff Stiegemeier	
1936-37	8	2	0	Cliff Stiegemeier	
Total	**25**	**11**	**2**	**Cliff Stiegemeier (4)**	**68.4%**
1937-38	6	1	1	Art Ruffini	
1938-39	4	3	1	Art Ruffini	
1939-40	2	3	4	Art Ruffini	
1940-41	3	4	2	Art Ruffini	
1941-42	1	6	1	Art Ruffini	
1942-43	0	7	1	Art Ruffini	
Total	**16**	**24**	**10**	**Art Ruffini (6)**	**42.0%**
1943-44	3	5	0	B.H. Gibbons	
1944-45	5	3	0	B.H. Gibbons	SCC Champions
1945-46	0	7	1	B.H. Gibbons	

Total	8	15	1	**B.H. Gibbons (3)**	35.4%
1946-47	6	1	1	Bob Maloney	
Total	6	1	1	**Bob Maloney (1)**	81.3%
1947-48	1	5	2	Joe Jurkanin	
1948-49	1	7	1	Joe Jurkanin	
1949-50	2	6	1	Joe Jurkanin	
1950-51	6	2	1	Joe Jurkanin	
1951-52	6	2	1	Joe Jurkanin	SCC Champions
Total	16	22	6	**Joe Jurkanin (5)**	43.2%
1952-53	1	8	0	Bill Edwards	
Total	1	8	0	**Bill Edwards (1)**	11.1%
1953-54	2	7	0	Jonas Lashmet	
Total	2	7	0	**Jonas Lashmet (1)**	22.2%
1954-55	4	5	0	Fred Brenzel	
1955-56	0	8	1	Fred Brenzel	
1956-57	5	5	0	Fred Brenzel	
1957-58	6	3	1	Fred Brenzel	
1958-59	5	3	1	Fred Brenzel	SCC Champions
1959-60	8	2	0	Fred Brenzel	SCC Champions
1960-61	7	3	0	Fred Brenzel	SCC Champions
1961-62	7	2	0	Fred Brenzel	SCC Champions
1962-63	7	3	0	Fred Brenzel	
1963-64	9	1	0	Fred Brenzel	SCC Champions
1964-65	9	0	1	Fred Brenzel	SCC Champions
1965-66	8	1	0	Fred Brenzel	SCC Champions
1966-67	8	1	1	Fred Brenzel	
1967-68	9	1	0	Fred Brenzel	SCC Champions
1968-69	6	4	0	Fred Brenzel	
1969-70	9	1	0	Fred Brenzel	SCC Champions
Total	107	43	5	**Fred Brenzel (16)**	70.6%
1970-71	8	0	1	Bob Chiti	SCC Champions
1971-72	5	5	0	Bob Chiti	SCC Champions
1972-73	6	4	0	Bob Chiti	
1973-74	7	3	1	Bob Chiti	
1974-75	4	5	0	Bob Chiti	
Total	30	17	2	**Bob Chiti (5)**	63.3%
1975-76	5	4	0	Barry Deist	
1976-77	5	4	0	Barry Deist	
1977-78	8	2	0	Barry Deist	Playoffs (1st Round)
1978-79	8	1	0	Barry Deist	
1979-80	7	2	0	Barry Deist	
1980-81	2	7	0	Barry Deist	
1981-82	6	3	0	Barry Deist	
1982-83	5	4	0	Barry Deist	
1983-84	6	3	0	Barry Deist	
1984-85	7	2	0	Barry Deist	
1985-86	4	5	0	Barry Deist	
1986-87	3	6	0	Barry Deist	
1987-88	2	7	0	Barry Deist	
1988-89	4	5	0	Barry Deist	

YEAR	W	L	T	COACH	TEAM NOTES / PERCENTAGE
1989-90	3	6	0	Barry Deist	
Total	**75**	**61**	**0**	**Barry Deist (15)**	**55.1%**
1990-91	0	9	0	Dave Martin	
1991-92	3	6	0	Dave Martin	
1992-93	5	4	0	Dave Martin	
1993-94	5	4	0	Dave Martin	
Total	**13**	**23**	**0**	**Dave Martin (4)**	**36.1%**
1994-95	4	5	0	Scott Tonsor	
1995-96	3	6	0	Scott Tonsor	
1996-97	6	4	0	Scott Tonsor	Playoffs (1st Round)
1997-98	10	1	0	Scott Tonsor	SCC East Champions, Playoffs (2nd Round)
1998-99	7	4	0	Scott Tonsor	Playoffs (2nd Round)
1999-00	4	5	0	Scott Tonsor	
2000-01	8	3	0	Scott Tonsor	SCC East Champions, Playoffs (2nd Round)
Total	**42**	**28**	**0**	**Scott Tonsor (7)**	**60.0%**
2001-02	0	9	0	Larry Caldieraro	
2002-03	1	8	0	Larry Caldieraro	
2003-04	1	8	0	Larry Caldieraro	
2004-05	1	8	0	Larry Caldieraro	
Total	**3**	**33**	**0**	**Larry Caldieraro (4)**	**8.3%**
2005-06	1	8	0	Mike Parmentier	
2006-07	3	6	0	Mike Parmentier	
2007-08	5	5	0	Mike Parmentier	Playoffs (1st Round)
2008-09	6	4	0	Mike Parmentier	Playoffs (1st Round)
2009-10	8	2	0	Mike Parmentier	PSC Champions, Playoffs (1st Round)
2010-11	10	2	0	Mike Parmentier	Playoffs (Quarterfinals)
2011-12	7	4	0	Mike Parmentier	Playoffs (2nd Round)
Total	**40**	**31**	**0**	**Mike Parmentier (7)**	**56.3%**
TOTAL	**488**	**371**	**40**	**FOOTBALL**	**56.5%**

Golf (Boys)

YEAR	W	L	T	COACH	TEAM NOTES / PERCENTAGE
1956-57*	0	0	0	Bill Schuetze	
1957-58*	0	0	0	Bill Schuetze	
1958-59*	0	0	0	Bill Schuetze	
1959-60*	0	0	0	Bill Schuetze	
Total*	**0**	**0**	**0**	**Bill Schuetze (4)**	
1960-75	N/A	N/A	N/A	N/A	No Team
1975-76*	0	0	0	Larry Kuba	
1976-77	10	2	1	Larry Kuba	District Champions, Sectional
1977-78	15	2	0	Larry Kuba	Sectional
1978-79	11	1	1	Larry Kuba	District Champions, Sectional
1979-80	12	2	0	Larry Kuba	District Champions, Sectional, State (7th)
1980-81	7	5	0	Larry Kuba	District Champions, Sectional
1981-82	2	7	1	Larry Kuba	
1982-83	6	5	0	Larry Kuba	
1983-84	3	7	1	Larry Kuba	
1984-85	3	13	0	Larry Kuba	

Year	W	L	T	Coach	Team Notes / Percentage
1985-86	6	8	0	Larry Kuba	
1986-87	4	7	0	Larry Kuba	
1987-88	6	9	0	Larry Kuba	
1988-89	7	7	0	Larry Kuba	
1989-90	12	7	0	Larry Kuba	
1990-91	22	1	0	Larry Kuba	SCC Champions, Sectional, State (14th)
1991-92	17	3	0	Larry Kuba	SCC, Regional Champions, Sectional, State (6th)
1992-93	15	6	0	Larry Kuba	SCC Champions
1993-94	16	3	0	Larry Kuba	SCC Champions, Sectional, State (5th)
1994-95	18	2	0	Larry Kuba	SCC Champions
1995-96	17	4	0	Larry Kuba	Sectional
1996-97	20	0	0	Larry Kuba	SCC Champions, Sectional, State (5th)
1997-98	17	1	0	Larry Kuba	SCC Champions, Sectional
1998-99	17	2	0	Larry Kuba	SCC Champions
1999-00	20	3	1	Larry Kuba	Sectional
2000-01	13	13	0	Larry Kuba	
Total*	**296**	**120**	**5**	**Larry Kuba (26)**	**70.9%**
2001-02	18	7	0	Dave Williams	
Total	**18**	**7**	**0**	**Dave Williams (1)**	**72.0%**
2002-03	12	14	0	Troy Redfern	
2003-04	6	20	0	Troy Redfern	
2004-05	14	18	0	Troy Redfern	
2005-06	16	18	0	Troy Redfern	
2006-07	21	17	0	Troy Redfern	Sectional
2007-08	9	26	0	Troy Redfern	
2008-09	11	23	0	Troy Redfern	
2009-10	10	22	0	Troy Redfern	
2010-11	7	15	0	Troy Redfern	
2011-12	6	23	0	Troy Redfern	
Total	**112**	**196**	**0**	**Troy Redfern (10)**	**36.4%**
TOTAL*	**426**	**323**	**5**	**GOLF**	**56.8%**

Golf (Girls)

YEAR	W	L	T	COACH	TEAM NOTES / PERCENTAGE
2005-06	17	10	0	Troy Redfern	
2006-07	21	12	0	Troy Redfern	
2007-08	20	3	0	Troy Redfern	Sectional
2008-09	20	4	0	Troy Redfern	Regional Champions, Sectional
2009-10	26	6	0	Troy Redfern	Regional Champions, Sectional
2010-11	15	9	0	Troy Redfern	
2011-12	8	16	0	Troy Redfern	Sectional
Total	**127**	**60**	**0**	**Troy Redfern (7)**	**67.9%**
TOTAL	**127**	**60**	**0**	**GOLF**	**67.9%**

Team Accompishments

Soccer (Boys)

YEAR	W	L	T	COACH	TEAM NOTES / PERCENTAGE
1999-00	4	12	0	Tim Smiddy	
2000-01	3	14	1	Tim Smiddy	
2001-02	4	12	0	Tim Smiddy	
2002-03	5	12	0	Tim Smiddy	
Total	16	50	1	**Tim Smiddy (4)**	**24.6%**
2003-04	10	6	2	Steve Moore	
2004-05	10	8	0	Steve Moore	
2005-06	8	9	3	Steve Moore	
Total	28	23	5	**Steve Moore (3)**	**54.5%**
2006-07	8	11	2	Ken Pelletier	
2007-08	3	15	1	Ken Pelletier	
2008-09	3	14	2	Ken Pelletier	
2009-10	2	16	0	Ken Pelletier	
Total	16	56	5	**Ken Pelletier (4)**	**24.0%**
2010-11	3	13	2	Brad Fulk	
2011-12	4	14	2	Brad Fulk	
Total	7	27	4	**Brad Fulk (2)**	**23.7%**
TOTAL	**67**	**156**	**15**	**SOCCER**	**31.3%**

Soccer (Girls)

YEAR	W	L	T	COACH	TEAM NOTES / PERCENTAGE
1993-94	5	6	1	Jennifer Dutko	
1994-95	6	7	1	Jennifer Dutko	
Total	11	13	2	**Jennifer Dutko (2)**	**46.2%**
1995-96	9	4	3	Tim Smiddy	
1996-97	10	5	2	Tim Smiddy	
1997-98	9	8	1	Tim Smiddy	
Total	28	17	6	**Tim Smiddy (3)**	**60.8%**
1998-99	9	7	2	Rob Werden	
1999-00	8	8	5	Rob Werden	
2000-01	12	7	2	Rob Werden	
2001-02	13	6	2	Rob Werden	
Total	42	28	11	**Rob Werden (4)**	**58.6%**
2002-03	15	5	1	Darrin Bonney	
Total	15	5	1	**Darrin Bonney (1)**	**73.8%**
2003-04	2	16	1	Andrea Williamson	
2004-05	5	14	1	Andrea Williamson	
2005-06	8	12	2	Andrea Williamson	
2006-07	8	11	1	Andrea Williamson	
2007-08	4	11	1	Andrea Williamson	
2008-09	13	6	1	Andrea Williamson	
2009-10	10	8	2	Andrea Williamson	
Total	50	78	9	**Andrea Williamson (7)**	**39.8%**
2010-11	9	10	0	Julie Tyler	
2011-12	7	13	2	Julie Tyler	Regional Champions

Total	16	23	2	Julie Tyler (2)	41.5%
TOTAL	**162**	**164**	**31**	**SOCCER**	**49.7%**

Softball

YEAR	W	L	T	COACH	TEAM NOTES / PERCENTAGE
1992-93	6	11	0	Jim Mathis	
1993-94	4	14	0	Jim Mathis	
Total	10	25	0	Jim Mathis (2)	28.6%
1994-95	9	9	0	Kyle Freeman	
1995-96	9	10	0	Kyle Freeman	
1996-97	12	13	0	Kyle Freeman	
1997-98	16	3	0	Kyle Freeman	SCC East Champions
1998-99	9	9	0	Kyle Freeman	
1999-00	9	16	0	Kyle Freeman	
2000-01	7	15	0	Kyle Freeman	
Total	71	75	0	Kyle Freeman (7)	48.6%
2001-02	11	12	0	Heather Ondes	
2002-03	11	13	0	Heather Ondes	
2003-04	1	21	0	Heather Ondes	
2004-05	5	15	0	Heather Ondes	
2005-06	4	17	0	Heather Ondes	
2006-07	4	16	0	Heather Ondes	
Total	36	94	0	Heather Ondes (6)	27.7%
2007-08	5	16	0	Doug Zehr	
2008-09	13	8	0	Doug Zehr	
2009-10	11	10	0	Doug Zehr	
2010-11	6	13	0	Doug Zehr	
Total	35	47	0	Doug Zehr (4)	42.7%
2011-12	10	13	0	Jennifer Brooke	
Total	10	13	0	Jennifer Brooke (1)	43.5%
TOTAL	**162**	**254**	**0**	**SOFTBALL**	**38.9%**

Track (Boys)

YEAR	W	L	T	COACH	TEAM NOTES / PERCENTAGE
1907-08	N/A	N/A	N/A	Bill Eccles	
1908-09	N/A	N/A	N/A	Bill Eccles	
1909-10	N/A	N/A	N/A	Bill Eccles	
1910-11	N/A	N/A	N/A	Bill Eccles	
1911-12	N/A	N/A	N/A	Bill Eccles	
1912-13	N/A	N/A	N/A	Bill Eccles	
1913-14	N/A	N/A	N/A	Bill Eccles	
1914-15	N/A	N/A	N/A	Bill Eccles	
1915-16	N/A	N/A	N/A	Bill Eccles	
1916-17	N/A	N/A	N/A	Bill Eccles	
1917-18	N/A	N/A	N/A	Bill Eccles	
1918-19	N/A	N/A	N/A	Bill Eccles	

Year				Coach	Accomplishments
1919-20	N/A	N/A	N/A	Bill Eccles	
1920-21	N/A	N/A	N/A	Bill Eccles	
1921-22	N/A	N/A	N/A	Bill Eccles	
1922-23	N/A	N/A	N/A	Paul Miller	
1923-24	N/A	N/A	N/A	Paul Miller	County Champions
1924-25	N/A	N/A	N/A	Byron Bozarth	
1925-26	N/A	N/A	N/A	Byron Bozarth	
1926-27	N/A	N/A	N/A	Carroll McBride	
1927-28	N/A	N/A	N/A	Carroll McBride	SCC, County, District Champions
1928-29	N/A	N/A	N/A	A.R. Pruitt	SCC, County Champions
1929-30	N/A	N/A	N/A	Judson Jones	
1930-31	N/A	N/A	N/A	Judson Jones	
1931-32	N/A	N/A	N/A	Judson Jones	
1932-33	N/A	N/A	N/A	Judson Jones	
1933-34	N/A	N/A	N/A	Cliff Stiegemeier	
1934-35	N/A	N/A	N/A	Cliff Stiegemeier	County Champions
1935-36	N/A	N/A	N/A	Cliff Stiegemeier	
1936-37	N/A	N/A	N/A	Cliff Stiegemeier	
1937-38	N/A	N/A	N/A	Art Ruffini	
1938-39	N/A	N/A	N/A	Art Ruffini	
1939-40	N/A	N/A	N/A	Art Ruffini	
1940-52	N/A	N/A	N/A	N/A	No Team
1952-53	N/A	N/A	N/A	Jonas Lashmet	
1953-54	N/A	N/A	N/A	Jonas Lashmet	
1954-55	N/A	N/A	N/A	Bill Edwards	
1955-56	N/A	N/A	N/A	Bill Edwards	
1956-57	N/A	N/A	N/A	Wayne Beach	
1957-58	N/A	N/A	N/A	Enno Lietz	
1958-59	N/A	N/A	N/A	Enno Lietz	
1959-60	N/A	N/A	N/A	Enno Lietz	
1960-61	N/A	N/A	N/A	Enno Lietz	
1961-62	N/A	N/A	N/A	Enno Lietz	
1962-63	N/A	N/A	N/A	Enno Lietz	
1963-64	N/A	N/A	N/A	Bill McCullough	
1964-65	N/A	N/A	N/A	Bill McCullough	
1965-66	N/A	N/A	N/A	Bill McCullough	
1966-67	N/A	N/A	N/A	Jim Haynes	
1967-68	N/A	N/A	N/A	Jim Haynes	
1968-69	N/A	N/A	N/A	Jim Haynes	
1969-70	N/A	N/A	N/A	Jim Haynes	
1970-71	N/A	N/A	N/A	Jim Haynes	
1971-72	N/A	N/A	N/A	Ward Derlitzki	
1972-73	N/A	N/A	N/A	Gale Bryan	
1973-74	N/A	N/A	N/A	Gale Bryan	
1974-75	N/A	N/A	N/A	Gale Bryan	
1975-76	N/A	N/A	N/A	Gale Bryan	
1976-77	N/A	N/A	N/A	Gale Bryan	
1977-78	N/A	N/A	N/A	Gary Baxter	SCC Champions
1978-79	N/A	N/A	N/A	Gary Baxter	
1979-80	N/A	N/A	N/A	Randy Legendre	

THE HISTORY OF STAUNTON HIGH SCHOOL SPORTS

YEAR	W	L	T	COACH	TEAM NOTES / PERCENTAGE
1980-81	N/A	N/A	N/A	Dave Martin	
1981-82	N/A	N/A	N/A	Dave Martin	
1982-83	N/A	N/A	N/A	Dave Martin	
1983-84	N/A	N/A	N/A	Dave Martin	
1984-85	N/A	N/A	N/A	Dave Martin	
1985-86	N/A	N/A	N/A	Dave Martin	
1986-87	N/A	N/A	N/A	Ron Sturomski	
1987-88	N/A	N/A	N/A	Ron Sturomski	
1988-89	N/A	N/A	N/A	Ron Sturomski	
1989-90	N/A	N/A	N/A	Ron Sturomski	SCC, County, Sectional Champions
1990-91	N/A	N/A	N/A	Ron Sturomski	
1991-92	N/A	N/A	N/A	Larry Caldieraro	
1992-93	N/A	N/A	N/A	Dave Williams	Sectional Champions
1993-94	N/A	N/A	N/A	Dave Williams	
1994-95	N/A	N/A	N/A	Dave Williams	
1995-96	N/A	N/A	N/A	Dave Williams	
1996-97	N/A	N/A	N/A	Dave Williams	
1997-98	N/A	N/A	N/A	Scott Tonsor	
1998-99	N/A	N/A	N/A	Scott Tonsor	
1999-00	N/A	N/A	N/A	Dave Williams	
2000-01	N/A	N/A	N/A	Tim Smiddy	
2001-02	N/A	N/A	N/A	B.J. Ogata	
2002-03	N/A	N/A	N/A	B.J. Ogata	
2003-04	N/A	N/A	N/A	B.J. Ogata	
2004-05	N/A	N/A	N/A	B.J. Ogata	County Champions
2005-06	N/A	N/A	N/A	B.J. Ogata	
2006-07	N/A	N/A	N/A	B.J. Ogata	
2007-08	N/A	N/A	N/A	B.J. Ogata	
2008-09	N/A	N/A	N/A	B.J. Ogata	
2009-10	N/A	N/A	N/A	B.J. Ogata	PSC Champions
2010-11	N/A	N/A	N/A	B.J. Ogata	PSC Champions
2011-12	N/A	N/A	N/A	B.J. Ogata	PSC Champions

Track (Girls)

YEAR	W	L	T	COACH	TEAM NOTES / PERCENTAGE
1972-73	N/A	N/A	N/A	Patty Rupert	
1973-74	N/A	N/A	N/A	Patty Rupert	
1974-75	N/A	N/A	N/A	Donna Ruehrup	SCC, County Champions
1975-76	N/A	N/A	N/A	Donna Ruehrup	SCC, County Champions
1976-77	N/A	N/A	N/A	Donna Ruehrup	SCC Champions
1977-78	N/A	N/A	N/A	Donna Ruehrup	SCC Champions
1978-79	N/A	N/A	N/A	Donna Ruehrup	SCC Champions
1979-80	N/A	N/A	N/A	Donna Ruehrup	
1980-81	N/A	N/A	N/A	Donna Ruehrup	SCC Champions
1981-82	N/A	N/A	N/A	Donna Ruehrup	
1982-83	N/A	N/A	N/A	Donna Ruehrup	
1983-84	N/A	N/A	N/A	Donna Ruehrup	
1984-85	N/A	N/A	N/A	Donna Ruehrup	

1985-86	N/A	N/A	N/A	Donna Ruehrup	
1986-87	N/A	N/A	N/A	Donna Ruehrup	
1987-88	N/A	N/A	N/A	Donna Ruehrup	
1988-89	N/A	N/A	N/A	Donna Ruehrup	
1989-90	N/A	N/A	N/A	Donna Ruehrup	
1990-91	N/A	N/A	N/A	Donna Ruehrup	
1991-92	N/A	N/A	N/A	Donna Ruehrup	
1992-95	N/A	N/A	N/A	N/A	No Team
1995-96	N/A	N/A	N/A	Dave Williams	
1996-97	N/A	N/A	N/A	Dave Williams	
1997-2002	N/A	N/A	N/A	N/A	No Team
2002-03	N/A	N/A	N/A	B.J. Ogata	
2003-04	N/A	N/A	N/A	B.J. Ogata	
2004-05	N/A	N/A	N/A	B.J. Ogata	
2005-06	N/A	N/A	N/A	B.J. Ogata	
2006-07	N/A	N/A	N/A	B.J. Ogata	
2007-08	N/A	N/A	N/A	B.J. Ogata	
2008-09	N/A	N/A	N/A	B.J. Ogata	
2009-10	N/A	N/A	N/A	B.J. Ogata	PSC Champions
2010-11	N/A	N/A	N/A	B.J. Ogata	
2011-12	N/A	N/A	N/A	B.J. Ogata	

Volleyball

YEAR	W	L	T	COACH	TEAM NOTES / PERCENTAGE
1974-75*	1	1	0	Sandal Herbeck	District Champions
Total*	1	1	0	Sandal Herbeck (1)	50.0%
1975-76	5	9	0	Donna Ruehrup	
1976-77	10	3	0	Donna Ruehrup	SCC Champions
1977-78	14	7	0	Donna Ruehrup	District Champions
1978-79	25	2	0	Donna Ruehrup	SCC, County, District, Sectional Champions
1979-80	20	5	0	Donna Ruehrup	District Champions
1980-81	28	3	0	Donna Ruehrup	SCC, County, District, Sectional Champions, State (Quarterfinals)
1981-82	26	2	0	Donna Ruehrup	SCC, County, District Champions
1982-83	19	10	0	Donna Ruehrup	Regional Champions
1983-84	22	5	0	Donna Ruehrup	SCC, County, Regional, Sectional Champions
1984-85	24	7	0	Donna Ruehrup	SCC, County, Regional, Sectional Champions
1985-86	5	21	0	Donna Ruehrup	
1986-87	19	6	0	Donna Ruehrup	SCC, Regional Champions
1987-88	8	16	0	Donna Ruehrup	
1988-89	10	15	0	Donna Ruehrup	
1989-90	16	11	0	Donna Ruehrup	County Champions
1990-91	25	5	0	Donna Ruehrup	SCC, County, Regional, Sectional Champions
1991-92	22	5	0	Donna Ruehrup	SCC, County, Regional, Sectional Champions
1992-93	16	12	0	Donna Ruehrup	
1993-94	14	11	0	Donna Ruehrup	
Total	328	155	0	Donna Ruehrup (19)	67.9%
1994-95	10	17	0	Kim Murray	
1995-96	15	14	0	Kim Murray	

Total	25	31	0	**Kim Murray (2)**	44.6%
1996-97	15	11	0	Becky Pepper	
1997-98	15	11	0	Becky Pepper	
Total	**30**	**22**	**0**	**Becky Pepper (2)**	**57.7%**
1998-99	16	9	0	Don Schaefer	
1999-00	27	6	0	Don Schaefer	SCC East, County, Regional Champions
2000-01	13	17	0	Don Schaefer	
Total	**56**	**32**	**0**	**Don Schaefer (3)**	**63.6%**
2001-02	12	16	0	Lana Odorizzi	Regional Champions
2002-03	16	12	0	Lana Odorizzi	
2003-04	5	23	0	Lana Odorizzi	
2004-05	6	15	0	Lana Odorizzi	
Total	**39**	**66**	**0**	**Lana Odorizzi (4)**	**37.1%**
2005-06	3	18	0	Bill Hanks	
Total	**3**	**18**	**0**	**Bill Hanks (1)**	**14.3%**
2006-07	6	15	0	Marvin Hayden	
Total	**6**	**15**	**0**	**Marvin Hayden (1)**	**28.6%**
2007-08	5	21	0	Amber Scruton	
Total	**5**	**21**	**0**	**Amber Scruton (1)**	**19.2%**
2008-09	15	11	0	Andrea Prante	
2009-10	23	6	0	Andrea Prante	PSC, Regional Champions
Total	**38**	**17**	**0**	**Andrea Prante (2)**	**69.1%**
2010-11	25	5	0	Mike Korte	County Champions
2011-12	16	8	0	Mike Korte	
Total	**41**	**13**	**0**	**Mike Korte (2)**	**75.9%**
TOTAL*	**572**	**391**	**0**	**VOLLEYBALL**	**59.4%**

* incomplete results

Conference Affiliation

Year	Conference	Teams
1926-32	SCC	Carlinville, Gillespie, Hillsboro, Litchfield, Mt. Olive, Nokomis, Pana, Shelbyville, Staunton, Taylorville
1932-34	SCC	Carlinville, Gillespie, Hillsboro, Litchfield, Mt. Olive, Nokomis, Pana, Staunton, Taylorville
1934-35	SCC	Carlinville, Gillespie, Hillsboro, Mt. Olive, Nokomis, Pana, Staunton, Taylorville
1935-44	SCC	Benld, Carlinville, Gillespie, Hillsboro, Mt. Olive, Nokomis, Pana, Staunton, Taylorville
1944-56	SCC	Benld, Carlinville, Gillespie, Mt. Olive, Staunton
1956-61	SCC	Benld, Carlinville, Gillespie, Mt. Olive, Nokomis, Southwestern, Staunton
1961-63	SCC	Carlinville, Gillespie, Mt. Olive, Nokomis, Staunton
1963-67	SCC	Carlinville, Gillespie, Mt. Olive, Nokomis, Springfield Feitshans, Staunton
1967-70	SCC	Carlinville, Gillespie, Mt. Olive, Nokomis, Staunton, Virden
1970-80	SCC	Carlinville, Gillespie, Mt. Olive, Nokomis, Southwestern, Staunton, Virden
1980-85	SCC	Carlinville, Gillespie, Litchfield, Nokomis, North Greene, Southwestern, Staunton, Virden
1985-93	SCC	Carlinville, Gillespie, Litchfield, Southwestern, Staunton, Triad
1993-97	SCC	Alton Marquette, Carlinville, Gillespie, Litchfield, Southwestern, Staunton
1997-09	SCC East SCC West	Greenville, Hillsboro, Litchfield, Pana, Staunton, Vandalia Alton Marquette, Carlinville, East Alton-Wood River, Gillespie, Roxana, Southwestern
2009-12	SCC East SCC West	Greenville, Hillsboro, Litchfield, Pana, Vandalia Alton Marquette, Carlinville, East Alton-Wood River, Roxana, Southwestern
2009-10	PSC	Gillespie, Girard, Kincaid South Fork, Mt. Olive, New Berlin (except football), Nokomis, Pawnee, Staunton, Virden
2010-12	PSC	Bunker Hill, Gillespie, Kincaid South Fork, Mt. Olive, Nokomis, North Mac, Pawnee, Staunton
2012-??	SCC	Carlinville, Gillespie, Greenville, Hillsboro, Litchfield, Pana, Roxana, Southwestern, Staunton, Vandalia

Basketball (County Champions)

Year	Boys	Girls	Year	Boys	Girls
1918-19	Benld	N/A	1965-66	Bunker Hill	N/A
1919-20	Mt. Olive	N/A	1966-67	Carlinville	N/A
1920-21	Brighton	N/A	1967-68	Carlinville	N/A
1921-22	Mt. Olive	N/A	1968-69	Gillespie	N/A
1922-23	Mt. Olive	N/A	1969-70	Bunker Hill	N/A
1923-24	Chesterfield	N/A	1970-71	Southwestern	N/A
1924-25	Mt. Olive	N/A	1971-72	Gillespie	N/A
1925-26	Mt. Olive	N/A	1972-73	Girard	N/A
1926-27	Mt. Olive	N/A	1973-74	Southwestern	N/A
1927-28	Staunton	N/A	1974-75	Southwestern	N/A
1928-29	Chesterfield	N/A	1975-76	Southwestern	N/A
1929-30	Chesterfield	N/A	1976-77	Virden	N/A
1930-31	Chesterfield	N/A	1977-78	Southwestern	N/A
1931-32	Gillespie	N/A	1978-79	Virden	N/A
1932-33	Virden	N/A	1979-80	Staunton	Carlinville
1933-34	Gillespie	N/A	1980-81	Bunker Hill	Carlinville
1934-35	Staunton	N/A	1981-82	Staunton	Bunker Hill
1935-36	Benld	N/A	1982-83	Bunker Hill	Carlinville
1936-37	Gillespie	N/A	1983-84	Bunker Hill	Bunker Hill
1937-38	Mt. Olive	N/A	1984-85	Staunton	Staunton
1938-39	Benld	N/A	1985-86	Staunton	Southwestern
1939-40	Gillespie	N/A	1986-87	Staunton	Staunton
1940-41	Gillespie	N/A	1987-88	Southwestern	Carlinville
1941-42	Mt. Olive	N/A	1988-89	Southwestern	Southwestern
1942-43	Gillespie	N/A	1989-90	Southwestern	Southwestern
1943-44	Gillespie	N/A	1990-91	Staunton	Southwestern
1944-45	Gillespie	N/A	1991-92	Staunton	Southwestern
1945-46	Staunton	N/A	1992-93	Virden	Carlinville
1946-47	Mt. Olive	N/A	1993-94	Southwestern	Gillespie
1947-48	Mt. Olive	N/A	1994-95	Gillespie	Gillespie
1948-49	Mt. Olive	N/A	1995-96	Bunker Hill	Gillespie
1949-50	Benld	N/A	1996-97	Carlinville	Gillespie
1950-51	Gillespie	N/A	1997-98	Bunker Hill	Southwestern
1951-52	Staunton	N/A	1998-99	Bunker Hill	Gillespie
1952-53	Gillespie	N/A	1999-00	Southwestern	Gillespie
1953-54	Gillespie	N/A	2000-01	Staunton	Southwestern
1954-55	Gillespie	N/A	2001-02	Gillespie	Gillespie
1955-56	Gillespie	N/A	2002-03	Gillespie	Southwestern
1956-57	Carlinville	N/A	2003-04	Mt. Olive	Southwestern
1957-58	Staunton	N/A	2004-05	Carlinville	Southwestern
1958-59	Carlinville	N/A	2005-06	Southwestern	Southwestern
1959-60	Gillespie	N/A	2006-07	Southwestern	Southwestern
1960-61	Carlinville	N/A	2007-08	Girard	Carlinville
1961-62	Carlinville	N/A	2008-09	Staunton	Southwestern
1962-63	Carlinville	N/A	2009-10	Girard	Southwestern
1963-64	Gillespie	N/A	2010-11	North Mac	Staunton
1964-65	Gillespie	N/A	2011-12	Staunton	North Mac

Football (Records vs. Opponents)

Opponent	W	L	T	Opponent	W	L	T
Albion Edwards County	1	0	0	Jerseyville	10	3	0
Alton Marquette	7	9	1	Johnston City	1	0	0
Alton Western Military Academy	4	3	0	Kincaid South Fork	3	0	0
Anna-Jonesboro	0	1	0	Kirkwood (MO)	3	0	0
Auburn	2	1	0	LeRoy	1	0	0
Belleville	0	4	0	Lincoln	0	1	0
Belleville East	0	3	1	Litchfield	55	17	1
Bement	0	1	0	Livingston	1	0	0
Benld	20	18	5	Modesto	1	0	0
Bethalto Civic Memorial	1	2	0	Mt. Olive	47	26	6
Blackburn College	2	0	0	Nokomis	38	13	2
Bismarck-Henning	0	1	0	North Greene	4	1	0
Bridgeport Red Hill	1	0	0	North Mac	0	3	0
Bunker Hill	3	0	0	Palmyra	5	2	0
Bunker Hill Military Academy	3	3	0	Pana	9	15	1
Carbondale	1	0	0	Pawnee	3	1	0
Carlinville	34	50	6	Petersburg PORTA	1	1	0
Carterville	0	1	0	Pittsfield	4	5	0
Casey-Westfield	0	1	0	Pleasant Plains	1	0	0
Centralia	1	1	0	Quincy CBC	4	2	0
Chatham Glenwood	1	0	0	Red Bud	1	0	0
Collinsville	0	4	1	Riverton	2	0	0
Columbia	0	7	0	Roxana	4	2	0
Decatur Lakeview	1	1	0	Rushville	0	1	0
Decatur St. Teresa	2	1	0	St. Louis CBC (MO)	1	0	0
Divernon	2	0	0	St. Louis Cleveland (MO)	1	0	0
DuQuoin	0	1	0	St. Louis DeAndreis (MO)	0	1	0
East Alton-Wood River	6	8	0	St. Louis University High (MO)	2	0	0
East St. Louis Senior	1	0	0	Shelbyville	1	0	0
East St. Louis Assumption	0	3	0	Southwestern	25	13	0
Edwardsville	15	20	3	Springfield Cathedral	2	5	0
Gillespie	45	35	7	Springfield Feitshans	5	0	0
Girard	5	0	0	Springfield St. James	1	0	0
Granite City	4	3	0	Stillman Valley	0	1	0
Greenfield	4	3	0	Stonington	1	0	0
Greenville	9	19	0	Taylorville	4	2	1
Hamilton	0	1	0	Tolono Unity	0	1	0
Hardin Calhoun	1	3	0	Triad	2	6	0
Highland	2	0	0	Troy	0	0	1
Hillsboro	31	28	1	Vandalia	5	7	0
Jacksonville ISD	2	2	0	Virden	28	4	3
Jacksonville Routt	1	0	0	TOTAL	488	371	40

Football (Conference Champions)

Year	Conference	Team(s)	Year	Conference	Team(s)
1926-27	SCC	Mt. Olive	1973-74	SCC	Gillespie
1927-28	SCC	Gillespie, Staunton	1974-75	SCC	Carlinville
1928-29	SCC	Staunton, Taylorville	1975-76	SCC	Carlinville
1929-30	SCC	Hillsboro	1976-77	SCC	Gillespie
1930-31	SCC	Hillsboro	1977-78	SCC	Nokomis
1931-32	SCC	Carlinville, Nokomis	1978-79	SCC	Carlinville
1932-33	SCC	Gillespie, Mt. Olive	1979-80	SCC	Carlinville
1933-34	SCC	Hillsboro	1980-81	SCC	Litchfield
1934-35	SCC	Hillsboro	1981-82	SCC	Gillespie
1935-36	SCC	Hillsboro	1982-83	SCC	Carlinville
1936-37	SCC	Mt. Olive	1983-84	SCC	Carlinville
1937-38	SCC	Mt. Olive	1984-85	SCC	Carlinville
1938-39	SCC	Hillsboro, Mt. Olive	1985-86	SCC	Carlinville
1939-40	SCC	Benld, Carlinville, Pana	1986-87	SCC	Carlinville
1940-41	SCC	Benld	1987-88	SCC	Triad
1941-42	SCC	Carlinville	1988-89	SCC	Triad
1942-43	SCC	Carlinville	1989-90	SCC	Carlinville
1943-44	SCC	Taylorville	1990-91	SCC	Gillespie
1944-45	SCC	Benld, Gillespie, Staunton	1991-92	SCC	Triad
1945-46	SCC	Benld	1992-93	SCC	Gillespie
1946-47	SCC	Benld	1993-94	SCC	Carlinville
1947-48	SCC	Mt. Olive	1994-95	SCC	Carlinville
1948-49	SCC	Gillespie	1995-96	SCC	Carlinville
1949-50	SCC	Mt. Olive	1996-97	SCC	Southwestern
1950-51	SCC	Benld	1997-98	SCC East	Staunton
1951-52	SCC	Gillespie, Staunton		SCC West	Southwestern
1952-53	SCC	Carlinville, Gillespie, Mt. Olive	1998-99	SCC East	Pana
1953-54	SCC	Mt. Olive		SCC West	Southwestern
1954-55	SCC	Gillespie, Mt. Olive	1999-00	SCC East	Hillsboro
1955-56	SCC	Mt. Olive		SCC West	EAWR, Southwestern
1956-57	SCC	Carlinville	2000-01	SCC East	Staunton
1957-58	SCC	Carlinville, Mt. Olive		SCC West	EAWR
1958-59	SCC	Staunton	2001-02	SCC East	Hillsboro
1959-60	SCC	Staunton		SCC West	Carlinville
1960-61	SCC	Staunton	2002-03	SCC East	Hillsboro
1961-62	SCC	Staunton		SCC West	Alton Marquette
1962-63	SCC	Carlinville	2003-04	SCC East	Hillsboro
1963-64	SCC	Staunton		SCC West	Roxana
1964-65	SCC	Gillespie, Staunton	2004-05	SCC East	Greenville
1965-66	SCC	Staunton		SCC West	EAWR
1966-67	SCC	Carlinville	2005-06	SCC East	Greenville, Hillsboro
1967-68	SCC	Staunton		SCC West	Gillespie
1968-69	SCC	Carlinville	2006-07	SCC East	Hillsboro
1969-70	SCC	Staunton		SCC West	EAWR
1970-71	SCC	Staunton	2007-08	SCC East	Greenville
1971-72	SCC	Carlinville, Nokomis, Staunton		SCC West	Carlinville
1972-73	SCC	Gillespie			

2008-09	SCC East	Greenville
	SCC West	Alton Marquette, Carlinville, Southwestern
2009-10	PSC	Staunton
	SCC	Greenville
2010-11	PSC	North Mac
	SCC	Carlinville, Greenville, Pana
2011-12	PSC	Pawnee
	SCC	Greenville

ATTACHMENT 2

Individual Accomplishments

Baseball

Year	Name	Accomplishment
1973-74	Bill Marcuzzo	SCC (1st Team)
	Eric Pingolt	SCC (Honorable Mention)
	Daryl Schuette	SCC (Honorable Mention)
	Vic Spagnola	SCC (1st Team)
1975-76	Kevin Barrett	SCC (Honorable Mention)
	Ron Heflin	SCC (1st Team)
	Dan McDole	SCC (1st Team)
	Eric Pingolt	SCC (1st Team)
	Phil Vesper	SCC (Honorable Mention)
	Bart Yakos	SCC (Honorable Mention)
1976-77	Kevin Barrett	SCC (Honorable Mention)
	Mark Bono	SCC (Honorable Mention)
	Bob Snell	SCC (1st Team)
	Bart Yakos	SCC (Honorable Mention)
1977-78	Bart Yakos	SCC (1st Team)
1978-79	Jay Meckles	SCC (1st Team)
	Brad Yakos	SCC (1st Team)
	Tim Yarnik	SCC (1st Team)
1979-80	Fred Brenzel	SCC (1st Team)
	Rich Fletcher	SCC (Honorable Mention)
	Mark Marcuzzo	SCC (Honorable Mention)
	Kevin Sievers	SCC (1st Team)
	Brad Yakos	SCC (1st Team)
	Tim Yarnik	SCC (1st Team)
1980-81	John Bond	SCC (Honorable Mention)
	Rich Fletcher	SCC (1st Team)
	Mark Vesper	SCC (1st Team)
1983-84	Roger Banovz	SCC (1st Team)
	Mike Bekeske	SCC (Honorable Mention)
	Larry Caldieraro	SCC (1st Team)
	Rich Garde	SCC (Honorable Mention)
	Randy Harbison	SCC (Honorable Mention)
	Dave Jones	SCC (1st Team)
1985-86	Bart Caldieraro	SCC (1st Team)
	Kevin Gockel	SCC (1st Team)
1987-88	Brian Barks	SCC (Honorable Mention)

	Kevin Dal Pozzo	SCC (Honorable Mention)
	Fred Harbison	SCC (1st Team)
	Darik Jones	SCC (Honorable Mention)
	John Rae	SCC (1st Team)
1988-89	Phil Deist	SCC (Honorable Mention)
	Ed Fletcher	SCC (1st Team)
1989-90	Ed Fletcher	SCC (1st Team)
1990-91	Scott Bremer	SCC (1st Team)
	Jason Huhsman	SCC (1st Team)
	Andy Kuba	SCC (Honorable Mention)
	Dan Lyday	SCC (1st Team)
	Nathan Spudich	SCC (Honorable Mention)
1991-92	Andy Kuba	SCC (1st Team)
	Jeremy May	SCC (1st Team)
1992-93	Mark Johnson	SCC (Honorable Mention)
	Andy Kuba	SCC (1st Team), Telegraph (Athlete of the Year - Finalist)
	Jeremy May	SCC (Honorable Mention)
	Chad Neuhaus	SCC (Honorable Mention)
	Tim Scheller	SCC (1st Team)
1993-94	Ron Hampton	SCC (Honorable Mention)
	Jeremy May	SCC (1st Team), Telegraph (1st Team), Telegraph (Athlete of the Year)
	Brian Murphy	SCC (Honorable Mention)
	Chad Neuhaus	SCC (Honorable Mention)
1994-95	Derek Allen	SCC (1st Team)
	Derek Brauer	SCC (1st Team)
	Steve Moore	SCC (Honorable Mention)
1995-96	Cory Callovini	SCC (1st Team)
	Ben Frank	SCC (Honorable Mention)
	Luke Melm	SCC (Honorable Mention)
	Steve Moore	SCC (1st Team), Telegraph (2nd Team), Telegraph (Athlete of the Year - Finalist)
1996-97	Ben Frank	SCC (1st Team)
	Ted Frank	SCC (1st Team)
	Ryan Machota	SCC (Honorable Mention)
	Luke Melm	SCC (1st Team)
	Steve Moore	SCC (1st Team), Telegraph (2nd Team), Telegraph (Athlete of the Year - Finalist)
	Beau Sievers	SCC (1st Team)
1997-98	Scott Billings	SCC East (1st Team)
	Brian Coalson	SCC East (1st Team)

Individual Accompishments

	Ben Frank	SCC East (1st Team), Telegraph (1st Team), Telegraph (Athlete of the Year - Finalist)
	Ted Frank	SCC East (1st Team)
	Luke Melm	SCC East (1st Team)
	Darren Ott	SCC East (1st Team)
	Vinnie Sanvi	SCC East (1st Team)
1998-99	Scott Billings	SCC East (1st Team)
	Ted Frank	SCC East (1st Team)
	Brett Herbeck	SCC East (1st Team)
	Terry Murphy	SCC East (1st Team)
	Darren Ott	SCC East (1st Team), Telegraph (2nd Team)
	Vinnie Sanvi	SCC East (1st Team), Telegraph (1st Team)
1999-00	Larry Senaldi	SCC East (1st Team)
2000-01	Brandon Fletcher	SCC East (Honorable Mention)
	John Moore	SCC East (Honorable Mention)
	Mike Rizzi	SCC East (Honorable Mention)
	Larry Senaldi	SCC East (Honorable Mention)
2001-02	Nathan Doherty	SCC East (Honorable Mention)
2002-03	Nick Jones	SCC East (Honorable Mention)
	Kyle Pirok	SCC East (Honorable Mention)
	Joe Scroggins	SCC East (1st Team)
2003-04	Mike Corby	SCC East (1st Team)
	Ricky Moulton	SCC East (Honorable Mention)
	Luke Pirok	SCC East (Honorable Mention)
2004-05	Ben Atwood	SCC East (1st Team)
	Joe Scroggins	SCC East (Honorable Mention)
2005-06	Ben Atwood	SCC East (1st Team)
	Kyle Pirok	SCC East (1st Team)
	Justin Revisky	SCC East (1st Team)
2006-07	Zack Arnett	SCC East (1st Team), SJ-R (Special Mention)
2007-08	Jake Langley	SCC East (1st Team), SJ-R (Special Mention)
2008-09	Zack Arnett	SCC East (Honorable Mention)
	Jake Langley	SCC East (Honorable Mention), Telegraph (1st Team), SJ-R (Special Mention)
2009-10	Kevin Billings	PSC (1st Team)
	Charlie Clark	PSC (1st Team), Telegraph (1st Team), SJ-R (Honorable Mention)
	Austin Hollaway	PSC (Honorable Mention)
	Jake Langley	PSC (1st Team), Telegraph (1st Team), SJ-R (Honorable Mention)
	A.J. Sitko	PSC (Honorable Mention)

2010-11　Larry Caldieraro　　PSC (Honorable Mention)
　　　　　Dillon Diesselhorst　PSC (2nd Team)
　　　　　Austin Hollaway　　PSC (1st Team), Telegraph (1st Team)
　　　　　Brady Moore　　　　PSC (2nd Team)
　　　　　A.J. Sitko　　　　　PSC (1st Team), Telegraph (1st Team), SJ-R (Honorable Mention)

2011-12　Sean Abernathy　　　PSC (2nd Team)
　　　　　Ryan Fretz　　　　　PSC (2nd Team)
　　　　　A.J. Sitko　　　　　PSC (1st Team)

Individual Accompishments

Basketball (Boys)

Year	Name	Accomplishment
1920-21	George Oehler	County (1st Team)
1925-26	Dave Wilson	County (2nd Team)
1927-28	Bernie Aschbacher	SCC (Honorable Mention), County (1st Team)
	Wellman France	SCC (1st Team), County (1st Team), District Tournament (1st Team)
	George Oehler	SCC (2nd Team), County (1st Team), District Tournament (1st Team)
	Don Overbeay	SCC (1st Team), County (2nd Team)
1928-29	Bill Moss	County (2nd Team)
	John Oehler	County (1st Team)
	Harry Walters	County (2nd Team)
1930-31	John Masser	County (1st Team)
1933-34	Norm Stolze	County (1st Team)
	? Westerman	County (1st Team)
1951-52	Len Renner	SHS (1000 Points)
1958-59	Don Kasubke	Chicago American (Special Mention), SHS (1000 Points)
1966-67	Al Culp	SCC (Honorable Mention)
	Tom Monschein	SCC (1st Team)
	Tom Oettel	SCC (1st Team)
1968-69	Brad Bahn	SCC (1st Team)
	Terry Best	SCC (2nd Team)
1970-71	Craig Schuette	County (Honorable Mention)
1971-72	Daryl Schuette	SCC (Honorable Mention)
	Bob Vesper	SCC (Honorable Mention)
1973-74	Daryl Schuette	SCC (1st Team)
	Mark Stein	SCC (2nd Team)
	Don Sullivan	SCC (Honorable Mention)
1975-76	John Clark	SCC (2nd Team)
	John Podwojski	SCC (Honorable Mention)
1977-78	Brad Yakos	SCC (1st Team)
1979-80	Troy Graves	SCC (Honorable Mention)
	Rich Link	SCC (Honorable Mention)

	Mark Marcuzzo	SCC (2nd Team), County (2nd Team)
	Brad Yakos	SCC (1st Team), County (1st Team), SHS (1000 Points)
	Tim Yarnik	SCC (1st Team), County (1st Team), SHS (1000 Points)
1980-81	Tom Coyne	SCC (1st Team), County (Honorable Mention), WSMI (3rd Team)
1981-82	Charlie Black	SCC (Honorable Mention)
	Tom Coyne	SCC (1st Team), County (MVP), WSMI (1st Team)
	Rich Fletcher	SCC (2nd Team)
	Bruce Kasubke	SCC (Honorable Mention), WSMI (2nd Team)
	Kelly Pieper	County (Honorable Mention)
1982-83	Jim Coyne	SCC (1st Team)
1983-84	Kevin Goebel	SCC (Honorable Mention)
	Jeff Paitz	SCC (1st Team), County (2nd Team)
	Tom Scherff	SCC (Honorable Mention)
	Deron Stein	SCC (1st Team), County (1st Team)
1984-85	Rick Landrem	SCC (1st Team), County (MVP)
	Jeff Paitz	SCC (1st Team)
	Deron Stein	SCC (2nd Team), County (1st Team)
1985-86	Kevin Gockel	SCC (Honorable Mention)
	Bret Kasubke	SCC (1st Team), County (MVP)
	Rick Landrem	SCC (1st Team), County (1st Team)
	Roman Meckles	SCC (2nd Team), County (2nd Team)
1986-87	Kevin Gockel	SCC (2nd Team), County (2nd Team)
	Bret Kasubke	SCC (1st Team), County (MVP), SJ-R (1st Team), IBCA (All-Star Game), SHS (1341 Points)
	Jeff Windau	SCC (2nd Team), County (2nd Team)
1987-88	Kelly Brown	SCC (Honorable Mention)
	Jeff Windau	SCC (1st Team), County (1st Team)
1988-89	Brad Best	SCC (2nd Team)
	Simon Hannig	SCC (1st Team), County (1st Team)
	Brad Hemann	SCC (Honorable Mention), County (1st Team)
1989-90	Brad Best	SCC (1st Team), County (1st Team), Telegraph (2nd Team), SJ-R (1st Team)
	Jeff Yarnik	SCC (Honorable Mention), County (2nd Team)
1990-91	Brad Best	SCC (1st Team), County (MVP), Telegraph (1st Team), SJ-R (1st Team), WSMI (1st Team), AP All-State (Honorable Mention), SHS (1681 Points)
	Kevin Hemken	SCC (1st Team), County (1st Team)
	Kevin Klein	SCC (2nd Team), County (2nd Team)
	Dan Lyday	SCC (Honorable Mention)
1991-92	Nathan Calcari	SCC (Honorable Mention), County (MVP)

Individual Accomplishments

	Kevin Hemken	SCC (1st Team), County (1st Team), Telegraph (1st Team), WSMI (1st Team), AP All-State (Honorable Mention)
	Andy Kuba	SCC (2nd Team)
	Kevin Meyer	SCC (1st Team), County (1st Team)
1992-93	Ron Hampton	SCC (Honorable Mention), Telegraph (2nd Team)
	Mike Kovaly	3-Point Shootout (State)
	Andy Kuba	SCC (1st Team), Telegraph (Player of the Year), Telegraph (Athlete of the Year - Finalist), SJ-R (1st Team), WSMI (1st Team), Sun-Times All-State (1st Team), AP All-State (Honorable Mention), State Tournament (1st Team)
	Kevin Meyer	SCC (1st Team), Telegraph (1st Team), SJ-R (Special Mention), WSMI (1st Team), AP All-State (Honorable Mention), State Tournament (2nd Team)
	Brad Skertich	SCC (Honorable Mention)
1993-94	Ron Hampton	SCC (2nd Team), County (2nd Team), WSMI (1st Team), AP All-State (Honorable Mention)
	Mike Kovaly	SCC (2nd Team)
	Jeremy May	Telegraph (Athlete of the Year - Winner)
1994-95	Derek Brauer	SCC (2nd Team)
	Mike Kovaly	SCC (Honorable Mention)
	Joe Odorizzi	SCC (Honorable Mention)
1995-96	Steve Moore	SCC (1st Team), County (1st Team), Telegraph (1st Team), Telegraph (Athlete of the Year - Finalist), WSMI (1st Team)
	Joe Odorizzi	SCC (2nd Team), County (2nd Team)
1996-97	Ben Frank	SCC (2nd Team), County (2nd Team), Telegraph (Honorable Mention)
	John Masinelli	SCC (Honorable Mention)
	Steve Moore	SCC (1st Team), County (1st Team), Telegraph (1st Team), Telegraph (Athlete of the Year - Finalist), SJ-R (1st Team), WSMI (1st Team), SHS (1208 Points)
1997-98	Brian Coalson	SCC East (2nd Team), County (1st Team)
	Ben Frank	SCC East (2nd Team), County (1st Team), Telegraph (2nd Team), Telegraph (Athlete of the Year - Finalist)
	Sam Miller	County (2nd Team)
1998-99	Ted Frank	SCC East (Honorable Mention), County (2nd Team)
	Zack Rigoni	SCC East (2nd Team), County (2nd Team)
1999-00	Zack Rigoni	SCC East (1st Team), County (2nd Team), SJ-R (Honorable Mention)
	Mark Sievers	SCC East (Honorable Mention)
2000-01	Chad Dugger	SCC East (Honorable Mention), County (2nd Team)
	Craig Phifer	SCC East (2nd Team), County (1st Team)
	Zack Rigoni	SCC East (1st Team), County (MVP), Telegraph (Player of the Year), SJ-R (1st Team), WSMI (1st Team), Post-Dispatch (Honorable Mention), SHS (1070 Points)
	Mark Sievers	SCC East (Honorable Mention)

2001-02	Mike Brown	SCC East (2nd Team)
	Craig Phifer	SCC East (1st Team), County (1st Team), Telegraph (1st Team)
2002-03	Mike Brown	SCC East (2nd Team)
	Doug Stiegemeier	SCC East (Honorable Mention)
2003-04	Luke Pirok	SCC East (2nd Team)
	Doug Stiegemeier	SCC East (Honorable Mention), County (1st Team), Telegraph (Special Mention)
2004-05	Scott Meyer	SCC East (2nd Team), County (1st Team)
	Doug Stiegemeier	SCC East (2nd Team), County (1st Team), Telegraph (2nd Team), SJ-R (Honorable Mention), WSMI (1st Team), SHS (1130 Points)
2005-06	Ben Atwood	SCC East (2nd Team), County (2nd Team)
2006-07	Chris Redfern	SCC East (Honorable Mention)
2007-08	Cody Best	County (1st Team), A Baseline View (Honorable Mention)
	Phil Rhodes	SCC East (2nd Team), County (1st Team), SJ-R (Honorable Mention), WSMI (1st Team), 3-Point Shootout (State)
2008-09	Cody Best	SCC East (1st Team), County (MVP), Telegraph (1st Team), SJ-R (2nd Team), WSMI (1st Team), A Baseline View (Special Mention), IBCA All-State (Honorable Mention), IBS All-State (Honorable Mention)
	Kevin Fuller	County (1st Team)
	Mike Mihelcic	SCC East (Honorable Mention), SJ-R (Honorable Mention), WSMI (1st Team)
2009-10	Andy Goebel	PSC (1st Team), SJ-R (Honorable Mention), 3-Point Shootout (State)
	Kevin Fuller	PSC (1st Team), County (1st Team), Telegraph (1st Team), SJ-R (Special Mention), A Baseline View (Special Mention), IBCA All-State (Special Mention)
2010-11	Kyle Brauer	County (1st Team)
	Devin Gerdes	PSC (1st Team), SJ-R (Honorable Mention), A Baseline View (Special Mention)
	Austin Hollaway	PSC (Honorable Mention)
	Brett Kinder	PSC (Honorable Mention), County (1st Team), A Baseline View (Special Mention)
2011-12	Billy Bartle	PSC (1st Team)
	Devin Gerdes	County (1st Team)
	Austin Hollaway	PSC (1st Team), County (1st Team), SJ-R (Honorable Mention), A Baseline View (Special Mention)

Basketball (Girls)

Year	Name	Accomplishment
1980-81	Evelyn Bean	SCC (Honorable Mention)
	Janis Treadway	SCC (1st Team), County (1st Team)
	Diane Williams	SCC (Honorable Mention)
1982-83	Sharon Bodi	SCC (1st Team)
	Mary Hering	SCC (Honorable Mention), County (1st Team)
1983-84	Mary Hering	SCC (2nd Team), County (1st Team)
	Lisa Kasubke	SCC (2nd Team), County (2nd Team)
1985-86	Dana Sievers	SCC (2nd Team), County (1st Team)
	Darla Sievers	SCC (Honorable Mention), County (2nd Team)
1986-87	Gayle Gusewelle	SCC (1st Team), County (1st Team)
	Tracy Kuba	SCC (2nd Team)
1987-88	Gayle Gusewelle	SCC (1st Team), County (MVP)
	Tracy Kuba	SCC (2nd Team), County (2nd Team)
	Kim Winslow	SCC (Honorable Mention), County (2nd Team)
1988-89	Jerri Hochmuth	SCC (Honorable Mention)
1989-90	Shayne Isbell	SCC (Honorable Mention), County (2nd Team)
	Glenda Kleeman	SCC (2nd Team), County (2nd Team), WSMI (1st Team)
	Kim Leaser	SCC (Honorable Mention)
	Debra Sievers	SCC (Honorable Mention), County (1st Team)
1990-91	Glenda Kleeman	SCC (1st Team), County (1st Team), Telegraph (Athlete of the Year - Finalist), WSMI (1st Team)
	Becky Miller	SCC (Honorable Mention), County (Honorable Mention)
	Debra Sievers	SCC (Honorable Mention), County (Honorable Mention)
1991-92	Sherry Masinelli	SCC (Honorable Mention)
	Angie Sievers	SCC (Honorable Mention)
1992-93	Angie Sievers	SCC (2nd Team), County (2nd Team), WSMI (1st Team)
	Janna Streif	SCC (Honorable Mention)
1993-94	Sara Zuber	SCC (2nd Team)
1994-95	Stefanie Kershaw	SCC (Honorable Mention)
	Marcy Molinar	SCC (2nd Team), County (1st Team), WSMI (1st Team)
	Pam Wieseman	SCC (1st Team), County (1st Team), WSMI (1st Team)
	Sara Zuber	SCC (Honorable Mention)

1995-96	Amber Brinson	SCC (Honorable Mention)
	Marcy Molinar	WSMI (1st Team)
	Stefanie Kershaw	SCC (Honorable Mention)
	Pam Wieseman	SCC (2nd Team), WSMI (1st Team)
1996-97	Becky Baum	SCC (Honorable Mention)
	Jacki Fritz	SCC (Honorable Mention)
1997-98	Beth Moore	County (2nd Team)
	Christie Partridge	SCC East (Honorable Mention)
1998-99	Katie Bequette	SCC East (2nd Team)
	Elaine Imhoff	SCC East (Honorable Mention)
	Robyn Painter	SCC East (Honorable Mention), County (2nd Team)
	Christie Partridge	SCC East (1st Team), County (1st Team)
1999-00	Katie Bequette	SCC East (Honorable Mention)
	Christie Partridge	SCC East (2nd Team), County (1st Team)
2000-01	Heather Caldieraro	SCC East (2nd Team), County (1st Team)
	Natalie Laurent	SCC East (2nd Team)
2001-02	Heather Caldieraro	SCC East (1st Team), County (1st Team), Telegraph (2nd Team)
	Jennifer Wyatt	SCC East (2nd Team)
2002-03	Heather Caldieraro	SCC East (1st Team), WSMI (1st Team), SHS (1000 Points)
	Jennifer Wyatt	SCC East (Honorable Mention)
2003-04	Kim Phifer	SCC East (2nd Team)
	Ashleigh Ries	SCC East (2nd Team), County (1st Team), WSMI (1st Team)
2004-05	Mallory Nathan	SCC East (Honorable Mention)
	Kim Phifer	SCC East (1st Team), County (MVP), Telegraph (2nd Team), SJ-R (Special Mention), WSMI (1st Team)
	Ashleigh Ries	SCC East (Honorable Mention), County (1st Team)
2005-06	Julie Hainaut	SCC East (Honorable Mention)
	Kim Phifer	SCC East (1st Team), County (1st Team), WSMI (1st Team) SHS (1000 Points)
2006-07	NONE	NONE
2007-08	Lauren Newbold	SCC East (Honorable Mention), County (1st Team), SJ-R (Honorable Mention)
2008-09	Lauren Newbold	SCC East (1st Team), County (1st Team), Telegraph (1st Team), WSMI (1st Team), SHS (1093 Points)
	Devin Painter	SCC East (Honorable Mention), County (1st Team)
2009-10	Briana Rae	PSC (1st Team), SJ-R (Special Mention)
	Kaitlin Schrader	PSC (1st Team), SJ-R (Honorable Mention)

2010-11	Sophie Fairman	PSC (1st Team), SJ-R (Honorable Mention)
	Briana Rae	PSC (1st Team), County (MVP), Telegraph (1st Team), SJ-R (3rd Team)
	Sam Senaldi	PSC (1st Team), County (1st Team)
2011-12	Kerstin Brown	PSC (Honorable Mention)
	Sophie Fairman	PSC (1st Team), County (1st Team), Telegraph (1st Team), SJ-R (1st Team), News-Gazette All-State (Honorable Mention), IBCA All-State (Special Mention), IBS All-State (Honorable Mention)

Bowling (Boys)

Year	Name	Accomplishment
2002-03	Nick Jones	12th State

Cross Country (Boys)

Year	Name	Accomplishment
1977-78	Tom Spears	30th State
	TEAM	Sectional
1978-79	Bob Cargnoni	Sectional
1999-00	Michael Williams	SCC (1st Team), Sectional
2004-05	Brad Pirok	Regional Champion, Telegraph (Runner of the Year), SJ-R (1st Team), All-State, 7th State
2006-07	Lucas Loots	SCC (1st Team), Sectional
	John Mihelcic	SCC (Champion), Telegraph (1st Team), 65th State
2007-08	Lucas Loots	SCC (Champion), Regional Champion, Telegraph (Runner of the Year), All-State, 22nd State
2008-09	Lucas Loots	SCC (1st Team), Telegraph (1st Team), All-State, 13th State
2010-11	NONE	NONE

Cross Country (Girls)

Year	Name	Accomplishment
2005-06	Alex Senaldi	SCC (1st Team), Sectional
2006-07	Kadambari Jain	Sectional
	Alex Senaldi	SCC (Champion), Sectional
2007-08	Alex Senaldi	SCC (1st Team)
	Katie Trettenero	SCC (1st Team), Telegraph (1st Team), 79th State
	TEAM	Sectional
2008-09	Alex Senaldi	SCC (Champion), Telegraph (Runner of the Year), 82nd State
	Mia Stefani	SCC (1st Team), Sectional
	Katie Trettenero	SCC (1st Team), Sectional
	TEAM	Sectional
2009-10	TEAM	Sectional
2010-11	Katie Trettenero	Telegraph (1st Team), Sectional
2011-12	Rachael Hoehne	Sectional

Football

Year	Name	Accomplishment
1922-23	Fred Arnicar	Illinois State Register (2nd Team)
	Dave Wilson	Illinois State Register (1st Team)
1923-24	George Oehler	Illinois State Register (Honorable Mention)
	Gerald Roberts	Illinois State Register (2nd Team)
	Art Ruffini	Illinois State Register (1st Team)
	Cliff Stiegemeier	Illinois State Register (1st Team)
	Mel Stiegemeier	Illinois State Register (1st Team)
	Dave Wilson	Illinois State Register (Honorable Mention)
1927-28	Bernie Aschbacher	SCC (1st Team)
	Wellman France	SCC (2nd Team)
	Roy Miller	SCC (1st Team)
	John Oehler	SCC (1st Team)
	Don Overbeay	SCC (1st Team)
	Bob Ramseier	SCC (2nd Team)
1931-32	Elmer Graham	SCC (1st Team)
	Layton Lamb	SCC (1st Team)
1932-33	Layton Lamb	SCC (1st Team)
1933-34	Frank Yakos	SCC (1st Team)
1934-35	Vic Bono	SCC (1st Team)
1937-38	Bert Bono	SCC (2nd Team)
	? Felchner	SCC (1st Team)
	Dom Fortuna	SCC (2nd Team)
	Ken Herbeck	SCC (1st Team)
	Ray Pesavento	SCC (1st Team)
	John Spagnola	SCC (1st Team)
1944-45	Bob Spagnola	All-State (1st Team)
1950-51	Dick Goehe	SCC (1st Team)
	John Johnson	SCC (1st Team), All-State (2nd Team)
	Dale O'Neal	SCC (1st Team)
	Fred Stein	SCC (1st Team)
	Jake Vezzoli	SCC (1st Team), All-State (1st Team)
	Charlie Yakos	SCC (1st Team)
1956-57	Chuck Frey	SCC (1st Team)
	Bernard Gaudi	SCC (1st Team)
	Leroy Luketich	SCC (1st Team)

	Wayne Masinelli	SCC (1st Team)
	Jim Oettel	SCC (1st Team)
	Wayne Zude	SCC (1st Team)
1958-59	Don Brewer	SCC (Honorable Mention)
	Barry Deist	SCC (1st Team)
	Dick Kapp	SCC (Honorable Mention)
	Larry Kuba	SCC (1st Team)
	Joe Mancewicz	SCC (2nd Team)
	Fred Marquis	SCC (1st Team)
	Leroy Schulte	SCC (1st Team)
1959-60	Fred Brauer	SCC (Honorable Mention)
	Don Brewer	SCC (2nd Team)
	Barry Deist	SCC (1st Team)
	Dick Kapp	SCC (Honorable Mention)
	Larry Kuba	SCC (1st Team), All-State (1st Team), SHS (1414 Yards Rushing)
	Joe Mancewicz	SCC (1st Team), All-Southern (1st Team)
	Leroy Schulte	SCC (1st Team), All-Southern (1st Team)
1960-61	Len Bednar	SCC (1st Team)
	Fred Brauer	SCC (1st Team)
	Barry Deist	SCC (1st Team), SHS (1259 Yards Rushing)
	Rick France	SCC (1st Team)
	Bill Knop	SCC (1st Team)
	Dean Oehler	SCC (1st Team)
	Leroy Schulte	SCC (1st Team), All-America (1st Team)
	Mike Yakos	SCC (1st Team)
1961-62	Barry Deist	SCC (1st Team), All-State (1st Team)
1964-65	Jim Arico	SCC (1st Team), All-State (1st Team)
	Rod Barnhart	SCC (1st Team)
	Ron Dustman	SCC (1st Team)
	Jim Goldasich	SCC (Honorable Mention)
	Larry Kleeman	SCC (1st Team)
	Dennis Kuba	SCC (1st Team), All-State (1st Team)
	Roger Kuba	SCC (1st Team), All-State (1st Team)
	Brian Machota	SCC (Honorable Mention)
	Jim Malek	SCC (1st Team), All-State (1st Team)
	Gary Oehler	SCC (Honorable Mention)
	Al Schuette	SCC (Honorable Mention)
	Lou Scroggins	SCC (1st Team)
	Tony Silvester	SCC (1st Team), All-State (1st Team)
1965-66	Jim Arico	SCC (1st Team)
	Rod Barnhart	SCC (1st Team)
	Ron Dustman	SCC (1st Team)
	Glen Herbeck	SCC (1st Team)
	Larry Kleeman	SCC (1st Team)

Individual Accompishments

	Dave Link	SCC (1st Team)
	Brian Machota	SCC (1st Team)
	Al Schuette	SCC (1st Team)
1966-67	Bob Barnhart	SCC (1st Team)
	Tony Bechem	SCC (1st Team)
	Phil Callovini	SCC (Honorable Mention)
	Al Culp	SCC (1st Team)
	Gary Frioli	SCC (1st Team)
	Ed Hilmes	SCC (Honorable Mention)
	Lyndall Kleeman	SCC (1st Team)
	Dave Link	SCC (1st Team)
1967-68	Phil Callovini	SCC (1st Team)
	Larry Grabruck	SCC (1st Team)
	Gary Herbeck	SCC (Honorable Mention)
	Bryan Kinnikin	SCC (1st Team)
	Lyndall Kleeman	SCC (1st Team), All-State (1st Team)
	Tom Kolkovich	SCC (Honorable Mention)
	Mike Pintar	SCC (1st Team)
	George Przymuzala	SCC (1st Team)
1968-69	Al Conroy	SCC (1st Team)
	Dean DeVries	SCC (1st Team)
	Gene Frioli	SCC (1st Team)
	Larry Grabruck	SCC (1st Team)
	Tom Kolkovich	SCC (1st Team)
	Dave Russell	SCC (1st Team)
	Jim Wilson	SCC (1st Team)
1969-70	Tom Brown	SCC (1st Team)
	Al Conroy	SCC (1st Team)
	Gene Frioli	SCC (1st Team)
	John Hochmuth	SCC (1st Team), SHS (1000 Yards Rushing)
	Steve Jarman	SCC (1st Team)
	Dennis Kellebrew	SCC (1st Team)
	Mike Kozemczak	SCC (1st Team)
	Dave Russell	SCC (1st Team)
	Craig Schuette	SCC (1st Team)
	Jim Wilson	SCC (1st Team)
1970-71	John Caldieraro	SCC (Honorable Mention)
	Rich Caldieraro	SCC (1st Team)
	Mike Dal Pozzo	SCC (1st Team)
	Dennis Felchner	SCC (1st Team)
	Roger Guennewig	SCC (Honorable Mention)
	Mike Kozemczak	SCC (1st Team), All-State (Honorable Mention)
	Gerald Moss	SCC (Honorable Mention)
	Craig Schuette	SCC (1st Team), All-State (1st Team)
	Rick Tsupros	SCC (1st Team)

	Don Warren	SCC (1st Team)
	Ron Warren	SCC (Honorable Mention)
	Mike Watkins	SCC (Honorable Mention)
1971-72	Mike Dal Pozzo	SCC (Honorable Mention)
	Paul Hiette	SCC (Honorable Mention)
	Brian Rotsch	SCC (Honorable Mention)
	Rick Tsupros	SCC (1st Team), All-State (Honorable Mention)
	Bob Vesper	SCC (Honorable Mention)
	Don Warren	SCC (1st Team)
	Mike Watkins	SCC (Honorable Mention)
1972-73	Randy Best	SCC (Honorable Mention)
	Gene Felchner	SCC (1st Team)
	Norm Heigert	SCC (Honorable Mention)
	Paul Hiette	SCC (1st Team)
	C.J. Kellebrew	SCC (Honorable Mention)
	Curt Kellebrew	SCC (Honorable Mention)
	Joe Kravanya	SCC (Honorable Mention)
	Daryl Schuette	SCC (Honorable Mention)
	Fred Stein	SCC (1st Team)
	Terry Tevini	SCC (1st Team)
1973-74	Randy Best	SCC (Honorable Mention)
	Norm Heigert	SCC (1st Team)
	Bob Lietz	SCC (Honorable Mention)
	Daryl Schuette	SCC (Honorable Mention)
	Don Sullivan	SCC (Honorable Mention)
1974-75	Rich Bednar	SCC (2nd Team)
	John Clark	SCC (Honorable Mention)
	Jeff Hebenstreit	SCC (1st Team)
	Ken Kleeman	SCC (Honorable Mention)
	Bob Lietz	SCC (Honorable Mention)
1975-76	Lou Cipriano	SCC (2nd Team)
	John Clark	SCC (1st Team)
	Mike Cockrell	SCC (Honorable Mention)
	Al DeVries	SCC (1st Team)
	Ron Heflin	SCC (Honorable Mention)
	Tony Muenstermann	SCC (2nd Team)
	Phil Vesper	SCC (2nd Team)
1976-77	Gilbert Best	SCC (3rd Team)
	Mark Bono	SCC (2nd Team)
	Lou Cipriano	SCC (1st Team)
	Mike Cockrell	SCC (3rd Team)
	Randy Foster	SCC (2nd Team)
	Ron Heflin	SCC (1st Team)
	Jay Meckles	SCC (Honorable Mention)
	Steve Wood	SCC (1st Team)

Individual Accompishments

1977-78	Brian Black	SCC (1st Team)
	Randy Foster	SCC (2nd Team)
	Terry Garino	SCC (2nd Team)
	Mike Heinemeyer	SCC (1st Team)
	Jim Holak	SCC (1st Team)
	Jay Meckles	SCC (Honorable Mention)
	Jack Vesper	SCC (1st Team)
	Bart Yakos	SCC (1st Team)
1978-79	Bob Carter	SCC (2nd Team)
	Bob Fletcher	SCC (1st Team)
	Mark Hebenstreit	SCC (Honorable Mention)
	Jim Holak	SCC (1st Team)
	Rich Link	SCC (1st Team)
	Jay Meckles	SCC (1st Team)
	Mark Sherfy	SCC (1st Team)
	Jim Strohkirch	SCC (Honorable Mention)
	Al Tebbe	SCC (1st Team)
	Tim Yarnik	SCC (Honorable Mention)
1979-80	Tom Allen	SCC (1st Team)
	Todd Anderson	SCC (2nd Team)
	Bob Chiti	SCC (Honorable Mention)
	Rich Link	SCC (1st Team)
	Craig Neuhaus	SCC (Honorable Mention)
	Joe Stranimeier	SCC (Honorable Mention)
	Brad Yakos	SCC (1st Team)
	Tim Yarnik	SCC (1st Team)
1980-81	Lonnie Colley	SCC (1st Team), All-State (Honorable Mention)
	Rich Fletcher	SCC (1st Team)
	Ron Siebert	SCC (Honorable Mention)
1981-82	Charlie Black	SCC (1st Team)
	Bart Brauer	SCC (1st Team)
	Lonnie Colley	SCC (1st Team)
	Chris Costley	SCC (2nd Team)
	Rich Fletcher	SCC (1st Team), All-State (1st Team), SHS (1000 Yards Rushing)
	Barry Wriede	SCC (2nd Team)
	Phil Yarnik	SCC (3rd Team)
1982-83	Russ Best	SCC (Honorable Mention)
	Larry Caldieraro	SCC (2nd Team)
	Damion Dobrinich	SCC (2nd Team)
	Fritz Musick	SCC (Honorable Mention)
	John Rabida	SCC (2nd Team)
	Tom Scherff	SCC (2nd Team)
	Brian Scrianko	SCC (1st Team)
	Randy Williams	SCC (1st Team)

1983-84	Roger Banovz	SCC (Honorable Mention)
	Mike Bekeske	SCC (Honorable Mention)
	Tony Bianco	SCC (1st Team)
	Larry Caldieraro	SCC (2nd Team)
	Don DeVries	SCC (Honorable Mention)
	Phil Evans	SCC (Honorable Mention)
	Randy Harbison	SCC (Honorable Mention)
	John Karl	SCC (2nd Team)
	Tom Scherff	SCC (1st Team)
	Deron Stein	SCC (Honorable Mention)
1984-85	Tim Bruhn	SCC (1st Team)
	Rich Deal	SCC (2nd Team)
	Don DeVries	SCC (2nd Team)
	Rich Garde	SCC (2nd Team)
	Kevin Goebel	SCC (2nd Team)
	Tim Gusewelle	SCC (2nd Team)
	John Isaacks	SCC (2nd Team)
	Dave Jones	SCC (2nd Team)
	Ray Rantanen	SCC (Honorable Mention)
	Joe Seketa	SCC (Honorable Mention)
	Deron Stein	SCC (1st Team)
	Adrian Vesper	SCC (2nd Team)
1985-86	Bart Caldieraro	SCC (1st Team)
	Greg Deist	SCC (1st Team)
	Kevin Gockel	SCC (Honorable Mention)
	Tim Gusewelle	SCC (1st Team)
	Jim Kinder	SCC (1st Team)
	Roman Meckles	SCC (2nd Team)
	Rick Miller	SCC (Honorable Mention)
	Ryan Ocepek	SCC (Honorable Mention)
	Ron Phillips	SCC (2nd Team)
	Joe Randle	SCC (1st Team)
	Jeff Ries	SCC (Honorable Mention)
1986-87	Bart Caldieraro	SCC (1st Team)
	Phil Callovini	SCC (Honorable Mention)
	Kevin Gockel	SCC (1st Team)
	Mike LaRosa	SCC (1st Team)
	John Rae	SCC (1st Team)
	George Wisnasky	SCC (2nd Team)
1987-88	John Rae	SCC (1st Team)
	Jeff Windau	SCC (Honorable Mention)
	Kelly Yeager	SCC (2nd Team)
1988-89	Brian Barks	SCC (1st Team), Telegraph (1st Team)
	Ray Cline	SCC (1st Team)

Individual Accompishments

	Phil Deist	SCC (1st Team), Telegraph (3rd Team)
	Ed Fletcher	SCC (2nd Team)
	Dave Gerdes	SCC (2nd Team)
	Simon Hannig	SCC (2nd Team), Telegraph (3rd Team)
	Fred Harbison	SCC (2nd Team)
	Brad Hemann	SCC (2nd Team)
1989-90	Phil Deist	SCC (1st Team), Telegraph (2nd Team)
	Ed Fletcher	SCC (1st Team), Telegraph (1st Team)
	Dave Gerdes	SCC (2nd Team)
	Brad Hemann	SCC (Honorable Mention)
	Bronson Painter	SCC (Honorable Mention)
1990-91	Dave Legendre	SCC (2nd Team)
	Craig Nolan	SCC (2nd Team)
	Matt Ray	SCC (Honorable Mention)
1991-92	Jeff Dal Pozzo	SCC (Honorable Mention)
	Ryan Kilduff	SCC (2nd Team)
	Bill Mosser	SCC (2nd Team)
	Tim Ott	SCC (2nd Team)
1992-93	Terry Albrecht	SCC (1st Team), Telegraph (2nd Team)
	Ryan Gusewelle	SCC (1st Team), Telegraph (3rd Team)
	Andy Kuba	SCC (2nd Team), Telegraph (Athlete of the Year - Finalist)
	Kevin Meyer	SCC (2nd Team)
	George Moore	SCC (Special Mention)
	Corey Painter	SCC (2nd Team)
	Matt Popovich	SCC (2nd Team)
	John Sharp	SCC (2nd Team)
	Brad Skertich	SCC (2nd Team)
1993-94	Dennis Bohlen	SCC (1st Team), Telegraph (2nd Team), SHS (1072 Yards Rushing)
	Derek Brauer	SCC (Honorable Mention)
	Mark Bruhn	SCC (2nd Team)
	Scott Colley	SCC (1st Team), Telegraph (2nd Team)
	Brian Herbeck	SCC (2nd Team)
	Brad LaRosa	SCC (Honorable Mention)
	Corey Painter	SCC (Honorable Mention)
	Jon Rondi	SCC (Honorable Mention)
	John Sharp	SCC (Honorable Mention)
1994-95	Derek Brauer	SCC (1st Team), Telegraph (2nd Team)
	Vic Buehler	SCC (1st Team), Telegraph (3rd Team)
	Lucas Calcari	SCC (1st Team), Telegraph (3rd Team)
	Tony Dal Pozzo	SCC (3rd Team)
	Jeff Hebenstreit	SCC (1st Team), Telegraph (3rd Team)
	Dean Heidke	SCC (Honorable Mention)
	Mike Kovaly	SCC (1st Team), Telegraph (2nd Team)
	Jim Sharp	SCC (3rd Team)

THE HISTORY OF STAUNTON HIGH SCHOOL SPORTS

		Matt Sievers	SCC (2nd Team)
1995-96		Charlie Best	SCC (Honorable Mention)
		Cory Callovini	SCC (1st Team), Telegraph (2nd Team), SJ-R (2nd Team)
		Jason Hebenstreit	SCC (Honorable Mention)
		Brad Legendre	SCC (Honorable Mention)
		Ryan Machota	SCC (Honorable Mention)
		Jeremy Molinar	SCC (2nd Team)
		Joe Odorizzi	SCC (2nd Team)
		Josh Rantanen	SCC (2nd Team)
		Greg Sievers	SCC (Honorable Mention)
		Harley Williams	SCC (Honorable Mention)
		Greg Wittman	SCC (2nd Team)
1996-97		Dustin Bramley	SCC (2nd Team)
		Matt Bruhn	SCC (2nd Team)
		Ben Frank	SCC (1st Team), Telegraph (1st Team), SJ-R (1st Team)
		Keith Gregory	SCC (1st Team), Telegraph (2nd Team)
		Brett Herbeck	SCC (2nd Team)
		Jarrod Leckrone	SCC (Honorable Mention)
		Josh Marquis	SCC (Honorable Mention)
		Alex Rigoni	SCC (1st Team)
		Billy Schuette	SCC (Honorable Mention)
		Jason Steinmeyer	SCC (1st Team)
		Greg Wittman	SCC (2nd Team)
1997-98		Dustin Bramley	SCC East (1st Team)
		Ben Frank	SCC East (1st Team), Telegraph (1st Team), Telegraph (Athlete of the Year - Finalist)
		Ted Frank	SCC East (1st Team)
		Brett Herbeck	SCC East (1st Team)
		Luke Melm	SCC East (1st Team)
		Alex Rigoni	SCC East (1st Team), Telegraph (1st Team)
		Billy Schuette	SCC East (1st Team), Telegraph (2nd Team), SHS (1371 Yards Rushing)
		Luke Schuette	SCC East (1st Team)
		Nathan Sievers	SCC East (Honorable Mention)
		Jason Steinmeyer	SCC East (1st Team), Telegraph (1st Team), IHSFCA All-State (1st Team)
1998-99		Ted Frank	SCC East (1st Team)
		Brett Herbeck	SCC East (1st Team), IHSFCA All-State (Honorable Mention)
		Brett Luster	SCC East (1st Team)
		Vinnie Sanvi	SCC East (1st Team)
		Billy Schuette	SCC East (1st Team), SHS (1247 Yards Rushing)
1999-00		Danny Feldmann	SCC East (1st Team), Telegraph (2nd Team)
		Brandon Fletcher	SCC East (Honorable Mention)
		Aaraon Hainaut	SCC East (Honorable Mention)
		Cory McCunney	SCC East (1st Team)
		Mike Popovich	SCC East (Honorable Mention)

262

Individual Accompishments

	Lance Semanek	SCC East (1st Team), Telegraph (2nd Team), IHSFCA All-State (Honorable Mention)
	Mark Sievers	SCC East (1st Team)
	Tyler Washburn	SCC East (1st Team)
2000-01	R.C. Belair	SCC East (Honorable Mention)
	Danny Feldmann	SCC East (1st Team)
	Brandon Fletcher	SCC East (1st Team), Telegraph (Honorable Mention)
	Cory McCunney	SCC East (1st Team)
	Donny Nicholas	SCC East (1st Team), Telegraph (1st Team)
	Zack Rigoni	SCC East (1st Team), Telegraph (1st Team), SJ-R (1st Team), Post-Dispatch (2nd Team), IHSFCA All-State (1st Team), SHS (1445 Yards Rushing)
	Lance Semanek	SCC East (1st Team), Telegraph (1st Team)
	Mark Sievers	SCC East (1st Team)
2001-02	Nick Baker	SCC East (1st Team)
	Richie Fletcher	SCC East (1st Team)
	John Molinar	SCC East (1st Team)
2002-03	Luke Pirok	SCC East (1st Team)
	Thomas Scroggins	SCC East (Honorable Mention)
2003-04	Luke Pirok	SCC East (1st Team)
	Josh Ohlinger	SCC East (1st Team), SHS (1189 Yards Rushing)
2004-05	Randy Large	SCC East (1st Team)
	Josh Ohlinger	SCC East (1st Team)
2005-06	David Hamilton	SCC East (1st Team)
	Kyle Pirok	SCC East (1st Team)
	Shaun Thomas	SCC East (Honorable Mention)
2006-07	Zach Bertels	SCC East (1st Team), Telegraph (1st Team), SJ-R (2nd Team)
	Josh Bruhn	SCC East (1st Team)
	Josh Revisky	SCC East (1st Team)
	Josh Teeske	SCC East (1st Team)
2007-08	Cody Best	SCC East (1st Team), Telegraph (1st Team)
	Todd Collins	SCC East (1st Team), Telegraph (1st Team)
	Justin Ladendorf	SCC East (Honorable Mention)
	John McMahon	SCC East (1st Team)
	Tyler Muenstermann	SCC East (1st Team), Telegraph (1st Team)
	Josh Teeske	SCC East (1st Team), Telegraph (1st Team), SHS (1380 Yards Passing)
	Zach Wisnasky	SCC East (Honorable Mention)
	Brad Wright	SCC East (1st Team), Telegraph (1st Team), SJ-R (1st Team), Post-Dispatch (Honorable Mention), News-Gazette All-State (1st Team), IHSFCA All-State (1st Team), Maxpreps All-State (1st Team)
2008-09	Kevin Ahrens	SCC East (1st Team), Telegraph (1st Team), SJ-R (2nd Team)
	Cody Best	SCC East (1st Team), Telegraph (1st Team)

	Adam Boston	SCC East (Honorable Mention)
	Mike Ebersohl	SCC East (1st Team)
	Gary Fuller	SCC East (1st Team)
	Dakota Kreger	SCC East (1st Team)
	Josh Teeske	SCC East (1st Team), Telegraph (1st Team), SHS (1105 Yards Passing)
2009-10	Kevin Billings	PSC (1st Team)
	Adam Boston	PSC (1st Team)
	Kyle Brauer	PSC (2nd Team)
	Dylan Caldieraro	PSC (2nd Team)
	Charlie Clark	PSC (2nd Team)
	Mike Ebersohl	PSC (1st Team), Telegraph (1st Team), SJ-R (1st Team)
	Kevin Fuller	PSC (1st Team), Telegraph (1st Team)
	Dusty Graves	PSC (Honorable Mention)
	Brady Moore	PSC (1st Team)
	Scott Prost	PSC (1st Team), Telegraph (1st Team)
	Blake Steele	PSC (1st Team), Telegraph (1st Team), SHS (1081 Yards Rushing)
	Nathan Ward	PSC (Honorable Mention)
	Zack Ward	PSC (2nd Team)
2010-11	Kole Billings	Telegraph (1st Team)
	Adam Boston	PSC (1st Team), Telegraph (1st Team), SJ-R (1st Team), IHSFCA All-State (1st Team), SHS (1186 Yards Rushing)
	Kyle Brauer	PSC (Honorable Mention)
	Dylan Caldieraro	PSC (1st Team), Telegraph (1st Team)
	Nick Dobrinich	PSC (2nd Team)
	Dusty Graves	PSC (1st Team)
	Brady Moore	PSC (1st Team), Telegraph (1st Team), SJ-R (2nd Team)
	Bryan Rucker	PSC (2nd Team)
	Kory Sczurek	PSC (2nd Team)
	Brad Seketa	PSC (2nd Team)
	Austin Sherfy	PSC (2nd Team)
	Andrew Slifka	PSC (Honorable Mention)
	David Vaughn	PSC (2nd Team)
	Zack Ward	PSC (2nd Team)
2011-12	Josh Barnes	PSC (Honorable Mention)
	Kole Billings	PSC (1st Team)
	Jake Bruhn	PSC (2nd Team), SHS (1815 Yards Passing)
	Larry Caldieraro	PSC (2nd Team)
	Austin Hollaway	PSC (1st Team), Telegraph (1st Team)
	Chaz Johnson	PSC (2nd Team)
	Jake Mahin	PSC (2nd Team)
	Kory Sczurek	PSC (1st Team), Telegraph (1st Team)
	Austin Sherfy	PSC (1st Team), Telegraph (1st Team), SJ-R (2nd Team)
	David Vaughn	PSC (Honorable Mention)
	Zack Ward	PSC (1st Team), Telegraph (1st Team), SJ-R (1st Team), IHSFCA All-State (Honorable Mention)

Golf (Boys)

Year	Name	Accomplishment
1976-77	TEAM	Sectional
1977-78	TEAM	Sectional
1978-79	Mark Marcuzzo	District (Medalist), Sectional (Medalist), 2nd State
	TEAM	Sectional
1979-80	Mark Marcuzzo	District (Medalist), 10th State
	TEAM	State
1980-81	John Bond	District (Medalist)
	TEAM	Sectional
1981-82	NONE	NONE
1982-83	Kevin Schulmeister	Sectional
1983-84	NONE	NONE
1984-85	NONE	NONE
1985-86	NONE	NONE
1986-87	NONE	NONE
1987-88	Brett Ahring	SCC (1st Team)
1988-89	Jim Williamson	SCC (Medalist), State
1989-90	Andy Kuba	SCC (1st Team)
	Jason Przymuzala	SCC (1st Team), State
	Nathan Spudich	SCC (1st Team)
1990-91	Nathan Calcari	SCC (1st Team)
	Jeremy May	SCC (Medalist)
	Jason Przymuzala	SCC (1st Team)
	Chris Schaeffer	SCC (1st Team)
	Nathan Spudich	SCC (1st Team)
	TEAM	State
1991-92	Nathan Calcari	SCC (1st Team), Telegraph (2nd Team), MEGCA (3rd Team)
	Brian Hughes	SCC (1st Team)
	Jeremy May	SCC (1st Team), Telegraph (Player of the Year), MEGCA (1st Team), Regional (Medalist)
	Jason Przymuzala	SCC (1st Team), Telegraph (1st Team), MEGCA (2nd Team)

	Chris Schaeffer	SCC (1st Team)
	Nathan Spudich	SCC (1st Team)
	TEAM	State
1992-93	Brian Hughes	SCC (Medalist)
	Andy Kuba	SCC (1st Team), Telegraph (Athlete of the Year - Finalist)
	Jeremy May	SCC (1st Team), State
1993-94	B.J. Brown	SCC (1st Team), Telegraph (2nd Team), MEGCA (2nd Team)
	Ron Hampton	SCC (1st Team)
	Brian Hughes	SCC (1st Team)
	Jeremy May	SCC (Medalist), Telegraph (1st Team), Telegraph (Athlete of the Year - Winner), MEGCA (1st Team)
	Kevin Mitchell	SCC (1st Team)
	TEAM	State
1994-95	B.J. Brown	SCC (Medalist), Telegraph (1st Team), News-Democrat (1st Team), MEGCA (1st Team), 6th State
	Elliot Kolkovich	SCC (1st Team)
	Brad Rizzi	SCC (1st Team)
	Brett Tevini	SCC (1st Team)
	Donnie Vazzi	SCC (1st Team)
1995-96	B.J. Brown	SCC (Medalist), Telegraph (Player of the Year), News Democrat (1st Team)
	Elliot Kolkovich	SCC (1st Team), Telegraph (Honorable Mention), News-Democrat (3rd Team)
	Brad Rizzi	News-Democrat (3rd Team)
	Brett Tevini	SCC (1st Team), Telegraph (Honorable Mention), News-Democrat (3rd Team)
	TEAM	Sectional
1996-97	B.J. Brown	SCC (Medalist), Telegraph (Player of the Year), News-Democrat (1st Team), MEGCA (1st Team), 2nd State
	John Caldieraro	SCC (1st Team), Telegraph (2nd Team), News-Democrat (2nd Team), MEGCA (3rd Team)
	Denny Conroy	SCC (1st Team), News-Democrat (Honorable Mention)
	Elliot Kolkovich	SCC (1st Team), Telegraph (1st Team), News-Democrat (2nd Team), MEGCA (2nd Team)
	Brad Rizzi	SCC (1st Team), News-Democrat (Honorable Mention)
	Brett Tevini	SCC (1st Team), Telegraph (2nd Team), News-Democrat (3rd Team), MEGCA (Honorable Mention)
	TEAM	State
1997-98	John Caldieraro	SCC (1st Team), Telegraph (1st Team), MEGCA (2nd Team)
	Elliot Kolkovich	SCC (1st Team), Telegraph (2nd Team), MEGCA (2nd Team)
	Brett Tevini	Telegraph (Honorable Mention), MEGCA (Honorable Mention)
	Brandon Young	SCC (1st Team), Telegraph (Honorable Mention), MEGCA (3rd Team)
	TEAM	Sectional
1998-99	Ryan Brown	SCC (1st Team)
	Andrew Caldieraro	MEGCA (2nd Team)
	John Caldieraro	SCC (Medalist), MEGCA (1st Team)

Individual Accompishments

	Mark Pirok	SCC (1st Team)
	Mike Rizzi	MEGCA (3rd Team)
1999-00	Ryan Brown	SCC (1st Team), MEGCA (2nd Team)
	Andrew Caldieraro	MEGCA (3rd Team)
	John Caldieraro	SCC (1st Team), MEGCA (1st Team)
	TEAM	Sectional
2000-01	Ryan Brown	SCC (1st Team)
2001-02	Ryan Brown	SCC (1st Team), Telegraph (1st Team), State Champion
2002-03	Drew Stiegemeier	Sectional
2003-04	Lucas Hemp	Sectional
2004-05	Chris Redfern	Sectional
2005-06	Chris Redfern	Sectional
	Tyler Zirges	SCC (1st Team), Sectional
2006-07	Mike Mihelcic	SCC (1st Team), Telegraph (1st Team)
	Chris Redfern	SCC (1st Team)
	TEAM	Sectional
2007-08	Mike Mihelcic	SCC (1st Team), Telegraph (1st Team), Sectional
	Phil Rhodes	SCC (1st Team)
2008-09	Mike Mihelcic	SCC (1st Team), Sectional
2009-10	NONE	NONE
2010-11	Ryan Fretz	Sectional
2011-12	NONE	NONE

Golf (Girls)

Year	Name	Accomplishment
1981-82	Patti Ruffini	Sectional
1996-97	Amanda Conroy	Telegraph (1st Team), News-Democrat (2nd Team), MEGCA (2nd Team), Sectional
2000-01	Ashley Goodman	SCC (1st Team), Sectional
2001-02	Ashley Goodman	SCC (1st Team)
2003-04	Heidi Caldieraro	SCC (1st Team)
2004-05	Heidi Caldieraro	SCC (1st Team), Sectional
	Christina Geisler	Sectional
2005-06	Heidi Caldieraro	SCC (1st Team), 46th State
	Christina Geisler	SCC (1st Team)
2006-07	Elyse Banovic	SCC (1st Team), Sectional
	Stormy Dufrain	Sectional
	Christina Geisler	SCC (1st Team), 28th State
2007-08	Elyse Banovic	SCC (1st Team), Telegraph (1st Team), 18th State
	TEAM	Sectional
2008-09	Elyse Banovic	SCC (1st Team), Telegraph (1st Team), 28th State
	Carmi Cioni	SCC (1st Team)
	Stormy Dufrain	SCC (1st Team), Telegraph (1st Team)
	TEAM	Sectional
2009-10	Elyse Banovic	Telegraph (1st Team), Regional (Medalist), 19th State
	TEAM	Sectional
2010-11	Cecily Haase	Sectional
	Courtney Redfern	Sectional
2011-12	Courtney Redfern	Telegraph (1st Team)
	TEAM	Sectional

Soccer (Boys)

Year	Name	Accomplishment
1999-00	Dave Hirschl	SCC (Honorable Mention)
	Joe Klein	SCC (1st Team)
	G.T. Prante	SCC (2nd Team)
2000-01	Brandon Kuba	SCC (2nd Team), Telegraph (Honorable Mention)
	Jonas Manka	SCC (2nd Team)
	Craig Phifer	SCC (Honorable Mention)
2001-02	Zac Bianco	SCC (Honorable Mention)
	Cody Gerdes	SCC (Honorable Mention)
	Mike Mansholt	SCC (Honorable Mention)
	Justin Wilhelm	SCC (Honorable Mention)
2002-03	Nino Cavataio	SCC (Honorable Mention)
	Derek Fey	SCC (2nd Team)
	Doug Watters	SCC (2nd Team)
2003-04	Cody Gerdes	SCC (1st Team)
	Matt Hainaut	SCC (2nd Team)
	Mike Moseley	SCC (1st Team)
	Brad Pirok	SCC (Honorable Mention)
2004-05	Tyler Bianco	SCC (Honorable Mention), Telegraph (Honorable Mention)
	Shawn Brodie	Telegraph (Honorable Mention)
	Cody Gerdes	SCC (1st Team), Telegraph (Honorable Mention)
	Mike Moseley	SCC (1st Team)
	Dan Podwojski	SCC (Honorable Mention)
2005-06	Tyler Bianco	SCC (1st Team)
	Dan Mathenia	SCC (Honorable Mention)
	David Podwojski	SCC (2nd Team)
2006-07	Adam Brackman	SCC (Honorable Mention)
	David Podwojski	SCC (2nd Team)
2007-08	Randall Hoehn	SCC (2nd Team)
	Andrew Milkovich	SCC (2nd Team)
2008-09	Anthony Fairman	SCC (2nd Team)
	Eric Yarnik	SCC (2nd Team)
2009-10	Devin Gerdes	Telegraph (1st Team)
2010-11	NONE	NONE
2011-12	NONE	NONE

Soccer (Girls)

Year	Name	Accomplishment
1996-97	Leslie Bono	Telegraph (1st Team)
1997-98	Leslie Bono	SCC (1st Team)
	Kristi Brown	SCC (Honorable Mention)
	Meaghan Calcari	SCC (2nd Team)
	Mickey Schutzenhofer	SCC (1st Team)
	Crista Straub	SCC (2nd Team)
	Rachel Streeb	SCC (2nd Team)
1998-99	Mickey Schutzenhofer	Telegraph (1st Team)
1999-00	Melissa Newbold	SCC (2nd Team)
	Danielle Stein	SCC (Honorable Mention)
	Bethany Stoverink	SCC (Honorable Mention)
	Stephanie Stoverink	SCC (2nd Team)
2001-02	Melissa Newbold	SCC (2nd Team)
	Danielle Stein	SCC (1st Team)
	Jessica Wieseman	SCC (Honorable Mention)
2002-03	Sarah Brodie	SCC (Honorable Mention)
	Julie Hainaut	SCC (Honorable Mention)
	Bethany Stoverink	SCC (Honorable Mention)
	Jessica Wieseman	SCC (Honorable Mention)
	Jennifer Wyatt	SCC (1st Team)
2003-04	Julie Hainaut	SCC (Honorable Mention)
	Melissa Vitiello	SCC (1st Team)
	Jessica Wieseman	SCC (Honorable Mention)
2004-05	Jackie DeVries	SCC (2nd Team)
	Julie Hainaut	SCC (Honorable Mention)
2006-07	Ali Neuhaus	SCC (1st Team)
	Sophia Roedel	SCC (2nd Team)
2007-08	Stephanie Darrah	SCC (2nd Team)
2008-09	Tara Allen	SCC (1st Team)
	Devin Bennett	SCC (Honorable Mention)
	Courtney Darrah	SCC (2nd Team)
	Lindsey Mathenia	SCC (Honorable Mention)
	Devin Painter	SCC (2nd Team)
2009-10	NONE	NONE

Individual Accompishments

2010-11   Sam Senaldi   IHSSCA All-Sectional (Honorable Mention)

2011-12   Lindsay Allen   Telegraph (1st Team), IHSSCA All-Sectional (Honorable Mention)

Softball

Year	Name	Accomplishment
1993-94	Emily Henry	SCC (Honorable Mention)
	Heather Kirkwood	SCC (Honorable Mention)
1994-95	Susan Fletcher	SCC (Honorable Mention)
	Maria Garbin	SCC (Honorable Mention)
	Emily Henry	SCC (Honorable Mention)
	Heather Kirkwood	SCC (Honorable Mention)
	Becky Roddick	SCC (Honorable Mention)
1997-98	Janey Best	SCC East (1st Team)
	Laura Bruhn	SCC East (1st Team)
	Stacey Fletcher	SCC East (1st Team)
	Susan Fletcher	SCC East (Honorable Mention)
	Natalie Laurent	SCC East (1st Team)
	Becky Roddick	SCC East (1st Team)
1998-99	Stacey Fletcher	SCC East (1st Team)
	Beth Moore	SCC East (1st Team)
1999-00	Natalie Laurent	SCC East (1st Team)
	Beth Wieseman	SCC East (1st Team)
2001-02	Kati Krivi	SCC East (1st Team)
	Ashleigh Ries	SCC East (1st Team)
2002-03	Kati Krivi	SCC East (Honorable Mention)
2003-04	Brittani Kreger	SCC East (1st Team)
	Dana Rigor	SCC East (1st Team)
2004-05	Charlie Barlow	SCC East (Honorable Mention)
	Brittani Kreger	SCC East (1st Team)
2005-06	Brittani Kreger	SCC East (1st Team)
	Lauren Newbold	SCC East (Honorable Mention)
	Dana Rigor	SCC East (1st Team)
2006-07	Brittani Kreger	SCC East (Honorable Mention)
2007-08	Rachel Hadjan	SCC East (1st Team), SJ-R (Special Mention)
	Lauren Newbold	SCC East (1st Team), SJ-R (Special Mention)
2008-09	Kayla Brown	SCC East (2nd Team), SJ-R (Special Mention)
	Rachel Hadjan	SCC East (2nd Team), SJ-R (Special Mention)
	Anna Kroeger	SCC East (1st Team), SJ-R (Special Mention)

Individual Accompishments

	Lauren Newbold	SCC East (1st Team), SJ-R (Special Mention)
2009-10	Kerstin Brown	PSC (1st Team)
	Rachel Hadjan	PSC (1st Team), SJ-R (Honorable Mention)
	Kim Machuga	PSC (Honorable Mention)
	Marissa Zirges	PSC (Honorable Mention)
2010-11	Kerstin Brown	PSC (2nd Team)
	Sarah Caldieraro	PSC (Honorable Mention)
	Melissa Heigert	PSC (1st Team), SJ-R (Honorable Mention)
	Dianna Highlander	PSC (2nd Team)
	Kim Machuga	PSC (1st Team), Telegraph (1st Team), SJ-R (Honorable Mention)
2011-12	Monica McMahon	PSC (1st Team)
	Kayla Rettig	PSC (1st Team)
	Katie Yakos	PSC (Honorable Mention)
	Marissa Zirges	PSC (Honorable Mention)

Tennis (Boys)

Year	Name	Accomplishment
1929-30	Al Haase	3rd State (doubles)
	Fred Schultz	3rd State (doubles)
1933-34	Art Ahrens	State (doubles)
	Roland Lippold	State (doubles)

Track (Boys)

Year	Name	Accomplishment
1907-08	Leslie George	County Champion (standing long jump)
1908-09	?	County Champion (100m)
	?	County Champion (200m)
	?	County Champion (discus)
	?	County Champion (shot put)
1909-10	Leslie George	County Champion (50m)
	Bob Woods	County Champion (triple jump)
1910-11	Art Goff	County Champion (standing long jump)
1911-12	NONE	NONE
1912-13	John Auer	County Champion (800m relay)
	Frank Godfrey	County Champion (shot put)
	? Handshy	County Champion (400m)
	Harry Hopper	County Champion (800m relay)
	Tie Kinnikin	County Champion (800m, 800m relay)
	John Luker	County Champion (1600m)
	? Nessel	County Champion (800m relay)
1913-14	Murrell Funderburke	County Champion (1600m)
1914-15	NONE	NONE
1915-16	Murrell Funderburke	County Champion (400m, 800m)
1916-17	NONE	NONE
1918-19	Byron Bozarth	County Champion (1600m)
1919-20	Byron Bozarth	State
	Jess Hastings	State
	Max Jones	State
1920-21	Max Jones	County Champion (1600m), 3rd State (1600m)
	Ervin McLauchlin	County Champion (javelin), 2nd State (javelin)
	Armond Sherman	County Champion (standing long jump)
1921-22	Max Jones	County Champion (800m)
	Roland Sawyer	County Champion (50m)
1922-23	Glen Hastings	County Champion (400m)
	George Oehler	County Champion (discus)

	Roland Sawyer	County Champion (standing long jump)
1923-24	Glen Hastings	County Champion (long jump, 800m)
	Roland Sawyer	County Champion (standing long jump)
1924-25	Fred Arnicar	County Champion (shot put, discus), 2nd State (shot put)
	Jim Peele	4th State (hurdles)
	Dave Wilson	County Champion (400m), 3rd State (400m)
1926-27	Wellman France	County Champion (high jump), District Champion (high jump, 800m relay), 6th State (high jump), State (800m relay)
	George McLauchlan	State (pole vault)
	Howard Meyer	District Champion (800m relay), State (800m relay)
	Don Overbeay	State (discus)
	Bob Ramseier	District Champion (800m relay), State (800m relay)
	Irwin Spotti	District Champion (800m relay), State (hurdles, 800m relay)
1927-28	Wellman France	SCC Champion (long jump, hurdles), County Champion (high jump, long jump, hurdles), 3rd State (high jump)
	Howard Meyer	SCC Champion (50m, 100m, 200m, 800m relay), County Champion (100m, 200m, 800m relay), District Champion (100m, 200m), 3rd State (100m), State (200m)
	Bob Ramseier	SCC Champion (800m relay), County Champion (800m relay)
	Irwin Spotti	SCC Champion (400m, 800m relay), County Champion (800m relay)
	Harold Walters	SCC Champion (800m relay), County Champion (800m relay)
1928-29	John Masser	SCC Champion (pole vault)
	Howard Meyer	SCC Champion (100m, 200m, 800m relay), County Champion (long jump, 50m, 100m, 200m, 800m relay), 2nd State (100m), 4th State (200m), 5th State (800m relay)
	Bob Ramseier	SCC Champion (400m, 800m relay), County Champion (400m, 800m relay), 5th State (400m), 5th State (800m relay)
	Irwin Spotti	SCC Champion (800m relay), County Champion (800m relay), 5th State (800m relay)
	Harold Walters	SCC Champion (800m relay), County Champion (800m relay), 5th State (800m relay)
1929-30	John Masser	SCC Champion (pole vault), State (pole vault)
1930-31	Elmer Graham	County Champion (hurdles)
	John Masser	SCC Champion (pole vault), County Champion (pole vault), State (pole vault)
	Ted Melton	County Champion (long jump, 400m)
	Bill Pervinsek	County Champion (shot put)
1931-32	Ted Melton	SCC Champion (long jump), County Champion (long jump)
	Bill Pervinsek	SCC Champion (discus, shot put), County Champion (discus, shot put)
1932-33	Ted Charley	County Champion (pole vault)
	Will Leonard	SCC Champion (400m)
	?	County Champion (800m relay)

	?	County Champion (800m relay)
	?	County Champion (800m relay)
	?	County Champion (800m relay)
1933-34	Pete Bono	SCC Champion (800m relay), County Champion (800m relay)
	Vic Bono	SCC Champion (800m relay), County Champion (50m, 100m, 800m relay)
	Will Leonard	SCC Champion (400m, 800m relay), County Champion (400m, 800m relay), State (400m)
	Norm Stolze	County Champion (pole vault)
	? Westerman	SCC Champion (800m relay), County Champion (800m relay)
1934-35	Vic Bono	SCC Champion (pole vault), County Champion (pole vault, 200m), District Champion (pole vault), State (pole vault)
	Ernest Grimm	County Champion (1600m), State (1600m)
	Norm Meyer	County Champion (100m)
	Jim Tietze	County Champion (400m)
	Frank Yakos	SCC Champion (800m)
1935-36	Vic Bono	SCC Champion (pole vault, 800m relay), County Champion (pole vault, long jump, 50m), State (pole vault)
	? Farris	SCC Champion (800m relay)
	Norm Meyer	SCC Champion (800m relay), County Champion (200m)
	Rich Stolze	SCC Champion (800m relay)
1937-38	Dom Fortuna	SCC Champion (200m, 400m), District Champion (400m), State (400m)
1955-56	Dick Coyne	SCC Champion (pole vault)
	Wayne Helm	SCC Champion (800m)
1957-58	Dick Coyne	SCC Champion (pole vault)
1958-59	Norm Wenner	SCC Champion (discus), County Champion (discus)
1959-60	Norm Wenner	SCC Champion (discus), State (discus)
1960-61	Barry Deist	State (200 meters)
1961-62	Barry Deist	SCC Champion (800m relay)
	Melvin Duda	SCC Champion (800m relay)
	Bill Knop	SCC Champion (800m relay)
	John Monroe	SCC Champion (hurdles, 800m relay)
1968-69	Terry Best	SCC Champion (high jump)
	Al Conroy	SCC Champion (1600m relay)
	Larry Grabruck	SCC Champion (discus), County Champion (shot put)
	John Hochmuth	SCC Champion (200m, 400m, 1600m relay), County Champion (200m, 400m, 1600m relay)
	Gene Roehl	SCC Champion (800m, 1600m relay), County Champion (800m, 1600m relay)
	Dave Russell	SCC Champion (1600m relay), County Champion (1600m relay)
	Kevin Sullivan	County Champion (1600m relay)

	Nick Wineburner	SCC Champion (long jump), County Champion (long jump)
1969-70	John Hochmuth	County Champion (200m, 400m)
1970-71	Gene Roehl	SCC Champion (800m)
	Jim Sitko	SCC Champion (1600m)
	Nick Wineburner	SCC Champion (100m)
	?	SCC Champion (800m relay, 1600m relay)
	?	SCC Champion (800m relay, 1600m relay)
	?	SCC Champion (800m relay, 1600m relay)
	?	SCC Champion (800m relay, 1600m relay)
1971-72	Dennis Crouch	County Champion (800m relay)
	Mike Dal Pozzo	SCC Champion (100m), County Champion (100m, 800m relay)
	John Skertich	County Champion (800m relay)
	Mike Watkins	County Champion (800m relay)
1972-73	Del Stiegemeier	SCC Champion (high jump)
1973-74	John Clark	SCC Champion (shot put)
	Daryl Schuette	SCC Champion (high jump)
	Don Sullivan	SCC Champion (triple jump)
1974-75	Jeff Hebenstreit	SCC Champion (800m relay)
	Greg Humphries	SCC Champion (high jump, 800m relay)
	Bob Lietz	SCC Champion (pole vault)
	Don Sullivan	SCC Champion (long jump, 800m relay), State (long jump)
	Brian Wall	SCC Champion (800m relay)
1976-77	Bob Cargnoni	State (3200m relay)
	Jay Edmiston	District Champion (1600m), State (1600m, 3200m relay)
	Mike Heinemeyer	State (3200m relay)
	John Hering	District Champion (triple jump), State (long jump, triple jump)
	Ed Ripperda	State (3200m relay)
	Tom Spears	District Champion (3200m), State (3200m)
	Steve Wood	State (hurdles)
	Paul Zimmer	State (200m)
1977-78	Bob Cargnoni	State (3200m relay)
	Dan Hartman	State (3200m relay)
	Mike Heinemeyer	State (3200m relay)
	Ed Ripperda	State (3200m relay)
	Tom Spears	State (1600m, 3200m)
1985-86	Greg Deist	State (400m relay, 800m relay)
	Tim Gusewelle	State (400m relay, 800m relay)
	Bret Kasubke	State (400m relay, 800m relay)
	Mike LaRosa	State (800m relay)
	Bill Scherff	SCC Champion (pole vault), County Champion (pole vault), Sectional Champion (pole vault), 5th State (pole vault), State (400m relay)

Individual Accompishments

1988-89	Greg Best	State (400m relay, 800m relay)
	Phil Deist	State (400m relay, 800m relay)
	Brian Dustman	State (400m relay, 800m relay)
	Chris Knowles	State (400m relay, 800m relay)
	Tim Straub	State (800m)
1989-90	Brad Best	County Champion (1600m relay)
	Greg Best	SCC Champion (400m relay, 800m relay), County Champion (400m relay, 800m relay), State (400m relay, 800m relay)
	Matt Bracht	County Champion (1600m relay)
	Dan Burgard	County Champion (1600m relay)
	Kevin Boeckenstedt	SCC Champion (300m hurdles), County Champion (300m hurdles, 1600m relay)
	Phil Deist	SCC Champion (400m relay, 800m relay), County Champion (400m relay, 800m relay), State (400m relay, 800m relay)
	Brian Dustman	SCC Champion (400m relay, 800m relay), County Champion (400m relay, 800m relay), State (400m relay, 800m relay)
	Dave Gerdes	SCC Champion (discus, shot put), County Champion (shot put), 7th State (shot put)
	Chris Knowles	SCC Champion (400m relay, 800m relay), County Champion (400m relay, 800m relay), State (400m relay, 800m relay)
	Tim Straub	SCC Champion (800m, 1600m), County Champion (800m, 1600m), 6th State (800m), State (1600m)
1990-91	Darrell Buffington	State (shot put)
	Nathan Calcari	State (3200m relay)
	Mark Rantanen	State (3200m relay)
	Blake Schuette	State (3200m relay)
	Tim Straub	3rd State (800m), State (1600m, 3200m relay)
1992-93	Brad Best	SCC Champion (200m), County Champion (200m), State (100m)
	Dennis Bohlen	SCC Champion (discus, hurdles, shot put), County Champion (hurdles), Sectional Champion (discus), State (discus, hurdles, shot put)
	Dean Heidke	Sectional Champion (200m), State (200m)
	Josh Schuette	SCC Champion (1600m), County Champion (1600m), Sectional Champion (3200m), State (1600m, 3200m)
1993-94	Dennis Bohlen	SCC Champion (discus, shot put), County Champion (discus, shot put), Sectional Champion (discus, shot put), State (discus, shot put)
	Josh Schuette	SCC Champion (3200m), County Champion (1600m), State (1600m)
	Dean Heidke	State (100m)
1994-95	Jason Foulk	State (100m, 200m)
1995-96	Dustin Bramley	SCC Champion (discus)
1996-97	John Masinelli	SCC Champion (high jump)
1997-98	Dustin Bramley	County Champion (shot put)

1998-99	Aaron Hainaut	County Champion (discus)
1999-00	Aaron Hainaut	County Champion (discus), Sectional Champion (discus), State (discus)
	Craig Phifer	State (800m)
	Michael Williams	SCC Champion (1600m), State (1600m)
2000-01	Doug Watters	State (1600m)
2001-02	Josh Ohlinger	County Champion (200m)
2002-03	Aaron Brashears	SCC Champion (3200m relay), State (3200m relay)
	Nino Cavataio	SCC Champion (3200m relay), State (3200m relay)
	Josh Ohlinger	SCC Champion (100m, 200m), County Champion (100m)
	Brad Pirok	County Champion (3200m), State (3200m)
	Doug Stiegemeier	SCC Champion (400m, 3200m relay), County Champion (high jump, 400m), State (400m, 3200m relay)
	Doug Watters	SCC Champion (1600m, 3200m relay), State (1600m, 3200m relay)
2003-04	Aaron Brashears	SCC Champion (3200m relay), County Champion (3200m relay), Sectional Champion (3200m relay), State (1600m relay, 3200m relay)
	Nino Cavataio	SCC Champion (3200m relay), County Champion (3200m relay), Sectional Champion (3200m relay), State (1600m relay, 3200m relay)
	Justin Embry	SCC Champion (3200m relay), County Champion (3200m relay), Sectional Champion (3200m relay), State (3200m relay)
	Mike Jurgess	Sectional Champion (400m relay), State (400m relay)
	Mike Moseley	Sectional Champion (400m relay), State (400m relay, 1600m relay)
	Josh Ohlinger	SCC Champion (100m, 200m), County Champion (100m, 200m), Sectional Champion (100m, 200m, 400m relay), State (100m, 200m, 400m relay)
	Brad Pirok	SCC Champion (3200m), County Champion (1600m, 3200m), 6th State (3200m), State (1600m)
	Joe Stranimeier	Sectional Champion (400m relay), State (400m relay)
	Doug Stiegemeier	SCC Champion (400m, 3200m relay), County Champion (400m, 3200m relay), Sectional Champion (3200m relay), State (high jump, 400m, 1600m relay, 3200m relay)
2004-05	Aaron Brashears	SCC Champion (3200m relay), County Champion (800m, 3200m relay), Sectional Champion (3200m relay), State (800m, 3200m relay)
	Justin Embry	SCC Champion (3200m relay), County Champion (3200m relay), Sectional Champion (3200m relay), State (3200m relay)
	Randall Hoehn	SCC Champion (3200m relay), County Champion (3200m relay), Sectional Champion (3200m relay), State (3200m relay)
	Mike Jurgess	County Champion (800m relay), Sectional Champion (800m relay), State (400m relay, 800m relay)
	Mike Moseley	County Champion (800m relay), Sectional Champion (800m relay), State (400m relay, 800m relay)
	Josh Ohlinger	SCC Champion (long jump, 100m, 200m), County Champion (100m, 200m), Sectional Champion (100m, 200m, 800m relay), 5th State (200m), 7th State (100m), State (400m relay, 800m relay)
	Brad Pirok	SCC Champion (1600m, 3200m), County Champion (1600m, 3200m), Sectional Champion (3200m), 2nd State (3200m)

Individual Accompishments

	Dean Sheffer	State (800m relay)
	Doug Stiegemeier	SCC Champion (400m, 3200m relay), County Champion (high jump, 400m, 3200m relay), Sectional Champion (3200m relay), State (400m, 3200m relay)
	Joe Stranimeier	County Champion (800m relay), Sectional Champion (800m relay), State (400m relay, 800m relay)
	Kevin Tucker	County Champion (800m relay)
2005-06	Aaron Brashears	SCC Champion (3200m relay), County Champion (800m, 1600m relay, 3200m relay), Sectional Champion (3200m relay), State (800m, 3200m relay)
	Justin Embry	County Champion (1600m), Sectional Champion (3200m relay), State (3200m relay)
	Aaron Foster	SCC Champion (3200m relay), County Champion (3200m relay)
	Randall Hoehn	SCC Champion (3200m relay), County Champion (1600m relay, 3200m relay), Sectional Champion (3200m relay), State (3200m relay)
	Mike Jurgess	County Champion (100m, 200m), State (200m)
	Lucas Loots	SCC Champion (3200m relay), County Champion (3200m relay), Sectional Champion (3200m relay), State (3200m relay)
	Brett Miller	County Champion (3200m)
	Dean Sheffer	County Champion (1600m relay)
	Kevin Tucker	County Champion (1600m relay)
2006-07	Randall Hoehn	County Champion (1600m), State (800m)
	Lucas Loots	State (1600m)
	Brett Miller	County Champion (3200m), State (3200m)
	Joe Stranimeier	SCC Champion (200m), County Champion (200m)
2007-08	Evan Allison	SCC Champion (3200m relay), County Champion (3200m relay), Sectional Champion (3200m relay), State (3200m relay)
	Aaron Foster	SCC Champion (3200m relay), County Champion (3200m relay), Sectional Champion (3200m relay), State (3200m relay)
	Randall Hoehn	SCC Champion (3200m relay), County Champion (3200m relay), Sectional Champion (3200m relay), State (3200m relay)
	Lucas Loots	SCC Champion (3200m relay), County Champion (1600m, 3200m), Sectional Champion (3200m relay), State (1600m, 3200m relay), Telegraph (1st Team)
	Scott Prost	County Champion (3200m relay)
	Dean Sheffer	State (200m)
2008-09	Evan Allison	State (3200m relay)
	Cody Drennan	State (3200m relay)
	Mitch Glisson	State (3200m relay)
	Lucas Loots	SCC Champion (1600m), County Champion (800m, 1600m, 3200m), State (1600m, 3200m, 3200m relay), Telegraph (Player of the Year)
	Eric Yarnik	State (3200m relay)
2009-10	Sam Allison	PSC Champion (1600m, 3200m relay)
	Nick Banovz	PSC Champion (3200m relay)
	Anthony Fairman	PSC Champion (high jump, triple jump, 400m), County Champion (high jump, triple jump), Sectional Champion (high jump), State (high jump, triple jump), Telegraph (1st Team)
	Andy Goebel	PSC Champion (800m, 3200m relay)

	Tom Homeier	PSC Champion (3200m)
	Brett Kinder	State (high jump)
	Dylan Rooney	PSC Champion (3200m relay)
2010-11	Sam Allison	PSC Champion (800m, 1600m relay), Sectional Champion (1600m relay), State (1600m relay), Telegraph (1st Team)
	Jordan Johnson	PSC Champion (triple jump)
	Brett Kinder	PSC Champion (1600m relay), Sectional Champion (1600m relay), State (1600m relay), Telegraph (1st Team)
	Jake Mahin	PSC Champion (discus, shot put), County Champion (discus, shot put), Sectional Champion (shot put), 7th State (shot put), State (discus), Telegraph (1st Team)
	Dylan Rooney	PSC Champion (1600m relay), Sectional Champion (1600m relay), State (1600m relay), Telegraph (1st Team)
	David Vaughn	PSC Champion (1600m relay), Sectional Champion (1600m relay), State (1600m relay), Telegraph (1st Team)
2011-12	Sam Allison	PSC Champion (pole vault, 400m), Sectional Champion (400m), State (400m)
	Dylan Bertels	PSC Champion (400m relay), County Champion (400m relay)
	Kyle Castaldi	PSC Champion (400m relay), County Champion (400m relay)
	Blake Kinder	PSC Champion (400m relay), County Champion (400m relay)
	Jake Mahin	PSC Champion (discus, shot put), County Champion (discus, shot put), Sectional Champion (discus, shot put), 2nd State (discus), 5th State (shot put), Telegraph (Player of the Year)
	Marcus Sitko	PSC Champion (triple jump, 400m relay), County Champion (triple jump, 400m relay)

Track (Boys Records)

Year	Name	Event (Time/Distance)
2004-05	Josh Ohlinger	100 Meter Dash (10.70)
2004-05	Josh Ohlinger	200 Meter Dash (22.20)
2004-05	Doug Stiegemeier	400 Meter Dash (50.30)
1990-91	Tim Straub	800 Meter Run (1:54.10)
1976-77	Tom Spears	1600 Meter Run (4:21.60)
2004-05	Brad Pirok	3200 Meter Run (9:21.98)
1992-93	Dennis Bohlen	110 Meter Hurdles (15.10)
1985-86	Bill Scherff	110 Meter Hurdles (15.10)
1985-86	Bill Scherff	300 Meter Hurdles (39.80)
2003-04	Mike Jurgess, Mike Moseley, Josh Ohlinger, Joe Stranimeier	400 Meter Relay (44.10)
1985-86	Greg Deist, Tim Gusewelle, Bret Kasubke, Bill Scherff	800 Meter Relay (1:31.50)
2010-11	Sam Allison, Brett Kinder, Dylan Rooney, David Vaughn	1600 Meter Relay (3:30.42)
2007-08	Evan Allison, Aaron Foster, Randall Hoehn, Lucas Loots	3200 Meter Relay (8:19.30)
2011-12	Jake Mahin	Discus (165'8")
2009-10	Anthony Fairman	High Jump (6'4")
1970-71	Nick Wineburner	Long Jump (22'0.5")
1985-86	Bill Scherff	Pole Vault (13'6")

2011-12   Jake Mahin   Shot Put (56'4")

1980-81   Bruce Kasubke   Triple Jump (42'11")

Individual Accomplishments

Track (Girls)

Year	Name	Accomplishment
1973-74	Paula Hering	State (long jump)
1974-75	Sheila Pingolt	District Champion (discus), State (discus)
1975-76	Chris Cordani	State (1600m relay)
	Lynne Eddington	State (400m relay, 800m relay)
	Karen Hering	State (400m relay, 800m relay, 800m medley)
	Liz Link	State (1600m relay)
	Sarah Link	State (1600m relay)
	Kathy Maxvill	State (400m relay, 800m relay, 800m medley)
	Kim Maxvill	State (400m relay, 800m relay, 800m medley)
	Sheila Pingolt	State (hurdles)
	Ellise Schuette	State (1600m relay, 800m medley)
1976-77	Bonnie Bruhn	State (400m relay)
	Deone Courtney	State (hurdles)
	Lynne Eddington	State (400m relay)
	Kim Maxvill	State (400m relay)
	Peggy Senaldi	State (400m relay)
1978-79	Brenda Bruhn	State (800m relay, 1600m relay)
	Deone Courtney	State (1600m relay)
	Kim Maxvill	State (800m relay)
	Patty Senaldi	State (1600m relay)
	Peggy Senaldi	State (800m relay, 1600m relay)
	Diane Williams	State (800m relay)
1979-80	Dori Hartman	State (800m)
1980-81	Nikki Coyne	District Champion (800m), State (800m)
	Dori Hartman	State (800m)
	Kim Mueller	State (long jump)
1981-82	Lynn Yakos	State (high jump)
1982-83	Lee Karl	Sectional Champion (shot put), State (shot put)
	Darla Sievers	State (400m)
	Lynn Yakos	Sectional Champion (high jump), State (high jump)
1984-85	Becky Coyne	State Champion (100m hurdles)
1985-86	Dana Anschutz	State (shot put)
1987-88	Becky Coyne	SCC Champion (200m, 100m hurdles), County Champion (100m hurdles, 300m hurdles), State Champion (100m hurdles), 3rd State (300m hurdles)

1988-89	Crystal Isbell	State (high jump)
2002-03	Jennie Satterlee	State (discus)
2003-04	NONE	NONE
2004-05	Kim Phifer	County Champion (800m), Sectional Champion (800m), State (800m)
	Jennie Satterlee	County Champion (discus), Sectional Champion (discus), State (discus)
2005-06	Kim Phifer	Sectional Champion (800m), State (800m)
	Jennie Satterlee	SCC Champion (discus), County Champion (discus, shot put), Sectional Champion (discus), 4th State (discus)
	Alex Senaldi	County Champion (800m), State (800m, 1600m)
2006-07	Alex Senaldi	State (1600m, 3200m)
2007-08	Kelsey Henke	County Champion (200m)
	Alex Senaldi	County Champion (800m, 1600m), State (3200m)
	Katie Trettenero	County Champion (3200m)
2008-09	Lika Hindi	State (3200m relay)
	Jessica Jarman	State (3200m relay)
	Kristen McDowell	State (high jump)
	Alex Senaldi	County Champion (3200m), State (3200m relay)
	Mia Stefani	SCC Champion (800m), State (3200m relay)
2009-10	Stephanie Becker	PSC Champion (400m relay, 800m relay)
	Claire Cioni	PSC Champion (100m, 400m relay, 800m relay)
	Amanda Cornell	PSC Champion (3200m relay)
	Sophie Fairman	PSC Champion (200m, 800m relay), County Champion (400m), Sectional Champion (400m), 6th State (triple jump), 8th State (400m), Telegraph (1st Team)
	Deirdra Fey	PSC Champion (400m relay), County Champion (long jump)
	Jordan Frye	PSC Champion (400m relay)
	Jessica Jarman	PSC Champion (3200m relay)
	Kristen McDowell	PSC Champion (800m relay), County Champion (high jump), Telegraph (1st Team)
	Ashley Rettig	PSC Champion (3200m relay)
	Katie Trettenero	PSC Champion (3200m relay)
2010-11	Brooke Buffington	PSC Champion (3200m relay), Sectional Champion (3200m relay), State (3200m relay), Telegraph (1st Team)
	Amanda Cornell	PSC Champion (800m), Sectional Champion (3200m relay), State (3200m relay), Telegraph (1st Team)
	Sophie Fairman	PSC Champion (triple jump, 100m, 200m), County Champion (triple jump, 200m, 400m), Sectional Champion (400m, 3200m relay), 3rd State (triple jump), 4th State (400m), State (200m, 3200m relay), Telegraph (1st Team)
	Yana Fairman	PSC Champion (3200m relay), State (3200m relay)
	Kristen McDowell	PSC Champion (high jump), County Champion (high jump), State (high jump)

Individual Accompishments

	Mia Stefani	PSC Champion (3200m relay), Sectional Champion (3200m relay), State (3200m relay), Telegraph (1st Team)
	Katie Trettenero	PSC Champion (3200m relay)
2011-12	Sophie Fairman	PSC Champion (long jump, triple jump), County Champion (long jump, triple jump, 200m, 400m), Sectional Champion (triple jump, 400m), 3rd State (triple jump), 4th State (400m), State (200m), Telegraph (1st Team)

Track (Girls Records)

Year	Name	Event (Time/Distance)
2011-12	Sophie Fairman	100 Meter Dash (12.9)
2011-12	Sophie Fairman	200 Meter Dash (26.49)
2010-11	Sophie Fairman	400 Meter Dash (58.05)
2011-12	Sophie Fairman	800 Meter Run (2:24.33)
2006-07	Alex Senaldi	1600 Meter Run (5:44.81)
2006-07	Alex Senaldi	3200 Meter Run (12:35.95)
2006-07	Sam Feldmann	100 Meter Hurdles (17.4)
1987-88	Becky Coyne	300 Meter Hurdles (44.87)
2009-10	Stephanie Becker, Claire Cioni, Deirdra Fey, Jordan Frye	400 Meter Relay (54.51)
2009-10	Stephanie Becker, Claire Cioni, Sophie Fairman, Kristen McDowell	800 Meter Relay (1:55.80)
1984-85	Shelia Banovz, Amy Clarkin, Chrissy Hughes, Dana Sievers	1600 Meter Relay (4:23.10)
2010-11	Brooke Buffington, Amanda Cornell, Sophie Fairman, Mia Stefani	3200 Meter Relay (10:28.60)
2005-06	Jennie Satterlee	Discus (120'7")
2010-11	Kristen McDowell	High Jump (5'4")
1974-75	Chris Cordani	Long Jump (16'9")
2009-10	Claire Cioni	Pole Vault (7'6")
1984-85	Lee Karl	Shot Put (36'10")
2011-12	Sophie Fairman	Triple Jump (37'2")

Volleyball

Year	Name	Accomplishment
1978-79	Bonnie Bruhn	SCC (Honorable Mention)
	Brenda Bruhn	SCC (Honorable Mention)
	Kelley Chiti	SCC (1st Team)
	Deone Courtney	SCC (1st Team), County (1st Team)
	Lisa Lovejoy	SCC (2nd Team)
	Peggy Senaldi	SCC (2nd Team)
	Linda Suhrenbrock	SCC (2nd Team)
	Lori Williamson	SCC (1st Team), County (1st Team)
1979-80	Evelyn Bean	SCC (Honorable Mention)
	Bonnie Bruhn	SCC (1st Team), County (1st Team)
	Brenda Bruhn	SCC (2nd Team), County (1st Team)
	Mary Henke	SCC (2nd Team)
	Janis Treadway	SCC (Honorable Mention)
	Diane Williams	SCC (1st Team)
1980-81	Evelyn Bean	County (1st Team)
	Diana Bruhn	SCC (1st Team)
	Stacy Stierwalt	SCC (1st Team), County (1st Team)
	Janis Treadway	SCC (2nd Team), County (1st Team)
	Diane Williams	SCC (1st Team), County (1st Team)
1982-83	Sharon Bodi	SCC (1st Team), County (1st Team)
	Kim Mueller	SCC (2nd Team)
	Lynn Yakos	SCC (Honorable Mention)
1983-84	Sharon Bodi	SCC (1st Team), County (1st Team), All-State (Honorable Mention)
	Denise Brown	SCC (Honorable Mention)
	Mary Hering	SCC (Honorable Mention)
	Lee Karl	County (1st Team)
	Kim Mueller	SCC (1st Team)
	Dimitria Sies	SCC (2nd Team)
1984-85	Janette Hughes	SCC (2nd Team)
	Lee Karl	SCC (1st Team), County (1st Team), All-State (1st Team)
	Lisa Kasubke	SCC (1st Team), County (1st Team)
	Dana Sievers	SCC (Honorable Mention)
1985-86	Dana Sievers	SCC (1st Team)
1986-87	Shelia Banovz	SCC (Honorable Mention)
	Jerri Hochmuth	SCC (2nd Team)
	Tracy Kuba	SCC (1st Team)
	Dana Sievers	SCC (1st Team), County (1st Team)

1987-88	Kris Goebel	SCC (1st Team)
1988-89	Angie Hainaut	SCC (2nd Team)
	Jerri Hochmuth	SCC (1st Team)
	Becky Miller	SCC (2nd Team)
1989-90	Janelle Franke	SCC (2nd Team)
	Glenda Kleeman	SCC (2nd Team)
	Sherry Masinelli	SCC (1st Team)
	Becky Miller	SCC (2nd Team)
1990-91	Sam Cooper	SCC (Honorable Mention)
	Janelle Franke	SCC (1st Team)
	Glenda Kleeman	SCC (Honorable Mention), Telegraph (Athlete of the Year - Finalist)
	Sherry Masinelli	SCC (1st Team), Telegraph (1st Team)
	Becky Miller	SCC (1st Team), Telegraph (2nd Team)
	Debra Sievers	SCC (Honorable Mention)
1991-92	Kristin Ahring	SCC (1st Team)
	Angela Bertolino	SCC (2nd Team)
	Sam Cooper	SCC (1st Team)
	Sherry Masinelli	SCC (1st Team)
	Alena Michuda	SCC (1st Team)
1992-93	Sam Cooper	SCC (1st Team)
	Alena Michuda	SCC (1st Team)
	Adrienne Spudich	SCC (2nd Team)
	Sara Zuber	SCC (2nd Team)
1994-95	Shannen Thomas	SCC (2nd Team), Telegraph (1st Team)
	Andrea Williamson	SCC (Honorable Mention)
	Sara Zuber	SCC (1st Team), County (1st Team), Telegraph (1st Team)
1995-96	Amber Brinson	SCC (1st Team), County (1st Team), Telegraph (1st Team)
	Stefanie Kershaw	SCC (Honorable Mention)
	Elena Tallman	SCC (1st Team)
	Andrea Williamson	SCC (2nd Team), County (1st Team)
1997-98	Katie Bequette	SCC East (2nd Team), County (1st Team)
	Leslie Bono	SCC East (1st Team), County (1st Team)
	Malinda Eller	SCC East (Honorable Mention)
	Christie Partridge	SCC East (2nd Team)
1998-99	Katie Bequette	SCC East (1st Team), County (1st Team)
	Robyn Painter	SCC East (2nd Team)
	Christie Partridge	SCC East (2nd Team), County (1st Team)
1999-00	Katie Bequette	SCC East (1st Team), County (1st Team), Telegraph (1st Team)
	Christie Partridge	SCC East (1st Team), County (1st Team), Telegraph (2nd Team)
	Andrea Snell	SCC East (2nd Team)

Individual Accomplishments

	Leticia Tevini	SCC East (2nd Team)
2000-01	Andrea Prante	SCC East (1st Team)
	Andrea Snell	SCC East (2nd Team), County (1st Team)
	Leticia Tevini	SCC East (Honorable Mention)
2001-02	Melissa Newbold	SCC East (Honorable Mention)
	Andrea Prante	SCC East (1st Team), Telegraph (2nd Team)
	Danielle Robeza	SCC East (2nd Team), Telegraph (Honorable Mention)
2002-03	Kelli Mueller	SCC East (Honorable Mention)
	Kelly Nicholas	SCC East (2nd Team)
	Jennifer Wyatt	SCC East (1st Team)
2003-04	Kayla Brown	SCC East (2nd Team)
	Ashleigh Ries	SCC East (2nd Team)
2004-05	Hilary Odorizzi	SCC East (2nd Team), County (1st Team)
	Kim Phifer	SCC East (2nd Team)
	Ashleigh Ries	SCC East (Honorable Mention), County (1st Team)
	Brittany Robeza	SCC East (2nd Team)
2005-06	Kim Phifer	SCC East (Honorable Mention)
2006-07	Lika Hindi	SCC East (Honorable Mention)
	Lauren Newbold	SCC East (Honorable Mention)
2007-08	Lika Hindi	SCC East (Honorable Mention)
	Lauren Newbold	SCC East (2nd Team)
2008-09	Lindsey Mathenia	SCC East (2nd Team)
	Kristen McDowell	SCC East (Honorable Mention)
	Lauren Newbold	SCC East (2nd Team)
2009-10	Yana Fairman	PSC (1st Team), SJ-R (1st Team)
	Kristen McDowell	PSC (1st Team), Telegraph (1st Team), SJ-R (Special Mention)
	Briana Rae	PSC (2nd Team), SJ-R (Special Mention)
	Sam Senaldi	PSC (Honorable Mention)
2010-11	Sophie Fairman	PSC (2nd Team), Telegraph (1st Team), SJ-R (Honorable Mention)
	Yana Fairman	PSC (2nd Team)
	Lindsey Mathenia	PSC (2nd Team)
	Kristen McDowell	PSC (1st Team), County (1st Team), Telegraph (Player of the Year), SJ-R (Honorable Mention)
	Briana Rae	PSC (1st Team), County (1st Team), Telegraph (1st Team)
2011-12	Kerstin Brown	PSC (2nd Team)
	Kassie Elliott	PSC (2nd Team)
	Sophie Fairman	PSC (1st Team), County (1st Team), Telegraph (Player of the Year), SJ-R (Honorable Mention)

Kim Machuga   PSC (Honorable Mention)
Katie Yakos   PSC (Honorable Mention)

Sources

Staunton Star Times

One of my two main sources, the local paper is available on microfilm at the Staunton Public Library. The publication was especially valuable in finding information for anything that happened before 1950, as yearbooks were scarce before that time.

Myrtle and Maroon and Echo yearbooks

My other major source, the school's annual yearbook was critical in determining who participated in each sport and for quick access to team results and individual accomplishments.

www.piasabirds.com

Brian Hanslow and Matt Hasquin run one of the best high school websites in the state, and the link was especially helpful in finding out which schools were part of the South Central Conference from its inception to present.

www.ihsa.org

The Illinois High School Association's website was helpful in verifying Staunton's postseason titles. Additionally, it was used to find or confirm team and individual record-setters throughout state history. It is worth noting that the website also contains information (wins/losses, coach, etc.) on each of its member schools, and most of what can be found on Staunton High School was submitted by me after conducting research for this book.

The Carlinville Cavaliers: A History of Football from 1913-1978 by Dick McLaughlin

I used this book to help compile a list of South Central Conference football champions, as well as to verify gridiron results between Carlinville and Staunton.